SALISBURY MUSEUM MEDIEVAL CATALOGUE

Part 4

edited by
Peter Saunders

with contributions by

David Algar, Allan Brodie, Tim Tatton-Brown, John Cherry, Anna Eavis, Geoff Egan, Alison Goodall, John McNeill, Lorraine Mepham, Beverley Nenk, Nigel Ramsay, Paul Robinson, Jörn Schuster, Brian Spencer and Diana Friendship-Taylor

drawings by
Nicholas Griffiths

and photography by
David Cousins

Published by
SALISBURY & SOUTH WILTSHIRE

SALISBURY & SOUTH WILTSHIRE

The King's House, 65 The Close, Salisbury, Wiltshire
SP1 2EN, England

ISBN 978-0-947535-26-1

Design and pre-production:
David Algar, David Cousins, David Pitt and
Peter Saunders

Printed by Salisbury Printing
Salisbury, Wiltshire, England

**The Trustees of Salisbury Museum are
grateful to The Marc Fitch Fund for a
generous grant towards the publication
of this catalogue.**

Front cover:
window glass Cat 96 showing St James wearing a pilgrim's hat with scallop shell
Back cover:
alabaster Cat 2; sculptured head Cat 149; bell Cat 22, bushel Cat 20; copper alloy brooches Cat 6, 12, buckle
Cat 102, strap-end Cat 125, finial Cat 252, candlestick Cat 254, parchment holder Cat 261, purse frame
Cat 169, iron shears Cat 78, knife Cat 48, padlock Cat 129, key Cat 181, shackles Cat 238, leather Cat 2;
porphyry Cat 8; wood panel Cat 5; enamel Cat 3

Contents

List of illustrations

Preface

This volume, the fourth in the *Salisbury Museum Medieval Catalogue* series, completes the publication of the Museum's entire collection of medieval objects, a publishing achievement believed to be unique by a UK museum, and one without an excavation team attached.

Although the growth of digital-format publishing suggests that the heyday of the printed catalogue may be past, the Museum felt a strong obligation, having already published three parts, to complete the catalogue in traditional form and has followed the style and format established by the first part, published in the 1990s, now to create a set.

The catalogue was originally conceived in the 1970s. Then, it was envisaged that this work would comprise a single volume modelled on the classic *London Museum Medieval Catalogue* which, though published as long ago as 1940, still found at that time little to rival or even complement it upon researchers' bookshelves. During the long gestation of the Salisbury catalogue it became apparent that it would be more practical to publish a number of separate volumes as and when sufficient content was gathered. Thus each volume comprises self-contained sections grouped together to make volumes of reasonable length and price. Whilst this approach has resulted in apparently random juxta-positions of disparate types of objects and classes of material (for example floor tiles and coins appeared in *Part I* whilst other ceramic types and jettons appeared in *Part 3*), it was nevertheless considered wiser to proceed this way than to delay further in the hope of producing an 'ideal' arrangement that might realistically never see the light of day. Contributors were generally persuaded generously to 'volunteer' their services to the task rather than be contracted and, all being busy people engaged in other projects or full-time employment, could not be expected to accept too rigid an imposed schedule. The untimely deaths of the project's instigator, Hugh Shortt and later its co-editor, Eleanor Saunders, together with the process of re-establishing the Museum in new premises, also conspired to delay its progress. Now complete, however, the series is a record of the scholarly expertise of some thirty three contributors, whose commitment and generosity in the gift of time has been remarkable. Hopefully too, it will stand as a fitting memorial to all those involved in this venture who are sadly no longer with us to celebrate its completion.

As before, each contributor has been given freedom to treat the subject matter as he or she thinks best, offering an introduction appropriate to their particular collection and a consideration of its relative importance to medieval studies followed by the detailed catalogue, bibliography and illustrations. A rigid date range for 'medieval' has not been imposed; authors have defined the period in the way they think most appropriate to their particular subject matter. Thus most sections conclude *c*.1500, whilst in *Part 3* Geoff Egan followed logic and pragmatically took cloth seals to 1724, the end of the alnage system. Some authors, like Allan Brodie on architectural stonework in this volume, have taken the opportunity to expand their basic catalogues with essays broadening the significance of their subject matter.

Objects acquired by the Museum since their class was published in earlier volumes are recorded here, for the sake of completeness, in extensive addenda.

By placing all the nationally-important medieval collections in Salisbury Museum in the public domain it is hoped that the four volumes collectively will prove invaluable as a definitive source to archaeologists, curators, historians and collectors alike in the tradition of the *London Museum Medieval Catalogue*, which pioneered the way.

Peter Saunders
Midsummer Day, 2012

Editor's acknowledgements

I am first and foremost grateful to all the contributors who have worked on the collections and who are the authors both of the new sections that form this part of the *Medieval Catalogue* and also the substantial addenda. My task has been made lighter by their scholarship and patience; it is their erudition which gives this work a stamp of authority that could not have been achieved by the editor and the Museum's staff alone. Brian Spencer's delivery of his draft text on the additional pilgrim souvenirs and secular badges when terminally ill was inspirational, and Geoff Egan's untimely death sadly prevented his seeing how influential his support was to prove.

In addition to those acknowledged by the various contributors within their respective sections I wish to thank all those who have given freely of their time, expertise and advice to assist in the preparation and production of this work: Louisa Burden, Sebastian Foxley, Beth Werrett, Helen Wilmott and Lynn Wootten (Wiltshire County Council Conservation Service) for conservation and other technical assistance; Steve Hobbs, Michael Marshman and Helen Rogers (Wiltshire and Swindon History Centre) and Lorna Haycock (Wiltshire Heritage Library) for archival and bibliographical assistance; Lisa Brown (Wiltshire Heritage Museum) for help with numismatica; Geoffrey Fisher (Conway Library, Courtauld Institute) for facilitating access to many of the images used in the architectural stonework section; Gilbert Green and Justin Delair for advice on the geological sources of architectural and domestic stonework; Roger Brownsword, Roderic Butler and Christopher Dalton for help with bronze vessels, church bells and casting methods; Suzanne Eward (Salisbury Cathedral Librarian) and Canon Edward Probert for providing access to the Cathedral chests and book chains; Lorrain Higbee (Wessex Archaeology) for bone identification; Professor Tom Beaumont James (Winchester University) for constructive comments on the text, especially that relating to Clarendon Palace; and Norman Hall and the late Catherine Saunders for proofing draft texts.

I repeat the acknowledgement made in *Part 3*, namely that I owe the greatest debt of gratitude, to David Algar, whose hands-on-help with the objects themselves and whose encouragement and the undertaking of innumerable editorial tasks, has done so much to ensure that this volume, like the last, has been brought to publication.

All parts of this catalogue series have benefited enormously from the drawing and photographic skills of Nicholas Griffiths and David Cousins. Nicholas, as in previous volumes, has not only rendered faithfully the wishes of contributors and editor but with his experienced eye has frequently detected more detail and information about an object than was at first apparent. David deserves special thanks for the meticulous care taken photographing difficult subjects, the cover design and especially his considerable practical assistance with production issues.

Present and past colleagues at Salisbury Museum have supported the editor in bringing this volume to production, particularly Janet Bell, Lindsay Guest, Katie Hinds, the late Eleanor Saunders and Jane Ellis-Schön (curatorially) and Pam Barton, Anne Jenson and Sara Willis (administratively).

The grateful thanks of the Museum is offered to all those who, since the 1860s, have donated the majority of the medieval objects here recorded. The Museum Publications Committee's recognition of the importance of publishing these and its support of its editor have been immensely significant. For him the task has largely been a labour of love squeezed into brief periods between more pressing demands on time, from his days as Assistant Curator in the 1970s to his present status in retirement as Curator Emeritus, and his pleasure and relief in its completion is profound.

Abbreviations used in the Catalogue

D.	diameter, except in architectural and sculptured stonework where depth is indicated
g	gramme
gr.	grain
H.	height
L.	length
Th.	thickness
W.	width
Wt.	weight
acc. no.	accession number
BM	British Museum
Cat, Fig and Pl	catalogue, figure and plate numbers (in this catalogue)
coll.	collection
Drainage coll.	Salisbury Drainage collection (see note on provenance)
DUA	Department of Urban Archaeology (Museum of London)
EH	English Heritage
MLA	Department of Medieval and Later Antiquities (in the British Museum)
MOL	Museum of London
MS	manuscript
O.S. Diary	*Old Sarum Diary:* Col. W. Hawley's manuscript diary of 1909-15 excavations, in Salisbury Museum
PAS	Portable Antiquities Scheme
pc	private collection
pers. comm.	personal communication

RCHM(E)	Royal Commission on the Historical Monuments of England
Sal. Mus. Cat.	*Catalogue of the Salisbury and South Wilts Museum*
Sal. Mus. Rep.	*Salisbury and South Wilts Museum Annual Report*
V. & A.	Victoria and Albert Museum
VCH	*The Victoria History of the Counties of England*
WA&NHS	Wiltshire Archaeological & Natural History Society
Wilts. Arch. Mag.	*Wiltshire Archaeological and Natural History Magazine*
W.R.O.	Wiltshire Record Office
WSA	Wiltshire and Swindon Archives

The abbreviated titles of periodicals, which appear in bibliographies, follow the standard list published by the Council for British Archaeology in *Signposts for Archaeological Publication* (London 1991) except as indicated above. The place of publication of works cited in bibliographies is London except where otherwise stated.

When Salisbury Museum internal catalogue and accession numbers are stated within catalogue entries, they appear in italics. Prior to the late 1990s the Museum's practice was to state an object's unique number first followed by the year of acquisition but for the sake of consistency this catalogue follows present-day practice of stating the year first.

Catalogue numbers are given in bold type preceding each object description. Each object that is illustrated has a figure or plate number, also in bold, following the catalogue entry.

Note on Provenance

All catalogued objects are of Wiltshire provenance unless otherwise stated. In common with most museum collections many are casual finds without archaeological context other than find-spot. Archaeological excavations at a number of important sites, including Old Sarum, Clarendon Palace and Gomeldon deserted medieval village, have, however, produced large groups of objects, some classes of which are included in this part of the *Medieval Catalogue*. Salisbury itself has been a constant source of medieval artefacts, a reflection of its size and importance (judged by the number of poll-tax payers assessed in 1377 it was then the sixth most populous English provincial town). Find spots and sites in the vicinity of Salisbury are shown in figure 84 (page 332).

The Salisbury Drainage collection was the foundation collection of the Museum and comprises discoveries, almost entirely of small metal objects, made during the laying of sewers and piped water supplies in Salisbury between 1852 and 1854, replacing the medieval system of open drainage channels which formerly ran through the city's streets. Given that the city was founded in the thirteenth century these discoveries were not mixed on the whole with earlier finds and they make an interesting series, though it should be stressed that they were recovered without regard to stratigraphy. Many were formed into a collection by Mr Edward Brodie, and others were added by the Museum's first curator, E. T. Stevens. Their names are recorded against individual catalogue entries where known. See also Peter Saunders, *Channels to the Past: the Salisbury Drainage Collection* (Salisbury, 2009). In the 1980s and early 1990s further finds were made by 'mud-larks', notably Tony Pilson and Ian Smith, chiefly from the river near Fisherton Bridge, Salisbury, and these have added significantly to the metalwork catalogued in this volume.

Old Sarum. In addition to casual finds the Museum also holds finds from the 1909-15 excavations by W. Hawley, W. St. J. Hope and D. Montgomerie (yearly reports in *Proc. Soc. Antiq.* 23-28 (1910-1916), from excavations in the east suburb 1933 (*Antiq. J.* 15 (1935), 174-92) and from excavations mostly in the east suburb 1957-61 by P. A. Rahtz and J. Musty (*Wilts. Arch. Mag* 57 (1959), 179-91 and 353-70; 59 (1964), 130-54). The names used in the catalogue for the buildings at Old Sarum are those used in the account of Old Sarum in the Royal Commission on Historical Monuments (England) *Ancient and Historical Monuments in the City of Salisbury* Vol. 1 (1980). The precise contexts at Old Sarum of some finds from the 1909-15 excavations are unknown but are given where they can be identified in the *Proc. Soc. Antiq.* reports or in Hawley's manuscript diary of the excavations (*O.S. Diary*). The principal occupation period was eleventh to fourteenth century.

Clarendon Palace. The finds from the royal palace at Clarendon are divided between the Salisbury Museum and the British Museum. The excavations of John Charlton and Tancred Borenius in the 1930s and of John Musty in 1961 are reported in T. B. James and A. M. Robinson, *Clarendon Palace: The History and Archaeology of a Medieval Palace and Hunting Lodge near Salisbury, Wiltshire* with a report on the 'Tile Kiln and Floor Tiles' by Elizabeth Eames (London, 1988). The principal period of occupation was from the early twelfth to later fifteenth century.

Gomeldon. J. Musty and D. J. Algar place the finds from this site in their full context in 'Excavations at the deserted medieval village of Gomeldon, near Salisbury' in *Wilts. Arch. Mag.* 80 (1986), 127-69. Occupation from twelfth to fourteenth century was evidenced.

Ivychurch Priory. Materials recovered at the time of demolition in 1888-9 and from subsequent fieldwork in 1986. No formal excavations have taken place on the site. See *Churches of South-East Wiltshire* (RCHM(E), 1987), 149-53.

Alabasters

by Nigel Ramsay

INTRODUCTION

The Museum possesses five pieces of carved alabaster. Four are fragmentary, but the fifth is a nearly complete panel representing the head of St John the Baptist. It is an assemblage such as might be expected in any English county museum with collections that were largely put together in the nineteenth century, when the greatest number of alabasters was unearthed as a result of building works or excavations in churches, monastic sites and private houses.

Alabaster is a fine-grained form of gypsum (chemically, a hydrated sulphate of calcium). It was dug up or quarried close to the surface in sites in and around Fauld, by Hanbury, Staffordshire, and Chellaston, Derbyshire; it was carved close to where it was quarried and in nearby towns such as Burton-on-Trent (Ramsay 1991).

Between the later fourteenth century and the 1530s, the carving of alabaster became a highly successful enterprise. The imagers who cut the panels and freestanding figures were seemingly quite different from the carvers of tomb effigies and the side-panels of tombs. Only a few hundred tomb effigies were carved (if one can safely assume that a large proportion of them still survive *in situ* in parish churches): 317 in England and Wales dating from before 1540 are listed by Gardner 1940. Several tens of thousands of the panels and figures were carved - perhaps two or three panels, or occasionally even a whole retable, were to be found by the end of the Middle Ages in every one of England's ten thousand or so parish churches and chapels, while many hundreds were in private ownership; as many more were sold abroad, throughout western Europe and as far afield as Iceland and along the Baltic and Croatian coasts.

In the fifteenth and early sixteenth centuries, alabaster panels were usually mounted in carved and painted wooden frames: five, seven, nine or more panels would make up a retable, with 'battlementing' or carved pinnacle-work, in separate pieces of the stone, set above them. No such complete retable survives intact from any English church, although there are at least 80 scattered across the European Continent and in Iceland (listed by Cheetham 2003, 161-77) and the Victoria and Albert Museum, London, has one seven-panel altarpiece, complete with seven canopies or battlements and mounted in its original wooden frame with painted Latin inscriptions (Cheetham 1984, 70-1).

Documented examples that were in Wiltshire include: a great [re]table on the upper part of the altar, with images of alabaster, also described as a [re]table of alabaster for the altar with seven images and surmounted by a Crucifix, valued at 10 *s.*, in inventories of Holy Trinity hospital, Salisbury, 1418 and 1436 (Baker 1910, 381 and 385); a Pietà in the 'capella bassa' of the deanery at Salisbury, 1440 (Drinkwater 1964, 57); a [re]table in the choir and 'eleven altars: two of them [re] tables, three imagery, one double table of alabaster, another large altar with Saint Barbara in the midst, [of] alabaster, three other [re]tables of alabaster' in the dissolution inventory of the Dominican friary, Salisbury, 1538 (Palmer 1879, 172, 173; spelling modernised); and 'iii fayer tabyls of alabaster [valued at] vi s. viii d.' in the dissolution inventory of the Carmelite friary, Marlborough (Walcott 1870, 360).

The Reformation both ended the production of religious imagery of all sorts and, increasingly, made it a matter of suspicion for a private individual to own such works of devotional art. The churchwardens of parish churches did away with their alabasters: they either destroyed them, sold them (for instance, to the French) or hid them (perhaps by burying them under the church floor); private owners followed suit, doubtless more slowly.

The history of the English alabaster carvers' activities was only gradually pieced together by antiquaries from the later eighteenth century onwards. Victorian church restorers' activities led to a flood of discoveries, and prompted research; alabasters began to be staple items in the collections of antiquaries such as the Revd Edward Duke (d. 1852), F.S.A., of Salisbury (Anon 1855, 186; this carving fetched £45 in the sale of Duke's collection at Sotheby's, 10 July 1895, as mentioned in *Wilts. Arch. Mag.* 28 (1896), 260-2; see further Cheetham 2003, 159, no. 34). A panel showing the Adoration of the Magi and now in Mere church (Wiltshire) is not from that church, however, but was found *c.*1860 in a garden a quarter of a mile away (Lloyd 1906). The alabasters that have been discovered in such ways have mostly been in a battered or broken condition; some, indeed, may have been buried precisely because they were already broken and it was felt to be wrong to throw them onto a common refuse heap.

One over-hasty piece of research led to an unfortunate misunderstanding. The publication of excerpts from the medieval records of Nottingham, with several mentions of 'alabastermen', resulted in the assumption by W. H. St J. Hope, a pioneer in the study of alabaster sculpture, that the stone was carved in Nottingham. This town was actually only a centre for the distribution and sale of the carvings: the 'alabastermen' were merchants, whereas the sculptors (in Derbyshire and Staffordshire) were simply known as 'imagers' or 'carvers' (Ramsay 1991).

CATALOGUE

1 St John the Baptist panel.
The head of St John the Baptist is represented on a dish. Above, two angels support a mandorla carved with rays, which contains a naked, standing figure, representing the soul of the saint. On the left stands the figure of St Peter with key and book and on the right, almost certainly St Thomas of Canterbury wearing mitre and with pastoral staff. Below, the figure of Christ rising from the tomb. Compare Cheetham 1984, 330 no. 254. 15th century. H. 258mm. W.176 mm (max), Th. 40mm. No traces of paint remains. Two lead dowel holes with traces of latten wires survive in the flat back of the tablet The back has been cut away at centre bottom. Exhibited at the inaugural (temporary) museum by the WA&NHS at Devizes in 1853 (*Wilts. Arch. Mag.* 1 (1854), 66), when it belonged to a Mrs Sanger and was stated to be from the Cathedral at Old Sarum, and also in 1855 at a meeting of the Archaeological Institute by the Wilton antiquary, James Edward Nightingale, see Anon 1855, fig. opposite p.184; *Sal. Mus. Cat.* 1864, 76 and fig.; Hope 1890, 695-6, no.18; Anon 1951, no. 33. *iiH4; 1876.2*   **Pl 1**

Carvings of the head of St John the Baptist were probably made for private devotional use

(Hope 1890, 707).

2 Fragment of a St John the Baptist panel.
This is the lower part of a panel similar to that above. The figure of Christ (wearing the crown of thorns and with a wound in his left breast), rising from the tomb is flanked by two trees. Much original colouring remains; the trees have red and white paint and the background white dots grouped around red dots, all on a green base; even Christ's hair and beard are green. Second half of the 15th century. H. 131mm. W. 170mm. Th. 40mm. There are roughly cut recesses in the back of the tablet which coincide with the thickest areas. These are perhaps to reduce the weight. There is one central lead dowel. In addition there are saw marks probably made when the alabaster was first cut into slabs. Found in the kitchen wall of the Old Parsonage (now The Grange), Winterbourne Dauntsey, in about 1860. *Sal. Mus. Rep.* 1950-1, 8 and pl. between 10 and 11; Shortt 1960, 31 no. 73; Anon 1951, no. 33a. *1951.47*
Pl 1 & cover

3 Fragment of a ?saint figure.
Left hand holding ?pastoral staff. It retains traces of dark green colour and gilding.

This is perhaps a fragment from the figure of a saint (such as Thomas Becket, Archbishop of Canterbury), approximately one half life size. H. 85mm. W. 50mm. Th. 25mm (max). Said to have been dug up at a church 'near Stonehenge' before *c.*1866, leading to the rather unlikely suggestion that it is from Amesbury Abbey. *iiH5; 1876.14*   **Pl 1**

4 Fragment of a Crucifixion panel.
Lower part of the figure of Christ with, to the right, a vertical shaft (i.e. lance) and a gloved right hand pointing upwards to the cross. Scrolls for lettering; but no trace of paint remains. This is a fragment of an early panel (*c.*1400) and the alabaster is very white. H. *c.*115mm. W. 190mm. Th. 45mm (max). The panel is basically 20mm. thick. The back is flat with chisel marks. From Stratford-sub-Castle. *Sal. Mus. Cat.* 1864, 78; *Sal. Mus. Cat.* 1870, 59 no. 5. *iiH2*   **Pl 1**

5 Corner fragment of an ?Adoration of the Magi panel.
Part of an angular, castellated canopy above a curtain, pulled aside to the left and revealing a red background (perhaps once gilded) flecked with white spots. On the curtain there is a right hand, palm outwards with the index finger pointing upwards. There are traces of gilding at the curtain edge and red paint in the crenellations. The panel must be of the Annuciation, Nativity or Adoration; almost certainly the Adoration of the Magi, the hand being that of one of the Magi pointing at a star (compare Cheetham 2003, illus. 54 and 55). *c.*1400? H. 115mm. W. 127mm. Th. 46mm (max). The back is smooth, apart from six (modern) scratches. Possibly from Ivychurch Priory (see *Proc. Soc. Antiq.* 13 (1891), 355). *Sal. Mus. Cat.* 1864, 78; *Sal. Mus. Cat.* 1870, 59 no. 4. *iiH1*   **Pl 1**

Another medieval alabaster was at one time in the Museum collection and is mentioned here for completeness of the record: a headless, handless, seated figure. H. 95mm. W. 76mm. Found in the church at Sturminster Marshall, Dorset, presented to the Museum in 1871 and transferred to Dorset County Museum in 1952. *iiH3*. It was suggested by W. L. Hildburgh that it was possibly St John, from a crucifixion scene, of late fourteenth-century date.

BIBLIOGRAPHY

Anderson, W. 2004: 'Re-discovery, collecting and display of English medieval alabasters', *J. Hist. Collections* **16(i)**, 47-58

Anon 1855: 'Notes on alabaster heads of St John the Baptist', *Archaeol. J.* **12**, 184-6

Anon 1951: *Salisbury - Festival of Britain 1951 - Catalogue of the Civic and Ecclesiastical Treasures* (Bennett Bros, Salisbury)

Baker, T. H. 1910: 'The Trinity Hospital, Salisbury', *Wilts. Arch. Mag.* **36**, 376-412

Cheetham, F. 1984: *English Medieval Alabasters: With a Catalogue of the Collection in the Victoria and Albert Museum* (Oxford)

Cheetham, F. 2003: *Alabaster Images of Medieval England* (Woodbridge)

Drinkwater, N. 1964: 'The Old Deanery, Salisbury', *Antiq. J.* **44**, 41-59

Gardner, A. 1940: *Alabaster Tombs of the Pre-Reformation Period in England* (Cambridge)

Hope, W. H. St J. 1890: 'On the Sculptured Alabaster Tablets called Saint John's Heads', *Archaeologia* **52**, pt. 2, 669-708

Lloyd, J. A. 1906: 'An Alabaster Panel at Mere, Wiltshire', *The Antiquary* **42**, 26-7

Oakes, C. 2006: 'Dr Hildburgh and the English medieval alabaster', *J. Hist. Collections* **18(i)**, 71-83

Palmer, C. F. R. 1879: 'The Black Friars of Wiltshire', *Wilts. Arch. Mag.* **18**, 162-76

Ramsay, N. L. 1991: 'Alabaster' in W. J. Blair and N. L. Ramsay (eds.), *English Medieval Industries: Craftsmen, Techniques, Products* (London and Rio Grande, Ohio), 29-40

Shortt, H. 1960: *The Collections Illustrated* (Salisbury)

Walcott, M. E. C. 1870: 'Inventories of Church Goods and Chantries of Wilts.', *Wilts. Arch. Mag.* **12**, 354-83

Pl 1. Alabasters: Cat 1 (scale 1:3), 2-5 (scale varies, see text)

Architectural and Sculptured Stonework

by Allan Brodie and David Algar

Editor's note:
To improve appreciation of the stonework, Allan Brodie includes essays on the architectural history of the various sites. That devoted to Old Sarum is detailed and may be of wider interest than purely as background to the catalogued fragments. The great importance of the Museum collection is emphasised and its interpretation is provided in a more easily accessible form than generally available in the published literature.

INTRODUCTION

Salisbury Museum contains a substantial collection of carved stone fragments from Old Sarum. Some of the stones came to the Museum as a result of excavations that took place in the early twentieth century while others arrived by a more circuitous route, being recovered from demolished buildings in and around Salisbury and Old Sarum. Most of the fragments originated from the former cathedral, though some fragments in the Museum and in the collection contained in the English Heritage (hereafter 'EH') stone store at Fort Cumberland, Portsmouth, probably came from the castle and the bishop's palace. Through studying these diverse fragments, in combination with the evidence of excavations and comparisons with contemporary buildings, it is possible to begin to visualise the scale and the detailed form of Old Sarum at its height in the twelfth century.

A smaller number of fragments from another great lost building in South Wiltshire, Clarendon Palace, provide hints of the scale and quality of the building campaigns during the twelfth and thirteenth centuries. When the finds from excavations at Clarendon were divided between the British Museum and Salisbury in 1957, the excavated stonework came to Salisbury Museum.

The Museum also holds fragments from other sites where there are more substantial remains. Most important is a small number of Purbeck marble carved stones from Salisbury Cathedral, and there is also a single, very high quality capital that originated from Glastonbury Abbey. The collection also possesses carved stone fragments recovered from a number of lesser buildings in and around Salisbury and South Wiltshire.

CATALOGUE

Editor's note:
The abbreviation 'D.' stands for 'depth' throughout this section of the catalogue. Where 'diameter' is abbreviated it appears as 'diam.' It has not proved practical to reproduce the pieces in photographic images to a common scale and individual dimensions should therefore be taken from catalogue entries.

OLD SARUM

The Foundation of Old Sarum

In 1075 an edict of the Council of London ordered the transfer of cathedrals to more populous places, leading to the unification of the sees of Ramsbury and Sherborne and the transplantation of the new see to Old Sarum (Report 1909, 191; RCHM(E) 1980, 15; Stroud 1986, 120). The site chosen for the new cathedral was an Iron Age hill-fort, which the Romans named Sorviodunum. It was probably the site of the battle of Searobyrg in 552 when the Saxons defeated the Britons. Following a Danish attack on the borough of Wilton in 1003, Old Sarum seems to have grown in importance, making it the most suitable location for a cathedral (RCHM(E) 1980, 1).

Immediately after the Norman Conquest, a timber, motte-and-bailey castle was established and ditches were dug running north to south, subdividing the area within the hill-fort. Within the north-west part of the fort the cathedral was erected (Report 1909, 191). In creating a cathedral beside a castle, the builders at Old Sarum were following a common procedure for dominating, practically and psychologically, the conquered population. Similar arrangements are found at Durham, Lincoln and Rochester, while at Malmesbury Bishop Roger of Salisbury erected a castle near the west end of the abbey.

Herman, who was the Bishop of Sherborne before 1075, then of Old Sarum from 1075 to 1078, probably began the construction of the new cathedral, but most of the work took place under his successor Bishop Osmund (1078-99) (Report 1909, 191; RCHM(E) 1980, 15). According to tradition Osmund was a nephew of William the Conqueror and by 1066 he was one of his chaplains. In 1070 or 1072 he became Chancellor, but in 1078 he relinquished the post to become bishop of Salisbury (Rogers 1978/9, 32; Oxford DNB online). However, he may have continued to be involved in royal administration and may have had a role in the compilation of Domesday Book (Oxford DNB online). Osmund was the bishop who probably produced the first elements of what became the Use of Sarum, a blueprint for the constitution of cathedrals (Greenaway 1996, 1). He also founded a library at the cathedral and established the song school (Rogers 1978/9, 34). He died in December 1099 after a long illness and was buried near the High Altar. His canonisation took place on 1 January 1457 and a shrine was created in the Lady Chapel of Salisbury Cathedral (Rogers 1978/9, 36; Oxford DNB online).

The cathedral at Old Sarum was consecrated on 5 April 1092, but five days later it was apparently struck by lightning and damaged, though this may be an attempt to gloss over a failure in the construction of the building. Excavators in 1914 believed that scorched and reddened stones in the excavations might date from this event, though the troubled later history of the site may be more likely to have been responsible (Report 1913-4, 102). The damage may not have been substantial as repairs were apparently completed before Osmund died seven years later.

The eleventh-century church had an apse-echelon plan with the apses of the aisles being enclosed externally within square walls, a form repeated in the early twelfth-century reconstruction (Report 1913-4, 103). Osmund's church did not have full transepts, but seems to have had side towers in the position of transepts. A similar arrangement existed in the slightly later Norman cathedral at Exeter until its reconstruction in the thirteenth century (RCHM(E) 1980, 17, Thurlby 1991, 37ff.). Excavations of the church revealed no other possible location for a tower. Therefore, it was presumably one of these transeptal towers that was damaged by lightning in 1092. When the choir was rebuilt in the early twelfth century the width of the central part of the east end was increased and large piers were built for a prominent central tower. Both these suggest that the intention was to replace the original, narrower, and presumably, lower nave of the eleventh-century church. However, the fall of Bishop Roger in 1139 allowed seven bays of the original nave to survive until the cathedral was abandoned in the thirteenth century. Excavations suggest that the original west façade was a simple screen, originally unembellished with towers.

Osmund's successor, Bishop Roger rebuilt the east end of the cathedral, creating one of the most richly decorated buildings of its day. Roger had served as a chaplain and steward to Henry I. In 1101 he was appointed as Chancellor, a position he relinquished when he became Bishop of Old Sarum in 1102, although his consecration did not take place until 1107 (Kealey 1972, 12 and 21). William of Malmesbury described how:

> 'king Henry had among his counsellors, Roger, bishop of Salisbury, on whose advice he principally relied; for, before his accession, he had made him regulator of his household; and, on becoming king, having had proof of his abilities, first made him his chancellor, and then a bishop.' (William of Malmesbury 1989, 142.)

During his thirty-five year reign, Henry I spent seventeen years in Normandy and therefore needed reliable advisers to manage royal affairs in England.

Henry appointed Roger as Regent during his absence in 1123–6 and probably on other occasions:

> 'Nor did he deceive the royal expectation; but conducted himself with so much integrity and diligence, that not a spark of envy was kindled against him. Moreover, the king was frequently detained in Normandy, sometimes for three, sometimes four years, and sometimes for a longer period; and on his return to his kingdom, he laid it to the credit of his justiciar's discretion that he found little or nothing to distress him.' (William of Malmesbury 1989, 143.)

In recognition of Bishop Roger's work, the King rewarded him with substantial estates:

> 'he [Henry I] gave him estates, churches, prebends, entire abbeys of monks; and lastly committed even the kingdom to his fidelity: he made him chancellor in the beginning of his reign, and not long after, Bishop of Salisbury. Roger, therefore, decided causes; he regulated the expenditure; he had charge of the treasury.' (William of Malmesbury 1988, 31.)

As long as Henry continued as monarch, Roger seems to have had an unassailable position, but the politics of the king's succession led to Roger's downfall. After Henry's death in 1135 Roger accepted Stephen of Blois' claim to the throne despite having sworn allegiance to Matilda in 1131. His reward included being granted the borough and hundred of Malmesbury. Roger attended Stephen's coronation at Christmas 1135; yet despite such a conspicuous show of allegiance, Stephen was still suspicious of Roger and his family. William of Malmesbury recorded that Alberic de Ver alleged that 'the bishop of Salisbury secretly favoured the king's enemies' and 'that it was in every person's mouth, that as soon as the empress should arrive, he would join her party, with his nephews and his castles'. (William of Malmesbury 1988, 27-8.)

In 1139 Roger was summoned to see King Stephen at Oxford. 'The bishop of Salisbury set out on this expedition with great reluctance', apparently suspicious of the king's motives. A dispute arose about accommodation at the assembly and the king ordered that the staff of the bishop should be punished as they had:

> 'infringed his peace; and that this satisfaction should be, the delivery of the keys of their castles, as pledges of their fidelity. Though prepared to make compensation, they hesitated at the surrender of their fortresses; and in consequence, lest they should depart, he ordered them into close confinement. So he took bishop Roger unfettered, but the chancellor, the nephew, (or as it was reported, more than a nephew,) of the bishop, in chains, to Devizes; intending, if he could, to get possession of the castle, which was erected at great and almost incalculable expense, not, as the prelate himself used to say, for the ornament, but as the real fact is, to the detriment of the church.'

(William of Malmesbury 1988, 25.)

Roger, his son, Roger the Chancellor, and his nephew Bishop Alexander of Lincoln were seized but his other nephew Nigel, Bishop of Ely, escaped to his uncle's castle at Devizes, though it was surrendered after a brief siege. Roger was returned to Old Sarum, effectively as a prisoner where he died on 11 December 1139 (William of Malmesbury 1988, 30). Roger was buried in the cathedral at Old Sarum, and on 14 June 1226 his remains were transferred to the new cathedral in Salisbury. When he died he left over 40,000 silver marks and a vast amount of gold, wealth derived from the properties granted to him by Henry I, supplemented by income probably obtained through his central position in the royal household (William of Malmesbury 1988, 28). Roger was a man with expensive tastes, with a liking for expensive works of art: 'His cathedral he dignified to the utmost with matchless ornaments' (William of Malmesbury 1988, 31). William of Malmesbury also recorded his admiration for Roger's buildings:

> 'With unrivalled magnificence in their construction, as our times may recollect, he erected splendid mansions on all his estates'. (William of Malmesbury 1988, 31.)

> 'He was a prelate of a great mind, and spared no expense in buildings, as may be seen in many places, but more particularly at Salisbury and at Malmesbury. For there he erected extensive edifices, at vast cost, and with surpassing beauty; the courses of stone being so accurately laid, that the line of juncture escapes the eye, and leads one to imagine that the whole wall is composed of a single block. He built anew the church of Salisbury, and beautified it in such a manner that it yields to none in England, but surpasses many; so that he had just cause to say "Lord, I have loved the glory of thy house."' (William of Malmesbury 1989, 143.)

Roger built castles at Sherborne, Malmesbury, Devizes, Old Sarum and perhaps Kidwelly. At Sherborne the buildings were arranged around a courtyard, a layout similar to the remains of the castle at Old Sarum (Stalley 1971, 68; RCHM(E) 1980, 8). The castle at Malmesbury, which was immediately to the west of the west front of the abbey, was demolished in 1216. Devizes Castle was demolished in 1646, though some Norman fabric has survived there and has been reused in a number of houses in the town. However, Bishop Roger's major architectural work was the rebuilding of the east end of the cathedral at Old Sarum.

Old Sarum Cathedral in the 12th Century

Bishop Roger rebuilt the choir, created full transepts with east and west aisles, built a treasury and laid out the cloister to the north of the new choir during the first four decades of the twelfth century (RCHM(E) 1980, 15). At his death there is conflicting evidence over whether the east end was fully completed. William of Malmesbury is clear that he 'built anew the church of Salisbury' but in the *Gesta Stephani* a small part of the bishop's fortune was left in his will to roof the church (Montague 2006, 52). Roofing may be a euphemism for finishing off the construction programme, but regardless of the actual state of the building in 1139, what is clear is that the building was conceived and driven forward to effective completion by Bishop Roger.

The church built in the late eleventh century was 173ft long from east to west and 113½ft across the 'transepts'. As a result of Roger's building campaign its overall size was increased to 316ft long and 138ft wide (Report 1913-4, 111). The plan of his church has been recovered through excavations, but no significant upstanding fabric of the church has survived. However, through examination of carved fragments combined with an examination of contemporary surviving churches, it is possible to begin to reconstruct some aspects of the cathedral's appearance.

The new, square, east end had a projecting central eastern chapel flanked by two smaller chapels. Though the chapels terminated in apses internally, externally they were treated as square blocks. Between the chapels, excavations revealed narrow spaces, the purpose of which is uncertain. A similar arrangement can be found in the later east end of Winchester Cathedral where the thickened sections between the chapels seem to be related to access to a proposed upper storey. An alternative interpretation is that the original layout included some form of raised floor within the central chapel that was removed later in the twelfth century (RCHM(E) 1980, 19).

The plan uncovered in the early twentieth century revealed the substantial piers of the crossing. These suggest that Roger had probably intended to rebuild the earlier nave, probably with a substantial central tower. The new constructions were considerably larger than their eleventh-century predecessors and therefore there would have been a notable disparity in size with the surviving nave, though not quite on the scale of Beauvais Cathedral where the thirteenth-century choir and sixteenth-century transepts tower over the Carolingian nave.

After Roger's death a narthex was built at the west end of the nave by Bishop Jocelyn de Bohun (1142-84) (RCHM(E) 1980, 16). It consisted of twin towers flanking a new west door and measured 75ft wide and 30½ ft deep (Report 1913-4, 110). It was built in front of the former simple screen façade from the early Norman cathedral. The towers were markedly rectangular in plan, and a tower of a similar shape was built at St John's in Devizes, a church which may have been associated with Bishop Roger.

Envisaging the elevations of the cathedral is inevitably more speculative than establishing the plan, but it is possible to describe some elements of the building with a degree of certainty. The east end would have probably been of three storeys, with a tall main arcade, a shorter triforium and a clerestory, probably with a single window and a tripartite arrangement of arches in front. This assertion can be made, both through the evidence of surviving fragments and by examining contemporary major churches. An alternative reconstruction is that the cathedral had a giant order, the form of elevation employed at St Frideswide, Oxford and perhaps at Reading Abbey (Thurlby and Baxter 2002, 291). Bishop Roger was a patron of Reading and therefore there could be links between the designs of the two buildings. However, the use of the giant order was always a minority approach and churches in the west of England influenced by Old Sarum reveal no obvious signs of this unorthodoxy.

The carved stone fragments that have survived reveal that the east end was very elaborate, probably with most significant features being embellished internally and probably externally. The original function of fragments is revealed by their form and by finding parallels in other churches to illustrate their potential position in the building. The nave at Malmesbury seems to have had many details in common with Old Sarum and although it was probably built in the third quarter of the twelfth century, its overall form may provide a suitable armature on which to apply the surviving carved detailing from Old Sarum. Features that were used on many occasions have survived in significant numbers while those that were used in only a few places may not have left any trace. For instance, in Roger's choir there were only six major pier capitals, three on each side of the choir and none still exist. However, dozens of small decorated roundels, which were probably around the exterior of the windows, have survived.

The main arcade may have been carried on circular columns with large scalloped capitals. There is nothing to indicate how tall these piers were, but if Old Sarum followed the practice of other major western English churches it could have had tall piers, like the naves of Gloucester, Tewkesbury, Pershore and perhaps Exeter cathedral. Alternatively the pier height may have been lower, similar to Malmesbury Abbey, as the arcades of both churches share a number of other features in common. For instance, a large stone decorated with a Greek-key pattern (Cat 29) may have originated in the arches of the main arcades of the east end. Alternatively this fragment may have been part of a substantial doorway, as this motif can be paralleled in the central western door at Lincoln Cathedral and Kenilworth Priory which both share other details with Old Sarum. Around the top parts of the main arcade arches there were probably hood moulds decorated with three rows of cylindrical billet (Cat 30) while at the apex there was a mask with teeth, biting the hood mould (Cat 16). Both these features appear in the nave of Malmesbury Abbey, though the mask biting the hood mould was also used in the nave of Gloucester Cathedral.

Two other features at Malmesbury may have been prominent on the lower storey of the elevation at Old Sarum. In the Museum (Cat 28), as well as in the EH stone store (no. 81109783), there are long narrow stones decorated with a Greek-key pattern consisting of alternating T-shapes and inverted T-shapes. This pattern is set on an angled surface, as if it was a string course designed to be seen from below. The same design was used as the string course between the nave arcades and the triforium in Malmesbury. However, in the same position in the choir at Malmesbury there was a small, arched, decorative frieze, similar to the form of a corbel table, and a stone with the same type of arrangement has been reset in the exterior of the east wall of the Cathedral Close at Salisbury. Therefore, there are two potential parallels at Malmesbury for treating the area between the arcades and triforium and it is unclear which was used in Old Sarum, or whether both were employed. Another possibility is that the Greek-key pattern was between the triforium and the clerestory, while the arched frieze was between the arcade and the triforium.

Above the main arcade there was probably a short triforium, the standard form found in churches in the west of England. The only fragments that may belong to its structure are two voussoirs, one being the junction between two arches (Cat 59 and 61). These are both decorated with a chevron pattern and the second voussoir appears to fit above the junction stone. The underside of the stones suggests that there was a second, inner order in the arch. Therefore, the triforium may have consisted of two pairs of arches, similar to, but more elaborate than in the nave of Gloucester Cathedral and comparable to one possible interpretation of the form of the former Romanesque Cathedral at Exeter (Thurlby 1991, 44). The alternative would be to have an arrangement similar to Malmesbury and Old Sarum's contemporary, St Bartholomew's at Smithfield, where the standard bay has four smaller arches set within a larger arch spanning the width of the bay.

Another piece in the Museum's collection may originate from the triforium. A surviving fragment, apparently shaped like a voussoir, has a raised quatrefoil similar to the numerous surviving roundels but decorated with lumpy foliage (Cat 21). There are also six examples of this form in the wall of the Cathedral Close and at least one in the EH stone store. Though a common fragment, it does not survive as frequently as the simpler roundels. Rather than being voussoirs, these stones may have been part of the tympana of the triforium. Similar foliage studs appear on the triforium of the two west bays of the nave of Worcester Cathedral and in the transepts, while comparable, but more elaborate forms appear in the triforium at Wells Cathedral and at Glastonbury Abbey. Although these are all considerably later, and probably not immediately related to Old Sarum, they do offer a parallel to explain these odd survivors from the demolished building.

No fragments survive from Old Sarum that can definitely be ascribed to the interior of the clerestory. However, vault ribs in the EH stone store, as well as the practice in the west of England in the early twelfth century, suggest that there were high vaults in the east end, as well as in the aisles (Report 1913-4, photograph opposite 112; Hoey and Thurlby 2004, 123; Thurlby and Baxter 2002, 297).

The form of the interior of the aisles is unknown though it is likely that there were single windows in each bay. In the Museum's collection and in the EH stone store there are remnants of elaborate string courses, particularly two sections in the Museum decorated with opposed, S-shaped motifs (Cat 26 and 27). The stones have the carving on an angled surface, while the quality of the detailing suggests that they were suitable to be seen close up.

Some fragments from Old Sarum retain traces of colour, although this is sometimes a result of their reuse. However, some of the traces clearly indicate that both internal and external sculpture was painted. One stone in the collection has the remains of a painted masonry pattern on it (Cat 34).

Externally the church was also elaborate and some of the most accomplished carving seems to have been reserved for the corbel table of the aisles and above the clerestory. The quality of the best carving suggests that the heads were expected to be seen relatively close up, probably along the eaves of the aisles. Corbel tables were features of some major cathedrals, such as Winchester and Ely, and at Reading Abbey, and they appear in Wiltshire churches such as St John, Devizes and Holy Cross, Sherston. A corbel table was also used at Lullington (Somerset). These local churches can be associated with Old Sarum through other details or in the case of Sherston with Old Sarum via Malmesbury Abbey.

Two voussoirs in the Museum's collection (Cat 14 and 15) have been shown to originate from a rose window, probably located in the transept façades (Thurlby 1981, 93-8). The presence of a rose window has been linked with Abbot Suger's west façade at St Denis (1137-40). Suger drew artists from all over Europe and could have attracted people familiar with Old Sarum, but the link could also be as a result of contacts between St Denis and Lincoln Cathedral where Bishop Roger's nephew, Alexander, was the bishop. A number of motifs link the 1140s west façade at Lincoln Cathedral to Old Sarum and buildings associated with it. The voussoirs from the rose window have extravagant mouthfuls of foliage, reminiscent of the beakheads on the inner order of the central door at Lincoln. Lincoln also has the large embattled motif and decorated roundels found at Old Sarum and churches derived from it. The hood mould of the central door of Lincoln Cathedral's west façade has dragons' heads as terminals, a motif found at Malmesbury and in a photograph in the National Monuments Record of a fragment from Old Sarum, which cannot be located at present. The likely mechanism for the dissemination of designs from Old Sarum in the 1140s is Roger's workshop being dispersed after 1139 to local churches and further afield through his family connections. However, knowledge of Old Sarum may have been acquired at Lincoln in the 1130s, though no fabric from this period survives to prove this.

Old Sarum had a major entrance in the south wall of the south transept, sheltered by a substantial porch. The practice of creating a major side entrance to a church became well established in the west of England by the late twelfth century, for instance at Wells and Salisbury Cathedrals and Malmesbury Abbey. These were side entrances to the nave rather than as at Old Sarum where it had to be in the south transept as the nave had not yet been rebuilt. The porch was dated by RCHM(E) to the episcopate of Bishop Jocelyn (RCHM(E) 1980, 20). The evidence they used was the date that they attributed to the fragment from a gable decorated with lions found in excavations (Cat 5). However, other fragments in the area and even this fragment could date from Bishop Roger's episcopacy. The excavation reports before World War I do not include any evidence to suggest that the porch was added to the transept. The angle of the sides of the gable decorated with two lions corresponds to the incline of the sides of a stone in the EH stone store, a stone decorated with a large, beaded roundel (no. 81109792). The moulding on the side of the gable stone is repeated in other fragments recovered from the excavations. These fragments would be visually effective over a porch rather than being from the apex of a tall transept. Two other stones from the tops of gables were also recovered in 1912, suggesting a series of gables on the porch or some other part of the façade (Report 1913-4, 115). There is also evidence to suggest that the interior of the porch was lavishly treated. Two stones from the broad order of a doorway, similar to the south door of Malmesbury Abbey, survive (Cat 24 and 25). If Old Sarum's south porch was the inspiration for Malmesbury, was there also a parallel for the large friezes in its side walls? The head of Christ (Cat 1) originated from a large frieze composed of a number of stones, an arrangement similar to Malmesbury but equally to Chichester where they were originally in the choir (Zarnecki 1953b, 108-13).

Another doorway with interesting parallels to Old Sarum, Malmesbury and Lincoln, is at Kenilworth, where the west door is set within a square surround edged with large, eight-lobed floral motifs. A strange four-lobed flower (Cat 23), probably originally from Old Sarum, may have performed a similar function. The outer order at Kenilworth, like the west door at Lincoln, has an embattled decoration. In the spandrels inside the surround at Kenilworth there are large beaded roundels similar to those in the nave clerestory at Malmesbury, Llandaff Cathedral, Portchester (Hampshire), Lullington (Somerset), the north portal of St Michael's, Bockleton (Worcestershire) and in fragments excavated at Newark Castle (Stalley 1971, 75; Thurlby 1981, 97). These beaded roundels are similar to the stone, in the EH stone store, from the porch gable at Old Sarum. There were also dozens of smaller roundels at Old Sarum. Lullington is important in the study of these circular decorations as its north door has beaded roundels in its gable, the smaller roundels decorated with quatrefoil-shaped 'ravioli' and a figure of Christ that has been linked to sculpture at Old Sarum.

The Sculptors of Old Sarum and the Characteristics of their Work

In 1971 Roger Stalley identified characteristics of the work of Old Sarum's leading sculptor and in 1990 James F. King christened him 'The Old Sarum Master' (Stalley 1971, 75-6; King 1990, 70). The characteristics of his work included bulbous eyes with large, drilled pupils and flat bands around the eyes. He also decorated some key lines of carvings with beading and often employed a design of hair with little curls at the end of each lock. Within the collection there are a number of fragments carved by a sculptor of great accomplishment, more 'realistic' in form, if that term can be applied to grotesques, as well as more three-dimensional. However, what the Museum's collection also demonstrates is that there were other sculptors working with him, carvers who deliberately mimic his overall style, but in a less accomplished fashion. This disparity is obvious in the figurative sculpture, but a similar difference in quality can be detected in some of the geometric fragments. It seems as

if the Old Sarum master set the form and style for other carvers to follow; in modern parlance he established the house style for the sculpture of the east end of the Cathedral.

The most skilful carver at Old Sarum seems to have been responsible for Cat 5, 7, 9, and 16. These sculptures have the characteristics described above combined with the plasticity of the leading sculptor. He was also probably the sculptor who produced the most accomplished corbel in English Heritage's collection (no. 81109754). However, Cat 10, 11, 13, 14 and 15 also have similar characteristics, but are obviously not of the first level of quality. Some fragments such as the stones from the rose window (Cat 14 and 15) are by a carver of considerable ability, though without the flare of the leading sculptor, and a corbel held by English Heritage seems to be by the same hand (no. 811 09855). At the bottom of the ability scale is the piper corbel (Cat 11) and the corbels (Cat 10 and 13) which are pale imitations of the master's work.

A similar difference in the skill of the execution can also be detected in one of the geometric emblems most frequently employed in the east end of the Cathedral. Dozens of examples of the small, four-lobed forms set within a circular frame appear in the wall around the Cathedral Close, in Salisbury Museum and in the EH stone store. Most examples consist of a diamond-orientated shape with curved sides, but Cat 19 in the Museum is an example of the more delicately-carved example. The four sides of the diamond are curved and are reminiscent of folded-over pasta, hence the nickname 'ravioli'. Each edge is also decorated with a line of drilled holes. These more skilful shapes account for about a quarter of the surviving examples.

The Influence of Old Sarum

Few pieces of mid twelfth-century sculpture and architectural detailing approach the general quality of Old Sarum, let alone the level of plasticity achieved by the leading carver. Therefore, when the Old Sarum workshop disbanded around 1139, its craftsmen would have been in demand. It has been argued by some authors that Old Sarum is connected to the major strands of sculptural and architectural thinking in large parts of England as well as in France and it is possible to find parallels for the detailed treatment of motifs in such distant workshops as St. Denis, in Burgundy and in south-western France. However, in some instances the normally elastic power of comparison is probably tested to breaking point, but the direct impact of the work at Old Sarum can be detected with confidence within local workshops, through territories subject to the influence of Old Sarum and through the family connections of Bishop Roger. Realistically, the influence of Old Sarum can be observed most strongly in sites in modern Wiltshire and eastern Somerset, in south Wales and Ireland, and, as has already been outlined, in a number of buildings in the Midlands.

In and around Wiltshire examples of the influence of Old Sarum can be divided into two distinct groups. In the southern half of the county and at nearby Lullington in Somerset, the influence is direct and immediate, probably dating from around the dissolution of the workshop in 1139. The highly-distinctive 'ravioli' appear at Durnford and Lullington. Berwick St Leonard can boast the simpler roundels, and at Codford St Peter a diaper circle and imbricated pattern are employed. Codford St Mary has two fragments that show some evidence of Old Sarum's influence. One stone is decorated with a beakhead with large oval eyes, drilled pupils and pointed ears, set within a strap-work pattern. A second fragment is a head with a large snout, and large oval eyes surrounded by beading and drilled pupils.

Further north at Chirton beakheads are employed, uncommon features in Wiltshire, and Devizes can boast two churches that differ from any others in the county. Their sophistication, including the employment of rib vaults, suggests they were created while the town felt the influence of Roger of Salisbury. There are also some motifs, such as the imbrication on walls, that appear at Old Sarum.

Old Sarum may have also had an impact on another major lost building of Wiltshire, Wilton Abbey. During repairs that took place in the 1990s the bottom of an elaborate door was revealed with a spiral-fluted, engaged shaft flanked by two orders decorated with geometric decoration including beaded strap-work. Although these motifs cannot be precisely paralleled at Old Sarum, the level of elaboration does reflect the cathedral and it is unlikely that Wilton could have been entirely immune from its influence.

Much of Old Sarum's local impact can be witnessed in churches in the northern half of Wiltshire later in the twelfth century and this is certainly the result of the transmission of ideas via Malmesbury Abbey. The abbey was rebuilt during the middle years of the twelfth century, and as its reconstruction is not referred to by William of Malmesbury, it may not have taken place until after 1143. However, the plan of the east end, and the few details that survive from it, could suggest a date earlier in the twelfth century, perhaps contemporary with the choir of Old Sarum. The church seems to have been complete or nearing completion in 1177 (Brodie 1988, 31ff.).

Excavations revealed that the choir of Malmesbury Abbey had a rounded east end with an ambulatory, not a square end as at Old Sarum. All that is known of its vertical form is contained in a narrow strip of masonry attached to the north-east crossing pier. This demonstrates that its overall form and proportions were similar to the later nave, but that its detailing was significantly earlier than the nave. The only motif with obvious links to Old Sarum is the remnant of the decorative, arched corbel table beneath the gallery which resembles a reset fragment in the wall of Salisbury Cathedral's Close. In the nave of Malmesbury Abbey many motifs seem to be derived from Old Sarum. However, it is the dragon-head terminal of the nave arcades that seem to have captured the imagination of northern Wiltshire sculptors. Similar, though less accomplished, versions of this form appear in parish churches at Castle Eaton, Hankerton, Bishopstone near Wanborough and Wroughton.

Old Sarum's influence can also be detected at Lullington (Somerset), a small church with an elaborate north door set in a gable, a corbel table and elaborate carvings to the arches around the central tower, especially the western arch. The door in the north side of the nave is set within a gable, the apex of which contains a niche with a seated figure of Christ flanked on either side by two pairs of beaded roundels. A similar gabled design appears at Roscrea (Tipperary), including two rather than four roundels flanking the niche above the door opening (Stalley 1971, 79; De Breffny and Mott 1976, 32-4; Henry 1970, 175-7). Old Sarum may have influenced another, more significant Irish church, which in turn influenced Roscrea. The north gable of Cormac's chapel at Cashel (Tipperary) is decorated with rosettes like those at Old Sarum (Stalley 1971, 80). This church was completed in 1134 and therefore may indicate that Old Sarum's impact was already being felt before Roger's demise (De Breffny and Mott 1976, 30; Henry 1970, 170). Gabled doorways become a popular feature in Irish churches and appear in the north of England at Kirkstall and at a number of churches in Scotland, but these do not share any of the distinctive motifs from Old Sarum. Although the figure of Christ at Lullington is eroded, it is possible to see echoes of the frieze on the west front of Lincoln Cathedral and of the later figures in the south porch at Malmesbury. The outer order of the north door at Lullington has beakheads strikingly similar in detail to the Old Sarum beakhead and the mask that decorated a label mould (Cat 9 and 16). To confirm the link to Old Sarum the sculptor has kindly set a couple of the distinctive 'ravioli' on the arch of the north door and on the jambs of the otherwise fairly plain south doorway. Internally the west arch of the crossing has capitals that also seem to be in a clear Old Sarum style. For instance, one capital has muscular lions with tufty manes and long curling tails, reminiscent of the gablet from Old Sarum with lions (Cat 5), while another has a pair of heads with the drilled, oval pupils characterised by the Old Sarum sculptors. The link with Old

Sarum seems incontestable and the quality of some of the sculpture suggests the presence of the leading sculptor from the cathedral or one of his most skilled assistants.

The beaded roundel motif at Lullington, which later adorns the exterior of the clerestory of the nave of Malmesbury, is also found at Llandaff Cathedral and a dragon-head terminal to a hood mould is also found in South Wales, at Ewenny Priory. Roger of Salisbury may have built a castle at Kidwelly and therefore there may be a plausible reason why craftsmen from Old Sarum might be present in Wales (Stalley 1971, 70-1). However, while some of these Welsh works may date from the time of Roger's episcopacy, others could date from after his downfall and the break up of the workshop.

In addition to an influence spreading westwards, a church in southern Gloucestershire, Leonard Stanley's priory church, also shares some characteristics in its sculpture with Old Sarum and Lullington. In two capitals in the north and south side of the choir, and in a reset tympanum in the south wall of the choir, there is sculpture of greater skill than the scallop capitals of the crossing. The tympanum has two lions with drilled oval eyes, muscular legs and the beaded mane. They resemble the lions of the gablet from Old Sarum (Cat 5) and are strikingly similar to a capital decorated with a pair of lions sharing a single head at Lullington. At Leonard Stanley two capitals depict Mary Magdalene washing Christ's feet and a nativity scene. Although nothing comparable survives from Old Sarum, the shape of the heads and eyes and the general plasticity of the carving probably indicate that the same sculptor as the tympanum was responsible for their execution. In the crossing and on the north door of the church, there are hood moulds treated with dragon-head terminals which also seem to originate from Old Sarum.

As well as clear links to churches in and around Wiltshire, in Wales and Ireland, there were a number of buildings in the Midlands where similar detailing can be found. Foremost amongst these was Lincoln Cathedral, but others included Newark Castle and Kenilworth Priory. There are also three isolated examples of mid twelfth-century sculpture with apparent links to Old Sarum. A carved, stone head in the Sainsbury Centre at the University of East Anglia may be related to Old Sarum (Zarnecki et al. 1984, 163; King 1990, 76-7). The basis for this assertion appears to be the general quality and the distinctive treatment of the band around the rim of the eyes. Although it seems possible that it was a work by the Old Sarum master, unfortunately the provenance of the piece is unknown. A corbel at Kilpeck (Herefordshire) employs the distinctive treatment of the eyes with the band around the pupil as well as the curly hair and the wide mouth found in Old Sarum's most accomplished corbel (Cat 7) (King 1990, 87-91). During the third quarter of the twelfth century the Old Sarum master could have also been working at Lewes Priory. A respond capital in the British Museum is decorated with a lion and a gryphon, both of which have strong muscular legs, tails curling over the body and the drilled oval eyes with a narrow band around them. The lion's mane is treated with small curls and the gryphon grabs a ball in one of its claws. The detailing of the animals is similar to the pair of lions on the apex of the gable (Cat 5).

Other 12th Century Buildings at Old Sarum

Roger was not content with a major reconstruction of the east end of the church. He also erected the cloister and a building that may have been a treasury and vestry on the north side of the cathedral. The irregular plan of the cloister was uncovered in the early twentieth century. The lengths of the four walks, clockwise from the south walk, measured 137ft, 113½ft, 133½ft and 125½ft on the east side (Report 1913-4, 104). The alleys were 12ft wide on three sides, but the south one was 13ft wide (Report 1913-4, 114). The irregular shape was not due to inept laying out, but may have been to maximize the use of the area between the north side of the choir and the southern edge

of the bishop's palace, as it existed when the cloister was laid out. An alternative explanation is that the south and west walks were laid out with reference to the new east end of the cathedral, while the northern and eastern walls were added later and were built in alignment with the rebuilt bishop's palace (Montague 2006, 50-1). What both explanations share is that there was a tension between aligning new buildings to the ancient earthworks and the existing buildings of the twelfth century.

The treasury was within a two storied structure attached to the north wall of the north transept. Its lower storey was four bays long and two bays wide, with a line of three central piers that were probably cylindrical in plan. Above the treasury was probably a vestry. The excavators in the early twentieth century did not attribute a definite function to this building, though they thought it might have been a chapter house (Report 1913-4, 105). However, there would have been problems with the level of the upper storey of this structure, the supposed chapter house, being above the probable floor level of the cloister. Normally the floor of both would have been on the same level. It has also been suggested that this building predated the construction of the north transept and was originally built as a freestanding building, but its form and position seem to be dependent on the construction of the new east end (RCHM(E) 1980, 15). Interestingly the new cathedral at Salisbury also included a two storied treasury and vestry structure attached, in this case, to the south-east transept.

Beside the cathedral and its monastic buildings, Bishop Roger and his successor built a large episcopal palace. It consisted of four ranges around a paved courtyard in the shape of an irregular quadrilateral. The east range was occupied by a large aisled hall with a nave 90-94ft long by 21ft wide, and aisles 11ft to 12ft wide. The piers of the arcades stood on 5ft wide sleeper walls and fragments found during the excavations suggested that the piers were square in plan with spiral shafts at the angles. Excavators believed that the aisles may have been vaulted and the arches of the arcades were moulded with an ornamental hood mould. In scale the hall probably resembled the surviving Great Hall at Oakham Castle, Rutland, dated to *c*.1180. However, the use of a central entrance, rather than a door into a cross-passage at one end of the hall, suggests that the Old Sarum hall may date from earlier in the twelfth century, though whether it dates from the episcopacies of Roger or Jocelyn is uncertain. The problems with aligning the cloister would seem to indicate that it was an addition after Roger's death in 1139.

Along the north end of the hall were the services including the kitchen. The south range of the palace was set along the north side of the cloister and the west range apparently contained a chamber and a private apartment of the bishop. However, in the interpretation at the time of the excavations, the latter range was supposed to have housed lodgings. Little on the north side of the courtyard has survived (RCHM(E) 1980, 21-2; Report 1914-5, 232-6).

Although the cathedral and the episcopal palace were probably the most elaborate buildings on the site, it was the castle that was at the heart of Old Sarum and the reason for the complex's existence in that location. The original building was a motte and bailey castle on an earthwork (RCHM(E) 1980, 2). The castle, which was always intended as a temporary measure, was originally held by the King and in 1129 the Sheriff of Wiltshire was carrying out building work there (Ashbee 2006, 76). It seems that, soon after, it had passed to Bishop Roger who replaced many of the early, purely-defensive structures with a substantial, fortified house, the 'Great Tower' and Herlewin's Tower in the northern half of the inner bailey. The Great Tower was first mentioned in 1130-1 and by the thirteenth century it was probably three storeyed (English Heritage 1994, 7; RCHME 1980, 8-11). The house had four ranges enclosing a rectangular, paved, inner courtyard. The major chambers were on the first floor, with the Great Hall occupying the west range and the Great Chamber the north one (English Heritage

1994, 7; Report 1909, 192; RCHM(E) 1980, 7). The eastern end of the south range was occupied by St Margaret's Chapel on the ground floor, with St Nicholas' chapel above. These chapels were three bays long with a short narrow chancel at the east end (RCHM(E) 1980, 8). At the north end of the east range there was a 'kitchen tower' and an east turret holding further garderobes (RCHM(E) 1980, 9). Although it was substantial and elaborate in plan, Roger's house does not seem to have been embellished with the same level of sculptural detail as the cathedral. Where sections of the walling survive, the remnants show that they were reinforced with pilaster buttresses and in the excavations fragments of stone shingles and ornate, red and green glazed ridge-tiles were discovered. The published reports suggest that the doors and windows were decorated with chevron, while it was surmised that the upper windows were subdivided by stone shafts with spiral grooves and other patterns. The chimney (Cat 80), which is the most elaborate surviving feature from the Great Tower, was discovered during the 1910 excavations and illustrated in the following year's report (Report 1909-10, 505; Report 1911-12, photograph opposite 60).

Pl 2. Stonework: Cat 80 chimney from Old Sarum

The photograph is reproduced, with background removed, as plate 2 left. The Great Tower and the adjacent narrow Postern Gate, as well as the East Gate, are the only significant, but ruinous, structures surviving from this period.

The Demise of Old Sarum

There is evidence that Roger would have continued the reconstruction of the cathedral to include the nave, but with his death in 1139 the rebuilding programme was scaled down. His successor, Bishop Jocelyn de Bohun (1142-84), built a large west façade, the last substantial building works that took place on the cathedral. In the early thirteenth century some new buildings were built on the site. A new hall was erected in the southern half of the inner bailey and a bakehouse was built south-west of the main gatehouse.

By the end of King John's reign the practical problems of the cathedral sharing a cramped, secure castle site were proving insurmountable for the clergy. Discussions about a move to the water meadows, where Salisbury is now located, were begun by Bishop Herbert Poore before his death in January 1217 (RCHM(E) 1980, 16). In a letter written at some time between 1182 and 1206, Peter de Blois mentions the poor environment on the hill, which was 'at the mercy of the wind, barren, dry, deserted and mean' (Frost 2005, 155-6). In April 1217 the Dean and Chapter petitioned to Pope Honorius III to move the cathedral:

> 'They state that the cathedral church, being within the line of defence, is subject to so many inconveniences, that the canons can not live there without danger to life.
>
> Being in a raised place, the continual gusts of wind and storm make such a noise that the clerks can hardly hear one another sing, and the place is so rheumatic by reason of the wind that they very often suffer in health.
>
> The church, they say, is so shaken by wind and storm that it daily needs repair; and the site is without trees and grass, and being of chalk has such a glare that many of the clerks have lost their sight.
>
> Water, they say, is only to be got from a distance, and often at a price that, elsewhere, would buy enough for the whole district.
>
> If the clerks have occasion to go in and out on business, they can not do so without leave of the castellan, so that on Ash Wednesday, Holy Thursday, and on synodal and ordination and other solemn days, the faithful who wish to visit the church can not do so, the keepers of the castle declaring that the defences would be endangered.
>
> Moreover, as many of the clerks have no dwellings there, they have to hire them from the soldiers, so that few are found willing or able to reside on the spot.' (Report 1909, 193).

Although the petition offers a colourful view of life at Old Sarum, the modern visitor to the site can still appreciate its windswept and slightly bleak quality. John Leland dismissed one of the reasons cited for wishing to move the cathedral: 'Sum think that lak of water caussid the inhabitants to relinquish the place; yet were ther many welles of swete water.' (Report 1909, 194.) However, it seems that the major problems were the restrictions on movement placed on the clergy by having to share a relatively small site with the occupants of the castle and the shortage of housing within the precinct. (Stroud 1986, 125). A contemporary poem by the court poet Henry d'Avranches, written c.1225-6, described the background to the translation of the cathedral to the new site and cited a range of biblical sources as a symbolic justification for the move (Frost 2005, 158ff.). Old Sarum was likened to the inhospitable mountains of Gilboa, whereas the new site was like Paradise (VCH 1956, 165).

On 29 March 1218 papal consent for the move was granted and by 1219 a cemetery and a wooden chapel had been built near the site of the Salisbury Cathedral (RCHM(E) 1980, 16). The foundation stone of the new church was laid on 28 April 1220 and in 1226 the bodies of three bishops, Osmund, Roger and Jocelin, were moved to the new cathedral. (Report 1913-4, 109). By 30 July 1227 the official translation from Old Sarum had taken place (Report 1909,

194). Part of the old cathedral was retained for use as the Chapel of St Mary and a chapel was still in use at Old Sarum as late as the sixteenth century (RCHM(E) 1980, 3, 16; Report 1913-4, 108). However, once the clergy had moved from the site, the slow but inevitable process of decline, ruination and the quarrying of stone began. In 1237 an order was given to take down the hall and other buildings belonging to the bishop to use the building material to repair the castle (RCHM(E) 1980, 3). In 1276 permission was given for stone from Old Sarum to be used in new buildings in Salisbury, but, judging from the buildings it was used in, it seems likely that Old Sarum was being used as a quarry earlier in the thirteenth century (RCHM(E) 1993, 22; Ayers and Sampson 2000, 81). In 1327 a licence was granted for the construction of a close wall and in 1331 Edward III allowed the chapter to use stone from the old cathedral and some of the former clergy houses for repairs to the new cathedral and the precinct wall (Report 1913-4, 102; Report 1909, 194; RCHM(E) 1993, 39).

The cathedral at Old Sarum was abandoned in the thirteenth century, but the castle remained in use though there are no indications of new, major building works. This is indicated both by documentary evidence and the paucity of later stone fragments that have survived. In 1247 a wheelhouse was built above the well, and the hall, the gaol and two kitchens in the castle were repaired (Report 1909, 193; RCHM(E) 1980, 3). In 1315 £60 of repairs were carried out followed in 1337-8 by repairs to the towers and walls, particularly the Great Tower (RCHM(E) 1980, 7). In 1366 a detailed indenture was compiled concerning the repair of the Courtyard House (RCHM(E) 1980, 3). Although some repairs were being undertaken the castle was still decaying. By 1307-8 the hall, chamber, kitchen and bakehouse had ceased to be used (RCHM(E) 1980, 3, 11). On 29 November 1399 a commission was appointed 'to inquire into divers wastes, dilapidations, and destructions committed in the King's Castle of Old Sarum.' (Report 1909-10, 510.) The introduction of artillery rendered the castle militarily ineffective and by 1446-7 it was described as 'now fallen into decay' (Report 1909, 194). In 1514 Thomas Crompton, Groom of the Chamber, was granted the right to use the castle for building materials. (RCHM(E) 1980, 4). In the 1530s John Leland described Old Sarum as 'This thing hath beene auncient and exceeding strong: but syns the building of New-Saresbyri it went totally to ruine.' (Report 1909, 194.) By 1832 Old Sarum was 'only a green mound without a habitation upon it', but it was famous, or more accurately infamous, as one of the notorious rotten boroughs abolished in that year (Stroud 1986, 120). On 9 June 1832 *The Times* published 'A Lament for Old Sarum', purporting to be written by the man who had bought the Parliamentary seat it had guaranteed:

'Farewell to thee, Sarum! for thousands I bought thee,
And hoped that a heir-loom thou long shouldst remain;
A provision for sons and for nephews I thought thee,
A fountain unfailing of honours and gains.
But the voice of the "Spolier" was heard to denounce thee,
A loud cry for "Plunder" arose in the land;
As a vote-giving mount, I at last must renounce thee,
And yield to the torrents I cannot withstand.'

Excavations of the Site

By the early twentieth century knowledge of the buildings at Old Sarum was limited to a small amount of above ground masonry, the appearance of parch marks in hot summers and small excavations. Bishop Richard Pococke visited Old Sarum in October 1754: 'The situation is very fine and elevated; it is defended by a double rampart and two deep ditches, and was walled round; great pieces of the wall are still to be seen.' (Cartwright, 1889, 131.) Following a period of severe frost and thaw during the winter of 1795, the entrance to a subterranean passage was revealed in the outer bailey. The presence of this tunnel was verified in 1957 (Rahtz and Musty 1960, 359). In 1834 the unusually dry summer weather exposed the outline of the church and prompted a small excavation (Report 1909, 191; Report 1912-3, 93-95; RCHM(E) 1980, 4).

The major campaign of excavations began on 23 August 1909 and would have lasted for a decade, but the outbreak of war in 1914 led to their immediate cessation. Initially the excavators concentrated on the interior of the earthwork of the Norman castle. When work began only a small part of the postern tower and the main gate were exposed, but by the end of the 1911 campaign a clear picture of the castle had emerged. The whole of the postern tower at the west side of the site was revealed while a structure occupying the northern half of the site, which they christened the 'Great Tower', was uncovered. To the south, excavations revealed a hall and a building with hearths, probably a bakehouse, near the gate. In 1912 excavations began on the cathedral and the monastic buildings to the north of it (Report 1912-3, 93). By the outbreak of World War I the plan of the church had been revealed, along with the treasury to the north of the north transept and several buildings to the west of the west façade (Report 1913-4, fig. 14).

Figurative Sculpture

1 Head of Christ. Sandstone; badly weathered. 1130-40. H. 280mm. W. 350mm. D. 290mm, relief projects 160mm. Removed in 1875 from an unknown location at the North Canonry, The Close, Salisbury, but probably originally from Old Sarum Cathedral. Zarnecki et al. 1984, 160, no. 114; King 1990 70, 77 et seq., pl. 2a. *OS.C54*   **Pl 3**

The head of Christ was from a large relief made up of a series of horizontal courses, an arrangement similar to the carvings from the screen at Chichester Cathedral. Its original location in the cathedral is unknown, but a possible option is that it came from within the south porch. This porch seems to have served as an exemplar for some part of the overall decorative

scheme of the later south porch of Malmesbury Abbey, though not its detailed execution. The porch was believed to have been added to the south transept of Old Sarum after 1139 and due to its weathered state it is difficult to compare this head with the style of other works by the leading sculptor at Old Sarum, the so-called 'Old Sarum Master'. However, the head is still likely to date from the era of Roger of Salisbury as it seems to be related to the figure of Christ above the door at Lullington Church (Somerset). This door also has a number of other motifs in common with Old Sarum and was probably a work by the Old Sarum Master, probably immediately after the cessation of work at the cathedral in 1139.

2 Left leg of figure with drapery. Traces of white paint. Mid 12th century. H. 215mm. W. 360mm. D. *c.*270mm. Probably from Old Sarum Cathedral; it was found incorporated in the 15th century building at 1 Castle Street, Salisbury. *1954.56*   **Pl 3**

This is the left upper leg of a figure covered in drapery. Its size suggests that it was part of a large scene, perhaps similar to the figures in the south porch of Malmesbury and may come from the south transept porch, like the head of Christ.

3 Fragment of figure. 12th century. H. 130mm. W. 93mm. D. 30mm. Found during the excavations at Old Sarum. *1945.269*

This small fragment may be part of a depiction of a priest wearing a stole decorated with circles. It has a small section of drapery on the left side, probably from the chest of the figure.

4 Feet of Christ from a crucifixion. 12th century. H. 65mm. W. 90mm. D. 95mm. Found during excavations at Old Sarum. *1945.268*

This fragment consists of the right foot and part of the left foot of a figure, presumably the crucified Christ. The size of the fragment suggests that it came from a substantial, near life-size figure. Is this related to the head of Christ, Cat 1 or a similar large relief?

5 Gablet flanked by crouching lions. Sandstone, weathered, especially the right hand lion. Legs of right hand lion broken off. 1130-40. H. 410mm. W. 400mm. D. 260mm. From Old Sarum Cathedral, possibly from the south transept porch. It was found in trial trenches south of the church, along with a number of corbels. *O.S. Diary* 1912, 15; Report 1912-3, 98; Report 1913-4, photograph opposite 114; Zarnecki et al. 1984, 176 no. 135a and 63, pl. 135a; King 1990, 70, pl. 2b. *1945.270*   **Pl 3**

The angle of the incline of the moulding beneath the lions is identical to the sloping edges of the large rosette in the EH stone store (no. 81109792), which suggests that this piece was at the apex of a gable and the rosette was set beneath it. Both fragments were found in the same excavation. The animals have beaded spines and the manes down their backs are treated as curly tufts, similar to the hair of the lion on corbel Cat 7. The legs are muscular with long claws, and elegant long tails curve over the lions' bodies. Zarnecki 1984 suggested that their form inspired an illustration in the *Shaftesbury Psalter* *c.* 1130-40.

6   Block decorated with two lions fighting an eagle. The upper parts of each animal are damaged. 1130-40. H. *c.* 210mm. W. *c.* 270mm. D. *c.* 210mm. From Old Sarum Cathedral, this was one of the stones found in excavations south of the south transept. *O.S. Diary* 1912, 15; Report 1912-3, 98 and photograph opposite 98. *1945.262*   **Pl 3**

This block was perhaps a finial at the apex of a gable designed to be seen from all directions and was only attached to a building beneath, and probably by a narrow piece of masonry between the lions. When it was excavated it was erroneously described as a capital. The backs of both lions have beaded spines with lines from them defining the musculature of the animals. On the more complete lion, the weathered head sits on a broad neck. The style of the animal and the beaded spine is similar to the lions flanking the gablet (Cat 5).

7   Corbel with a lion's head. Damaged at rear where it was attached to a wall. *c.* 1120-40. H. 235mm. W. 200mm. L. 200mm. This was one of

the corbels found in excavations south of the south transept of Old Sarum Cathedral. Report 1912-3, 98 and photograph opposite 98; Stalley 1971, 75; Zarnecki et al.1984, 177 pl. 135d; RCHM(E) 1980, pl. 29f; King 1990, 70, pl. 1a. *1945.274.1*   **Pl 4**

This fragment is the most accomplished corbel surviving from Old Sarum, carved by a sculptor able to create a strong, very plastic image. This lion's head has the distinctive wide mouth, curly locks, small ears and large eyes with drilled pupils found in many other heads that are not carved with the same skill level. There are two similar corbels in the EH stone store (no. 81109753 and 81109854).

8   Corbel with a youthful head. Sandstone, weathered, minor damage to front but cut off at back. *c.* 1120-40. H. 180mm. W. 180mm. From Old Sarum Cathedral, this was one of the corbels found in excavations south of the south transept. Report 1912-13, 98 and photograph opposite 98; Zarnecki et al. 1984, 176 pl. 135c; Stalley 1971, 75; RCHM(E) 1980, pl. 29a; Thurlby 1981 93-8; King 1990, 70, pl. 1a. *1945.273*   **Pl 4**

9   Beak-head. Beak-head with large eyes with drilled pupils, biting a short section of shaft. Rough at rear where fixed into wall. Discolouration on left side of beak suggests traces of pigment. H. 200mm. W. 145mm. D. 200mm. *c.* 1120-40. From Old Sarum Cathedral. Stalley 1971, 77-9; Zarnecki et al. 1984, 174 no.130; King 1990, 73, pl. 4b. *1945.275*   **Pl 4**

This is the only beak-head in surviving fragments from Old Sarum. It has been compared with similar carvings from Reading Abbey and Sherborne Castle, the former being supported by Bishop Roger and the latter having been built by him. King and Zarnecki suggest it was from a door but it could have been a corbel. The quality of the carving suggests it was probably a work by the most accomplished sculptor.

10   Corbel, with bearded, animal's head with cat's ears. *c.* 1120-40. H. 200mm. W. 200mm. D. 240mm. (broken off at rear). From the excavations at Old Sarum. RCHM(E) 1980, pl. 29b. *1945.272*   **Pl 4**

The style of this corbel is related to others surviving in the collection. It has the bulbous eyes with drilled pupils and strong ridges around the eyeball and the short pointed ears. Compared to the lion's head corbel (Cat 7) it is rigid in its form, though the flourish at the end of the handlebar moustache is in marked contrast to the coarse, almost geometric facial features.

1 Corbel with a trumpeter. Sandstone, weathered and damaged. This corbel is fairly crudely carved compared to some others (e.g. Cat 7 and 8). The large eyes have drilled pupils and ridges around them (similar to Cat 8 and 9). The figure uses both his arms to support the top of the corbel and therefore implausibly manages to play the trumpet with no hands! *c.*1120-40. H. 220mm. W. 250mm. D. 380mm. From Old Sarum Cathedral. This could be one of the corbels found in excavations south of the south transept. Zarnecki et al. 1984, 176 no. 135b. *1945.276*   **Pl 3**

2 Fragment of a corbel with an animal's head. This small fragment has a broad nose, bulging drilled eyes and ridges on the forehead. In form it can be seen as derived from the more accomplished corbels from the cathedral. 12th century. H. 155mm. W. 110mm. D. 90mm (max). From the excavations at Old Sarum. *1945.265*

3 Corbel decorated with crude human head, long moustaches. Weathered. Traces of paint in the beard. This is a crude head but with features derived from the more accomplished corbels. *c.*1120-40. H. 180mm. W. 185mm. D. 225mm. From the excavations at Old Sarum. RCHM(E) 1980, pl. 29c. *1945.274.2*   **Pl 4**

4 Voussoir with grotesque animal head with a fluted tongue. This item and the next voussoir formed part of the surround of a rose window. *c.*1120-40. H. 480mm. W. 280mm (max), 200mm (min). From Old Sarum Cathedral. Report 1913-4, 14; Zarnecki 1953a, 7, pl. 43; Stalley 1971, 75; Zarnecki et al. 1984, 177 no. 135f; RCHM(E) 1980, pl. 29(e); Thurlby 1981, 93-8. *1945.280*

Pl 5

15 Voussoir with a woman trying to open the mouth of a monster. This item and the previous voussoir formed part of the surround of a rose window. *c.*1120-40. H. 480mm. W. 270mm (max), 210mm (min). From Old Sarum Cathedral. Report 1913-4, photograph opposite 114; Zarnecki 1953a, 22 and 56, pls. 42, 43 and 45; Stalley 1971, 75; Zarnecki et al. 1984, 177 no. 135g; RCHM(E) 1980, pl. 29(g); Thurlby 1981 93-8. *1945.281*   **Pl 5**

These two fragments originated from the same feature at Old Sarum and were probably carved by the same sculptor. Although both are skilfully carved, they are not of the highest quality found in Old Sarum fragments and are probably not by the leading sculptor. Originally said to have been from a door, Thurlby has proposed that they came from the surround of a large rose window in the east end. He argues that the heads would have been upside down if they were on a door and that the voussoirs would be too large for a doorway. The creatures on both voussoirs have short ears, strong mouths and bulging eyes with drilled pupils. They have strong noses and eyebrows with notches carved in them to simulate hair. Cat 14 has a strange fluted tongue, as if breathing fire, while Cat 15 has a small figure hanging from its mouth.

16 Mask with a lion's head. Damage at rear where attached to walls and at sides where a label mould extended from it. Evidence of red colouration survives between the teeth. *c.*1120-40. H. 230mm. W. 260mm. From Old Sarum Cathedral, this was one of the fragments found in excavations south of the south transept. Report 1912-13, 98 and photograph opposite 98; Zarnecki 1953a, 22, pls. 45, 46; Stalley 1975, 75; Zarnecki et al. 1984, 177 no. 135e. *1945.271*   **Pl 4**

This fragment was originally at the apex of a label moulding, probably above the main arcade of the east end. A similar motif is used in the nave of Gloucester Cathedral and in the later nave of Malmesbury Abbey, which has many forms derived from Old Sarum. The labels at Malmesbury have dragons' heads as label stops and in the National Monuments Record a similar head appears in a photograph labelled as a fragment from Old Sarum. However, today this fragment does not appear to survive in the EH stone store or in the Museum.

17 Fragment of capital with two birds and section of chamfered abacus. H. 190mm. W. (surviving) 160mm. D. 120mm. Column diam. approximately 140mm. From the excavations at Old Sarum. *1945.261*

This is a small capital decorated with the body and two wings of a bird, and the wing of a second bird. It has approximately the same diameter as a group of engaged capitals (Cat 44, 45 and 46) and this is the diameter of the sections of kidney shaped shafts in the collection. However, apart from this possible coincidence, it is difficult to link this capital with any other fragments.

18 Small corbel with grotesque head. This is a small head with a grotesque face; probably from a corbel. It has protruding eye balls, bared, sharp teeth, a large nose and hair streaming back. H. 155mm. The corbel top is 125mm x 95mm. Labelled 258 in red paint. From the excavations at Old Sarum. *1945.264*

Though the fragment originated from Old Sarum it does not appear to be Romanesque in date and may originate from a later building on the site.

Non-figurative Sculpture

19 Voussoir decorated with quatrefoil in a roundel. *c.*1120-40. H. 215mm. W. 240mm top, 165mm base, D. 160mm. From the excavations at Old Sarum. King 1990, 73, pl.3. *1945.284* **Pl 5**

In the wall of the cathedral close, in Salisbury Museum and in the EH stone store there are dozens of voussoirs decorated with quatrefoils. Most are simple geometric forms (e.g. Cat 20) but a significant number, around twenty-five, are treated as more elaborate, curved forms nicknamed 'ravioli'. These quatrefoils have curved sides with small drilled holes along their edge and resemble pinched and folded sheets of pasta. The fluidity of the form, compared with the simple geometric form in some stones, suggests carvers with a higher skill level created these voussoirs.

The narrower face of the voussoir has a slight but deliberate curve, suggesting that it was from around an arch. Perhaps it was a decoration around a window, similar to the function of Cat 22 and the 'paterae' around the nave clerestory of Malmesbury Abbey. The large number of surviving quatrefoils suggests that the motif was used around a common feature, such as a decoration around the choir windows (Report 1913-4, photograph opposite 110; Brakspear 1931, 1-18; Wilson 1975, 80-90; Brodie 1988, 34).

20 Voussoir with roundel containing a diamond shape with curved faces. Limestone block from a frieze. *c.*1120-40. Traces of plaster with colour wash. A cut away behind carving probably dates from reuse. H. 268mm. W. 200mm. D. 260mm broken off. From 1 Castle Street, Salisbury - originally from Old Sarum Cathedral. *1954.54*   **Pl 6**

This is one of three stones with this design apparently from Old Sarum Cathedral that were found incorporated in the fifteenth-century building at 1 Castle Street, Salisbury. There are also thirty-one examples of this motif on stones in the east wall of the cathedral close.

This version of the diamond motif is similar in form to the more elaborate voussoir (Cat 19), the so-called 'ravioli'. If both were around a clerestory window, their forms would have been superficially similar if observed from the ground. Perhaps one was used in the choir while the other was used on the transepts, or alternatively the 'ravioli' were at a lower level than these simpler designs.

21 Voussoir decorated with a projecting quatrefoil. Traces of later white paint. *c.*1120-40. H. 220mm. W. 245mm top, 205mm base, D. 280mm (broken off at rear). Carving projects 40mm. From the excavations at Old Sarum. Report 1913-4 photograph opposite 110. *1945.282*   **Pl 6**

This voussoir is another variation of the themes in Cat 19 and 20, and is also related to the voussoir with the roundel (Cat 22). It is decorated with a quatrefoil, similar in form to the 'ravioli' on Cat 19, but with a lumpy surround. However, unlike Cat 19 and 20, this item projects from the surface of the stone 40mm as in Cat 22. There are six examples of this type of voussoir in the east wall of the cathedral close and at least one in the EH stone store. Like the other voussoirs there is a definite, though slight curve on the narrower face, suggesting it was around an arched opening. However, the best parallel may be found in the triforia of Worcester Cathedral, Wells Cathedral and Glastonbury Abbey.

22 Voussoir decorated with a garb of wheat and leaves. *c.*1120-40. H. 220mm. W. 245mm top, 200mm base, D. 360mm. Carving projects 40mm. From the excavations at Old Sarum. Report 1913-4, photograph opposite 110. *1945.283*
Pl 5

This voussoir has a slightly curved lower face indicating that it was from around an arched opening, such as a window. The carved roundel projects 40mm from the surface of the stone. The carving is well drawn but roughly finished as if the piece was never expected to be seen close up. For instance, the bundle of wheat, which is similar in form to the Roman fasces, is bound by a square clip coarsely decorated with small squares created by criss-cross lines. Perhaps this fragment, and other decorated roundels came from around clerestory windows. A similar, but more elaborate arrangement is found in the later nave at Malmesbury Abbey where flat dishes decorated with semicircles are arranged around the windows. The form of these circular dishes, christened 'paterae', is similar to a large circular decoration on a stone from a gable from the south transept at Old Sarum. Report 1913-4, photograph opposite 112; Brakspear 1913, 399-437; Stalley 1971, 75-6; Wilson 1975, 80-90; Brodie 1988, 34.

23 Block with quatrefoil flower. This stone is decorated with a large four-lobed, floral motif. At the centre there is a large drilled bead and the leaves

each have a central spine of beads. Two similar flowers are held by English Heritage (no. 81109702). This floral motif is part of a larger decoration, as at one side of the stone there is a small projection, as if there was an adjacent carved form. H. 210mm. W. 295mm. D. 180mm. From the yard of Church House, Crane Street, Salisbury. Originally from Old Sarum. *1951.51*
Pl 6

Was it from a door surround, as a similar floral motif is used around the outside of the west door of Kenilworth Priory?

24 Engaged column with elaborate carving. Traces of red colouration survive in the recesses. H. 145mm. W. 330mm. D. 280mm. Column diam. *c.*310mm. From a cottage opposite Avon Farm, Stratford-sub-Castle. *1937.22.2*
Pl 6

25 Engaged column with elaborate carving. Incised star, probably a mason's mark on one face. H. 190mm. W. 365mm. D. 265mm. Column diam. *c.*310mm. From a cottage opposite Avon Farm, Stratford-sub-Castle. *1937.22.3*
Pl 6

Cat 24-25 must originally have come from Old Sarum. They are semicircular in plan and decorated with large trilobed leaves along the sides and a criss-cross, strap-work pattern decorated with drilled beads. The form of the shafts and the general type of decoration though not the detail, resembles some of the orders in the south porch of Malmesbury Abbey.

26 String course decorated with opposed S-curved foliage forms. H. 120mm. W. 423mm. D. *c.*420mm. From the excavations at Old Sarum. *c.*1120-40. *1945.278*
Pl 7

27 String course decorated with palmettes. Incomplete on right-hand side. H. 120mm. W. (surviving) 390mm. D. *c.*190mm. From the excavations at Old Sarum. *c.*1120-40 *1945.279*
Pl 7

This and Cat 26 are remnants of elaborate string courses from the east end of the cathedral. Their elaboration and their detailed finish suggest they were at a relatively low level, possibly in the aisles.

28 Block with Greek key pattern. Traces of red colouration survive in the recesses. H. 180mm.

L. 300mm. D. 310mm. From the excavations at Old Sarum. *1945.277*   **Pl 7**

This is a section of an elaborate string course which retains traces of red paint. It consists of two interlocking T-shaped forms probably with the remnant of another simpler decoration above it. At Malmesbury Abbey the string course above the nave arcades has the same pattern of decoration, suggesting a possible location for the motif in the east end of Old Sarum Cathedral (Stalley 1971, 76).

29 Voussoir with Greek key pattern. This is a very large stone decorated with a Greek key pattern but with an irregular finish to the pattern. The line effectively returns and continues at right angles to the main pattern. The block is shaped as if it was a keystone but its size and the pattern does not seem to accord with just being a straightforward arch. H. 420mm. W. 430mm. D. 290mm. Found re-used in the north wall of Old Sarum Farm (Wingrove's Barn) within the East Suburb of Old Sarum. Musty and Rahtz 1964, 143 and fig. 5 no. 1. *OS.C96; 1959.10.1; 1963.73*   **Pl 7**

Was it part of a door surround, similar to decoration found at Lincoln and Kenilworth?

30 Voussoir from hood moulding with four alternating rows of cylindrical billet. H. 140mm. W. 490-420mm. D. 255mm. See also Cat 24, 25 and 36. From a cottage opposite Avon Farm, Stratford-sub-Castle. *1937.22.1*

This stone is probably from a section of a hood moulding.

31 Two stones forming a block with interlaced arcading. H. 350mm. W. 887mm. D. 130mm at top, 200mm at base. From the excavations at Old Sarum. RCHM(E) 1980, pl. 29(d). *1945.263*   **Pl 7**

These two stones formed a single panel decorated with a small, intersecting arcade with simple cushion capitals and simple arches decorated with a small roll moulding. Was it a panel from the side of a tomb?

32 Palmette moulding. 12th century. H. 115mm.

W. 150mm. D. 48mm (max). From the excavations at Old Sarum. *1945.266*

This is a small piece of moulding that came from a horizontal feature, such as a string course.

33 Vine moulding. 12th century. H. 52mm. W.120mm. D. 55mm (max). From the excavations at Old Sarum. *1945.267*

This fragment has a small leaf beside a bunch of grapes. Its original function is unknown.

34 Irregular block with painted lines. This block has dark red paint depicting the outline of stone blocks on one surface. H. 215mm. W. 290mm. D. 215mm. From the excavations at Old Sarum. *1945.258*

Along with the frequent traces of paint on carved fragments this provides some insight into the highly coloured interior of the twelfth-century church.

35 Voussoir with chevron moulding on two faces. This voussoir differs from any others as it has chevron carved on two faces. Both faces have two bands of chevron but the 'front' face has an additional narrower, smaller band of chevron along the bottom of it. H. 240mm. W. 185mm. D. 420mm, of which 130mm is the moulding. From Stratford-sub-Castle. *1949.132*

36 Engaged column base. Engraved P on one flat surface. H. 180mm. W. 480mm. D. (max.) 370mm. From a cottage opposite Avon Farm, Stratford-sub-Castle, originally from Old Sarum. *1937.22.4*

This large base is from a semicircular shaft and is the only base in the collection.

37 Wedge-shaped section of large cylindrical shaft. Approximately one quarter of its circumference. H. 300mm. The original diam. of the shaft appears to have been *c*.400mm. Mortar on 'inner' face. Apparently from Musty and Rahtz excavations in the East Suburb of Old Sarum. *1959.10.2*

38 Wedge-shaped block with three layers of imbricated feather moulding. *c*.1120-40. H. 196mm. W. 260mm. D. (max) 160mm. Length of imbricated surface 250mm. From Old Sarum Cathedral. Report 1913-4, photograph opposite 110. *1945.260*

The function of this stone is unclear but it resembles a coping stone from the top of a buttress.

39 Fragment with beading. H. 140mm. W. 95mm. D. 90mm. Small fragment with paper label: 'Found in Old Sarum moat - piece of Cathedral wall? March 20th. 1918?' From Old Sarum. *1947.53*

This is a small piece of a stone decorated with a hollow chamfer and a line of small beads.

40 Stone with hollow chamfered moulding. H. 200mm. W. 155mm. D. 125mm. From the excavations at Old Sarum. Probably *1945.259*

This is a small piece of a stone decorated with a hollow chamfer.

Fragments from Toone's Court, 14 Scot's Lane, Salisbury

Toone's Court was a group of sixteenth-century houses on Scot's Lane that was demolished in 1972 (RCHM(E) 1980, 142-3). The chimney-breast in no. 14 was found to include a large number of carved stones including three engaged columns, four engaged capitals, six sections of 'kidney-section', spiral shafts, ten voussoirs with chevron moulding, ten similar parallel-sided blocks, five blocks decorated with diaper pattern and one other fragment. The diversity, quality and date of the fragments suggests that they probably originated from Old Sarum. As there is considerable consistency in the type of fragments used in the chimney this suggests that they came directly from Old Sarum and specifically from one or two buildings. Therefore, although the first robbing of stone from the site took place as early as the thirteenth century, this suggests that significant buildings were still standing in the sixteenth century, available to be quarried. An alternative, though less likely, explanation is that the chimney breast was built from stone taken from a previous building in the town, which itself was built from stone robbed from Old Sarum. One wonders how many houses in Salisbury have reused stone within them!

41 Engaged shaft and a quarter with spiral moulding and imbricated panel on lateral face. H. 180mm. W. 260mm. D. 270mm. Shaft diam. 110mm. *1972.21* (stone 6)   **Pl 7**

42 Engaged shaft and a quarter with spiral moulding and imbricated panel on lateral face. H. 200mm. W. 200mm. D. 350mm. Shaft diam. *c.*120mm. *1972.21* (stone 5)

43 Engaged shaft and a quarter with spiral moulding and strap-work panel on lateral face. H. 200mm. W. 200mm. L. 360mm. Shaft diam. *c.*120mm. *1972.21* (stone 7)

These three fragments from the chimney at 14 Scot's Lane, Salisbury have a similar plan. They have an engaged shaft and part of another one decorated with spiral fluting. Cat 41 and 42 have beading included in the decoration. On the flat, originally exposed sides of the stone, there is an area of decoration. Cat 40 is decorated with rows of geometric forms, resembling a five lobed leaf. Each row consisted of three or two and two halves of these motifs. Cat 41 has a similar imbricated, almost feathered pattern but with less elaborate elements. The most elaborate decoration appears on Cat 43. The panel is decorated with a beaded strap-work motif enclosing two beaded leaves with pointed lobes, a leaf form resembling ivy.

44 Engaged capital with volutes. H. 175mm. W. 230mm. D. 275mm. Shaft diam. *c.*160mm. Late 11th century. RCHM(E) 1980, 143. *1972.21* (stone 1)   **Pl 7**

This small capital probably dates from the episcopate of Bishop Osmund (1078-99) and may have come from the nave which was not rebuilt by Bishop Roger.

45 Engaged capital. Part cut away when re-used and heavily sooted. H. 180mm. W. 230mm. D. (surviving) 300mm. Shaft diam. *c.*140mm. *1972.21* (stone 3)

This is a small engaged, scalloped capital with four scallops on each face.

46 Engaged capital. H. 175mm. W. 230mm. D. 320mm. Shaft diam. *c.*140mm. Part cut away when reused. *1972.21* (stone 2)

This small engaged, scalloped capital has the scallops carved as if emerging from a shallow sheath around the base of the capital.

47 Engaged capital. Partly cut away when re-used. H. 170mm. W. 235mm. D. (surviving) 310mm. Shaft diam. *c.*140mm. *1972.21* (stone 4)

This small engaged capital is decorated with parallel curved grooves as if portraying stiff, vertical leaves. Cat 45, 46 and 47 performed the same function in the building from which they originated, though their original location is unclear.

48 Column of kidney section with opposed spiral moulding. L. 335mm. W. 130mm. D. 145mm. *1972.21* (stone 8)

49 Column of kidney section with opposed spiral moulding. L. 329mm. W. 140mm. D. 130mm in two fragments. *1972.21* (stone 9)   **Pl 8**

50 Column of kidney section with opposed spiral moulding. L. 283mm. W. 140mm. D. 130mm. *1972.21* (stone 10)

51 Column of kidney section with opposed spiral moulding. L. 340mm. W. 145mm. D. 130mm. *1972.21* (stone 11)

52 Column of kidney section with opposed spiral moulding. L. 270mm. W. 143mm. D. 130mm. *1972.21* (stone 12)

53 Column of kidney section with opposed spiral moulding. L. 290mm. W. 145mm. D. 135mm. *1972.21* (stone 13)

In plan the shafts have two lobes at the front, decorated with spiral mouldings in opposite directions. There is a piece of a similar shaft in the EH stone store (no. 811 09852). Sections of shafts with spiral grooves were described in the excavation reports as having perhaps originated from work carried out in 1130-1 on the Great

Tower but these shafts seem too elaborate and lack grooves or holes for window fittings. The function of the shafts is unknown but was probably part of Bishop Roger's elaborate east end or cloister.

54 Voussoir with chevron moulding. H. 190mm. W. 250-190mm. D. 350mm. *1972.21* (stone 14)

55 Voussoir with chevron moulding. H. 200mm. W. 180-140mm. D. 270mm. *1972.21* (stone 15)

56 Voussoir with chevron moulding. H. 200mm. W. 175-130mm. D. 290mm. *1972.21* (stone 16)

57 Voussoir with chevron moulding. H. 200mm. W. 210-160mm. D. 200mm. *1972.21* (stone 17)

58 Voussoir with chevron moulding. H. 200mm. W. 285-220mm. D. 210mm. There is a slot cut into the back of the stone about 130mm x 130mm. *1972.21* (stone 18)

59 Voussoir with chevron moulding. H. 200mm. W. 190-140mm. D. 240mm. *1972.21* (stone 19)

60 Voussoir with chevron moulding. H. 200mm. W. 145-115mm. D. 280mm. *1972.21* (stone 20)

61 Voussoir with chevron moulding. H. 230mm. W. 220-165mm. D. 260mm. *2002.55*

These are a group of voussoirs from arches decorated with a chevron pattern consisting of a roll, a hollow and a roll. As the fragments came from the dismantled chimney, some have soot on them. Cat 60 is a junction piece between a pair of arches and Cat 58 is shaped to be the voussoir immediately above it. On the underside of the voussoirs there are projections which were attached to another chevron on a separate block, as if they originated from the outer order of a multiple order arch. The fragments are consistent with a decorated outer order of a substantial arch, probably a gallery rather than the main arcade.

62 Voussoir with chevron moulding. Damaged when reused. H. 180mm. W. (estimated) 190-120mm. D. 305mm. *1972.21* (stone 21)

This voussoir is superficially the same as the main group of voussoirs but the chevron pattern is different.

63 Rectangular block with chevron moulding. H. 305mm. W. 200mm. D. 250mm. *1972.21* (stone 22)

64 Rectangular block with chevron moulding. Inner surface sooted through being in chimney. H. 370mm. W. 190mm. D. 150mm. *1972.21* (stone 23)

65 Rectangular block with chevron moulding. H. 330mm. W. 180mm. D. 220mm. Notch roughly cut at back from one edge, 110 x 90 x 40mm. *1972.21* (stone 24)

66 Rectangular block with chevron moulding. H. 270mm. W. 180mm. D. 220mm. *1972.21* (stone 25)

67 Rectangular block with chevron moulding. H. 230mm. W. 200mm. D. 260mm. *1972.21* (stone 26)

68 Rectangular block with chevron moulding. Grey encrustation on carved face, possibly lime wash. H. 280mm. W. 200mm. D. 260mm. *1972.21* (stone 27)

69 Rectangular block with chevron moulding. H. 330mm. W. 150mm. D. 280mm. *1972.21* (stone 28)

70 Rectangular block with chevron moulding. H. 285mm. W. 125mm. D. 300mm. *1972.21* (stone 30)

71 Rectangular block with chevron moulding. H. 200mm. W. 300mm. D. 295mm. *1972.21* (stone 31)

Some of these blocks, which came from the dismantled chimney have soot on them. There is a very slight taper on some of the blocks but it is too slight to suggest that they were voussoirs from an arch. They seem to have originated from a flat surface, like a wall rather than a pier. The chevron is formed with an alternating pattern of three shallow rolls and two hollows.

72 Rectangular block with chevron moulding. H. 230mm. W. 210mm. D. 270mm. There is a notch 90mm x 90mm x 70mm cut out of one corner of the moulded face. *1972.21* (stone 29)

This fragment is similar in form to the group of chevron decorated blocks but it is only moulded with two shallow hollows with a roll between.

73 Fragment with diagonal grooves. Corner of block, 140mm x 120mm surviving, with maximum thickness 200mm. *1972.21* (stone 37)

This is a small part of a larger block with shallow, diagonal grooves cut into the surface.

74 Block with diaper pattern. H. 175mm. W. 290mm. D. 230mm. Similar to Cat 64. *1972.21* (stone 34)

75 Block with diaper pattern. H. 175mm. W. 325mm. D. 250mm. Stone 32. *1972.21* (stone 32)

76 Block with diaper pattern. Possibly a cut-down voussoir. H. 80mm. W. 240. D. 230mm. *1972.21* (stone 36)

77 Block with diaper pattern. H. 105mm. W. 330mm. D. 230mm. *1972.21* (stone 33)

78 Block with diaper pattern. H. 155mm. W. 420mm. D. 180mm. Similar to Cat 64. *1972.21* (stone 35)

These blocks are decorated with a surface pattern of diamond-shaped diaper. Although one block was damaged and therefore seems to have a curved edge, they appear to come from a flat surface. The diaper in Cat 77 is more irregular and elongated than in the other blocks.

79 Rectangular block with chevron mould-ing. A trimmed voussoir. H. 200mm. W. 85mm. D. 175mm (max). A slot has been cut into the back of the stone. *2008.14*

Fragments from the Courtyard House at Old Sarum

80 Part of a chimney. Twenty-five blocks from the conical top and upper section of chimney, ten with carved decoration. External diameter *c.*910 mm. Wall thickness *c.*175 mm. Course height *c.*140-180 mm. Found during excavation on the outside the north side of the Courtyard House at Old Sarum. Early 12th century. *1945.257*   **Pl 2**

The chimney as reconstructed in the Museum is based on the excavators' photograph (Report 1911-2, photograph opposite 60). The conical top is represented by three blocks with angled mouldings, smoke holes and with mortar joints angled at 30° from the vertical. The upper part of the chimney itself is of four courses. The uppermost course, decorated with a projecting chevron pattern, is 150mm high. Under this, and of the same height, is a course containing a series of circular smoke holes; apparently in alternate stones the holes are blind. The next course has a curved strap-work pattern decorated with beads. At the base there is a plain course 172mm high. (Report 1909-10, 505). The chimney illustrates that while the cathedral was very richly decorated, Bishop Roger also expended considerable money on the domestic buildings of Old Sarum.

Fragments from site of Gibbs Mew Brewery, Gigant Street, Salisbury

These are a series of fragments recovered from excavations on the site of the Gibbs Mew brewery in Gigant Street, Salisbury, conducted by the Trust for Wessex Archaeology (site code W192, small finds 7-11). They consist of two blocks with engaged shafts at one corner, two sections of a shaft with a similar diameter and a piece of Purbeck marble. Although most fragments found in buildings in Salisbury were quarried

from buildings at Old Sarum, the piece of Purbeck marble is more likely to originate from the cathedral.

81 Block with engaged shaft. H. 130mm. W. 150mm. D. 150mm. Column diam. about 120mm. *1991.54*

82 Block with engaged shaft. H. 130mm. W. 180mm. D. 220mm. Column diam. about 120mm. *1991.54*

83 Fragment of shaft. H. 125mm. Column diam. about 120mm. *1991.54*

84 Fragment of shaft. H. 110mm. Column diam. about 120mm. *1991.54*

85 Purbeck marble block. Sub-rectangular block, H. 350mm. W. 250mm. D. 150mm with axing marks. *1991.54*

CLARENDON PALACE

The collection of Old Sarum fragments in the Museum is sufficiently large and diverse to allow some, hopefully intelligent, speculation about the form of the buildings that once occupied the site. However, the same cannot be said of the remains of Clarendon Palace. The Museum contains the finds deposited after the excavations that first took place between 1933 and 1939 and continued intermittently in the 1950s and 1960s. The 1930s finds were divided up in 1957 and the stonework was deposited in the Museum (James and Robinson 1988, 234). Although the stone fragments cannot help with reconstructions, some of them do provide hints of the quality of the buildings erected in the twelfth and thirteenth centuries.

It is not the intention here to provide a detailed description of the history and development of the palace but a broad understanding of the form of the house and how it developed during the twelfth to fourteenth centuries is necessary to appreciate the surviving fragments. For a more detailed discussion of Clarendon

Palace Howard Colvin's medieval volumes of *The History of the King's Works* published in 1963 and the excavation report of 1988 should be consulted (Colvin 1963 A, B; James and Robinson 1988). However, a clear and concise image of the size and extent of the palace can be gleaned from an examination of the excavation plan supplemented by the plausible, though necessarily speculative, reconstruction by A.C. Garnett published in 1988 (James and Robinson 1988; James 1988). In 2007 a new study was published, describing how the Palace functioned within its landscape (James and Gerrard 2007). Today some pieces of wall survive above ground level, including the east wall of the hall, but most of the palace has been destroyed (Borenius and Charlton 1936, pl. XIX).

Clarendon Palace was a series of visually piecemeal buildings that evolved predominantly during the twelfth and thirteenth centuries. Though they might have looked haphazard to the modern eye for symmetry, the buildings expressed the functions of the medieval house very clearly. Services and the kitchen were at the lower end of the Great Hall and there were two sets of royal apartments at the upper end of the hall. The hall lay on the north side of the palace complex and was aligned approximately east to west; therefore the services were to the west and the royal apartments to the east. The main buildings, where not directly interconnecting, were linked by a series of pentices and covered walkways. Life for the monarch and his retinue was conducted at first floor level, with rooms below being for storage and other lower status functions. The king's oldest son, visitors and staff supporting the King and Queen were housed in buildings further from the hall, on the east and west sides of the courtyard. Clarendon's buildings reflected the form of complex medieval houses prior to the evolution of the compact, familiar medieval house during the twelfth century, with its combination of hall, services and solar in one unified structure (Blair 1993, 6-7).

The palace was first referred to in 1072 as a lodge used by William I when he was hunting in Clarendon Forest, though the site may have been inherited from his Saxon predecessors (James and Robinson 1988, 1, 267). In the 1930s excavations traces of the early house were found underlying the later palace (Colvin 1963 vol. 2, 910). Henry II transformed the status of the site from an occasional private residence to a palace capable of hosting major councils (James and Robinson 1988, 4; 267 Colvin 1963 vol. 2, 910). Documentary sources point to work on the palace beginning in 1155-6, with improvements to the King's chamber in 1167-8, and a wine cellar was excavated in *c.*1172 (Borenius and Charlton 1936, 58; James and Robinson 1988, 5; Colvin 1963 vol. 2, 910-1). In 1175-6 £343 was spent on buildings, including importing Purbeck columns that may have been destined for All Saints Chapel which was first referred in 1178-9. Payments to the canons of Ivychurch Priory to serve the palace first occur immediately after this substantial expenditure. A Purbeck column and flat leaf capital was excavated in the 1930s, but this is now lost (James and Robinson 1988, pl. LXb). The chapel apparently had a nave and chancel and the existence of the column demonstrates that part of the chapel had aisles (Colvin 1963 vol. 2, 915).

Major expenditure continued into the 1180s (James and Robinson 1988, 5). In 1181-3 over £200 was spent on the palace, perhaps on the new hall (Colvin 1963 vol. 2, 910-1). This new building was at the heart of the palace and remained so even after the mid thirteenth-century alterations and extensions. It was a four-bay, aisled hall (82ft x 52ft, 25m x 15.9m) and probably resembled the surviving hall at Oakham Castle, Rutland (James and Robinson 1988, 10). At the west end of the hall, its lower end, was a screens passage leading to the services. The principal dating evidence came from a scalloped capital found in the east wall of the hall, in line with the north arcade of the hall and some fragments in the Museum which came from excavations also point to a similar date (James and Robinson 1988, 235).

Although the Palace continued in use during the reigns of Richard I and John, it was during

Henry III's reign that there was a strong, renewed interest in the site. Between £3,000 and £4,000 was spent on enlarging and refurbishing the Palace (Colvin 1963 vol. 2, 912; James and Robinson 1988, 7-8). Henry II's hall, updated or rebuilt, remained the nucleus of the house and two-light windows were inserted where there had previously been smaller, single light Romanesque openings. (Colvin 1963 vol.1, 123; Colvin 1963 vol. 2, 912; James and Gerrard 2007, 74). Two louvers were set into the roof of the hall in 1231-3 and a new porch was added in 1246. A number of stones in the Museum's collection, which resemble fragments of ceiling bosses, apparently came from the refurbishment of the Great Hall. However, as the hall would have had a timber roof rather than vaults, perhaps the fragments were from corbels.

After his marriage in 1236 Henry III erected a new chamber and wardrobe for his Queen at all his manor houses, but at Clarendon a Queen's chamber already existed and therefore was extended and altered after his marriage in that year (Colvin 1963 vol. 1, 121). The King's and Queen's suite of rooms each included a hall, wardrobe, chambers and a chapel, with the King's suite of rooms being larger (James 1988, 10; Colvin 1963 vol. 2, 915). The Queen's chapel was dedicated to St Katherine and scenes from her life were painted on its walls in 1236. The King's chapel was built by Master Elias of Dereham in 1234-7 and was decorated with gilded angels and images of Saint Mary and Saint Edward (Colvin 1963 vol. 2, 914). In 1244 a new stable was created, as the old one, which was an old hall, was to be converted into a chamber with a fireplace. (James and Gerrard 2007, 74-6).

Beginning in 1246, Henry III also undertook a ten-year refurbishment and rebuilding programme of his private apartments (Alexander and Binski 1987, 323). The palace was redecorated in a contemporary style, probably much as at other royal residences (James and Robinson 1988, 267). Rooms had elaborate tiling and paint schemes like at Westminster Palace, including chambers decorated with scenes

from the story of Antioch, the duel of Richard and Saladin and the life of Alexander (Colvin 1963 vol. 1, 128-9). The Queen's Hall had a new fireplace built in 1251 with marble columns and the twelve months of the year carved into the mantel.

Although Henry III spent lavishly on Clarendon Palace, some of the basic maintenance was apparently neglected, perhaps particularly late in his reign when he was at loggerheads with his barons (James 1988, 5). A survey compiled at the beginning of Edward I's reign listed the problems with the roofs and the rainwater goods, as well as itemising some recent fire damage to the Queen's inner chamber (Colvin 1963 vol. 2, 916-7; James and Robinson 1988, 32-4). Although a series of repairs was immediately undertaken, a subsequent survey in 1315 still identified the need for £1830 of repairs. In 1327 a new gate was built and in the 1350s the King's chapel, the Great Chamber and the kitchen were reroofed, All Saints chapel was altered in 1355-6 and the Great Hall was repaired in 1358-9 (Colvin 1963 vol. 2, 917). A new stable was built near one of the gates in 1399 and in 1448-9 one of the gates was pulled down and rebuilt (Colvin 1963 vol. 2, 918). The 'Bolpit', the prison for offenders who breached Forest law, was rebuilt in 1477.

These modest changes suggest the palace was still in use, though probably not a leading royal residence. However, after 1485 the palace was ignored by Tudor rulers, though some of the buildings were still in use in 1574 when Queen Elizabeth I took shelter there (James and Robinson 1988, 40ff., 268). In the seventeenth century the estate passed out of royal hands, through a tortuous route, to the Bathurst family who built Clarendon House in 1717 (James and Gerrard, 2007, 134). The palace was a sad ruin when it was first excavated in 1821. Major excavations took place under the direction of Dr Tancred Borenius and John Charlton between 1933 and their premature cessation in September 1939. Further excavations were conducted in the 1950s by Elizabeth Eames in search of tile pavements and John Musty in the

1960s (James 1988, 12). However, it was only in 1988 that a collected report of these excavations was published.

Editor's note:

The numbers given to stones in Ashurst and James 1988 are captured within the references below in order to facilitate cross referencing to individual catalogue entries here. Most of the stones are fragments and the measurements given indicate little more than the relative size of the piece.

Plain Ashlar Stones

86 Plain ashlar with obtuse angle. This wedge-shaped block, with a concave soffit, may have originated from a vault or a window arch. It has diagonal tooling and is decorated with paint and plaster. On what would have been its exposed faces, it had originally had a red surface on a white ground with a darker red block of paint. This has been plastered over with a fine lime or gypsum plaster finished with a red motif that resembles small semicircles. H. 140-160mm. W. 120mm. D. 100mm. Ashurst and James 1988, 238 no. 1, fig. 88 (where the illustration has been reversed). *1957.47*

The following ashlar fragments were excavated in the 1930s. They are all of Chilmark-type stone with undecorated chiselled or axed faces, though due to their fragmentary condition it is impossible to tell on some of them how many faces were dressed. The majority of the pieces were painted and appear to show evidence of various schemes of decoration.

87 Plain ashlar, a weathered and irregularly shaped piece, mortared on several sides, suggesting it has been reused as core filling. H. 110mm. W. 110mm. D. 100mm. Ashurst and James 1988, 238 no. 2. *1957.47*

88 Plain ashlar, with traces of mortar, probably original. There are remnants of a painted linear pattern: blue, green, yellow, red and another yellow stripe. One end is broken into a whitewashed triangular face. H. 120mm. W. 65mm. D. 80mm. Ashurst and James 1988, 238 no. 3. *1957.47*

89 Plain ashlar. This obtuse-angled stone is worked on three surfaces with one axed face and it is painted on two surfaces. One is blue, green and yellow, the other is yellow. H. 45mm. W. 75mm. D. 90mm. A coating of modern varnish has distorted the colour of the original colour scheme. Ashurst and James 1988, 238 no. 7. *1957.47*

90 Plain ashlar, with a painted surface 45mm x 40mm of rcd on a white ground. This has been varnished in modern times. Ashurst and James 1988, 238 no. 8. *1957.47*

91 Plain ashlar, decorated with some red paint on a white ground. H. 95mm. W. 55mm. D. 45mm. Ashurst and James 1988, 238 no. 9. *1957.47*

92 Plain ashlar. H. 110mm. W. 90mm. D. 52mm. This stone has traces of red and yellow bands on one surface, with a white ground on the return face. Ashurst and James 1988, 238 no. 10. *1957.47*

93 Corner of block with three axed faces, red colouration on one face, mortar adhering to another. H. 65mm. W. 80mm. D. 40mm. From the Musty 1961 excavations. Ashurst and James 1988, 238, fig. 88, no. 11 (where the illustration has been reversed). *1990.24*

94 Plain ashlar. H. 70mm. W. 70mm. D. 105mm. Course height possibly 70mm. From the Musty 1961 excavations. Ashurst and James 1988, 238 no. 12. *1990.24*

95 Plain ashlar. Two axed faces give a course height of 130mm. H. 130mm. W. 120mm. D. 150mm. From the Musty 1961 excavations. Ashurst and James 1988, 238 no. 13. *1990.24*

96 Plain ashlar, The block indicates a course height of 140mm. The block is broken to form a rough wedge shape and there are three dressed surfaces. Joggles, measuring 25mm x 10mm deep, have been cut into the upper and lower surfaces to receive mortar or lead. There are traces of mortar and on one surface there are traces of fire-reddening. Ashurst and James 1988, 238 no. 14, fig. 88 (where the illustration has been reversed). From the Musty 1961 excavations, labelled 'corner stone from GH' (Great Hall). *1990.24*

Moulded Stones

97 Complete jamb stone of a large doorway. The face of the stone had been covered by a fine lime-wash but there are no traces of polychrome decoration. The stone has rough axed surfaces with finer diagonal axing and vertical tooling on exposed faces. The moulding consists of a large quadrant framed by two flat bands, suggesting a quarter-round door opening possibly of the first half of the 14th century. It is a Chilmark-type stone. H. 212mm. W. 210mm. D. 295-170mm. Ashurst and James 1988, 241 no. 15, fig. 89. *1984.234*

98 Fragment of door or window jamb. It is a hollow-chamfered stone with a small, approximately circular bowtell. H. 120mm. W. 50mm. D. 90mm. Ashurst and James 1988, 241 no. 16, fig. 89. *1957.47*

The collection contains eight fragments of scroll moulding which may be fragments of hood moulds. Seven fragments show evidence of more or less heavy lime-washing.

99 Scroll moulding. L. 80mm, moulding 40mm x 50mm. There are remnants of dark red paint overlying a white ground. Ashurst and James 1988, 241 no. 17. *1957.47*

100 Scroll moulding. L. 80mm, moulding 40mm x 50mm. This stone has traces of red paint overlaid by white and heavy lime-washing suggests that this may have been an external moulding. Ashurst and James 1988, 241 no. 18. *1957.47*

101 Scroll moulding. This is the smallest fragment. L. 43mm, moulding 30mm x 40mm. Ashurst and James 1988, 241 no.19. *1957.47*

102 Scroll moulding. L. 70mm, circular moulding diam. *c*.25mm. Ashurst and James 1988, 241 no.20. *1957.47*

103 Scroll moulding, the largest fragment, L. 170mm, moulding *c*.40mm x 80mm. Heavy limewash suggests that this may have been an external moulding. Ashurst and James 1988, 241 no. 21, fig. 89. *1957.47*

104 Scroll moulding. L. 140mm, circular moulding diam. *c*.55mm. Ashurst and James 1988, 241 no. 22. *1957.47*

105 Scroll moulding. L. 65mm, moulding 30mm x 30mm. Ashurst and James 1988, 241 no. 23. *1957.47*

106 Scroll moulding, possibly a fragment of an arch. L. 95mm, moulding *c*.50mm x 50mm. This displays toothed axe-work on the undamaged end. Ashurst and James 1988, 241 no. 24, fig. 89. *1957.47*

There are three fragments of filleted roll mouldings which seem to come from another type of hood mould.

107 Filleted roll moulding. It has traces of yellow overlying white on the inner face of the curve. L. 130mm, moulding 50mm x 70mm. Ashurst and James 1988, 241 no. 25, fig. 89. *1957.47*

108 Filleted roll moulding. It has a rebated lap joint, and it originally joined Cat 109. There are traces of yellow overlying white on the inner face of the curve. L. 75mm, moulding 60mm x 65mm. Ashurst and James 1988, 241 no. 26. *1957.47*

109 Filleted roll moulding. This originally joined fragment Cat 108. L. 75mm, moulding 60mm x 65mm. Ashurst and James 1988, 241 no. 27. *1957.47*

There are three fragments consisting of a large filleted roll, with an adjacent, small, roll moulding. All these pieces retain evidence of paint and there is visible tooling on the bed face and finer tooling on the dressed faces. They may have formed part of an arch rather than a rib, judging by the angle at which the main filleted roll is set.

110 Large filleted roll, H. 100mm, moulding *c.*120mm x 80mm. It retains traces of a black linear design on a white ground, the whole later limewashed over. Ashurst and James 1988, 241 no. 28, fig. 89. *1957.47*

111 Filleted roll moulding, which has been painted yellow. L. 110mm, moulding 90mm x 75mm. Ashurst and James 1988, 241 no. 29. *1957.47*

112 Filleted roll moulding, covered with yellow paint. L. 83mm, moulding 130mm x 80mm. Ashurst and James 1988, 241 no. 30. *1957.47*

113 Purbeck marble moulding fragment, perhaps part of the base of an attached shaft. The stone is damaged so that it is now roughly triangular in shape with two broken faces. Three surfaces are worked, one of which is rubbed and polished and there is a moulding channel on one side. L. 87.5mm. W. 78mm. H. 45mm. Ashurst and James 1988, 241 no. 31, fig. 89. *1957.47*

114 Fragment of pink Chilmark stone with a groove forming the edge of a simple moulding. Irregular fragment 75mm x 65mm x 35mm. From the Musty 1961 excavations. Ashurst and James 1988, 241 no. 32. *1990.24*

Carved Stones

115 Chevron string course moulding. L. 90mm. H. 65mm. D. 35mm. This is probably a remnant of a piece of chevron and therefore dates from the 12th century. It was discovered in 1934 and may be one of the pieces of chevron moulding recovered from excavations in the west kitchen. Ashurst and James 1988, 241 no. 33, fig. 89. *1957.47*
A number of fragments of attached columns, originating from a doorway leading from the Great Hall were unearthed during the 1930s excavations of the Great Hall (Borenius and Charlton 1936, 72-3, fig. 3). The suggested date, based on documentary sources, for this work was *c.*1250, though the fragments may have been reused (James and Robinson with Eames 1988, 93 and 244). The columns are more likely to date from the twelfth century and

may have been attached shafts to support roof timbers of the aisles.

116 Attached column fragment. A tapered half cylinder, this was possibly part of an attached column with a moulded astragal, or annulet, at the neck of the shaft. It may have been burnt and shows no sign of paint or lime-wash. It is similar in form to three other pieces (Cat 117, 118 and 110). L. 210mm. W. 75-115mm. D. 40mm, column diam. 90mm (max). Ashurst and James 1988, 241 no. 34, fig. 90. *1957.47* **Pl 8**

117 Small attached column fragment. It has a triple ring-moulded astragal or annulet similar to Cat 116. H. 60mm. W. 82mm (max). D. 45mm, column diam. 82mm (max). It was excavated from the south west corner of the Great Hall. Ashurst and James 1988, 244 no. 35, fig. 90; Borenius and Charlton 1936, 72-3 and fig. 3. *1957.47*

118 Attached column fragment with painted decoration. This stone corresponds in size with the broad end of Cat 116. It is finely tooled and has a red painted pattern of stylised wing-shapes on a pale background. L. 85mm. W. 105mm. D. 40mm, column diam. *c.*125mm. Ashurst and James 1988, 244 no. 36, fig. 90. *1957.47* **Pl 8**

119 Attached column fragment, similar to Cat 118. It retains some evidence of lime-wash, but the mortar adhering to the face suggests it has been reused as core filling. This stone was recovered from the solar. L. 45mm. W. 122mm. D. 65mm, column diam. *c.*130mm. Ashurst and James 1988, 244 no. 37. *1957.47*

Four fragments of attached column shafts, measuring 40-45mm in radius, were excavated in the 1930s.

120 Attached column fragment. L. 50mm. W. *c.*60mm. D. 20mm, shaft diam. *c.*70mm with blue paint on a white ground, varnished in modern times. Ashurst and James 1988, 244 no. 38. *1957.47*

121 Attached column fragment, decorated with red paint on a white ground. Apparently from 'solar U' (perhaps an unstratified location in the solar). L.

112mm. W. 82mm. D. 35mm. Ashurst and James 1988, 244 no. 39. *1957.47*

122 Attached column fragment, L. 180mm. W. 90mm. D. 80mm, shaft diam. 90mm. No evidence of painting. From their proportions this stone and Cat 123 may have been components in a compound pier or cluster of shafts. Ashurst and James 1988, 244 no. 40, fig. 90. *1957.47*

123 Attached column fragment, L. 185mm. W. 90mm. D. 90mm, shaft diam. 90mm. No evidence of painting, encrustations of mortar suggesting it may have been reused. Ashurst and James 1988, 244 no. 41. *1957.47*

124 Multi-angular stone, possibly part of an octagonal base or a capital, or less likely a padstone for a timber pier. It consists of a larger hollow moulding with two fillets. There are traces of mortar on the bottom face and traces on the carved faces. H. 75mm. W. 170mm. D. 100mm. Ashurst and James 1988, 245 no. 42, fig. 90. *1957.47*

125 Multi-angular stone, possibly from the base of a pier. Similar in form to Cat 124. Unlabelled, possibly from Clarendon. H. 115mm. W. 170mm. D. 50mm. *2008R.1438*

126 Shaft with fillet. This was described as a fragment of a column capital (Ashurst and James 1988, 245 no. 43, fig. 90). It has painted decoration with a white ground and a red overlay. L. 180mm. W. 105mm. D. 65mm. *1957.47*

It seems to resemble a shaft with a fillet ending in a v-shaped fork, as if it was located near the point where a small vault or arch sprang from the upright.

127 Purbeck marble, scroll moulded rib, possibly from an arch, excavated from the Queen's chamber. 70mm x 30mm x 20mm. Ashurst and James 1988, 245 no. 44. *1957.47*

128 Purbeck marble, scroll moulded rib, possibly from an arch, excavated from the Queen's chamber. L. 70mm. W. 30mm. D. 20mm. Ashurst and James 1988, 245 no. 45. *1957.47*

129 Corbel or vault springer with a cat's

head. The cat has pointed ears, oval eyes with thick bands around them and a strange nose with diagonal grooves. It is made of siliceous limestone, and is broken away below the nose. H. 210mm. W. 200mm. D. 150mm. Ashurst and James 1988, 245 no. 46, fig. 91 and pl. LXIa. *1956.92*   **Pl 8**

This stone was found during the excavations of the 'chapel' in late August 1939. It was dated in James and Robinson 1988 to the twelfth century and stylistically it probably dates from the mid twelfth century. It should be part of Henry II's building campaigns of the 1160s and 1170s, but it seems archaic in style. In its broadest form it is reminiscent of some of the carved heads from Old Sarum, though its quality does not match that of the former cathedral.

130 Ear of an animal. Some mortar adheres to the rear of the stone. The whole piece measures 150mm x 130mm x 70mm, the ear only 90mm x 57.5mm. Ashurst and James 1988, 245 no. 47 and fig. 91, where it is dated to the 13th or 14th century. *1957.47*   **Pl 8**

131 Fragment of stiff-leaf foliage capital. Although heavily weathered, it was originally a piece of elaborate, mid 13th-century foliage, possibly from a capital. H. 152mm. W. 142mm. D. 162mm, depth of abacus 35mm. Ashurst and James 1988, 245 no. 48, fig. 91. *1957.47*   **Pl 8**

132 Roof boss or capital fragment decorated with stiff-leaf forms. This stone was excavated from the Great Hall, and in style dates from the mid 13th century, possibly the 1230s. It was carved from a dense and glauconitic limestone, 170mm x 140mm. D. 90mm. Ashurst and James 1988, 245 no. 49, fig. 91 and pl. LXIb. *1956.93*

133 Part of capital or a boss with a ribbed and leaf pattern. 80mm x 50mm. D. 70mm. It has a central mortice hole, 15mm in diameter and 5mm deep. Ashurst and James 1988, 245 no. 50, fig. 91. *1957.47*

134 Fragment of a capital or a boss? It is decorated with an intertwining, floral motif, resembling a spade in a pack of cards. It was excavated from the

Great Hall and therefore probably dates from work of the 1230s. There is still some mortar attached to it. L. 155mm. W. 110mm. D. 80mm. Ashurst and James 1988, 245 no. 51, fig. 92 and pl. LXIb. *1957.47*

135 Volute from a capital or corbel There are three small indentations in the centre of the volute, probably the centres of radii for inscribing the design. There is still some mortar adhering to the former, unexposed faces of the stone. H. 120mm. W. 65mm. D. 120mm. Ashurst and James 1988, 245 no. 52, fig. 92. *1957.47*

The next group of fragments are decorated with stiff-leaf foliage and three (Cat 137-9) are recorded as having been excavated from the south west corner of the Great Hall, hence dating from the thirteenth century. More precisely the fragments probably date from the 1230s.

136 Fragment of stiff-leaf crocket. H. 75mm. W. 100mm. D. 80mm. Borenius and Charlton 1936, 73 and fig. 3; Ashurst and James 1988, 245 no. 53. *1957.47*

137 Stiff-leaf crocket. H. 98mm. W. 85mm. D. 75mm. Ashurst and James 1988, 245 no. 54. *1957.47*

138 Stiff-leaf crocket. H. 90mm. W. 75mm. D. 85mm. On this carving there are traces of red colour on a white ground. Ashurst and James 1988, 245 possibly no. 55, 56 or 57. *1957.47*

139 Stiff-leaf carving. H. 135mm. W. 115mm. D. 85mm. This fragment retains traces of red and white coloration. Ashurst and James 1988, 245 possibly no. 55, 56 or 57. *1957.47*

140 Stiff-leaf carving. H. 130mm. W. 115mm. D. 110mm. Ashurst and James 1988, 245 possibly no. 55, 56 or 57. *1957.47*

141 Stiff-leaf foliage. H. 48mm. W. 76mm. D. 30mm. Ashurst and James 1988, 245 no. 58. *1957.47*

142 Crocket with leaf and ball design. According to Borenius and Charlton it was excavated

from the south-west corner of the Great Hall (see Cat 117) and was originally a decoration from a doorway. It would date from the 1230s and is carved in a particularly compact Chilmark-type stone, H. 85mm. W. 64mm. D. 62mm. Borenius and Charlton 1936, 73 and fig. 3; Ashurst and James 1988, 245 no. 59. *1957.47*

143 Fragment of pink Chilmark stone, perhaps foliage carving. H. 70mm. W. 100mm. D. 35mm. From the Musty 1961 excavations. Ashurst and James 1988, 245 no. 60. *1990.24*

144 Fragment of a beaded string course or arch moulding. This stone is decorated with a beaded, hollow-chamfer and probably dates from the third quarter of the 12th century. H. 120mm. W. 100mm. D. 55mm. Ashurst and James 1988, 245 no. 61. *1957.47*   **Pl 8**

145 Fragment of a beaded string course or arch moulding. This stone is decorated with a beaded, hollow-chamfer and probably dates from the 12th century, probably from the campaign of the third quarter of the 12th century. Mortar adhering to the finished face suggests it was reused as core filling. H. 150mm. W. 132.mm. D. 62mm. Ashurst and James 1988, 245 no. 62 and fig. 92 (where erroneously illustrated as no. 61). *1957.47*   **Pl 8**

146 Fragment of incised and relief ball design. H. 85mm. W. 40mm. D. 40mm. Ashurst and James 1988, 245 no. 63. *1957.47*

147 Fragment of cornice, string course or capital with flattened bead design. H. 110mm. W. 72mm. D. 80mm. Traces of black and red coloration on end face. Ashurst and James 1988, 245 no. 64, fig. 92. *1957.47*

148 Fragment of cornice or string course. It is decorated with cylindrical billet set into a hollow chamfer, with adjacent smaller billets. H. 85mm. W. 125mm. D. 66mm. Mortar on two faces. Ashurst and James 1988, 245 no. 65, fig. 92. *1957.47*

149 Head of a Youth. *c.*1246-56. Found in 1935 in the solar. The head was carved from a block of

Chilmark stone which measured at least 250mm x 200mm x 140mm. The carved part of the block is H. 190mm, W. 140mm and D. 125mm. The carving of the rather attenuated head, with its furrowed brow, teeth and curly hair has a naturalistic, almost portrait-like quality. There are traces of an orange or light brown colouring on the hair, which may be the remains of gilding. The pupils have a spot of black paint and the lips, when the piece was found, were painted pink. *Sal. Mus. Rep.* 1955-56, 9 and pl.1; 1 Stone 1972, 118-19 and pl. 92; Ashurst and James 1988, 246 no. 66, frontispiece and pl. LXII; Alexander and Binski 1987, 323. *1956.80*   **Pl 9 & cover**

This head may have been a label stop of a hood mould, suggesting that this was one of a pair. In 1246 Henry III began to improve his private apartments. In 1249 a fireplace in the King's wardrobe was repaired and improved while in 1252-3 a window was provided for the King's wardrobe, with a pillar, a seat and a bench for his clothes. Could this be the window from which the head originated? (Alexander and Binski 1987, 323.) Henry's improvements to Clarendon echoed the programme of refurbishment that took place at Westminster Palace, and therefore it is perhaps no surprise that heads with comparable detailing survive at Westminster Abbey (most of the adjacent medieval palace having now been replaced). In the Abbey the depiction of a head with a line of visible teeth, hair ending in rows of curls and a long face are found in corbel heads in St Faith's Chapel, while the furrowed brow appears in a corbel in St Benedict's Chapel and in the combat bosses in the Muniment Room.

In the report of the excavation the head was thought to represent 'the dead', and so may have been balanced by a second head representing 'the quick' (Ashurst and James 1988, 246). Another interpretation is that the head depicts 'anguish' suggesting its pair may have been 'joy' (Alexander and Binski 1987, 323).

Fragments of Carved Figures from the Great Hall

The next six items were excavated apparently from the south west corner of the Great Hall, beneath a fourteenth-century floor. However, some of the fragments seem to have come from the solar that would have been at the east end of the hall. They have been compared with the double capital from the cloister of Ivychurch Priory (see Cat 200). As the canons of the priory served the chapel of the palace a further link through shared craftsmen seems plausible (Borenius and Charlton 1936, 67 and pl. XII, 2).

The size of these pieces suggests that they may have been part of the decoration of historiated capitals. They were dated to *c.*1155-60 in the catalogue of the English Romanesque Sculpture exhibition (Zarnecki et al. 1984, 189-90). However, the hall seems to have been built in the early 1180s though the report of the excavations did emphasise that fragments could have been moved there from one of the chapels (James and Robinson 1988, 246). A date of around 1160 seems more plausible.

150 Half figure in profile. The torso and left hand of a human figure with drapery decorated with a beaded border. H. 150mm x 85mm x 45mm. Correspondence suggests this fragment may have been found in the solar. Zarnecki et al. 1984, 190 pl. 155b; Ashurst and James 1988, 246 no. 67, fig. 93 and pl. LXIIIa; Borenius and Charlton 1936, 67 and fig. 2(b). *1957.47*   **Pl 9**

151 Upper part of a male torso holding a sword. Broken in two fragments. The drapery is decorated with beaded hems. H. 120mm x 110mm x 40mm. Zarnecki et al. 1984, 189 pl. 155a; Ashurst and James 1988, 246 no. 68, fig. 93 and pl. LXIIIb; Borenius and Charlton 1936, 67 and fig. 2(e). *1957.47*   **Pl 9**

152 Seated Figure. H. 112mm. W. 110mm. D. 45mm. Correspondence suggests this fragment may have been found in the solar. Zarnecki et al. 1984, 190 pl. 155f; Ashurst and James 1988, 246 no. 69, fig. 93 and pl. LXIVa; Borenius and Charlton 1936, 67 and fig. 2(f). *1957.47*   **Pl 9**

153 Legs of a seated figure. H. 100mm x

60mm x 45mm. Zarnecki et al. 1984, 190 pl. 155c; Ashurst and James 1988, 246 no. 70, fig. 93 and pl. LXIVb; Borenius and Charlton 1936, 67 and fig. 2(d). *1957.47* **Pl 9**

154 Harpy or Siren. Legs, tail, head and one arm broken off. This fragment was described by Borenius as an angel. H. 155mm x 140mm x 50mm. Zarnecki et al. 1984, 190 pl. 155e; Ashurst and James 1988, 246 no. 71, fig. 94 and pl. LXVa; Borenius and Charlton 1936, 67 and fig. 2(a). *1957.47* **Pl 10**

155 Feline head. It has a wide mouth with prominent teeth and large oval eyes. In overall form, though not in its detailed execution, it is similar to heads from Old Sarum. Was this part of a beak-head voussoir, a corbel or a historiated capital? H. 70mm x 65mm x 40mm. This fragment apparently came from in or near the solar. Zarnecki et al. 1984, 190 no. 155d; Ashurst and James 1988, 246-9, no. 72, fig. 94; Borenius and Charlton 1936, 67 and fig. 2(c). *1957.47* **Pl 10**

156 Fragment of bird or angel wing. 75mm x 45mm x 50mm. This fragment has traces of red coloration on a white ground and there is clear evidence of gilding on the feathers. It was excavated from the Queen's chambers, but the King's chapel, built in 1234-7, was known to have been decorated with gilded angels. Could this be a fragment from one of these angels or a similar scheme in the Queen's chambers? James and Robinson 1988, 249 no. 73, fig. 94 and pl. LXVb. *1957.47* **Pl 10**

157 Fragment of a head? This stone resembles a large set of teeth, but may simply be two bands of irregular beads. Probably 12th century. H. 45mm. W. 70mm. D. 65mm. Ashurst and James 1988, 249 no. 74, fig. 94. *1957.47*

158 Fragment of drapery. L. 110mm. W. 50mm (max). D. 25mm. Ashurst and James 1988, 249 no. 75. *1957.47*

159 Fragment of drapery, including a line of beading. Probably 12th century. L. 90mm. W. 25-33mm. D. 40mm. Ashurst and James 1988, 249 no. 76. *1957.47*

This fragment appears to be related to Cat 169.

160 Fragment of spiral-shaped drapery or leaf. H. 55mm. W. 60mm. D. 25mm. Ashurst and James 1988, 249 no. 77. *1957.47*

161 Fragment with intertwined leaf trails. H. 120mm. W. 80mm. D. 50mm. Ashurst and James 1988, 249 no. 78. *1957.47*

162 Fragment with overlapping beaded border. Probably 12th century. H. 75mm. W. 70mm. D. 30mm. Ashurst and James 1988, 249 no. 79. *1957.47*

163 Fragment of rib or arch moulding with beaded border. H. 70mm. W. 40mm. D. 35mm. Ashurst and James 1988, 249 no. 80. *1957.47*

164 Fragment with beaded border. Probably 12th century. H. 45mm. W. 40mm. D. 30mm. Ashurst and James 1988, 249 no. 81. *1957.47*

165 Fragment with beaded border. Probably 12th century. H. 55mm. W. 40mm. D. 15mm. Ashurst and James 1988, 249 no. 82. *1957.47*

166 Carved fragment with roll moulding. H. 95mm. W. 85mm. D. 50mm. Ashurst and James 1988, 249 no. 83. *1957.47*

167 Fragment with radiating ribs. H. 30mm. W. 40mm. D. 15mm. Ashurst and James 1988, 249 no. 85. *1957.47*

168 Purbeck marble, unworked fragment, 60mm x 40mm x 15mm. Ashurst and James 1988, 249 no. 92. *1957.47*

Cat 169-176 are fragments that cannot be related to those published by Ashurst and James 1988.

169 Fragment of arch or rib. H. 43mm. W. 85mm. D. 23mm. *1957.47*

This may be part of a tracery arch. See also Cat 159.

170 Moulded fragment. H. 70mm. W. 40mm. D. 28mm. *1957.47*

171 Carved fragment. A stone with shallow carving but no obvious function. H. 60mm. W. 20-35mm. D. 35mm. *1957.47*

172 Crocket with trilobed leaf form. H. 75mm. W. 70mm. D. 50mm. *1957.47*

173 Moulded stone. H. 36mm. W. 50mm. D. 55mm. *1957.47*

174 Carved stone. This stone is pink/red in colour, possibly as a result of being burnt. H. 58mm. W. 36mm. D. 36mm. *1957.47*

175 Fragment of a beaded string course. This stone is decorated with a beaded hollow chamfer similar to Cat 144. H. 75mm. W. 75mm. D. 30mm. Unlabelled, but apparently from the Musty 1961 excavations as with other stones from this source. *1990.24*

176 Block with an incised cross. Mortar adhering to one face. 185mm x 185mm x 170mm. Probably from the salsary. Unpublished. *1964.59*

SALISBURY CATHEDRAL

Within the Museum's collection there are a number of fragments that originated from Salisbury Cathedral. These seem to have predominantly originated from the vestibule to the chapter house and the west wall of the chapter house where it adjoined the vestibule. Purbeck marble was used selectively in the building to provide accents to the rest of the carved stone, but more Purbeck was employed around the entrance from the vestibule.

The construction of the cathedral was underway by the end of the 1210s and the symbolic laying of the foundation stone took place on 28 April 1220. By 1226 the building was sufficiently advanced to allow the first of the bishop's tombs from Old Sarum to be moved into the cathedral. According to an early fourteenth-century source, the cathedral was consecrated in 1258, though it was apparently not completed until 1266 (VCH 1956, 165; Cocke and Kidson, 1993 3-4 and 8; Spring 1987, 10-5; Blum 1991, 22). However, the tower and the spire, as well as the statues of the west front belong to later in the thirteenth and fourteenth century. The cloister and chapter house were usually an integral part of the building programme, so that, if the 1266 date is broadly accurate, the chapter house was complete by that date. However, recent research has suggested that at Salisbury the construction of the cloister and chapter house was not undertaken until the last two decades of the thirteenth century (Blum 1991, 25-36).

By the end of the seventeenth century the chapter house was in need of repairs but nothing appears to have been done until the mid nineteenth century (Cocke and Kidson 1993, 22). Repairs to the cloister were begun in 1850 by Bishop Denison who died in 1854. As a tribute to the bishop a restoration of the chapter house was funded through public subscriptions. This campaign is dated by various authors to 1855, 1856, 1855-6 or 1855-61 (Whittingham 1979; Slocombe 1996, 30; Spring 1987, 26; Cocke and Kidson 1993, 29). The architect responsible was Henry Clutton (1819-93) though the sculptor John Birnie Philip (1824-75) and William Burges were also involved (Slocombe 1996, 30 and 72; Cocke and Kidson 1993, 29; Whittingham 1974; Spring 1987, 26). After the repairs, fragments of the original fabric were deposited in the Victoria and Albert Museum: Cat 177-194 are now on long term loan.

177-80 Four mouldings. Purbeck marble, decorated with cusps, from an arch. Maximum width at the spandrels *c.*290mm and at the cusps 130mm. L. *c.*700mm. D. max. 220mm. V & A: A40.1916. *1971.38*   **Pl 10**

These four stones formed a single arch with stiff leaf carving in the spandrels of the cusping originally on both sides of the opening, though one side is badly damaged. They were originally part of one of the two arches between the chapter house and the vestibule.

181 Male head. H. 180mm. W. 130mm. D. 110mm. The face and hair both retain traces of gilding. V & A: A44.1916. *Sal. Mus. Rep.* 1970-1,

21 and pl. IIIA. *1971.37* **Pl 10**

At the rear of this head are the remains of the hood moulding to which the head was attached. This indicates that it came from one of the decorative arches, presumably from one of the arches at the west side of the chapter house.

182 Quarter capital with stiff leaf carving. Purbeck marble. H. 150mm. Column diam. *c.*160mm. V & A: A49.1916. *1971.42* **Pl 10**

This stiff-leaf capital, which has its crockets broken off, is a quarter of a circle in plan, suggesting that it came from a corner. The most likely location is where the arcading above, and flanking, the entrance to the vestibule adjoined the vault shafts.

183 Capital with stiff leaf carving. Damaged. Purbeck marble. H. 220mm. Column diam. *c.*100 mm. V & A: A48.1916. *1971.42*

This capital, which is similar in form to Cat 182 but is more circular in form, probably originated from the same arcading above the vestibule.

184 Annulet for connecting group of three, or more shafts. 420mm (max.) x 260mm (max.) x 80mm thick. The central column diam. 115mm, the flanking ones 100mm. Purbeck marble. 13th century. V & A: A43.1916. *1971.39* **Pl 10**

This stone was one of the connecting annulets to join lengths of Purbeck marble. Although it is not possible to point to its precise original location, it is clear that it was one of the connecting pieces in a group of vault shafts, probably where the shafts passed through the string course above the dado arches.

185 Base. Purbeck marble. H. 140mm. W. 270mm. D. 400mm. The moulding is 230mm x 190mm. A recess indicates that it was a base for a quatrefoil-shape shaft 115mm x 85mm. V & A: A45.1916. *1971.40*

186 Base. Purbeck marble. H. 140mm. W. 270mm. D. 285mm. A recess indicates that it was a base for a quatrefoil-shape shaft 115mm x 85mm. V & A: A46.1916. *1971.40* **Pl 10**

This fragment and Cat 185 are bases of small shafts, which were quatrefoil in plan. Similar shafts appear in the west side of the chapter house.

187 Capital. Purbeck marble. Rounded square H. 130mm. W. 220mm. V & A: A47.1916. *1971.41*

This capital has a recess to take a column of quatrefoil section, similar to the bases Cat 188 and 189.

188 Engaged capital. Purbeck marble. H. 150mm. W. (max.) 210mm. Column diam. 75mm. V & A: A53.1916. *1971.46*

189 Engaged capital. Purbeck marble. H. 200mm. W. 210mm. Column diam. 75mm. Identical to Cat 188 except for length of column. V & A: A54.1916. *1971.46*

190 Engaged capital. Purbeck marble. H. 260mm. W. 210mm. Column diam. 75mm. Identical to Cat 188 except for length of column. V & A: A55.1916. *1971.46*

These capitals differ in height but were all carved to fit columns of approximately 75-80mm in diameter and share the same profile. They may have come originally from the tracery or vault shafts of the chapter house.

191 Engaged capital. Purbeck marble. H. 110mm. W. 145mm. Column diam. 80mm. Flat at the back with a slot 30mm wide and 20mm deep cut into the top. V & A: A51.1916. *1971.44*

This capital also topped a shaft 80mm in diameter, but is simpler in profile than the previous group.

192 Annulet. Purbeck marble. H. 80mm. W. 200mm. D. 180mm. V & A: A52.1916. *1971.45*

This annulet is a junction piece to join two length of Purbeck marble shaft 100mm in diameter.

193 Engaged capital. Purbeck marble. H. 300mm. W. 400 mm. D. 450mm. Column diam. *c.*130mm. V & A: A50.1916. *1971.43* **Pl 11**

This capital is much larger than the other fragments from the chapter house. This indicates that it either came from part of the vaulting system or more plausibly from the vaulting of the vestibule to the chapter house. The dimensions of the capitals of this section of vaulting are close to the size of the fragment.

194 Engaged base. Purbeck marble. H. 130mm. W. 205mm. D. 270mm. Diam. of column base 140mm. V & A: A56.1916. *1971.47*

Other Fragments from the Cathedral
There are fragments from buildings in and around the city that are presumed originally to have come from the Cathedral.

195 ?Corbel with a female head in wimple. Limestone. H. 230mm. W. 170mm. D. 240mm. Mid to late 13th century. This head was re-used decoratively in the Crown Hotel, High Street, Salisbury, which was demolished in 1969. *Sal. Mus. Rep.* 1969-70, 18 and pl. IIa. *1970.52*   **Pl 11**

196 Corbel with human head. Purbeck marble. A very large corbel, of which only the lower part survives. H. 140mm. W. (at shoulders) 290mm. D. 260mm. From Harnham. *1937.109*

197 Fragment of simple moulding with ?ivy-leaf frieze. Surface mortar suggests reuse as rubble. L.185mm. W. 170mm. D. 100mm. This moulded string course is decorated with two stiff leaves and the carving retains traces of red, blue and yellow/brown colouration. From the garden of 11 The Close, Salisbury. *2003.11*

The Hungerford Chantry Chapel
The Hungerford Chantry Chapel occupied the angle between the north wall of the Lady Chapel and the east wall of the north aisle of the choir. The chapel, built in 1464-1471, commemorated Robert Lord Hungerford (pre 1413-1459) (Cocke and Kidson 1993, 14.) His widow Margaret de Botreaux spent £497 on the construction of the chapel and £250 on ornaments and furniture. To maintain the chantry she provided extensive endowments and a house in The Close for its two priests (VCH 1956, 181, 200; White 1898, 46).

Between 1789 and 1792 an extensive campaign of 'improvements' to the cathedral took place including the demolition of the thirteenth-century choir screen, the removal of most medieval glass, the opening of the Lady Chapel to the Choir and externally the demolition of the thirteenth-century belfry. The Hungerford Chapel and its counterpart on the south side of the Lady Chapel, which were in poor condition, were also demolished (VCH 1956, 200; Strong 1987, 22; Cocke and Kidson 1993, 28). Other fragments from the Hungerford chapel can be found in the west walk of the cloister (Spring 1987, 146).

198 Raven in cusped quadrilobe. The raven gorged and chained was one of the badges of the Hungerford family. Thus it is most likely that this stone came from the Hungerford Chantry Chapel. H. 385mm. W. 285mm. D. *c.*110mm. Very weathered. From the garden of 48 The Close, Salisbury. *1937.148*   **Pl 11**

IVYCHURCH PRIORY, ALDERBURY

Ivychurch Priory was founded in the middle of the twelfth century, probably during the reign of King Stephen. From 1154 until its dissolution in 1536 it received an annual grant from the Royal treasury in exchange for saying the offices in the chapel of nearby Clarendon Palace. After the Dissolution the site was converted into a large house, but this was largely demolished in 1889. See RCHM(E) 1987, 148-153; Nightingale 1891, 352-5. Today the remains of the north aisle and north transept of the priory church have been incorporated into a farmhouse. This building contains a number of reset fragments and parts of walls and piers survive around the farmhouse. There is also a fountain in the nearby village that incorporates double capitals that may have come from the cloister.

199 Capital of respond. H. 300mm. W. 336mm

D. 460mm. Column diam. >350mm. From Ivy-church Priory, Alderbury.. Possibly *1888-89.2* or *1890-91.2*

This substantial scalloped capital is from a large respond, probably from an aisle of the church. It has plain scallops whereas the sur-viving capitals on the site have small, v-shaped sheaths around the scallops.

200 Double capital. H. 200mm. W. 510mm. D. 260mm. Column diam. *c.*130mm. Figure carving is badly damaged. From the cloisters of Ivychurch Priory, Alderbury. *1934.67*   **Pl 11**

This eroded double capital depicts a series of small seated figures set within arches. Borenius and Charlton (1936, 67 and pl. XII, 2) referred to this piece as possibly illustrating the use of the historiated fragments from Clarendon Palace, Cat 150-55. It is clearly from a cloister with double shafts, and a number of similarly-shaped capitals survive in the farmhouse and surround-ing walls, while four are incorporated into the water fountain of the village. They are mostly decorated with scalloped forms and many make use of beaded strap-work, but none of these has figures set within arches.

201 Sundial, possibly formerly a capital. H. 165mm. W. 145mm. D. 145mm. From Ivychurch Priory, Alderbury. *1890-9.2*

This strange stone, which has had a sundial set into it, may be a cut-down capital, or a stone that has been discarded and adapted. All the faces are different including one with a recessed crescent, while the opposite face is decorated with a heart. The carvings on the other faces are clear, but are not specific forms. The piece retains traces of several iron pins, perhaps a post-medieval adaptation.

202 Ridge stone with ?finial socket. Ironstone. H. 240mm. W. (max.) 250mm. Diam. of socket 90mm. From Ivychurch Priory, Alderbury. *1890-91.2*

IMBER

Imber was a small village requisitioned by the military during World War II. Residents were informed at a meeting on 1 November 1943 that they had until 17 December 1943 to va-cate their homes, the pub and the church. They expected to be able to return after the war, but apart from occasional open days the village has remained the sole preserve of the military (Sawyer 1987, 97ff.).

Some of the buildings, including the church, survive from the historic village, but many of the buildings were built to simulate the conditions that soldiers would face in a European land war. The church had a Norman font, now in Brixton Deverill, suggesting a Norman origin for the building. However, it was rebuilt in the late thirteenth century and its fenestration was altered during the fifteenth century. The early chancel was rebuilt in 1849 and the church was restored in 1895 (Sawyer 1987, 5-6; Pevsner 1975, 276).

203 Block with human face. H. 250mm. W. 240mm. D. 200mm. Late 13th or early 14th century. Found built into a stone wall of a building known as the Imber Post Office. *1965.3*   **Pl 11**

This block is decorated with an eroded and damaged female face. Although it was built into the Post Office, it probably originally came from the church and dates from the main building campaign.

EAST KNOYLE

Two fragments from the garden of Knoyle Place at East Knoyle. Knoyle Place is a large house with late fourteenth-century origins, but with major additions in the seventeenth and eight-eenth centuries. It was the home of Christopher Wren's family at the time of his birth in 1632.

204 Central part of Trinity group. 'Knees of the Father and lower part of Crucifix.' 15th century. From the garden of Knoyle Place, East Knoyle. *1959.20.1*

Un-located in the Museum since at least 1974; description is based on a note by Hugh Shortt, confirmed by a photograph (acc. no. *2009R.125.2537*).

205 Carving of outstretched left hand, possibly the hand of the Father blessing his Son. 15th century. L. 120mm. W.110mm. D.80mm. From the garden of Knoyle Place, East Knoyle. *1959.20.2*   **Pl 12**

GLASTONBURY ABBEY

The Museum has a fine capital from the cloister of Glastonbury Abbey. It was built while Henry of Blois was the abbot (1126-71). Henry, a nephew of Henry I, was the Bishop of Winchester from 1129 onwards, but he never relinquished control of the abbey. No documents record the dates of the construction of the cloister, but it is attributed to the middle of the twelfth century. The cloister was destroyed by a devastating fire in 1184.

206 Part of double capital. Blue Lias limestone. This was originally a free-standing double capital supported by two colonnettes, but only half of the capital survives. Column diam. *c*.40mm. H. 230mm. *c*.1150. *OS.C53*   **Pl 11**

The capital has no provenance, but the material from which it is made and the style of the decoration are identical to fragments from the cloister sculpture of Glastonbury Abbey. They share similar curling leaf forms, the stalks of which are decorated with beading, zigzag and decorated clasps. The capital featured in the 1984 'English Romanesque Art 1066-1200' exhibition alongside capitals that came from Glastonbury. See *Sal. Mus. Cat.* 1870, 60 no. 3; Zarnecki et al. 1984, 184-5 no. 149a; Radford 1981, 131, pl. XXIVF.

OTHER PIECES

After the catalogue above was completed three additional pieces came to light:

207 Head of a grotesque. 12th century. H. 240 mm. W. 200 mm. D. 450 mm. The head of what appears to be a grimacing man was recovered from a trench dug at The Market House, Salisbury (built 1859), itself on the site of the former Maidenhead Inn. In style it has some affinities with figural carving from Old Sarum though its relationship to it cannot be demonstrated. *1973.138*   **Pl 12**

208 Boss. Mid-13th century. L. 340 mm. W. 320 mm. H. 180 mm. Found in the garden of 97 Exeter Street, Salisbury. Although very eroded that are signs that it was decorated with stiff-leaf foliage and presumably originally came from a building within The Close, which is adjacent to this street. *1932.1*   **Pl 12**

209 Part of a chimney capstone. Max. diam. at base 230 mm. H. 190 mm. With one complete aperture (W. 130 mm and H. 140 mm.) and traces of two others at right angles. Although the capstone appears to be oval, damage prevents certainty over whether it may originally have been circular. Upper surface appears to have supported a finial. 13th century. Found reused in the east wall of the hall of The Old Deanery, The Close, Salisbury. Drinkwater 1964, 55 and pl. 32b. *1962.86*   **Pl 12**

BIBLIOGRAPHY

Alexander, J. and Binski, P. (eds.) 1987: *Age of Chivalry: Art in Plantagenet England 1200-1400* (exhibition catalogue, Royal Society of Arts, London)

Ashbee, J. 2006: 'Cloisters in English Palaces in the Twelfth and Thirteenth Centuries', *Journal of the British Archaeological Society* **159**, 71-90

Ashurst, J. and James, T. B. 1988: 'Stonework and Plasterwork' in T.B. James and A.M. Robinson with Elizabeth Eames, *Clarendon Palace: the History and Archaeology of a Medieval Palace and Hunting Lodge near Salisbury, Wiltshire.* Soc. Antiq. Res. Rep. **45**, 234-258

Ayers, T. and Sampson, J. 2000: 'The Medieval Period' in Tim Ayers (ed.), *Salisbury Cathedral: The West Front* (Chichester)

Blair, J 1993: 'Hall and Chamber: English Domestic Planning 1000-1250' in Gwyn Meirion-Jones and Michael Jones (eds.), Manorial Domestic Buildings in England and Northern France, Soc. Antiq. Occ. Pap. **15**, 1-21

Blum, P. Z. 1991: 'The sequence of the building campaigns at Salisbury', *Art Bulletin*, **73**, no. 1 (March), 6-38

Borenius, T. and Charlton, J. 1936: 'Clarendon Palace: an interim report', *Antiq. J.* **16**, 55-84

Brakspear, H. 1913: 'Malmesbury Abbey' *Archaeologia* **64**, 399-436

Brodie, A. 1988: 'Malmesbury Abbey', *Proc. Royal Arch. Inst. - The Cirencester Area*, (supplement to *Archaeol. J.* **145**) (London), 31-5

Cartwright, J. J. (ed.) 1889: *The Travels Through England of Dr Richard Pococke, vol. 2.* The Camden Society, New Series **44**

Cocke, T. and Kidson, P. 1993: *Salisbury Cathedral: Perspectives on the Architectural History* (HMSO)

Colvin, H. M. (ed.) 1963: *The History of the King's Works: The Middle Ages.* vols. 1 and 2 continuously paginated

De Breffny, B. and Mott, G. 1976: *The Churches and Abbeys of Ireland*

Drinkwater, N. 1964: 'The Old Deanery, Salisbury', *Antiq. J.* **44**, 41-59

English Heritage 1994: *Old Sarum Guidebook*

Frost, C. 2005: 'The Symbolic Move to New Sarum', *Wilts. Arch. Mag.* **98**, 155-164

Greenway, D. E. 1996: '1091, St Osmund and the Constitution of the Cathedral', in Laurence Keen and Thomas Cocke (eds.), *Medieval Art and Architecture at Salisbury Cathedral*, Brit. Archaeol. Assoc. Conf. Trans. **17**, 1-9

Henry, F. 1970: *Irish Art in the Romanesque Period (1020 – 1170 AD)*

Hoey, L. R. and Thurlby, M. 2004: 'A Survey of Romanesque Vaulting in Great Britain and Ireland', *Antiq. J.* **84**, 117-84

James, T. B. 1988: *Clarendon: a Medieval Royal Palace* (Salisbury)

James, T. B. and Robinson, A. M. with Eames, E. 1988: *Clarendon Palace: the History and Archaeology of a Medieval Palace and Hunting Lodge near Salisbury, Wiltshire.* Soc. Antiq. Res. Rep. **45**

James, T. B. and Gerard, C. 2007: *Clarendon: Landscape of Kings* (Macclesfield: Windgather Press)

Kahn, D. 1992: 'Anglo-Saxon and Early Romanesque Frieze Sculpture in England' in Deborah Kahn (ed.), *The Romanesque Frieze and its Spectator*, 61-74

Kalinowski, L. 1992: 'The 'Frieze' at Malmesbury' in Deborah Kahn (ed.), *The Romanesque Frieze and its Spectator* (London), 84-96

Kealey, E. J. 1972: *Roger of Salisbury, Viceroy of England* (Berkeley)

King, J. F. 1990: 'The Old Sarum Master: A Twelfth-Century Sculptor in South-West England', *Wilts. Arch. Mag.* **83**, 70-95

Montague, J. 2006: 'The Cloister and Bishop's Palace at Old Sarum with Some Thoughts on the Origins and Meaning of Secular Cathedral Cloisters', *Journal of the British Archaeological Society* **159**, 48-70

Nightingale, J. E. 1891: 'The Priory of Ivychurch and its Wall-Paintings', *Proc. Soc. Antiq.* **13**, 352-5

Oxford DNB online: see Webber, T. 2004

Pevsner, N. 1975: *Wiltshire*. The Buildings of England (2nd ed., revised by B. Cherry, Harmondsworth)

Radford, C.A.R. 1981: 'Glastonbury Abbey before 1184: Interim Report on the Excavations, 1908-64' in N. Coldstream and P. Draper (eds.), *Medieval Art and Architecture at Wells and Glastonbury*, Brit. Archaeol. Assoc. Conf. Trans. **4**, 110-34

Rahtz, P. A. and Musty, J. W. G. 1960: 'Excavations at Old Sarum 1957', *Wilts. Arch. Mag.* **57**, 353-370

RCHM(E) 1980: *Ancient and Historical Monuments in the City of Salisbury* **1** (HMSO)

RCHM(E) 1987: *Churches of South-East Wiltshire* (HMSO)

RCHM(E) 1993: *Salisbury: The Houses of the Close* (HMSO)

Report 1909: 'Report on the Excavations at Old Sarum in 1909', *Proc. Soc. Antiq.* **23**, 190-200

Report 1909-10: 'Report on the Excavations at Old Sarum in 1910', *Proc. Soc. Antiq.* **23**, 501-517

Report 1911-2: 'Report on the Excavations at Old Sarum in 1911', *Proc. Soc. Antiq.* **24**, 52-65

Report 1912-3: 'Report on the Excavations at Old Sarum in 1912', *Proc. Soc. Antiq.* **25**, 93-104

Report 1913-4: 'Report on the Excavations at Old Sarum in 1913', *Proc. Soc. Antiq.* **26**, 100-119

Report 1914-5: 'Report on the Excavations at Old Sarum in 1914', *Proc. Soc. Antiq.* **27**, 230-240

Rogers, H. 1978-9: 'Saint Osmund of Salisbury *c.*1040-1099', *Hatcher Review* **6**, 32-7

St. John Hope, W. H. 1904: 'Notes on the Abbey Church of Glastonbury Abbey', *Archaeol. J.* **61**, 185-96

Sawyer, R. 1987: *Little Imber on the Down* (East Knoyle)

Slocombe, P. (ed.) 1996: *Architects and Building Craftsmen with work in Wiltshire* (Trowbridge)

Spring, R. 1987: *Salisbury Cathedral* (London)

Stalley, R. A. 1971: 'A Twelfth-Century Patron of Architecture: a study of the buildings of Roger, Bishop of Salisbury 1102-1139', *J. Brit. Archaeol. Assoc.* 3rd series, **34**, 62-83

Stone, L. 1972: *Sculpture in Britain: The Middle Ages* (Harmondsworth)

Stroud, D. 1986: 'The Site of the Borough of Old Sarum 1066-1226: an Examination of some Documentary Evidence', *Wilts. Arch. Mag.* **80**, 120-6

Thurlby, M. 1981: 'A note on the twelfth-century sculpture from Old Sarum Cathedral', *Wilts. Arch. Mag.* **76**, 93-8

Thurlby, M. 1991: 'The Romanesque Cathedral circa 1114-1200' in Michael Swanton (ed.), *Exeter Cathedral: A Celebration* (Exeter), 37-44

Thurlby, M. and Baxter, R. 2002: 'The Romanesque fabric of Reading Abbey Church' in Laurence Keen and E. Scarff (eds.), *Wind-sor: Medieval Archaeology, Art and Architecture of the Thames Valley,* Brit. Archaeol. Assoc. Conf. Trans. **25** (London and Leeds), 282-301

VCH Wilts. 1956: R.B. Pugh and E. Crittall (eds.), 'The Religious Houses of Wiltshire' in *A History of Wiltshire* (Victoria History of the Counties of England) **3,** 289ff.

Warry, D. R. 1893: 'Ivy-Church, Co. Wilts.', Wiltshire Notes and Queries **1**, 24-9

Webber, T. 2004: 'Osmund [St Osmund] (d. 1099)' in *Oxford Dictionary of National Biography* online (http://dx.doi.org/10.1093/ref:odnb/20902)

White, G. 1898: *The Cathedral Church of Salisbury*

Whittingham, S. 1974: *Salisbury Chapter House* (Salisbury)

William of Malmesbury 1988: *A History of His Own Times, from 1135 to 1142* in J. Stevenson (ed.), *Contemporary Chronicles of the Middle Ages* (Llanerch Enterprises, Felinfach)

William of Malmesbury 1989: *A History of the Norman Kings 1066-1125* (Llanerch Enterprises, Felinfach)

Willis, R. 1866: *The Architectural History of Glastonbury Abbey* (Cambridge)

Wilson, C. 1978: 'The Sources of Late Twelfth-Century Work at Worcester Cathedral' in G. Popper (ed.), *Medieval Art and Archaeology at Worcester Cathedral*, Brit. Archaeol. Assoc. Conf. Trans. **1** (Leeds), 80-90

Zarnecki, G. 1953a: *Later English Romanesque Sculpture 1140-1210*

Zarnecki, G. 1953b: 'The Chichester reliefs', *Archaeol. J.* **110**, 106-119

Zarnecki, G., Holt, J. and Holland, T. (eds.) 1984: *English Romanesque Art 1066-1200* (exhibition catalogue Hayward Gallery, Arts Council, London)

Pl 3. Stonework: Old Sarum? Cat 1; Old Sarum Cat 2, 5-6, 11

Pl 4. Stonework: Old Sarum Cat 7-10, 13, 16

14   15   15

14   15

19   22

Pl 5. Stonework: Old Sarum Cat 14-5, 19, 22

Pl 6. Stonework: Old Sarum Cat 20-1, 23-5, 29

26

27

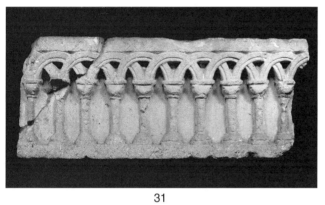

31

28

41

44

Pl 7. Stonework: Old Sarum Cat 26-8, 31; other provenance Cat 41, 44

Pl 8. Stonework: Other Cat 49; Clarendon Palace Cat 116, 118, 129-31, 144-5

149

149

150

151

152

153

Pl 9. Stonework: Clarendon Palace Cat 149-53

154   155   156

177   181   182

184   186

Pl 10. Stonework: Clarendon Palace Cat 154-6; Salisbury Cathedral Cat 177, 181-2, 184, 186

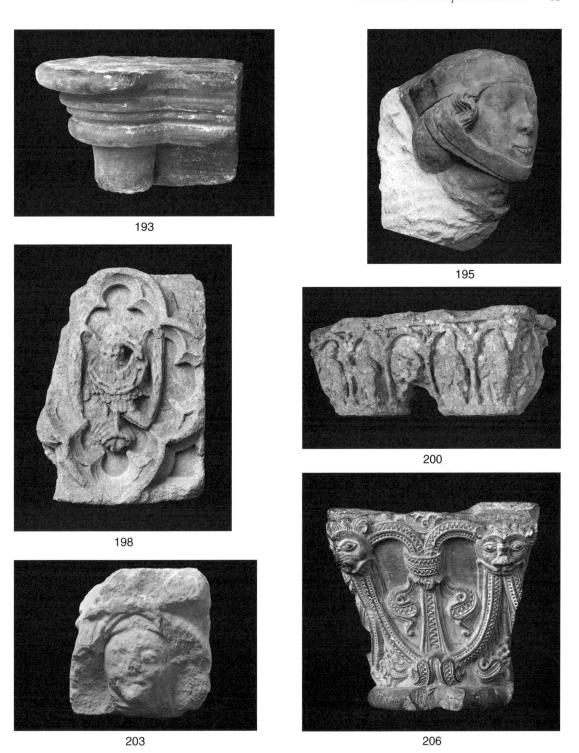

Pl 11. Stonework: Salisbury Cathedral Cat 193; Ivychurch Priory Cat 200;
other provenances Cat 195, 198, 203, 206

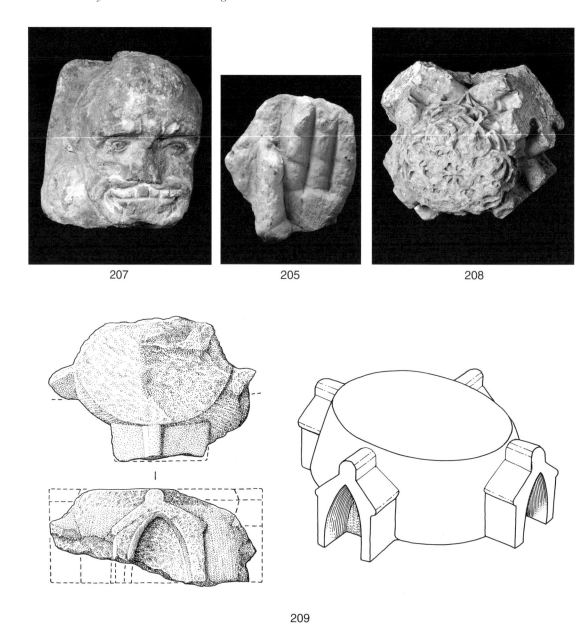

207   205   208

209

Pl 12. Stonework: Other provenances Cat 205, 207-8; Cat 209 chimney capstone (1:8)
(with reconstruction)

Church Bells and Cast Copper-alloy Vessels

by David Algar and Peter Saunders

INTRODUCTION

The majority of the objects of copper alloy in the Museum collection are catalogued by Alison Good-all (see pages 90-142). As the result of research arising from salvage excavation in Salisbury, church bells and cast vessels are treated separately here. Until the 1970s, the evidence for the existence of a bell-foundry in medieval Salisbury was limited to documentary references and to the survival of numerous church bells. Then the construction of the inner ring road and redevelopment of consid-erable areas of the eastern part of Salisbury led to the identification of the remains of copper alloy working sites. Foundry waste, mainly in the form of mould debris, derived from the casting of bells and domestic vessels, was recovered (Algar 1973) and is illustrated here for the first time.

Information about copper alloy foundry work in Salisbury, previously scattered, is brought to-gether here, and the Museum's collection of medieval bells, of which two were almost certainly cast (as parts of the same peal) in the local foundry, are recorded, as are the wooden frames that held these bells. We also catalogue fragments of cast vessels, many of which must be from the products of braziers working in the city; some can be closely related to surviving mould fragments. The Win-chester bushel, the lone survivor of the official weights and measures issued to Salisbury c.1497, is described. The opportunity is also taken to list in summary form inscribed bells and domestic vessels of post-medieval date that were made in Salisbury by the same techniques as were used in the medieval period.

We are grateful to Geoff Egan for many helpful comments.

Copper-alloy casting in Salisbury

Bell-founders and braziers

In the medieval period, the principal names for craftsmen associated with the working of copper alloys were potters, braziers, founders and belyeters. The casting of vessels was apparently the main trade of braziers and potters, as is supported by the meagre evidence from Salisbury. By the time of the earliest surviving records here, the term potter had been replaced by brazier. This term, with that of founder, appears in the will of John Barbur, 1404 (Tyssen 1908). Barbur is spelt Barbor in his will but Barbvr on a bell (Walters, 1927-9, 257-8 and fig. 43) and Barbur in documents recording his occupation (Ward List WSA G23/1/236, 1399/1400). Given the interchangeability of 'v' and 'u' in medieval hands and the lack of standardized spelling, we take Barbur as our preferred spelling. The Salisbury Guild of Smiths referred to in the Corporation Ledger as early as 1440 included 'goldsmythes, blacksmythes and brayziers'. At this time some braziers were also apparently founding bells and only later were the trades separated. In Salisbury the word belyeter or belliator does not seem to occur until late in the fifteenth century (Swayne 1896, 361). In 1612, the City received its Charter of Incorporation from James I. Subsequently the new constitutions of the 'Companye of Smythes' were the first to be ratified by the Mayor under the new Charter. It now included twelve trades, among which were braziers and bell-founders.

History

The relocation and growth of the new city of Salisbury from its beginnings in the first quarter of the thirteenth century would have attracted peripatetic craftsmen with foundry skills not only through commissions to provide bells for the cathedral and the city churches but also to exploit the ever ex-panding market for domestic vessels. In the medieval period it is known that many church bells were cast on site by founders based elsewhere. A Salisbury foundry would have served not only the needs of the city but of the whole diocese (Walters 1927-9, 255ff.). There is evidence that metal cooking vessels became increasingly common during the thirteenth and fourteenth centuries and that some were made by the founders of bells. The earliest Salisbury founder presently known is John Barbur who lived in Milford Street (then called Winchester Street) and whose will was proved in 1404. This suggests that a foundry was well established in Salisbury by the middle of the fourteenth century.

The accounts of the churchwardens of St. Edmund's parish contain many references to the activities of braziers and bell-founders, and, during the last quarter of the fifteenth century, to the numerous records of brass vessels being bequeathed to and sold for the benefit of the church (Swayne 1896).

Braziers (bell-founders) known to have worked in Salisbury during the medieval period are: John Barbur (bell-founder and brazier) - late fourteenth century (Tyssen 1908); Peter Brazier (presumed brazier, apparently the eldest son of John Barbur) - early fifteenth century (Tyssen 1908, 354); John Barbur II, the second son of John Barbur (a later John Barbur is associated with braziers in Shaftes-bury in the 1450's) - early fifteenth century (Tyssen 1908, 363 and 357); John Founder ('brasyer') – Salisbury Ward List, 1399/1400 (Chandler 1983, 271); Humfrey the founder - early fifteenth century (Tyssen 1908, 354); John and Richard Peccham (presumed braziers) - early fifteenth century (Tyssen 1908, 354); William Bokebrigge (brazier) - *fl.* 1443-6 (Swayne 1896, 358); Lucas Hope (bell-founder and brazier) - *fl.* 1461-76 (Swayne 1896, 361); Thomas Hamelyn - *fl.* 1464-6 (Salisbury Cathedral Fabric Accounts, where the entry suggests that Hamelyn may have been a bell-founder, but not necessarily based in Salisbury); Richard Thomas (bell-founder) - *fl.* 1476-7 (Swayne 1896, 362, 248); and Henry Pinker (bell-founder) - *fl.* 1475-95 (Swayne 1896, 43). Walters 1927-29, 255-6 mentions other bells probably from the Salisbury foundry, one of which bears the names Agnes Honehiness, John Chaple and Alis Chaple.

Bells and cast vessels continued to be made in Salisbury throughout the sixteenth and seventeenth centuries. Documentation and inscriptions on surviving bells provide a continuous list of founders for the post-medieval period: Thomas Skelton, *c.*1512; Roger Ellis, 1530-6; Thomas Warre, died 1578; John Wallis, *fl.*1581-1624 with and succeeded by John Danton, *fl.*1624-40; Francis Foster, 1654-75; Thomas Thresher, described as a bell-founder in his will, proved in 1674; William Purdue, *fl.*1656-64 with Nathaniel Bolter; Richard Florey, *fl.*1671-79, succeeded by his widow Elizabeth Florey, 1679-80 initially with Clement Tosear I, 1679-95; John Tosear I, *fl.*1679-87; Clement Tosear II, 1679-1718; William Tosear, 1695-1730 and John Tosear II, *fl.*1723-33. Thus bell-founding in Salisbury survived until the early eighteenth century at which time the foundry closed and bells were only cast again in the late nineteenth century, when a few were cast by Thomas Blackbourn (1883-1904) at the Friary Works in St Ann Street. For bell-founding in Wiltshire see VCH 1959, 252-3.

Location

Culver Street was referred to as 'Bell-founder's Street' in a deed of 1624 (VCH 1962, 80). In medieval times Culver Street was known to include what subsequently became Guilder Lane. Archaeological salvage work in 1972 revealed a widespread scatter of foundry waste across the eastern part of the city within the line of the surrounding medieval rampart. Foundry waste was also found in some of the earliest infilling, perhaps of fifteenth-century date, of the ditch adjacent to Milford Street and thinly scattered in the eighteenth-century levels along the west side of Rampart Road. The earliest topographical information is contained in the will of John Barbur, 1404 and that of his wife Alice, 1407, where the bounds of their property in Milford Street are described in some detail (Tyssen 1908, 355 and 361-2).

The site of the Barbur foundry in the angle between the east side of Guilder Lane and the north side of 67 Milford Street was confirmed archaeologically. From the late thirteenth century this site had been occupied by potters, most probably related in some way to those working at Laverstock, who had attempted to establish themselves in the new city. This enterprise appears not to have thrived or was bought out. Copper alloy founding, the subsequent industrial activity on the site, largely destroyed the potters' working area and a kiln. The earliest foundry waste can be dated not only stratigraphically to later than about 1350 but also by the presence of the fourteenth-century pottery associated with it. It is of interest to note that, most unusually, on this site potters in metal replaced potters in clay. Both of these industries were seen as a fire hazard and were thus located on the eastern side of the city away from the prevailing wind. The most interesting feature revealed was a well, abandoned and filled in, probably in the late fourteenth century, which contained foundry waste in the form of broken mould fragments from the production of tripod cauldrons (see page 70). No other structures were discovered, the most numerous features being partially inter-cut pits containing black soil and mould fragments similar to those from the well. One pit contained foundry waste associated with a few fragments of German stoneware with brown salt glaze. This suggests that bronze founding here may well have continued into the sixteenth century.

On the site of 81 Milford Street there were perhaps the last traces of what was a virtually-destroyed furnace, and to the east, at the back of the site of 83 Milford Street, the base of a bell-casting pit, which had several stake-holes in its flat base and a large fragment of clay bell cope (Cat 21) in the fill. This pit, about two metres in diameter and which had almost certainly been used for the casting of bells, was subsequently in-filled with mould fragments from the casting of tripod skillets. It is likely that the material is late medieval or just post-medieval (the few indeterminate body sherds therewith lack dating precision). The location of the bell pit is of some interest as it lay on ground that at one time would have been occupied by the city rampart. This indicates that by the time of the construction of the bell pit the rampart had already been considerably reduced and the foundry had been extended in an easterly direction onto land that had become available. This supports the apparent late medieval dating of the material from this pit.

Thus the land behind what became 67-83 Milford Street was used extensively for the working of copper alloys. Further south, to the east side of 41 Culver Street, there was another area devoted to this, the most obvious feature recorded being the remains of what was probably a reverberatory furnace, which on the evidence of a few small pottery sherds may be of thirteenth/fourteenth-century date. The site of the seventeenth/eighteenth-century bell-foundry is unknown but traditionally thought to have been in Culver Street.

Other evidence of medieval/late-medieval copper alloy working was found on the site at the north-west corner of the junction of Winchester Street and Greencroft Street. A small ill-defined pit at the rear of 92 Winchester Street contained braziers' mould fragments and fifteenth/sixteenth-century potsherds.

Production methods

For the methods of working in copper alloys and bell-founding see Blair and Blair 1991, 85-93. The methods used to cast bells in places such as Exeter and Winchester, where remains of casting pits and mould fragments have been excavated, are described in Scott 1968, Blaylock 2000 and Davies and Ovenden 1990a, and those used in Salisbury will have differed little. The casting of copper-alloy vessels would likewise have followed traditional methods. Cauldrons, for example, were cast upside down in two part moulds around a solid core. The core and the outer mould (the cope) were separated by a series of chaplets (small pieces of metal), which it was hoped would melt during the casting process but often remain visible in the surface of the completed casting. A round mark in the base is often apparent where the molten metal flowed in and the sprue had been removed, as is also a vertical line on the vessel body resulting from inaccuracies in the joining of the two halves of the outer mould and both may show signs of filing.

A rare example of a bell-foundry still employing medieval founding methods is to be found at Villedieu les Poeles, Manche, France.

CATALOGUE

The catalogue comprises foundry waste, domestic vessels and bells.

FOUNDRY WASTE (vessels)

The foundry waste derived from the production of domestic vessels is listed first, followed by fragments of vessels, and that from bell-founding is on page 75.

Tripod cauldron casting waste of late 14th/early 15th-century date.

The construction of the inner ring road across the eastern side of Salisbury in 1972 led to the discovery of features associated with the working of copper alloy. The best recorded of these was a chalk-lined well on the site of the workshops of John Barbur in present day Milford Street. From internal evidence this well was most probably filled in about the end of the fourteenth century, an event which may well have happened with a change of ownership following Barbur's death in 1404. Apart from building rubble, re-used roof tile, animal bones, a pen made from a goose bone (see page 237) and the fragments of one green glazed jug (Musty 2001, 160 and fig. 63, no.178), the well contents yielded 15kg of fragments of broken-up mould, discarded from the casting of mostly one form of domestic vessel, the tripod cauldron.

The mould may be divided into core, cope, leg and handle fragments. There are also pieces of tube, which appear to be from ingates or sprue cups. All this material is accession

2008.21.

These fragments reveal that the diameters of the cauldrons at the everted rim vary from *c.*240-310mm. Only one fragment preserved the angle of *c.*100° between the body wall and the outward-flaring rim. In this case the opening at the neck of the vessel would have been *c.*220mm in diameter. The majority of the cauldrons appear to have been bag-shaped with a maximum diameter between *c.*320-340mm with a few up to *c.*400mm. Most seem to have had two horizontal wire lines below the handle, 15-16mm apart, with another at the basal angle. They had two rounded handles of circular section and three broad and only slightly-splayed legs. The general vessel form is best paralleled by Butler and Green 2003, 171 no. 184. See fig. below for a schematic illustration of this type of vessel.

Fig 1. Tripod cauldron

Core fragments.

These are all derived from solid one-piece cores, which are distinguished by their having only one smoothed convex surface and by their reduced grey/dark brown coloration throughout. Fragments from near the rim have a raised rib, the notch below which results in the thickening to the inside of the cauldron rim. There are also plain wall fragments with convex curvature at right angles to the circumference; these appear to be from inside the bases of cauldrons.

Cope fragments.

Derived from the outer parts of moulds, these are distinguished by their smoothed concave inner surface, which is always reduced to a grey colour, gradually changing to the reddish brown coloration of the oxidized rough outer surface. Most fragments are *c.*15-20mm thick with a few as much as 30mm. Depressions in the inner surface of some of the cope fragments indicate the position of the raised wire lines on the casting. The outer surface of some thicker pieces from near to the cauldron base and across the leg moulds has a horizontal recess 3mm wide and *c.*4mm deep, which probably held a metal band strengthening the outer mould at this point.

1 A combination of three fragments of core and cope. A raised rib from near the cope rim fits into a channel in the core and, when assembled for use, would have formed a tight-fitting seal between the two parts of the mould, through which metal would not pass. *2008.21*   **Fig 3**

A cauldron rim fragment found at Milford Farm, Salisbury (see Cat 8 below) fits within these mould parts and indicates the sort of vessel being cast.

Leg mould.

There are fragments from the junction where the leg mould and cope mould for the wall of the vessel are joined together. These indicate that the vessel legs were rather flat and parallel sided except for a slight widening at the lower end. There is no evidence for the existence of feet. The legs vary in width between 44-48mm, with more of the smaller size. There is always a central rib on the outside 9-10mm wide and standing proud about 3-4mm. This decreases in width and height as it merges into the vessel wall. See Guildhall Museum 1908, 289 no. 43 and pl. 92 no. 8. The leg thickness cannot have been less than *c.*10mm and would have been greater nearer to the body.

2 Two fragments of leg mould. Although not directly related, they do indicate that the castings were of similar section to surviving cauldron leg fragments and fit closely one from Catherine Street, Salisbury (Cat 10 below). *2008.21*   **Fig 3**

Handle mould.

The evidence from mould fragments is slight but handles appear to have been rounded with a rod diameter of about 13mm. Rounded handles are normally associated with early cauldrons; the more familiar angular handles with cauldrons of the sixteenth or seventeenth century. See Butler and Green 2003, 171 no. 184.

3 Fragment of handle mould. This fits precisely a cast handle fragment from Clarendon Palace (Cat 18 below). *2008.21*   **Fig 3**

In-gates (sprue cups).

There are a small number of fragments which appear to be parts of two tubes with internal diameters calculated to be in the range 30-50mm and maximum surviving lengths up to 85mm. These are parts of the in-gates through which molten metal was run into the mould.

4 Fragment of in-gate. Flaring tube. L. (surviving) 85mm. D. (internal) 40mm. *2008.21*   **Fig 3**

For comparable material from Exeter see Blaylock 2000, 36ff. and from Winchester see Davies and Ovenden 1990b, 168-70, fig. 36.

Tripod cauldron casting waste of late 15th/16th-century date.

This material comes from a pit containing mould fragments from the casting of large tripod cauldrons with a rim diameter of about 280mm. The presence of three non-joining fragments from the top part of a handled brown-glazed Raeren stoneware mug suggests a date at the end of the fifteenth century, perhaps 1475-1510. See the note by Duncan Brown (Cat 403 on pages 314-5).

5 Cope mould body fragment with attached leg; retains curve of profile of lower body of tripod cauldron with the three ribs of a three-ribbed leg merging into it. The total leg length of 80mm is present, of which the lower 40mm is five-ribbed below a collar. Diameter of the base of the vessel is *c.*180mm. Late 15th or early 16th century. From a pit to the east of 29 Guilder Lane, Salisbury. *2009. 5*   **Fig 4**
          The form and length of the leg is very similar to those on the Henry VII bushel measure of 1497 (Cat 20 below).

6 Cope mould body fragment with attached leg. This piece is essentially the same as Cat 5, from the bottom of a tripod cauldron with leg attached. The outer angle of the leg continues up to merge with the wall of the vessel, L. (overall) 95mm. Late 15th or early 16th century. From a pit to the east of 29 Guilder Lane, Salisbury. *2009. 5*   **Fig 4**
          The mould fragment is from a miscast vessel as there still remains inside it the hollow imperfect casting of a triangular leg, *c.*30 x 30 x 30mm. There is *c.*1mm of copper alloy adhering to the inner surface of the mould. For a similar failed leg-casting see Blaylock 2000, fig. 24, 109.

Tripod skillet casting waste, possibly of 16th-century date.

Fig 2. Tripod skillet

This material comes from the upper fill of a disused bell pit. The waste mould is mostly from the casting of vertically-sided vessels about 220mm in diameter with legs about 80 mm in length and strip handles about 30mm wide, the upper surface bearing a type of herringbone decoration lacking a central rib. Fragments of in-gate were also present here. The only pottery found was a few body sherds of local earthenware with flecks of amber glaze. The mould fragments should be later than the bell cope, Cat 21 below. See fig. 2 for a schematic illustration of this type of vessel.

7 Cope mould body fragment with attached leg; retains curve of profile of lower body of tripod skillet with the ribs of a three-ribbed leg merging into it; there are no wire lines. The surviving leg length of 50mm bears no evidence of either collar or foot. Other fragments from the same group indicate that the D-section legs terminated in a five-ribbed foot about 35mm in length below a collar. Possibly 16th century. From the infilling of a disused bell-casting pit behind 83 Milford Street, Salisbury. *2008. 20*
          Fig 4
          Compare Blaylock 2000, fig. 25, 113.

Other mould waste.
The collection contains other mould waste from the casting of copper-alloy vessels, including some from excavations at 49-51 Brown Street, Salisbury (acc. no. *1991.56*), but as this is essentially undated and residual it is not further described.

DOMESTIC VESSELS
By the fourteenth century all but the poorest of kitchens would have contained at least one cast copper-alloy vessel. There are few forms, the most common being the tripod, double handled cauldron, the skillet and the posnet, a smaller version of the cauldron with a single strip handle (Butler and Green 2003, 35).
          Complete medieval vessels are very rare as the metal would have been methodically recycled. The Museum collection bears witness to this; cauldrons are represented by one body and one handle fragment only. There are ten leg fragments from vessels, which although unidentified are most likely to have been cauldrons. Several of these fragments show bubbles in the broken

section, perhaps the location of inclusions or where lead has concentrated, indicating the probable reason for the breakage. Three fragments come from useful contexts: Old Sarum, Clarendon Palace and a medieval level in Scot's Lane, Salisbury, but most are chance finds some of which may be of post-medieval date. The find spot of the two apparently unworn leg fragments, Cat 15 and 16, suggests that they may have been acquired as scrap for recycling by metal workers known to have been located adjacent to the River Avon. Butler, Green and Payne 2009, 3-6 make useful comment on the classification of vessel fragments. Also catalogued here is the Henry VII bushel measure issued to the City of Sarum in 1497, Cat 20.

The Museum possesses no copper-alloy cooking vessels of medieval date. There is, however, a toy example in lead/tin alloy (Egan 2001, fig. 38, no. 173) and a contemporary ceramic cauldron which probably mirrors the rounded form of the fourteenth-century type (Musty 2001, fig. 48, no. 31).

8 Cauldron rim fragment from the everted rim of a cauldron with a diameter of *c.*270mm. There is a pre-discard saw mark at right angles to the rim near one side of the fragment, showing how the vessel was cut up, perhaps for the melting pot. The inner face has a smooth green patina; the outer has circumferential striations under sooting. From Milford Farm, Salisbury. *1980.55*   **Fig 4**

By comparison with fourteenth-century mould fragments (see Cat 1), this is probably of similar date and, as are most or all of the other fragments listed here, cast by the lost wax process.

9 Cauldron leg fragment. Massive lump of copper alloy weighing *c.*460g. (1lb). L. *c.*55mm, of tapering triangular section, at max. *c.*60mm x 40mm, with traces of crude fluting on the two outer faces.?15th century. From Wylye. Shortt 1956, 393 and fig. 5. *1955.43*   **Fig 4**

This appears to be from near to the top of a moulded leg from an exceedingly large and heavy vessel. Compare Anon 1803.

10 Cauldron leg end. Corroded fragment, L. 50mm, plano-convex section *c.*48mm x 15mm with a rough central rib vertically *c.*9mm x 3mm, and slightly splayed at the foot. From Catherine Street, Salisbury. *1972.140*   **Fig 5**

This appears to be a piece of a vessel leg very similar in form to that suggested by the fourteenth-century mould fragments (Cat 2), and is probably of similar date.

11 Cauldron leg fragment. L. 45mm, plano-convex section *c.*36mm x 10mm with a central rib vertically *c.*8 x 2 mm. The fragment splays slightly to the point of attachment to the vessel; here a small area of the body wall survives. Shows signs of heating and sooting from use. From Durrington Walls. Shortt 1956, 393 and fig. 3. *1956.12*   **Fig 5**

Probably fourteenth or fifteenth century. This fragment is very much like Cat 10 in section but appears to be part of a slightly more angled leg.

12 Leg fragment from the end of a leg, perhaps similar to Cat 11, L. 22mm, rectangular section 33mm x 10mm with traces of a raised rib on one side. From Toone's Court, 12 Scot's Lane, Salisbury. *1972.13*   **Fig 5**

From its excavated context this piece is probably of fourteenth-century date.

13 Leg fragment possibly from a posnet or ewer. L. 27mm, trapezoidal section 10-20mm in width and 6mm thick that expands at the end. Unstratified. From Old Sarum. Shortt 1956, 393 and fig. 4. *OS.C151; 1920-1.30.27*   **Fig 5**

From the provenance this fragment should be thirteenth or fourteenth century.

14 Skillet leg fragment. Rather slender leg, plano-concave section 20mm x 4mm. with a worn outer rib vertically. The end splayed out and thickened to give a rectangular foot *c.*30mm x 20mm. ?15th century. From Dinton allotments. Shortt 1956, 392-3 and fig. 2. *1947.109*   **Fig 5**

Compare with the legs on a cauldron in the British Museum, Butler and Green 2003, 166, fig. 1.

15 Cauldron leg fragment. L. (surviving) 87mm, triangular section, 38mm x 18mm, with a central rib vertically, and a well-formed, five-toed animal foot terminal below a collar. No trace of wear. From the River Avon, Bridge Street, Salisbury. *1993.1*

Fig 5

Probably late medieval.

16 Skillet or posnet leg terminal. Smaller version of Cat 15 but with a smoother surface. This leg end, L. 36mm is of triangular section, 17mm x 13mm; a horizontal band defines a paw with five toes. No trace of wear. From the River Avon, Bridge Street, Salisbury. *1993.1*   **Fig 5**

Probably late medieval. Three voids in the fractured surface may perhaps be for tenons and indicate a failed repair.

17 Skillet leg fragment. Sub-trapezoidal section, L. 60mm, 40mm x 20mm at the broken face where there are traces of a large concavity possibly a gas bubble or other inclusion. Equally this may, as above, be evidence for a repair. The leg has a central rib and tapers to a plain rounded foot. From Stratford-sub-Castle. *2008R.1437*   **Fig 5**

18 Cast handle/lug. Almost complete lug from a cast vessel, the fragment sinuous and worn at the top perhaps by friction with an iron bail. H. 75mm. D. *c*.12mm. From the excavations at Clarendon Palace in 1961, midden 1. *1990.24; 2000R.54*   **Fig 5**

The curved handle of round section is paralleled on a cauldron with almost spherical body. See Butler and Green 2003, no. 184. Cauldrons of this form were dated by Dresher 1968 as earlier than the fifteenth century. Egan illustrates a cauldron fragment still retaining its pivoting iron looped handle (Egan 1998, 163, no. 446).

19 Skillet handle fragment. L. 60mm, plano-concave section 20mm x 5mm, which tapers slightly to the handle end. Upper surface decorated with a series of rather crude saltires between lateral grooves. The saltires seem to be over some inscription, possibly ISA...., perhaps to erase it. The surface has apparently been finished with a fine file. Drainage coll. Shortt 1956, 392, and fig. 1; Shortt 1949, 74. *2010R.221*   **Fig 5**

Late medieval or possibly seventeenth century. Some of the Florey and Tosear skillet handles have saltires as legend stops. See Butler and Green 2003, no. 142 for a similar handle on a mid-seventeenth century skillet.

20 A 'Winchester' bushel measure. This is a standard vessel dating from the reign of Henry VII. It is cast in leaded bronze and weighs 36 kilos (73.25 lbs). D. (at rim) 486mm, depth at centre 224mm. H. (including legs) 264mm and wall thickness 6-10mm. Its capacity is 35.01 litres (0.96 bushels or 7.69 gallons). There are two opposed horizontal handles, which divide an inscription. This blackletter inscription is separated by Tudor badges: on one side (a greyhound) HENRICUS SEPTIMUS (a single rose) DEI and on the other GRA REXCIA REX HANGLIE (a portcullis) ET FRANCIE . The human error of an additional misplaced REX within GRACIA is surprising. The privy mark of the founder, a cross over a 'v', formed by scratching into the face of the mould, appears by the greyhound and the letter S (presumably for Sarum or Salisbury) is engraved beneath GRA. The measure stood originally on three short legs, which terminated in collars above five-toed paw feet. Only two of these legs now remain; the third was broken off at some unknown date and replaced in iron. This ancient repair consists of a leg attached to an angled bracket riveted to the bowl of the measure. The percentage composition of the metal is copper 81.1, lead 10.1, antimony 4.54, tin 2.23 and arsenic 1.06, with smaller quantities of zinc, nickel, iron and silver in that order. This analysis of heavily-leaded bronze is similar to other Henry VII bushel and gallon measures (pers. comm. R. Brownsword). The heavily-leaded copper with arsenic and antimony impurities was probably available as a by-product of silver extraction from copper ores (see Brownsword 2001, 5). The City of Salisbury presented the measure, which had been on loan since 1865, to the Museum in 1973. *Sal. Mus. Cat.* 1870, 61 no. 27; Haskins 1912, 250 and pl. opposite; Shortt 1973, 34 pl. 78. *1973.203*   **Fig 5-6 & cover**

From the time of Alfred the Great, Winchester was of great importance as a centre of government and of commerce. Under Edgar it was decreed that all measures must agree with the standards kept at Winchester and in London. From that time the bushel and its divisions became known as 'Winchester measure' and were to be used for all grain and agricultural produce. Throughout the medieval period, legislation continued to be passed to ensure that weights and measures conformed to national standards and in 1491, following a period of rapid economic growth, Parliament petitioned the king, Henry VII to make new 'weights and measures of brass according to the very true standard . . .' In c.1497 these measures were delivered to thirty seven county towns and five other important cities and ports (Stevenson n.d., 6). From the standards issued to Salisbury, the bronze bushel is the sole survivor. It is a rare but not unique survival of the largest of the set of official measures issued in accordance with Statute 12 Henry VII of 1496. Other bushel measures survive, notably one issued to Winchester, now in the city's museum (Wilde 1931, 241, 247 no. 40 & fig. opposite 241), and another, from the Exchequer, in the Science Museum, London (Skinner 1967, 100; Connor 1987, fig. 34).

The Museum collection includes several post-medieval domestic vessels by Salisbury makers and these are listed below as a record of the Museum's holding for the benefit of those studying the industry irrespective of period. The lettering on the skillet handles is incuse.

Skillet with handle inscribed XX ROBERT FLOWER REE XX. *MiiiA 242; 2009R.219.216*

Skillet with handle inscribed CLEMANT X TO-SEAR....... *1971.138*

Skillet with handle inscribed CLEMANT X TOSEAR X...... *MiiiA 239; 2009R.219.213*

Mortar, made by Clement Tosear II and bearing the inscription R LONG CLEMENT TOSIEAR CAST ME IN THE YEAR 1717. *Sal. Mus. Cat.* 1870, no. 27. *2008R.1450*

FOUNDRY WASTE (bells)

21 Bell cope (outer mould from the side of a bell)
Fragment of cope, the outer mould with the impres-

sion of the side of a bell. This would have been formed over the model of the bell, retaining in its surface the group of four wire lines spaced at 9mm intervals, which would have been above the sound bow. The fragment is approximately 350mm x 165mm overall and *c*.95mm thick. Possibly 15th-16th century. From a bell-founding pit at rear of 83 Milford Street, Salisbury. *2008.20* **Fig 7**

The restored profile suggests that this piece of cope comes from a large casting such as that of the tenor bell made by Thomas Warre in 1572 and noted below (p. 77). The dimensions of this bell are 1010mm in overall height and 975mm in diameter at lip, with the same number of wire lines above the sound bow.

BELLS

Salisbury, at the focal point of a large diocese, is known to have been associated with the casting of church bells most probably from soon after the city's foundation in 1220. Bells with the names of Salisbury founders are known from the fourteenth century. The Museum collection contains three medieval bells, comprising what is probably the earliest surviving inscribed bell in Wiltshire and the only surviving pair of bells cast by John Barbur. Much of the detailed information about these bells is derived from correspondence between George Elphick and Hugh Shortt, filed in the Museum.

22 Turret bell. H. (excluding argent and canons) 377mm, (including argent and canons) 540mm, (crown to lip on surface) 385mm, D. (at lip) 435mm. A small bell of long waisted profile with two plain wire lines around the shoulder. Inscribed +AV : E MARIA in Lombardic letters. Elphick 1960, 404 and fig. (1); Walters 1927-9, 156 and 251 (where it is incorrectly stated to possess no inscription); Pevsner 1963, 329; *Sal. Mus.Rep.* 1973-4, 18 and pl. IIIA. From St Peter's Church, Pertwood. *1973.190* **Fig 7**

The oldest inscribed bell in Wiltshire and possibly the earliest bell surviving from the Salisbury foundry. *c*.1300. Described by George Elphick in 1973 (pers. comm.) as "the only bell we now have with this type of lettering. The other specimen was at Chaldon in Kent [actually Surrey] but this has been stolen and broken up."

Pair of John Barbur bells from the same peal

23 Tenor bell. H. (excluding argent and canons) 540m, (including argent and canons) 710mm, (crown to lip on surface) 489mm. D. (at lip) 700mm. Estimated weight *c*.4cwt. The bell is complete except for the loss of all but two of its canons. It has an iron clapper. It is un-inscribed but marked with a hexagon divided into six triangles, see *Sal. Mus. Rep.* 1974-5, front cover. From the church of St Mary Magdalene, North Wootton, Dorset. RCHM(E) 1952, 268. *1974.127*   **Fig 7**

Late fourteenth/early fifteenth century. Probably cast by John Barbur. The mark occurs on a bell at Chitterne, Wiltshire, which also bears the inscription: IHON BAR BVR ME MADE. See Walters 1927-9, 257-8 and fig. 43 and Dalton 2001, 495-7.

George Elphick said (pers. comm. 1972) that "only two founders used the trade mark (hexagon) on the tenor bell; John Barbur of Winchester Street, Salisbury, whose will was dated 1st February 1404, and Thomas Gefferies, who was Sheriff of Bristol in 1525 and who died in 1545/6. John Barbur mentioned in his will the father of John Gosselin who was a Bristol founder apparently inheriting the trade mark. He would not have used it as no founder would use another man's trade mark until it carried no significance. This would explain why it was not used in the period 1404-1509. I have studied the design characteristics of most of the bells by John Barbur and a number by Thomas Gefferies and am quite certain that the second and tenor at North Wootton are John Barbur's work. Each of these founders used a different type of sound bow, a different form of internal curve to their bell shape and a different section of canon. The recess in the crown is normal on the Gefferies bells but unusually small on the Barbur bells which also have a crown staple of distinctive shape and of heavy section."

24 Second bell. H. (excluding argent and canons) 500mm, (including argent and canons) 680mm, (crown to lip on surface) 470mm. D. (at lip) 640mm. Estimated weight *c*.3.5cwt. The bell is badly cracked with a fragment missing from the lip and there are only two canons remaining. It has an iron clapper. From the church of St Mary Magdalene, North Wootton, Dorset. *1974.127*   **Fig 7 & cover**

Late fourteenth/early fifteenth. RCHM(E) 1952, 268, Dalton 2001, 495-7. Probably cast by John Barbur.

George Elphick, as we noted above in the discussion of Cat 23, argued that there is little doubt that this bell and Cat 23 were the work of John Barbur and that they were cast as a pair. The type of sound bow, the form of the internal curve to the bell shape and the section of the canon all conformed to John Barbur's work. In addition the recess to the crown was unusually small as might be expected and the crown staple was of distinctive shape and of heavy section. These are the only known pair of Barbur bells and demonstrate how he set out to cast a pair of bells a whole tone apart.

Bell-frame for the Barbur bells

25 Three of the original four oak trusses which formed the framing for the bells from the church of St Mary Magdalene, North Wootton, Dorset (Cat 23-24). The trusses consist of sills, tall king-posts, curved braces and short heads. The transoms have not survived but two transom-struts showed that the transoms had been placed unusually low down the braces. Some of the timbers bear carpenter's assembly marks, names, initials and other marks. *1974.128*   **Fig 8-9**

The trusses are recorded in Dalton 2001 496-7 where there is also a photograph of one of the end trusses still in position in the church tower. He describes the bell-frame as one of only four pre-Reformation bell-frames surviving in Dorset and the only virtually unaltered example He dismisses the seventeenth century date given to it in RCHM(E) 1952, 268. The bell-frame is considered to be late medieval but in the absence of examination by dendrochronology this remains unproven.

Two of the trusses, supporting a replica bell

have been displayed in the Museum.

There are also five post-medieval church bells and a fire bell. They are noted here for completeness as they too derive from the Salisbury foundry.

Tenor bell. H (excluding argent and canons) 800mm, (including argent and canons) 1010mm, (crown to lip on surface) 780mm. D. (at lip) 975mm. Thomas Warre 1572. Inscribed on band +ANNO:M:D:LXX:II (all letters crowned). From St. Michael's Church, Wilsford cum Lake. *Sal. Mus. Rep.*1972-3, 18 and pl.IIIA. *1972.141*

Walters 1927-9, 232 says this bell is probably by Thomas Warre and, if so, it is the only existing example of his work.

Treble bell. H (excluding argent and canons) 680mm, (including argent and canons) 860mm, (crown to lip on surface) 630mm. D. (at lip) 842mm. John Wallis 1585. Inscribed on band GOD BE OVR GVYD I W 1585. From St. Michael's Church, Wilsford cum Lake. Walters 1927-9, 232. *1973.43*

Tenor bell. H. (excluding argent and canons) 460mm, (including argent and canons) 590mm, (crown to lip on surface) 430mm. D. (at lip) 590mm. Clement Tosear II 1698. Inscribed on band in two lines WILLIAM LOCKIER CHURCH WARDEN above CLEMENT TOSIEAR CAST MEE IN THE YEAR 1698. From the church of St Mary, East Stoke, Dorset. RCHM 1970, 274. *2009.4*

Treble bell. H. (excluding argent and canons) 635mm, (including argent and canons) *c.*740mm, (crown to lip on surface) 600mm. D (at lip) 750mm. Clement Tosear II 1704. Inscribed on band in two lines I:AM:THE:FIRST:ALL:THOVGH:BVT:SMALL:IT:WILL:BE:HARDE: above ABOVE:YOV:ALL:THOMAS:READ:THOMAS:LAWES:CT:1704: From All Saints Church, Broad Chalke. Walters 1927-9, 41; *Sal. Mus. Rep.* 2002-3, 17 and pl. on 16. *2003.19*

Turret bell. H. (excluding argent and canons) 265mm, (including argent and canons) 350mm. D. (at lip) 315mm. William Tosear 1719. Inscribed on band W T 1719 W B S Z. The chapel bell from the clock at Meyrick Close, formerly the Salisbury workhouse. *1996R.2659*

Walters 1927-9, 194 says that it was thought to have come from Longford Castle.

Fire bell with wooden stock and bell wheel. H. (excluding argent and canons) 280mm. D. (at lip) 370mm. William Purdue 1663. Inscribed on band H V SAR 1663 bell W bell P bell. From Salisbury Guildhall. *1973.197*

BIBLIOGRAPHY

Algar, D. J. 1973: 'Wiltshire archaeological register for 1972: medieval Salisbury', *Wilts. Arch. Mag.* **68,** 137

Anon. 1803: Appendix - 'Ancient hunting pot of bell-metal' exhibited by Hon. Col Greville, May 7 1801, *Archaeologia* **14,** 278 and pls. LI-LIII

Blair, B. and Blair, J. 1991: 'Copper Alloys' in J. Blair and N. Ramsay (eds.), *English Medieval Industries*, 81-106

Blaylock, S. 2000: ' Excavation of an early post-medieval bronze foundry at Cowick Street, Exeter, 1999-2000', *Proc. Devon Archaeol. Soc.* **58,** 1-92

Brownsword, R. 2001: 'Mortars, Skillets and the Silver Dollar', *J. Antique Metalware Soc.* **9,** 5-7

Butler, R. and Green, C. 2003: *English Bronze Cooking Vessels and their Founders 1350-1830* (Honiton)

Butler, R., Green, C. and Payne, N. 2009: *Cast copper-alloy cooking vessels*, Finds Research Group AD 700-1700 Datasheet **41**

Chandler, J. H. 1983: *Endless Street* (Salisbury)

Connor, R. D. 1987: *The Weights and Measures of England*

Dalton, C. 2001: *The Bells and Belfries of Dorset Part 2* (Upper Court Press, Ullingswick, Hereford)

Davies, R. M. and Ovenden, P. J. 1990a: 'Bell-founding in Winchester in the tenth to thirteenth centuries' in Biddle, M. (ed.), *Object and Economy in Medieval Winchester*, Winchester Studies **7ii (i)** (Oxford), 100-124

Davies, R. M. and Ovenden, P. J. 1990b: 'Copper-alloy Casting Moulds from Trafalgar (*Gar*) Street' in Biddle, M. (ed.), *Object and Economy in Medieval Winchester*, Winchester Studies **7ii (i)** (Oxford), 124-9

Dresher, H. 1968: 'Mittelalterliche Dreibeintöpfe aus Bronze' in J. G. N. Renaud (ed.), *Rotterdam Papers* (**1**), 23-33

Egan, G. 1998: *The Medieval Household*, Medieval Finds from Excavations in London **6**

Egan, G. 2001: 'Lead/Tin Alloy Metalwork' in Peter Saunders (ed.), *Salisbury Museum Medieval Catalogue Part 3*, 92-118

Elphick, G. P. 1960: 'The Oldest Wiltshire Bells', *Wilts. Arch. Mag.* **57**, 404-5

Graham, A. H. 1982: 'Excavations in the Nave of the Parish Church of Sydling St. Nicholas, Dorset', *Proc. Dorset Natur. Hist. Archaeol. Soc.* **104**, 127-136

Guildhall Museum 1908: *Catalogue of the Collection of London Antiquities in the Guildhall Museum* (2nd ed.)

Harding, J. 1896: 'The Belfry formerly standing in the Close, Salisbury and its Bells', *Wilts Arch. Mag.* **28**, 108-120

Haskins, C. 1912: *The Ancient Trade Guilds and Companies of Salisbury* (Salisbury)

Hawthorne, J. G. and Smith, C. S. (trans.) 1963: *On Diverse Arts. The Treatise of Theophilus* (Chicago), 167-176

Musty, J. 2001: 'Pottery, Tile and Brick' in Peter Saunders (ed.), *Salisbury Museum Medieval Catalogue Part 3*, 132-212

Nevill, E. R. 1910: 'Salisbury. A royal aid and supply for 1667', *Wilts. Arch. Mag.* **36**, 413-434

Pevsner, N. 1963: *Wiltshire* (The Buildings of England)

Raven, J. J. 1905: 'The Church Bells of Dorset', *Proc. Dorset Nat. Hist. Antiq. Field Club* **25**, 33-128

RCHM(E) 1952: *An Inventory of the Historical Monuments in Dorset, Volume 1 – West* (HMSO)

RCHM(E) 1970: *An Inventory of the Historical Monuments in Dorset, Volume 2 – South East, Part 2* (HMSO)

Scott, Rev. J. G. M. 1968: 'Casting of a bell for Exeter Cathedral 1372', *Trans. Devonshire Assoc.* 100, 191-203

Shortt, H. de S. 1949: 'Bronze founders moulds from Romsey', *Proc. Hants. Field Club* **17**, 72-6

Shortt, H. de S. 1956: 'Scrap bronze from south Wiltshire', *Wilts. Arch. Mag.* **56**, 392-4

Shortt, H. de S. 1973: *Salisbury Heritage: The Collections Illustrated* (Salisbury)

Skinner, F. G. 1967: *Weights and Measures: their ancient origins and their development in Great Britain up to AD 1855*

Stevenson, M. n.d.: *Weights & Measures of the City of Winchester* (Winchester)

Swayne, H. J. F. 1896: *Churchwardens' Accounts of S. Edmund and S. Thomas, Sarum 1443-1702* (Wiltshire Record Society, Salisbury)

Tyssen, A. D. 1908: 'John Barbor of Salisbury, Brasier', *Wilts Arch. Mag.* **35**, 351-369

VCH 1959: 'Bell-founding' by J. E. Buckley in Elizabeth Crittall (ed.), *A History of the County of Wiltshire* (The Victoria History of the Counties of England) **4**

VCH 1962: 'The City of Salisbury' by M. K. Dale in Elizabeth Crittall (ed.), *A History of the County of Wiltshire* (The Victoria History of the Counties of England) **6**

Walters, H. B. 1927-9: *The Church Bells of Wiltshire* (Devizes, issued in three parts)

Wilde, E. E. 1931: 'Weights and Measures of the City of Winchester' in *Pap. & Proc. Hants. Field Club & Archaeol. Soc.* **10**, 237-48

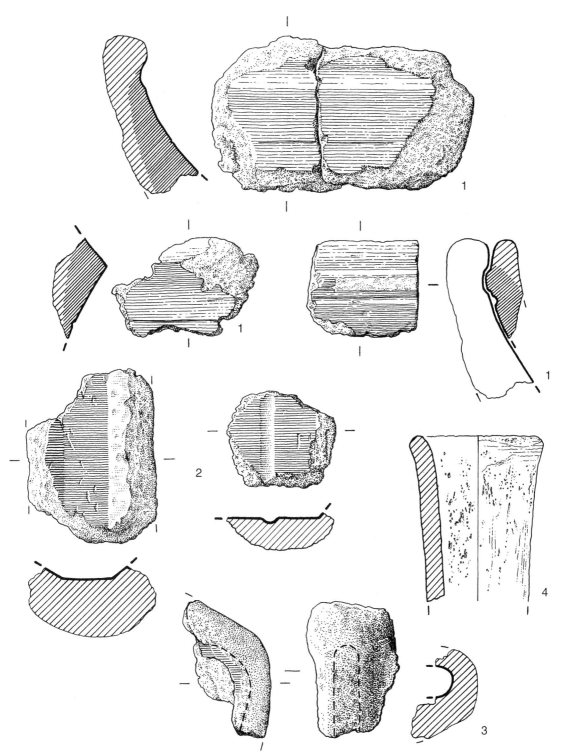

Fig 3. Cast vessels: Cat 1-4, mould from tripod cauldron casting and in-gate, 14th/15th century (1:2)

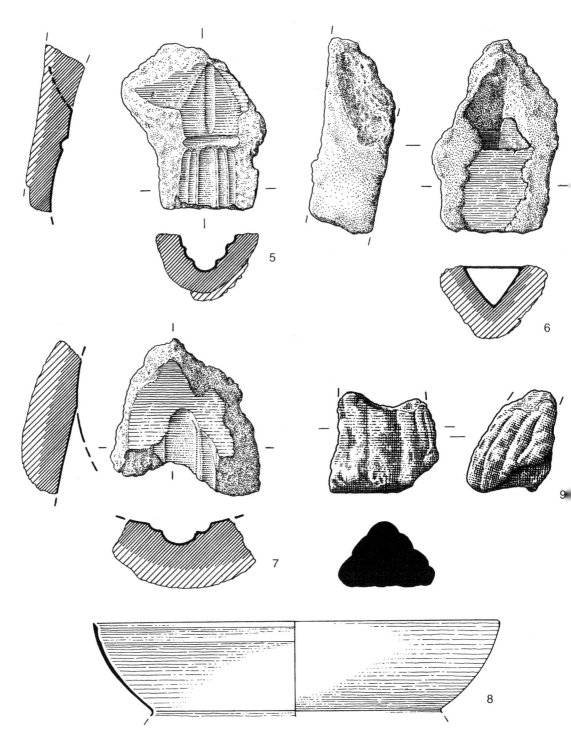

Fig 4. Cast vessels: Cat 5-7, mould fragments from tripod skillet leg casting, 15th/16th century; Cat 8-9, fragments of cauldron (1:2)

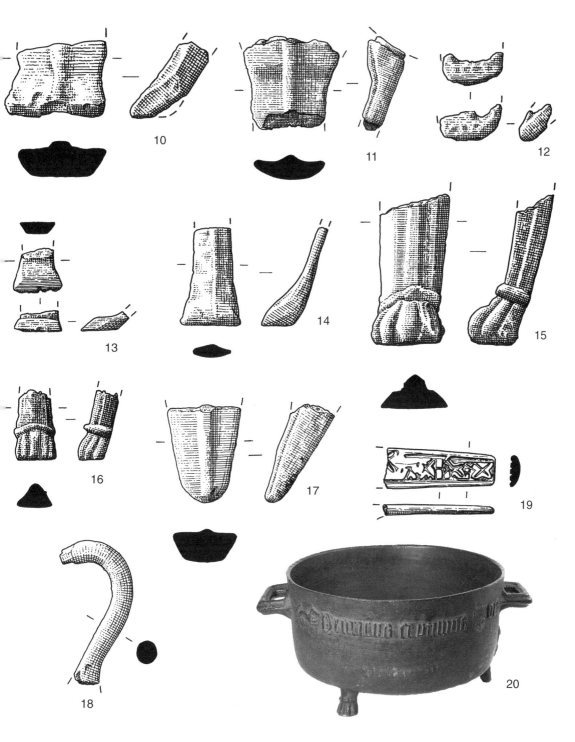

Fig 5. Cast vessels: Cat 10-17, leg fragments; Cat 18, cauldron handle; Cat 19, skillet handle fragment (1:2); Cat 20, Winchester bushel of Henry VII (1:8)

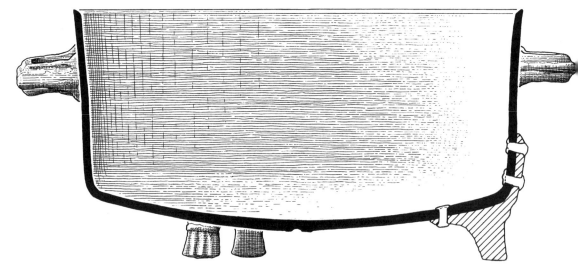

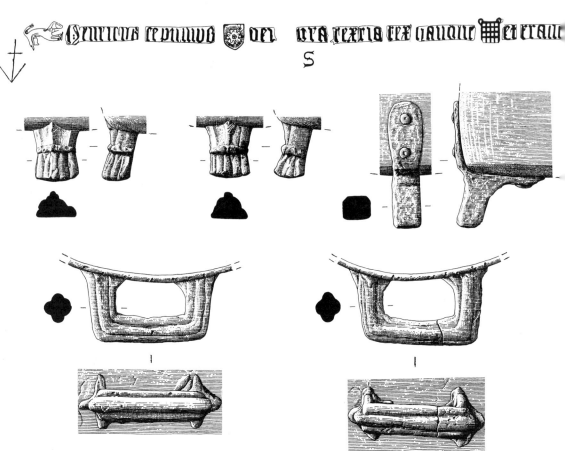

Fig 6. Cast vessel: Cat 20, Winchester bushel of Henry VII (1:4); inscription (1:8)

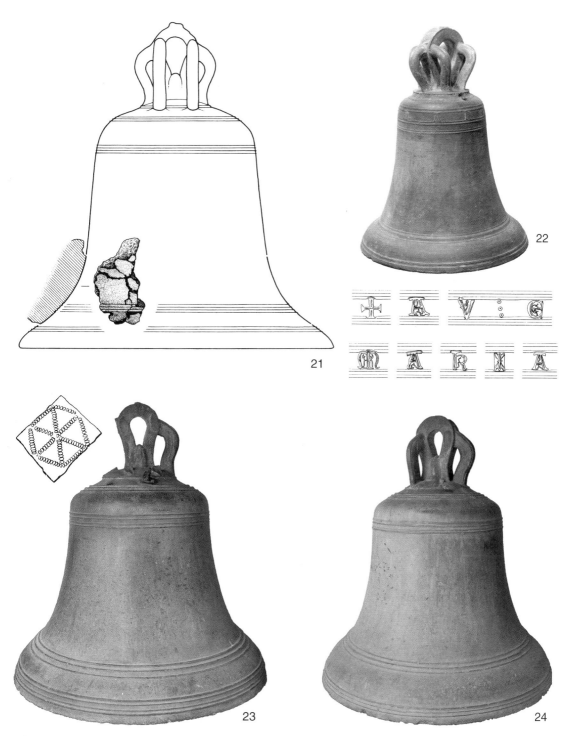

Fig 7. Church bells: Cat 21, mould, cope fragment, 15th/16th century (1:12); Cat 22, turret bell from St Peter's, Pertwood, *c.*1300 (H. 540mm), inscription (1:4); Cat 23-4, tenor and second bell from St Mary Magdelene's, North Wootton, Dorset, *c.*1400 (H. 710mm & 680mm), founder's mark (1:2)

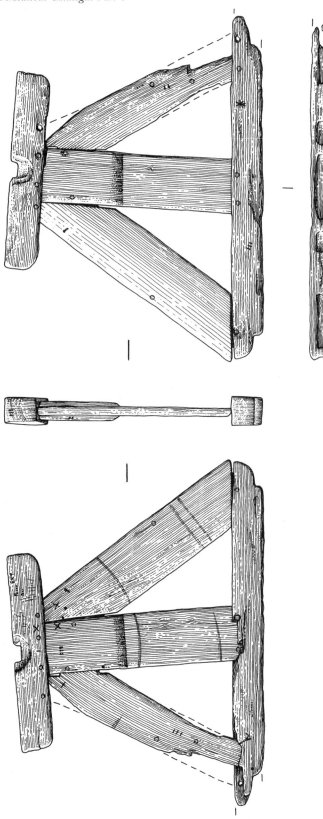

Fig 8. Church bells: Cat 25, one truss from the bell-frame of St Mary Magdelene's, North Wootton, Dorset (1:20)

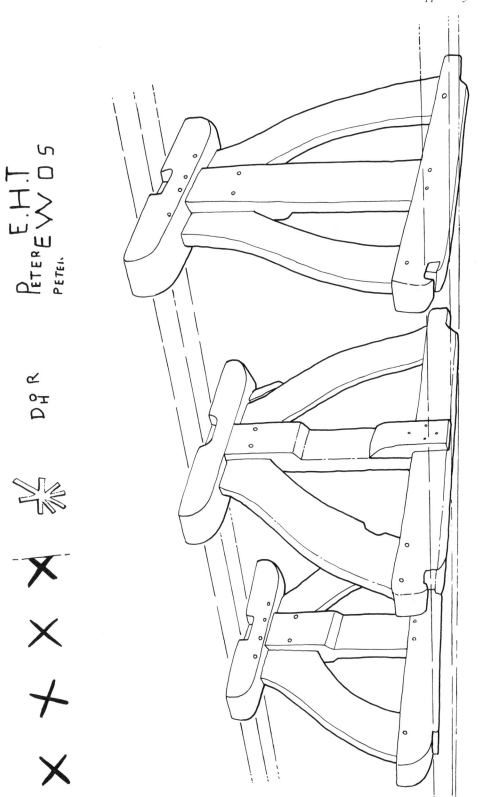

Fig 9. Church bells: Cat 25, bell-frame from St Mary Magdelene's, North Wootton, Dorset: carpentry marks on the truss in fig 8 (1:4); suggested reconstruction of three of the original trusses, showing likely arrangement in use (not to scale)

Leather Shoes

by Diana Friendship-Taylor

INTRODUCTION

Leather survival

Leather can survive in anaerobic (oxygen-free) waterlogged or sealed wet environments, where the biological and physical elements of decay are absent, although some chemical deterioration (hydrolysis) may continue. Tanning agents and oils are reduced during burial, so the water maintains the fibrous structure. Leather conservation is based on the principles of preventing the collapse of collagen fibres and further decay and, hence, the character and integrity of objects made of leather.

Information derived from shoe components

In a unique way among the artefacts which we wear, shoes assume something of the character and circumstances of the wearer - the size and shape of the foot and how the wearer walks. They may show evidence of the diseases and deformities that the wearer suffered in life through distortions in the leather, unusual wear patterns or deliberate modifications to ease pressure on the foot. Shoes can also display the owner's wealth, fashion-consciousness or poverty. They may provide evidence as to the wearer's occupation, or conversely, from the circumstances of burial, we know the wearer's rôle in life and may be able to characterise the type of footwear which someone in that position could be expected to wear.

Shoe construction and style

Before *c.* 1500, medieval shoes were made by the turn-shoe method: the sole and upper parts were sewn together and then literally turned inside out. A rand was often included in the seam, to fill the 'gape' between the upper and bottom components, to make them more water resistant. Soles were usually of one thickness (unless repaired), though they could be quite substantial, until the method of construction changed from the turn-shoe to a welted construction and the insole was introduced. Raised heels did not appear until towards the end of the sixteenth century. Whether shoe or boot, of varying leg lengths, the toe and sole shape, upper style, method of fastening (whether front- or side-laced, fastened with toggles or buckles, or slip-on), were all factors subject to fashion, the style of the monarch, the political climate and the needs and means of the wearer. As today, fashions become extreme, such as the exaggerated toe lengths during periods of the fourteenth and fifteenth centuries. Periods of war tended to produce more sober attire. For full explanation of terminology see Grew and de Neergaard 1988, 123-5 and Thornton 1975. Doughty 1975 and Mould, Carlisle and Cameron 2003 are additional useful references.

Source and date of the material

The small quantity of medieval leather in the collection was salvaged from waterlogged graves on the site of the Dominican Friary in Fisherton Street, Salisbury. In association were an ash bowl (see page 207) and fragments of rope, perhaps from friars' habits (see page 330). Between two and four shoes are represented, all of pre-Dissolution date. Where determinate, the shoe sizes are approximately adult sizes 1 and 5 respectively. A striking feature of all the components is their pale red-brown colour, possibly due to the shoes being dyed, or to the burial conditions.

The context naturally suggests that the graves are those of friars. The shoes are restrained in style, the earliest example being a very 'sensible' working shoe, but the types are those which ordinary members of the population would have worn at the respective periods. Two of the shoe components fall within the date range, *c*.1480-1500. They do not belong to the same shoe, but may represent each of a pair. An almost complete shoe is probably of thirteenth-century date, but a fourteenth or fifteenth-century date cannot be ruled out.

The Dominican Order (Black Friars) was introduced into Britain in the 1220s, the first house being established at Oxford, with 50 houses in existence by the end of the century. The foundation in Salisbury (see Galbraith 1956, 331-3) is most likely to have taken place within the decade 1270-80, (moving from nearby Wilton), which gives a guide *terminus post quem* for the proposed thirteenth-century shoe. If it does belong to this earlier period, it may have been part of a burial disturbed by grave digging in the late fifteenth century.

I am grateful to David Algar for information about the Black Friars in Salisbury.

CATALOGUE

1 **Left foot turned ankle boot**, of true one-piece wrap-around upper construction, joined with an inside butted seam (stitch holes at 3mm spacing). The toe is very rounded, with a wide waist and broad heel seat; sole seams at 5mm spacing. The sole is absent, but the estimated total length is 220mm, 92mm. across the tread, and 55mm at the waist: approximate modern adult size 1. The rand impression is visible around the upper margin of the upper and the detached portion of rand fits into position. There is a slit at the centre of the throat, with a lace hole in the opposite angle, formed by slight extensions of the top edge on each side. A lace would presumably have been tied through the holes across the instep (damage has blurred the exact fastening arrangement). The vamp and backpart are cut quite high. There is no heel stiffener. There was some wear at the outside heel seat, extending above the lasting margin. The associated heel seat repair may belong: there is some evidence for tunnel-stitch holes, just above the lasting margin, with which the repair would have been attached to the heel seat. Probably 13th century, but possibly 14th or 15th century. *1983.11*

Fig 11 & cover

2 **Shoe vamp**, possibly from a right foot shoe, with symmetrical vamp wings, which would have joined to one-piece quarters, with butted seams (stitch holes at 3mm spacing): sole seam holes at 5mm spacing. A slit, 70mm long, has been made from the centre of the throat towards the toes and the throat has been enlarged, perhaps to accommodate a growing, spreading or swollen foot. On the flesh side (inside) is a marginal whipped seam, from the outside throat edge/butted seam angle, around the throat, probably to secure a (missing) tongue. It has been partly cut away with the alteration. Alternatively, the whip stitching may have secured a thin cord to stiffen the throat edge. The outside lasting margin has been worn away and part of the upper abraded, where a wide foot has put extra pressure on this side. *c*.1480s-*c*.1500. *1983.11*   **Fig 11**

3 **Right foot randed turnshoe sole**, in two parts, with a transverse butted seam at the waist. The toe is oval in shape, the sole slender, with a narrow waist and heel seat: length 254mm, 77mm across the tread, 30mm at the waist: approximate modern adult size 5; edge/flesh sole seam holes at 6mm spacing. The heel seat is delaminated, with a hole worn through the seat; there is a tack hole near the waist position. A fragment of heel seat rand is present. The toe end of the vamp has survived, though damaged during wear or through deterioration during burial. *c*.1480s-*c*.1500. *1983.11*   **Fig 11**

All the fragments are most probably pre-Dissolution; from burials on the site of the Dominican Friary, Fisherton Street, found during redevelopment of the site in 1977.

There are no other shoes of medieval date in the Museum collection.

BIBLIOGRAPHY

Doughty, P. S. (ed.) 1975: *Transactions of the Museum Assistants' Group* **12** (for 1973) (Belfast)

Goubitz, O., van Driel-Murray, C. and Groenman-van Waateringe, W. 2001: *Stepping Through Time: Archaeological Footwear from Prehistoric Times until 1800,* Foundation for Promoting Archaeology (Stichting Promotie Archeologie), Zwolle

Galbraith, G. 1956: 'The Dominican Friars of Salisbury' in *A History of Wiltshire* **3** (Victoria History of the Counties of England)

Grew, F. and de Neergaard, M. 1988 & 2001: *Shoes and Pattens,* Medieval Finds from Excavations in London **2**, Museum of London

Mould, Q., Carlisle, I. and Cameron, E. 2003: 'Craft, Industry and Everyday Life: Leather and Leatherworking in Anglo-Scandinavian and Medieval York' in *The Archaeology of York, The Small Finds* **17/16**, CBA for York Archaeological Trust (York)

Thornton, J. 1975: 'A glossary of shoe terms' in Doughty 1975, 44-48

Fig 10. Images taken from the *Luttrell Psalter,* c.1340, ff. 207b and 208, depicting servants preparing and serving food, all wearing shoes of the period

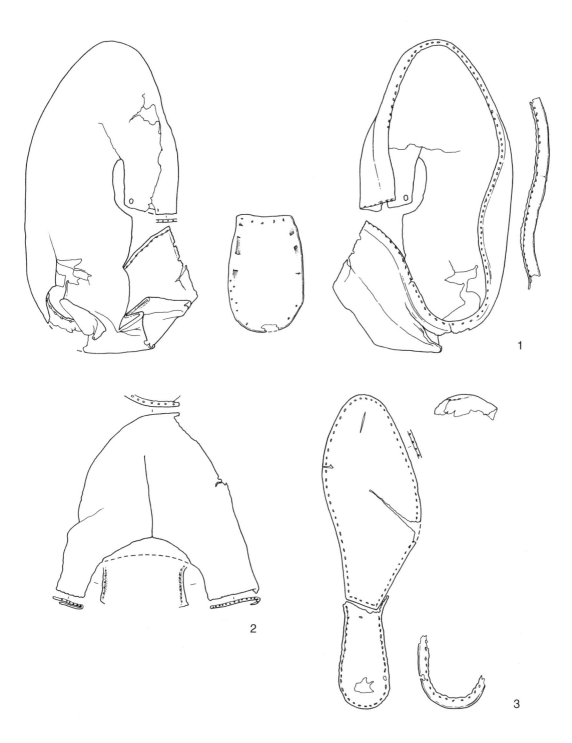

Fig 11. Leather shoes: Cat 1-3 (1:3)

Objects of Copper Alloy

By Alison Goodall

INTRODUCTION

The copper alloy objects in Salisbury Museum have been collected over a long period and represent both casual finds and those retrieved by systematic excavation, including those recovered from the mid-nineteenth century drainage works and excavations at Old Sarum in the early part of the twentieth century. In latter years, the popularity of responsible metal detection has increased not only the rate at which metal objects have been brought into the Museum, but also the range of objects represented. Compared, therefore, with the assemblage of copper alloy finds from a modern excavation, the collection shows a bias in favour of quality objects, such as buckles and brooches, and complete objects, rather than unidentifiable fragments and there is a lack of general debris and fragments. The number of brooches is particularly notable and may either be due to this bias or may reflect the wealth and status of Salisbury and its surrounding towns and villages.

Although the collection does not represent a single excavated assemblage, nevertheless it demonstrates a range of both decorative and utilitarian objects in use during the medieval period. The copper alloy brooches imitate those of gold or silver worn by the more-wealthy. Large numbers of buckles and strap-ends reflect the belted tunics and robes illustrated on memorial brasses and monuments. Household activities are shown by the copper alloy pins and thimbles, and fragments from cooking and other vessels, while the small bells may be evidence of keeping pet animals and of hunting with birds of prey. The inscriptions on some of the brooches, strap-ends and purse frames show that not only was religion more important then, but that religious spells and talismans were much more common in an age before modern medicine and scientific knowledge.

As in previous volumes of this catalogue, the term 'medieval' is not closely defined and no definite cut-off date has been imposed. Some objects of sixteenth century date have been included where they follow the tradition of their medieval precursors, while others, which form part of a later type sequence, have been excluded.

Copper alloy keys and the copper alloy fittings from knife handles have been catalogued with the more numerous iron keys and knives (see pages 158-67 and 146-51), while brooches of silver-gilt and iron purse frames are included here for ease of comparison. Cast vessels are catalogued on pages 72-5.Certain categories of objects, such as miscellaneous plain rings and pieces of sheet metal, have been omitted altogether as it was felt that they did not have a place in a catalogue of this nature.

CATALOGUE

Dress Accessories

Brooches

Brooches in the medieval period were used not just for ornament, but as garment fastenings, often at the neck. At the upper end of the social scale they were made of gold and set with precious stones, but they were imitated in base metal and might be variously inlaid with glass or enamel. The most usual form in the thirteenth and fourteenth centuries was the annular brooch with a separately-made pin swivelling on a constricted area of the frame, but closed forms with pins attached at the back also existed, although these are not represented in the collection. Variants of annular brooches had frames which might be four-, six- or eight-sided, lobed, star- or heart-shaped, like those of Cat 5-6 and 16. Some brooches were obviously love gifts and bear appropriate messages inscribed on the frame; others, like Cat 5 and 10, bear devotional inscriptions which served as charms or talismans.

To fasten the brooches, a section of material was pulled up through the middle of the frame and pushed onto the pin, and then pulled back again so as to hold the pin in place with its point resting on the frame. The collar or moulding frequently found on the pins prevented the fabric from getting caught in the hinge of the brooch.

It can sometimes be difficult to distinguish between the plainer forms of annular brooch and some types of annular buckle with pins which swivel on the frames. The distinction is made easier when the objects are found *in situ*, as for instance when they are found in burials. The evidence suggests that those objects which were used as brooches almost always had a constriction on the frame to take the pin: those used as buckles, on the strap of a waist or hip belt, generally did not, thus allowing the frame to turn freely. The pins of annular buckles are often thicker and blunter than those of brooches, since they could be used with pre-punched holes, and they often have a distinctive boss-like moulding as opposed to the collar or quillon-like mouldings found on brooch pins.

1 Annular brooch with the pin attached to a recessed bar. The brooch has a rectangular section and is decorated with what appears to be an indecipherable inscription, starting with 'AVE'; the 'inscription' may be inlaid or just filled with dirt and corrosion products. The pin has a simple collar moulding. The metal has a bright brassy colour but does not appear to have been gilded. D. 26.5mm. From the River Avon, Bridge Street, Salisbury. *1987.92*
                                                   Fig 13

False inscriptions are not uncommon as deco-

ration on medieval brooches and must be the attempts of illiterate or semi-literate craftsmen to imitate the fine inscribed brooches like Cat 5 and Cat 10. A brooch with similar decoration on a flattened rectangular-sectioned frame was found in excavations on the Thames foreshore in London (Egan and Pritchard 1991, 250, fig. 160.1313) and dated to the late thirteenth to early fourteenth century.

2 Very small annular brooch with shallow D-shaped section. The front is decorated with raised zig-zag lines and pellets. The pin is attached to a recessed bar and is corroded but may have had a simple collar moulding. D. 18.5mm. Found at Old Sarum during the 1909-1915 excavations. *O.S.C31*   **Fig 13**

A similar decorative scheme, albeit executed in inlay rather than relief, is seen on a brooch from Swan Lane, London found in a late thirteenth to early fourteenth-century context (Egan and Pritchard 1991, 250, fig. 161.1314). The decoration may be purely geometric, but it could represent a ribbon-bound wreath or chaplet.

3 Annular brooch with lobed decoration. The pin, which seems to have been made from flattened wire, is attached to a recessed bar and has a pair of transverse incisions at its head instead of a collar moulding. D. 25mm. Found near south wall of the church at Gussage St Andrew, Dorset. *1967.22*   **Fig 13**

4 Small annular brooch with six raised collets cast in one piece with the loop, and a triangular arrangement of three punched dots between the collets. The collets contain a white substance which may be the degenerated remains of 'gemstones' or of an adhesive material used to secure the stones. The pin is attached to a recessed bar; it has been cast with an open end to the head which has subsequently been closed round the bar. D. 20mm. Found at Bridge Farm, Britford. *1983.23*   **Fig 13**

At Exeter, the collets on a slightly larger brooch contained a pale green glass-like material; the brooch was dated to the mid-thirteenth century (Goodall 1984, 339, fig. 190.51). Similar brooches of similar date are known from other sites, for example, a small one from

Norwich, dated 1275-1400 (Margeson 1993, 14-16, fig. 7.58; for others see Goodall 1984, 339). A brooch of related type, having similar decoration but with the pin swivelling not on a recessed bar but in a perforation in the frame, comes from Faccombe Netherton in Hampshire, in an unstratified context (Goodall 1990, 427, fig. 9.12.21).

5 Quatrefoil-shaped brooch with leaf-like projections between the lobes. The brooch is inscribed with the names traditionally given to the Three Wise Men of the Nativity: 'IA/SPAR B/ALTA[SA]R/ MELCHI/OR'. The pin has a collar moulding and is attached to a recessed bar. L. 37mm. Drainage coll. *üK4; SD585; 2009R.61*   **Fig 13**

This brooch probably dates from the fourteenth century. While many brooches bear amatory inscriptions and may have been love gifts, others such as this bear devotional inscriptions and may have had magical or prophylactic significance. The names of the Magi, for example, were thought to protect against the falling sickness (Evans 1970, 47).

An un-inscribed quatrefoil-shaped brooch, of silver-gilt and with leopard masks at the cusps, was found in an early fourteenth to mid fifteenth-century context at Rattray Castle, Aberdeenshire (Goodall 1993, 189, fig. 40.181).

6 Hexagonal brooch with trapezium-shaped cross-section, probably having the front and back sections separately made. The back plate has a lobed outer edge which gives a decorative border to the brooch. The front section is decorated with leaf-scrolls and incised lines, possibly representing an indecipherable inscription, starting with 'AVE'. The pin is attached to a mounting which passes through the frame of the brooch, apparently reformed from another object. W. 48mm. Drainage coll. *üK5; SD586; 2009R.62*
Fig 13 & cover

Joan Evans illustrates a silver hexagonal brooch, which she ascribes to the fourteenth or fifteenth century (Evans 1970, pl. 14b). Alternate sides are undecorated, the other three sides bearing the inscription 'IHESVS NASERENE'. The Salisbury brooch appears to imitate this form.

7 Annular brooch, undecorated. The pin is attached to a recessed bar and its head is ornamented with longitudinal ridges. D. 23mm. Drainage coll. *SD588; 2008R.627*   **Fig 13**

8 Annular brooch with two opposing projections in the form of snakes' heads. The pin is missing. L. 33mm. From the garden of Avon Cottage, Lower Woodford. *1962.8*   **Fig 13**

A similar brooch with snakes' head projections was excavated at Abingdon from a ditch containing pottery of the early- to mid-thirteenth century (Parrington 1975, 77, fig. 55.1).

9 Annular brooch, D-shaped in section and with gilding. The front is decorated with impressed dots and is divided into sections by plain diagonal strips. The pin has a simple moulding. The surface is pitted with corrosion. D. 28mm. From The Moot, Downton. *1974.91*   **Fig 13**

10 Annular brooch of silver gilt. On one face the brooch is decorated with a number of rectangular bosses each with a quatrefoil impressed into it: the reverse is inscribed 'IESVSИASAREИVN'. The pin is mounted so that the inscribed face, which was probably the back of the brooch, appears to be at the front. D. 23mm. From Allotment Gardens, Amesbury. Saunders 1983, 146-7 and fig. 1. *1981.46*
Fig 13

Although this brooch seems to have been made so that it could be worn with either side facing the front, the inscription was probably worn to the back. It represents a contracted and slightly blundered version of the legend: *Iesus Nazarenus Rex Iudaeorum*, one of the most commonly found on brooches, which was thought to offer protection against sudden death (Evans 1970, 47) and in combination with the names of the Magi, to be a cure for epilepsy (Campbell, 2009, 90). Joan Evans has suggested that brooches with this inscription were made in the fourteenth century for magical purposes from five pennies (Evans 1922, 127). An annular silver brooch from London, dated to the second half of the fourteenth century, carries a similar inscription (Egan and Pritchard 1991, 255, fig. 164.1337).

11 Annular brooch with four decorated panels on the frame, each decorated with three depressions possibly containing inlay. The pin has a moulded stop to prevent it getting caught in the fabric of the garment to which it was attached. D. 35mm. From the Laverstock kiln site excavations, found near building 1. Musty et al. 1969, 147, pl. XVb and fig. 28, no. 2. *Sal. Mus. Rep.* 1959-60, 18 and pl. 3a. *1960.12*
Fig 13

The decoration on this brooch may be compared with the panels of notched decoration on an annular brooch from Exeter from a context dated to the second half of the thirteenth century (Goodall 1984, 339, fig. 190.52).

12 Small annular brooch of silver gilt, possibly composite with a flat back part and a scrolled and pelleted filigree front. Early 13th century? D. 17.5mm. From the Laverstock kiln site excavations, found near kiln 2 but not necessarily associated with it. Musty et al. 1969, 147, pl. XVa and fig. 28, no.1; *Sal. Mus. Rep.* 1959-60, 18 and pl. 2b. *1960.11*
Fig 13 & cover

A close parallel was recovered before 1970 from the moat around Peterborough Abbey (pers. comm., letter from G. W. Abbott to John Musty dated 9.12.1970) and was dated to the first half of the thirteenth century.

13 Annular brooch with D-sectioned frame. The flat upper face is decorated with crudely incised scroll ornament; the convex face is undecorated. D. 27.5mm. Found in the garden of King John's House, Tollard Royal in 1894. *TR49*
Fig 14

14 Small annular brooch of silver with shallow incisions and pelleted moulding on the pin. D. 21mm. Found at Bugley Barton Farm, Cley Hill, Corsley. Treasure 2001 M&ME 412. *Treasure Annual Report 2001* (DCMS), 59 no. 91. *2002.11*
Fig 14

15 Annular brooch of copper alloy. The flat-backed frame is decorated with notches and collar mouldings. It has a narrow pin. D. 37mm. From 'near Salisbury'. *2007.11*
Fig 14

16 Small seven-lobed annular brooch of silver gilt. The frame is flat-backed and it has a broad dagger-shaped pin. D. 14mm. Found at Codford. Treasure 2006 T237. *Treasure Annual Report 2005/6* (DCMS), 108 and 348, no. 336. *2007.43* **Fig 14**

Like the quatrefoil brooch (Cat 5), annular brooches were made with varying numbers of lobes. A more ornamental gold sexfoil brooch is shown by Joan Evans (Evans 1970, pl. 14d); it has a suggested date in the fourteenth century.

17 Annular brooch of silver, somewhat irregularly made. There is a hint of a moulding either side of the hinge and on the pin, otherwise the brooch is undecorated. D. 24mm. Found at Durnford. Treasure 2006 T129. *Treasure Annual Report 2005/6* (DCMS), 109 and 349, no. 342. *2007.65* **Fig 14**

Ear-ring

Ear-rings are very uncommon finds on archaeological sites of the medieval period, and they are not shown in contemporary illustrations, although there are references in literature. Joan Evans quotes lines from the early thirteenth-century *Roman de la Rose* which appear to refer to ear-rings (Evans 1970, 47). Ear-rings were probably therefore less popular than brooches or finger rings. Many of the headdresses and hairstyles fashionable during the medieval period would in any case have rendered ear-rings hardly visible.

18 Possible ear-ring; penannular ring with overlapping tapered ends. Heavy lozenge-shaped section. Maximum D. 21.5mm. Brodie coll. Drainage coll. *SD802; 1999R.1065* **Fig 14**

Buckles

The collection contains a large number of buckles, reflecting their popularity as a dress accessory throughout the medieval period. Belts with metal buckles, and often with pendent strap-ends, were worn by both men and women. Buckles are found as fastenings on armour, spurs and sword belts, and small buckles, most often of lead-tin alloys, were used on shoes. Buckles were also used on horse harness. They were made in a wide variety of forms which developed according to use and fashion. The first authoritative study of these forms was made by Fingerlin 1971 and, more recently, publications such as Whitehead 2003 have appeared as a result of the increasing number of finds made by metal detectorists.

Annular buckles

Annular buckles may sometimes be difficult to distinguish from plain annular brooches (see above). Those identified as buckles have simple annular frames without decoration and without a recessed bar for the pin to swivel on. They also often have simpler pins, without a moulding at the hinge. An annular buckle from Exeter was found in a context dated 1450-1500 although the evidence from London suggests that smaller annular buckles date from the later thirteenth/ early fourteenth century and larger ones from the late fourteenth century (Egan & Pritchard 1991, 58). Two annular buckles were found in situ halfway down the femurs of a skeleton in a grave at Pontefract Priory (Bellamy 1962-4, 124) suggesting that they might have been used to support hose. Another was found in what was probably a female grave, possibly of the fourteenth century, at the Austin Friars, Leicester, with leather still attached, indicating that it was a belt buckle (Mellor and Pearce, 1981, 133, fig. 24).

19 Annular buckle with no decoration on the ring and a pin with a simple collar moulding. D. *c.*35-40 mm. Found at Old Sarum during the 1909-1915 excavations. *OS.C31*

20 Annular buckle, undecorated, with simple collar moulding on the pin. D. 38mm. Found at Old Sarum during the 1909-1915 excavations. *OS.C75*
Fig 14

21 Annular buckle, undecorated, with a moulded pin. D. 39mm. Drainage coll. *SD587; 2008R.626*
Fig 14

22 Annular buckle with a decorative moulding on the pin. D. 40mm. From the site of the Franciscan Friary, Salisbury. *1969.81*   **Fig 14**

23 Annular buckle. The pin has simple moulding and scratch or file marks on the shaft. D. 41mm. From Bilbury Rings, Wylye. *iiK6; 1999R.1060*

24 Annular buckle, possibly of iron. Pin has no moulding. D. 43mm. Drainage coll. *SD626; 1999R.114.3*

25 Annular buckle with simple pin. File marks on surface. D. 45mm. From Clarendon Palace. *Sal. Mus. Rep.* 1956-7, 15 and pl. IIIa; Goodall et al. 1988, 204 and fig. 69, no.9; Shortt 1960, fig. 61(5). *1957.47*
Fig 14

Miscellaneous buckle forms

26 Trapeze-shaped buckle and plate of gilded copper alloy. The frame has panels of traced zigzag in the corners. There is a border of similar decoration on the plate. The plate is secured by three dome-headed rivets. L. 43mm. From King John's House, Tollard Royal. Pitt Rivers 1890, pl.XIX, no.19. *TR111*   **Fig 15**

27 Trapeze-shaped buckle frame cast to look as if made from a folded strip. There is incised geometric decoration on three sides of the frame. L. 36mm. From River Avon, Salisbury. *1993.1*

28 Square buckle frame with scallop-mouldings at the corners and a central pin bar. Simple buckle plate with three rivet holes. L. 33mm. From River Avon, Salisbury. *1993.1*   **Fig 15**

29 Well-made buckle with oval/D-shaped frame decorated with scroll ornament in fine, high relief. Plate originally with five dome-headed rivets and traced zigzag border, broken at the end. Pin has collar moulding. Possible traces of white metal plating. L. 37mm. From 3 Meadow Cottages, Laverstock. *1946.128*   **Fig 15**

The form of the buckle and the scroll decoration may be compared with two incomplete buckle frames, one from Exeter (Goodall 1984, 339, fig 190.71) found in a late thirteenth/early fourteenth-century context, the other from Faccombe Netherton (Goodall 1990, 427, fig. 9.13.37) from a context dated *c.*1180-1280. Similar scroll ornament also occurs on Limoges enamelled buckles from the first half of the thirteenth century (see for example Fingerlin 1971, 38, fig. 15). However, scroll ornament is also found on a pair of D-shaped, silver-gilt and enamel buckles from a later fifteenth-century grave in the cathedral of Novara, northern Italy (Fingerlin 1971, 417-8, pls. 488 and 490).

Buckles with integral buckle plates

30 Buckle with oval frame and integral plate. Plate has collar moulding at junction with frame and fleur-de-lis shaping at end; pin attached through a hole in the plate; two further holes containing rivets. Traces of gilding. L. 42mm. From Harnham, Salisbury. *1940.60*   **Fig 15**

An almost identical buckle was found in York in a context dated to the fifteenth century (Ottaway and Rogers 2002, 2889, fig. 1467.13336).

31 Large undecorated buckle with a pointed front and an integral plate. The iron pin is attached through a hole in the plate; there is an iron rivet in the plate and another rectangular hole. There are remains of gilding. L. 54mm. Found during excavations at an enclosure at Wick Farm, Tisbury. Fowler 1963, 290-3. *1990.36*   **Fig 15**

32 Cast plate from a buckle with an integral plate, or possibly a binding strip; it is bent and if there was a buckle frame it is now missing. It has a shaped and pierced terminal at one end and collar mouldings at the broken end. L. 41mm. From 2 Meadow Cottages, Laverstock. *1968.76.2*   **Fig 15**

Buckles with bow-shaped frames

33 Buckle with bow-shaped frame made from a strip of metal with the ends rolled round the ends of the iron pin-bar; the frame is decorated with traced zigzag lines and dots. The buckle plate is approximately D-shaped with two projecting perforated lugs for attachment to the strap, and a third one missing; the plate is decorated with repoussé scrolls and bosses which are outlined and in-filled with traced zigzags. The pin rotates in a slot in the plate which has been set eccentrically. L. 46mm. Drainage coll. *SD538*
Fig 15

34 Large bow-shaped buckle made from sheet metal, the back part of the frame rolled to form the pin-bar. The frame and plate are decorated with incised and traced zigzag lines. Two rivet-holes close together on the plate indicate that one is a replacement. L. 55mm, H. 73mm. Found near Crane Bridge, Salisbury. *Sal. Mus. Rep.* 1970-1, 22 and pl. IVB. *1970.123*   **Fig 16**

Tall, bow-shaped buckles first appear in the middle of the fifteenth century and continue into the early sixteenth century. The frames are frequently made from sheet metal, as in the case of the examples described above, but cast examples are also known. They may be associated with ornate, often pierced, buckle plates and strap-ends as on a buckle from Norwich and also a group of unfinished buckles and plates from Cheapside, London (Margeson 1993, 24-25, pls. VII and IX). A similar buckle is also shown on a German altarpiece dated 1500-1504 by the Master of the Holy Family (illustrated in Fingerlin 1971, 421, pl. 494).

35 Buckle frame with bow-shaped front; front has pin-rest flanked by splayed grooves. Found near Old Sarum. *OS.E7; 1946.128*   **Fig 16**

Buckles with moulded frames

Buckles with single-looped frames and various forms of moulding, including lobes and large projecting knops, on the front of the frame are common throughout the thirteenth and fourteenth centuries. It has been suggested that the type may have been in use from the late twelfth century (Egan and Pritchard 1991, 76). Egan (ibid, 72) has argued that many of these buckles would have had metal buckle plates to attach them to the end of the strap. Although only about half of the examples in the Salisbury collection have surviving plates, the rebated pin-bars that are often seen on these types of buckle would sit well with a metal plate. However, the folded hinge of a sheet metal buckle plate is its weakest point, as evidenced by the many broken examples that are found, so the absence of a plate does not imply that there never was one.

36 Small buckle frame with moulded front. L. *c.*14mm. Probably from the Roman villa site at Holbury, East Dean, Hampshire. *1950.28.3*   **Fig 16**

A circular strap-end with acorn knop (Cat 126 below) appears to have been found at the same time but the forms of the buckle and the strap-end and their relative sizes confirm that they could not have been used together.

37 Buckle with oval frame, the front with decorative moulding; cast in two-piece mould. Plate with incised zigzag decoration; single damaged rivet-hole at end has been replaced by another. L. 62mm. From Gomeldon, building 1. Musty and Algar 1986, 153 and fig. 12, no. 17. *1964.76*   **Fig 16**

38 Rectangular buckle frame with moulded front and ridge mouldings on sides; deep pin-rest. L. 14.5mm. From Ebbesbourne Wake. *1983.141.1.1*   **Fig 16**

39 Buckle frame with heavily moulded front and incised decoration. L. 18.5mm. From Ebbesbourne Wake. *1983.141.1.2*   **Fig 16**

40 Buckle with moulded front forming pin-rest; pin incomplete. Plate has decoration of traced zigzag lines and three rivets. Found at Old Sarum during the 1909-15 excavations. *OS.C.29*   **Fig 16**

41 Buckle with trapezoid frame; front bar broader, with pin-rest flanked by pairs of grooves. Cast pin with collar moulding. Undecorated plate with single rivet-hole. Found at Old Sarum during the 1909-15 excavations. *OS.C.32*   **Fig 16**

42 Oval buckle frame; front moulded to provide

a pin-rest and projecting knops. Found near Old Sarum. *OS.E8; 1946.128*   **Fig 16**

43 Buckle with oval frame, moulded with pin-rest and ridges. Plate has hole for missing pin and two rivet-holes; decorated with two pairs of transverse incised lines. L. 37mm. From Porton. *1935.159*

44 Buckle with lobed frame and mouldings between the lobes. The pin is dagger shaped and swivels on a straight, slightly recessed pin bar. 18mm x 16mm. From Old Sarum, east suburb. *2006.7.4*   **Fig 16**

45 Buckle frame with mouldings on the front corners and either side of the pin rest. L. 24mm. From River Avon, Salisbury. *1993.1*   **Fig 16**

Buckles with rollers or revolving arms

A cylinder or roller on the front bar of a buckle frame would have facilitated tightening of the strap and reduced wear on the leather. Large iron buckles sometimes have rollers but more commonly have a revolving arm in place of the front bar of the frame (see Cat 51-53). These were probably used on horse harness where the ability to tighten for instance a girth strap without chafing the leather would have been particularly useful. On smaller copper alloy buckles lost rollers can often be inferred from the narrower front bar of the frame, often with stop mouldings at its ends (see for example Cat 46). These should not be confused with clasps with a folding end in place of the roller, which may look similar but do not have a pin (see Cat 137).

46 Buckle with stirrup-shaped frame; front bar narrower and may originally have had roller on it. Pin missing, but a hole in the plate for it to swivel in. Plate undecorated, with single rivet-hole. L. 16mm. Found at Old Sarum during the 1909-15 excavations. *OS.C.33*   **Fig 16**

47 Buckle with stirrup-shaped frame and simple buckle plate. There is a roller on the front bar of the frame. L. 42mm. From River Avon, Salisbury. *1993.1* **Fig 16**

48 Trapeze-shaped iron buckle with pin. It may originally have had a roller on the shorter side of the frame, as on Cat 49 and 50. L. 54mm. Drainage coll. *SD488; 2007R.168* **Fig 17**

49 Trapeze-shaped iron buckle frame with roller on shortest side. Pin missing. L. 52mm. From Clarendon Palace. Goodall 1988, 218 and fig. 81, no. 103. *1957.47* **Fig 17**

50 Iron buckle frame with roller on shortest side. Pin missing. 82mm x 67mm. From Clarendon Palace. Goodall 1988, 218 and fig. 81, no. 105. *1957.47* **Fig 17**

51 Iron buckle with separate, revolving baluster-shaped arm, and broad pin. Decoration of transverse grooves on the frame. L. 92mm. From Old Sarum, east suburb. *OS.C106; 1932.8* **Fig 17**

52 Iron buckle of similar type to above. L. 69mm. From Gomeldon. Musty and Algar 1986, 153 and fig. 12, no. 16.

53 Iron buckle of similar type to above. The revolving arm is straight rather than baluster-shaped. L. 60mm. From east of St Mary's Church, Winterbourne Gunner. *1991.21*

D-shaped buckles

Many of the simplest buckles of the medieval period are included within this category, which broadly consists of those buckles with a more or less straight pin bar and a simple curved frame. The zoomorphic buckle (Cat 54) and the buckle resembling a Lombardic letter D (Cat 61), as well as buckle types which have elsewhere been described as oval, have also been included in this section.

54 D-shaped buckle frame with animal head mouldings at the junctions with the pin-bar and a pin-rest on the front of the frame between two cast

ridges. H. 45mm, W. 31mm. From allotments at Dinton, *1954.29* **Fig 18**

The mouldings on this buckle frame are not as clearly zoomorphic as those on a D-shaped buckle from Winchester dated to the eleventh-twelfth century (Hinton 1990, 514, fig. 129.1110) but it probably dates to the same period.

55 Small D-shaped buckle frame with a pin-rest on the front. L. 18mm. From 3 Meadow Cottages, Laverstock, *1946.128.8*

56 Buckle with pointed front and pin-rest. Plate with single rivet-hole and larger hole for the pin. L. 26mm. From Ebbesbourne Wake. *1983.141.1.3*

57 Oval buckle with tapering plate; pin missing. Plate has two rivet-holes and white metal plating. Found at Old Sarum during the 1909-15 excavations. *OS.C.30* **Fig 18**

58 Buckle with thick, D-shaped frame; pin-rest on front. Pin missing. Plate has incised line outlining the edge and four rivets with domed heads. Found at Old Sarum during the 1909-15 excavations. *OS.C35* **Fig 18**

59 D-shaped buckle frame with chamfered edges and scratch or file marks. Pin-rest for missing pin. Found at Old Sarum during the 1909-15 excavations. *OS.C51* **Fig 18**

60 Buckle with slightly pointed front and chamfered edge. H. 22mm. Drainage coll. *SD628; 1999R.126*

61 Buckle shaped like a Lombardic 'D'. Chamfered edge and shallow pin-rest. Scratch or file marks on surface. H. 37mm. From Clarendon Palace. *Sal. Mus. Rep.* 1956-7, 15 and pl. IIIa; Goodall et al. 1988, 204 and fig. 69, no. 7; Shortt 1960, fig. 61(1). *1957.47* **Fig 18**

62 Iron D-shaped buckle with pointed pin rest. Traces of transverse-grooved decoration on the frame. L. 84mm. From Old Sarum, east suburb. *OS.C107; 1932.8* **Fig 18**

Buckles with forked spacers

These buckles are cast with a pair of prongs projecting back from the pin bar and onto which the buckle plates were soldered. The buckle frame commonly has a pointed or ogee shape at the front. The prongs acted as a spacer to separate the plates and to enclose the end of the strap. The assemblage was attached to the strap by means of rivets passing through the plates. A similar method of construction was used for strap-ends (see Cat 121-8 below) but there is insufficient evidence to suggest that buckles and strap-ends with forked spacers were always used together. Both the buckles and the strap-ends occur throughout the fourteenth century.

63 Buckle with pointed front to the frame and a plate with forked spacer. The plate has traced geometric decoration and an ornamental cut-out at the end. L. 67mm. From River Avon, Salisbury. *1993.1*
Fig 18

64 Buckle with pointed front and integral forked spacer for attaching the plates. Slender. L. 58mm. Drainage coll. *SD640; 1999R.116.1*

65 Buckle with integral forked spacer. L. 54mm. Drainage coll. *SD641; 1999R.116.2*

66 Buckle frame with pointed front and forked extension; one prong broken or damaged in casting. L. 56mm. From Bilbury Rings, Wylye. *1999R.1077*

Rectangular pewter buckle

67 Rectangular buckle of pewter with an iron pin attached to a bent pin bar. The point of the pin rests in a groove on the frame. L. 52mm. OS *Diary* 1910, 20. From Old Sarum (probably garderobe pit 1). *OS.C37*
Fig 19

Double looped buckles

Buckles with two loops either side of a pin bar become more common in the later part of the medieval period although an example from London dates to the mid-thirteenth century (Egan and Pritchard 1991, 53). These forms continue into the post-medieval period and may be highly elaborated, with rosettes and other mouldings on the loops.

Circular double looped buckles

68 Circular buckle with central pin bar. The frame is bevelled alternately on the inner and outer edges. D. 50.5mm. From River Avon, Salisbury. *1993.1*
Fig 19

69 Circular buckle similar to above. D. 45mm. Drainage coll. *SD494*

70 Circular buckle similar to above but of iron. The outer edge of the frame is notched. D. 50mm. Drainage coll. *SD493*

71 Circular buckle with central pin-bar. D. 36mm. From near Crane Bridge, Salisbury. *1963.26*

Double oval buckles

72 Iron double-looped buckle. There are two perforations on the frame forming an integral strap distributor. In one of the perforations is an oval strap attachment. L. 50mm. Drainage coll. *SD546; 2007R.186*
Fig 19

73 Two double-looped buckles made from oval-sectioned rods bent to form a ring. The ends overlap and are flattened and perforated; there is a corresponding, opposing flattened and perforated area and a separate pin-bar would have been inserted through the perforations. One buckle has incised radiating lines on the loops. L. 25mm. Drainage coll. *SD646; 1999R.117*

74 Double-looped buckle with slightly pointed loops and projecting ends to pin bar. L. 36mm. Drainage coll. *SD531; 1999R.108.3*   **Fig 19**

75 Double-looped buckle with pointed loops. L. 36mm. Drainage coll. *SD532; 2007R.172*

76 Two plain double-looped buckles. L. 38 and 40mm. Drainage coll. *SD530; 2007R.173* (figured) and *SD497; 2007R.174*   **Fig 19**

77 Double-looped buckle with shaped loops decorated with shallow engraving. The pin appears to be of iron. Drainage coll. *SD533*   **Fig 20**

78 Double-looped buckle. Flat-backed, with no decoration; shallow V-shaped profile. L. 28mm. From Gomeldon. Musty and Algar 1986, 153 and fig. 12, no. 15. *1964.83*   **Fig 20**

79 Double-looped buckle with iron pin; V-shaped profile. L. 25mm. From Clarendon Palace. Goodall et al. 1988, 204 and fig. 69, no. 8. *1957.47*

80 Small double-looped buckle with chiselled decoration. ?16th century. L. 21mm. From 20 Park Lane, Salisbury. *1972.75*   **Fig 20**

81 Incomplete double-looped buckle; a very thin casting. L. 73mm. From River Avon, Salisbury. *1993.1*   **Fig 20**

82 Double-looped buckle. L. 21mm. From the Millstream near St Thomas's Square, Salisbury. *1987.101.7*

83 Double-looped buckle with three incisions on each loop. L. 36mm. Drainage coll. *SD498; 1999R.108.1*   **Fig 20**

84 Double-looped buckle. L. 31.5mm. Drainage coll. *SD629; 1999R.12*

85 Two double-looped buckles of almost circular form; no decoration; file marks on surface. One has a pin of iron wire. L. 27mm. Drainage coll. *SD630; 1999R.124.5* (with pin) and *SD637; 1999R.124.2*   **Fig 20**

86 Double-looped buckle with three ornamental grooves on each loop. Broken and distorted. L. 27.5mm. Drainage coll. *SD631; 1999R.124.3*

87 Small double-looped buckle. L.

18.5mm. From 3 Meadow Cottages, Laverstock. *1961.126.4*

88 Double-looped buckle; undecorated. L. 24mm. From Stockton Earthworks, Stockton. *1949.62*

Asymmetrical buckles

89 Asymmetrical double-looped buckle; one loop is D-shaped; the other, to which the strap would have been attached, is smaller and rectangular. L. 34mm. From the North Canonry, Salisbury. *1946.128.7*

90 Asymmetrical double-looped buckle: one loop is rectangular, the other D-shaped. L. 29mm. From River Avon, Salisbury. *1993.1*   **Fig 20**

In excavations on the site of the Augustinian Friary at Hull buckles of this form made up the majority of the buckles. Many were found in graves of the monastic period, up to the Dissolution, 1316/17 – c.1600. The burials were mostly male and were clothed, some of the buckles still being attached to the remains of leather straps and found in positions suggesting that they were from belts worn round the waist or hips (Goodall forthcoming a); see also the interim report by David Evans (2000, 18-23).

91 Buckle with separate pin-bar and broad-hinged pin attached to it. The frame projects back beyond the pin-bar as two pierced lugs, intended to hold another bar to which the strap would have been attached. Uncertain date. Probably Drainage coll. *1999R.1057*   **Fig 20**

92 Asymmetrical buckle with central pin-bar and corrosion indicating that the pin would have been of iron. One loop of the buckle has transverse notches dividing it into lobes, the other is shaped. L. 35mm. From Woodgreen, Hampshire. *Sal. Mus. Rep.* 1975-6, 19 and pl. III. *1975.120*

Buckles in the form of cinquefoils

This form of buckle probably dates from the

end of the medieval period, in the fourteenth to fifteenth centuries. It is tempting to link it to the roses of York and Lancaster, united as the Tudor rose from 1485, but this is merely guesswork.

93 Circular buckle in the form of a five-petalled flower, with central pin-bar and an iron pin with a curved profile. D. 41mm. Drainage coll. *SD541*
Fig 20

94 Circular buckle in the form of a five-petalled flower. Pin missing. D. 28mm. Drainage coll. *SD542; 1999R.110.1*

Rectangular buckles

95 Square buckle with central pin-bar. Frame decorated with an incised border and rough diagonal incisions. L. 49mm. Drainage coll. *SD557; 1999R.110.6*
Fig 21

96 Rectangular buckle with central pin-bar and pin. The sides have baluster mouldings. L. 45mm. Drainage coll. *SD545*

97 Rectangular buckle with central pin bar. The sides of the frame are notched and would have been set with wires to give a decorative edging. L. 36mm. From River Avon, Salisbury. *1993.1*
Fig 21

A similar but more corroded buckle without the inlaid wires was found at Swan Lane, London in a late thirteenth to mid fourteenth-century context (Egan & Pritchard 1991, 97 and fig. 62, no. 443). Another, with the wire inserts, came from Burton Dassett, Warwickshire (Goodall forthcoming b) where metallurgical analysis suggested a date in the fifteenth or sixteenth centuries. This later date seems more probable for this form of buckle.

98 Rectangular buckle with central pin-bar and rectangular loop below for the attachment, for example, of another strap, or for attachment to a spur. The buckle appears to be unfinished and retains the casting flashes from the mould. L. 32mm. From River Avon, Salisbury. *1993.1*
Fig 21

Two further examples of this type of buckle

are in the collection: one from Drainage coll. (*SD642; 1999R.123*) and one from the River Avon, Salisbury (*1993.1*).

99 Buckle with almost rectangular frame, with concave sides and central pin-bar; quatrefoil bosses at corners. Incised Vs on sides of frame. H. 65mm. Drainage coll. *SD537; 2007R.179* **Fig 21**

100 Rectangular buckle frame with central pin bar and cut-away corners; part of leather strap remains riveted over the bar. The frame is decorated with small stamped circles. L. 44mm. From River Avon, Salisbury. *1993.1*
Fig 21

101 Buckle of similar form to above but with the frame decorated with incised V-shaped notches. L. 47mm. From River Avon, Salisbury. *1993.1*

Buckle with swivelling hook

102 Rectangular double-looped buckle with a broad pin. The pin-bar extends below the buckle frame to form a swivelling hook with a moulded finial, which rests against a flange on the buckle frame. 30mm x 39mm. Found in the garden at Brecklands, Laverstock Park, Salisbury. *1969.101* **Fig 21 & cover**

It has been suggested that the hook on this type of late medieval buckle was a locking device, but it is difficult to imagine how it would have operated. More likely it formed a hook, for instance for a purse.

Strap-ends and buckle plates

It is not always easy to distinguish between strap ends and buckle plates, especially if they are incomplete. Plates may also come from clasps and hinges. The simplest buckle plates and strap ends consist of a long rectangular strip folded in the middle. Buckle plates will normally have a slot cut through the fold to accommodate the buckle pin and the corners may be cut away to take the angle of the pin bar. It is not unusual for the plates to break along the line of the fold.

103 Decorated strap-end plate with three rivets

holes, one containing an (?)iron rivet. Pronounced convex curve may not be original. The front is decorated with an incised 'ihc' against a traced zigzag background and there is a trace of white metal plating or solder round one of the rivet holes. It is possible that this has been cut down from a larger object for re-use since the decoration has not been placed centrally and seems to run off the edge of the object. L. 41mm. From Amesbury. *1989.80* **Fig 22**

The inscription is probably a corruption of the more common motto 'IHS' representing either the first three letters of the name of Jesus in the Greek alphabet or 'in hoc signo [vinces]' (by this sign you will conquer) allegedly seen in a vision by Constantine before his victory in AD312. The name of Jesus was thought to protect against sudden death (Campbell 2009, 90).

104   Simple folded sheet strap-end with two rivets. W. 21.5mm. From Clarendon Palace. Goodall et al 1988, 201 and fig.69, no.3. *1957.47; 2000R.71*

105   Small strap-end comprising two plates, riveted together, and cut at the bottom to form a simple knop. L. 28mm. From River Avon, Salisbury. *1993.1* **Fig 22**

106 Small buckle plate comprising a single sheet folded and with two rivets. L. 21mm. From River Avon, Salisbury. *1993.1* **Fig 22**

107   Possibly a strap-end with hooked end, or a broken hook or a hinge loop from a small wooden box; two large holes, possibly for rivets. L. 57mm. From the excavations at Clarendon Palace, from N. end of cellar. Goodall et al 1988, 201 and fig. 72, no. 22. *1957.10*

108   Strap-end plate with rivet-hole at each end. Traced decoration on one side indicates plate is incomplete; it may have been cut down for re-use from a larger strap-end or it may be scrap metal. L. 39mm. Found at Old Sarum during the 1909-1915 excavations. *OS.C158; 1920-1.30.34* **Fig 22**

109   Crescent shaped strap-end plate with three rivets. W. 32mm. From River Avon, Salisbury. *1993.1* **Fig 22**

110   Strap-end plate with pointed end; top edge with ornamental shaping and two rivet-holes. Remains of solder on back. L. 41mm. From Gomeldon. Musty and Algar 1986, 153 and fig. 12, no. 20. *1964.71* **Fig 22**

111   Incomplete strap-end plate with ornamental trefoil opening at top edge. Originally with four rivet holes. White metal plating on front face. L. 32mm. From Clarendon Palace. Goodall et al. 1988, 201 and fig. 69, no. 2. *2000R.74*

112   Incomplete strap-end or buckle plate with traced or punched border; border of incised lines on back. Three surviving rivet-holes, one with impression made by dome-shaped rivet head; probably originally had five rivets. L. 28mm. From the Gomeldon excavations. Musty and Algar 1986, 153 and fig. 12, no. 21. *1964.93* **Fig 22**

113   Long tapering strap-end made from pair of plates with two rivet-holes at top. Front decorated with pairs of incised lines running along long edges. L. 87mm. From Clarendon Palace. Goodall et al. 1988, 201 and fig. 69, no. 4. *1957.47* **Fig 22**

114   Strap-end or scabbard chape. Single-sided, cast with the ornamental upper edge defined by a raised ridge. A strip at the back for attaching to the strap or scabbard. The surface has a black patina which may be due to corrosion or to a decorative finish. L. 46mm. From the River Avon, Bridge Street, Salisbury. *1993.1* **Fig 22**

115   Strap-end or clasp plate of folded sheet. Both faces decorated with traced or punched border. Five rivet-holes but only one rivet retains its domed head. L. 23mm. From Clarendon Palace. Goodall et al. 1988, 201 and fig. 69, no. 5. *1957.47* **Fig 22**

116   Strap-end attached to leather by two rivets secured by washers. Terminates in loop and ring. Possibly 16th or 17th century. L. 37mm. From River Avon, Salisbury. *1993.1* **Fig 22**

117 Strap-end of unidentified metal with trefoil-shaped strap distributor attached. L. 44mm. From River Avon, Salisbury. *1993.1*   **Fig 22**

Lyre-shaped strap-ends

118 Lyre-shaped strap-end with vine leaf terminal. Lyre-shaped plate shows figure of St Christopher holding a staff and carrying Christ on his shoulders. L. 65mm. From Brown Street, Salisbury. *2008R.615*   **Fig 23**

What may be a similar strap-end is mentioned in the will of Thomas Bathe of Bristol, dated 1420: it specifies a girdle with forty six silver studs, a gold buckle and a pendant with an image of St Christopher in it. A similar one is illustrated by Ward Perkins (1940, fig. 85, no. 1). Fingerlin dates this type of strap-end to the late fourteenth to early fifteenth century and gives a number of St Christopher examples, all from Britain (Fingerlin 1971, 163, figs. 274-6).

119 Cast strap-end, or buckle plate, with box-like fitting to hold the end of the strap, secured by two rivets. The front is decorated with a quatrefoil motif. The lower end is incomplete but would have ended in an elaborate finial, perhaps lyre-shaped as above or foliate. L. 29mm. From the River Avon, Bridge Street, Salisbury. *1993.1*   **Fig 23**

120 Terminal from lyre-shaped strap-end decorated with a swan-like bird. L. 35mm. From the River Avon, Bridge Street, Salisbury. *1993.1*   **Fig 23**

Strap-ends with forked spacers

These strap-ends correspond with the buckles with integral forked spacers catalogued above (Cat 63-6 above) and probably date to the fourteenth century.

121 Composite strap-end with acorn knop and forked extension forming a spacer onto which two plates are soldered. One plate has faint traced zigzag lines decorating it. Two rivets to hold strap-end onto end of belt. L. 85mm. From the Millstream behind 43 Castle Street, Salisbury. *Sal. Mus. Rep.* 1956-7, 15. *1957.88.7*   **Fig 23**

122 Strap-end with forked spacer and small acorn knop. Ornamental cut-out at the top of the plates. L. 60mm. From River Avon, Salisbury. *1993.1*   **Fig 23**

123 Forked spacer from a strap-end similar to above. L. 65mm. From River Avon, Salisbury. *1993.1*   **Fig 23**

124 Central part of composite strap-end; collared knop and forked spacer. Rectangular cross-section. L. 30mm. Found at Old Sarum during the 1909-1915 excavations. *OS.C48; 1920-21.30.16*   **Fig 23**

125 Strap-end with forked spacer and ornamental finial consisting of lozenge-shaped plate with quatrefoil and a pierced animal head; the ears of the animal (rabbit?) lie back along the lower edges of the lozenge and it would probably have held a ring. L. 189mm. From the River Avon, Salisbury. *1987.94*   **Fig 23 & cover**

Simpler, acorn-shaped knops are the most common form of terminal but this strap-end can perhaps be compared with an ornate forked spacer from London illustrated by Fingerlin (1971, p. 115, fig. 190, cat. no. 303) which she dates to the second half of the fourteenth century.

126 Circular strap-end with acorn knop and forked spacer. Lug with single rivet for attachment to strap. L. 40mm. Probably from the site of the Roman villa at Holbury, East Dean, Hampshire. *1950.31*   **Fig 24**

127 Circular strap-end similar to above except that the rivet holes for attachment to the strap are in the circular plates. There is an ornamental perforation in the plates. L. 39mm. From the River Avon, Bridge Street, Salisbury. *1993.1*   **Fig 24**

128 Circular strap-end similar to above. L. 42mm. From River Avon, Salisbury. *1993.1*

129 One part of a two-part stone mould fo

casting the forked core of strap-end with circular expansion and small knop. The incomplete mould is of fine-grained sandy limestone *c.*75mm x 50mm x 26mm. The flat face bears a shallow recess for the casting the forked cores of strap-ends. The core terminates with a circular expansion D. 30mm. and small knop. There are two small holes for locating pins. The source of the stone is possibly Jurassic and from Vale of Wardour. From River Avon, Salisbury. *1987.96*   **Fig 24**

The help of Justin Delair in the identification of this stone is gratefully acknowledged.

Miscellaneous plates possibly from strap-ends

130 Strap-end with three rivet-holes and border of traced zigzags; possible ferrous corrosion at the rivet-holes. At one end is a projecting ring, possibly for use with a hook. Gilding on outer face. L. 56mm. From Standen, Chute. *1972.120*   **Fig 24**

131 Plate, possibly from a strap-end. May be incomplete. Decorated with three rings of repoussé dots and possible gilding. Attached to leather by two iron rivets secured on underside by washers. L. 20mm. From the Millstream near St Thomas's Square, Salisbury. *1987.101.23*   **Fig 24**

Buckle plates

132 Buckle plate with traced or punched border decoration; originally five dome-headed rivets, only one complete one remaining. L. 26mm x 13mm. From the Laverstock kiln site excavations, found on the floor of kiln 6. Musty et al. 1969, 149, pl. XV and fig. 28, no. 4; *Sal. Mus. Rep.* 1959-60, 18 and pl. 3a. *1960.13.2*   **Fig 24**

133 Buckle plate with traced border decoration that has cut through the thin metal in places. Five rivet holes, three containing large headed rivets. L. 44mm. From King John's House, Tollard Royal. Pitt Rivers 1890, pl. XIX, no. 23. *TR169*

134 Buckle plate, incomplete, with traced or

punched border on long edges, single rivet-hole. L. 30.5mm. From Gomeldon. Musty and Algar 1986, 154 and fig. 12, no. 19. *1964.81*   **Fig 24**

Belt loop

135 Trapeze-shaped belt loop with internal lugs and flat boss on front. L. 15mm. Found at Old Sarum during the 1909-1915 excavations. *OS.C34*   **Fig 24**

Miscellaneous dress fastenings

136 Rectangular clasp or connecting link with hooked attachment riveted onto leather. Both parts have transverse mouldings. Gilded. D-shaped section and transverse mouldings reminiscent of gilded strips. L. 64mm. Found at Old Sarum during the 1909-1915 excavations, from garderobe pit 5/6. *O.S.* Diary 1910, 32. *OS.C1*   **Fig 24**

137 Clasp with stirrup-shaped frame with a folding end with lozenge-shaped mount. The plate is made from folded sheet. The folding end would have locked into a corresponding strap-end plate. L. 40mm. From Clarendon Palace. Goodall et al. 1988, 204 and fig. 69, no. 6. *Sal. Mus. Rep.* 1956-7, 15 and pl. IIIa; Shortt 1960, fig. 61(4). *1957.47*   **Fig 24**

The way these clasps functioned is illustrated in Egan and Pritchard (1991, 116). The short strap-end plate at the other end of the strap would have passed through the frame of the clasp and the points on the folding end would have hooked into the material of the belt to hold it secure. Any pressure on the belt served to hold it more securely onto the points.

138 Button with domed head and cast floral motif. Long pierced shank at back. D. 13.5mm. From the River Avon, Salisbury. *1987.210.5*

Brian Spencer (pers. comm.) suggested a sixteenth-century date for this button.

139 Ten small buttons, almost identical, with globular/bun-shaped heads and loops. Average L. 17mm. From River Avon, Salisbury. *1993.1*
    Fig 25

140 Small button with daisy motif on head and a pierced shank. L. 15mm. From River Avon, Salisbury. *1993.1*   **Fig 25**

Decorative mounts and strap ornaments

Mounts and studs were used to decorate and reinforce belts and straps and also other larger items, such as caskets, chests and book bindings. It is not always possible to distinguish between those that were attached to dress or harness and those attached to other objects unless they are found *in situ*. Size is not necessarily significant since large mounts were often used on belts, such as the armorial mounts from London (Egan and Pritchard 1991, 181-84). Belt and strap ornaments are likely to have shorter shanks or rivets, more suitable for attaching to leather or woven braid, while longer shanks, of 10mm and more, are more consistent with having been mounted on wood or other non-dress items.

   Decorative mounts are found in a great variety of forms and may be made from cast or repoussé sheet metal. Simple shapes such as sexfoils are common, but naturalistic forms like leaves, or the acorn below, are also known.

141   Bar mount with chamfered edges and a rivet at each end secured by washers. L. 48mm. From Clarendon Palace, room west of the kitchen wall. Goodall et al. 1988, 201 and fig. 69, no. 1. *2000R.73*   **Fig 25**

142   Bar mount from a strap, or possibly from a casket, with floreate or scallop-shaped ends and two rivets. L. 35mm. From Old Sarum, probably from the excavations. Possibly *O.S. Diary* 1912, 4. *OS.A15*
                                                     Fig 25
   A very similar mount was found in the bailey area of Goltho Manor, Lincolnshire, in a context dated *c.*1080-1150, together with quantities of gilt binding strip (Goodall 1987, 173, fig. 154.17). This may suggest that mounts of this type were not necessarily used on belts and straps, although similar-looking mounts are shown on a shoulder strap supporting a shield on the mid thirteenth-century effigy of a knight in the Temple Church, London (illustrated in Egan and Pritchard 1991, 210, fig.132).

143   Eyelet of repoussé thin sheet. Two peripheral rivet-holes and larger central opening. D. 24mm. From the River Avon, Salisbury. *1987.101.22*

144 Repoussé stud head with central perforation. D. 16mm. From River Avon, Salisbury. *1993.1*
                                                     Fig 25

145   Circular mount with champlevé enamel design of a bird with its tail ending in a leaf scroll. Small amounts of the enamel background survive, now showing as bluish green and brownish red. There are three perforations for attachment. D. 34.5mm. From Amesbury. *1989.60*   **Fig 25**

146 Circular repoussé mount with central rivet and decoration of a 10-petalled rosette within a pelleted border. D. 19mm. From the River Avon, Bridge Street, Salisbury. *1993.1*   **Fig 25**

147   Circular mount with cut edges and a central shallow repoussé 'S' within a broad border. No visible rivet or other means of attachment. D. 20mm. From the River Avon, Bridge Street, Salisbury. *1993.1*
                                                     Fig 25

148 Small quatrefoil mount. 8.5mm x 9.5mm, with single rivet hole. From the River Avon, Bridge Street, Salisbury. *1993.1*   **Fig 25**

149 Fragment of ornamental disc with incised Lombardic 'h' on a ground of traced zigzags. Border consisting of a pair of concentric incised lines with some traced zigzags. Two rivet-holes. Suggested 14th century date. L. 63mm. From Clarendon Palace, north-east corner of Queen's 'chapel'. *Sal. Mus. Rep.* 1955-6, 10 and pl. IIB; Shortt 1960, fig. 62; Goodall et al. 1988, 204 and fig. 70, no. 13. *1956.87*
                                                     Fig 25

150 Rectangular mount with a rivet at each end one secured with a small rove or washer. The front is decorated with what may be a Lombardic 'i' or 'l' against a traced zigzag background. L. 30mm. From the River Avon, Bridge Street, Salisbury. *1993.1*

Fig 25

151 Mount in the form of an acorn with two shanks at the back for attachment. L. 38mm. From River Avon, Salisbury. *1993.1*   **Fig 25**

Once considered medieval but more common from Tudor times.

152 Decorative fragment with incised linear ornament and one rivet-hole. L. 41mm. From the River Avon, Salisbury. *1987.107.8*

153 Mount or pin head of repoussé sheet with remains of iron pin at back. In the form of a heraldic cross-crosslet. L. 24mm. From the River Avon, Salisbury. *1987.107.7*   **Fig 25**

154 Decorative strip with four rivet holes and traced linear decoration. Possibly from a strap-end or an ornamental binding. In places it is convex in section. L. 70mm. From Clarendon Palace, midden 1. Goodall et al. 1988, 207 and fig. 71, no. 20. *2000R.53*

155 Annular mount with a hinge and three rivet holes, one containing a 7mm long rivet. Gilding on surface. The hinge may possibly have been for attachment of e.g. a pendant. D. 36mm. From King John's House, Tollard Royal. Pitt Rivers 1890, pl. XIX, no. 20. *TR112*   **Fig 26**

156 Part of a similar object to above, with two large rivets. No gilding. L. 46mm. From King John's House, Tollard Royal. Pitt Rivers 1890, pl. XIX, no. 22. *TR168*

157 Small square plate with central perforation and punched decoration. 14.4mm x 14.5mm. From River Avon, Salisbury. *1993.1*   **Fig 25**

158 Small square plate with ring-and-dot decoration. 14mm x 15mm. From River Avon, Salisbury. *1993.1*   **Fig 25**

159 Stud with domed centre to head. D. 23mm. From River Avon, Salisbury.

Dress Pins

160 Twelve pins with lengths between 50 and 70mm. Two have approximately globular heads with a longitudinal notch on one side and with the end of the shank projecting just above the head. These have lengths of 54 and 55mm. Another has an irregular, probably corroded, head of unknown alloy and is 54mm long. Seven pins have composite heads consisting of two convex discs with a heavy (lead/tin?) filling. Their lengths are 54, 55, 57, 59, 65, 66 and 67mm. Two more pins are of similar composite construction but the upper plates of their heads are decorated with repoussé pellets. They are both 51mm long. Drainage coll. *SD900-911; 1999R.49.6-17*

These pins were probably used to hold and decorate costume, such as the wimples and veils worn by women in the late medieval and early post-medieval periods. It is possible that most of them are of post-medieval date: pins with composite heads filled with solder-like material were found at Henry VIII's Whitehall Palace and a single example was found in excavations at Exeter in a context of the second half of the sixteenth century (Goodall 1984, 345, fig. 193.175).

161 Pin with flat round head and swelling in middle of shank. Tip missing. L. 95mm. Found at Old Sarum during the 1909-1915 excavations. *OS.C81*   **Fig 26**

162 Possibly a dress pin or a tool. At one end is a globular head with a globular collar below it. The other end is incomplete. The whole object is decorated with incised cross-hatching. Uncertain function and date. L. 125mm. From Chilmark. *1992.13*

Fig 26

Personal Accessories

Toilet implements

163 Hinged mirror case, characteristically decorated with punched lines. The mirror does not survive. L. 43mm. Found at Wilton. *1998.12*

Fig 26

164 Part of small mirror case, oval in shape with broken hinge at one end and projection or clasp at the other. Outer face decorated in characteristic style with punched lines. L. 40mm. From Willoughby Hedge, West Knoyle. *1978.114*   **Fig 26**

Small cased mirrors of this type were popular in the later thirteenth and fourteenth centuries. The decoration frequently takes the same form as on the examples above, four arcs of traced zigzag lines outlining a rough cross, and another traced line running between the hinge and the fastening. They appear to have been mass-produced with a wide distribution. An example of a similar mirror case comes from Heybridge, Essex and has been discussed by Bayley et al. who list a number of other similar mirrors (Bayley, Drury and Spencer 1984, 399, figs. 11-2, and pl. LIIIa). Three further examples were found in London in contexts dated to 1270-1350 (Egan and Pritchard 1991, 361-3, fig. 241.1714-1716).

165 Hinged toilet set consisting of spoon-shaped ear-scoop, curved nail cleaner or toothpick and a pointed implement. L. 60mm. Drainage coll. *SD597*   **Fig 26**

166 Toilet set consisting, at one end, of tweezers with bowed profile, closing ring and traced or pecked zigzag decoration and, at other end, of an ear-scoop with three ornamental grooves. L. 68mm. Found at Old Sarum during the 1909-1915 excavations. *OS.A6a*   **Fig 27**

Toilet or cosmetic sets, consisting of tweezers, ear-scoops and toothpicks are found in various forms. Two hinged sets and various combined tools were found in medieval deposits in London and are discussed by Egan and Pritchard (1991, 377-83).

167 Tweezers with bowed profile and ornamental traced or pecked zigzag lines. L.70mm. Found at Old Sarum during the 1909-1915 excavations. *OS.A6b*   **Fig 27**

168 Tweezers made from a strip of metal, slightly narrower at the hinged end and flattened at the tips. Incised or punched guilloche decoration. L. 60mm. From the River Avon, Bridge Street, Salisbury. *1993.1*   **Fig 27**

Purse frames

Purses consisting of a fabric bag suspended from a metal frame or hoop are shown in European manuscript illustrations of the later fifteenth century, such as a miniature showing a market scene from *Le Gouvernement des Princes* (MS 5062, fol. 149v, Bibliothèque de l'Arsenal, Paris, illustrated in Evans 1966, 263, pl. 53). They are generally thought to be a late medieval to early post-medieval type. However, it is possible that they may have been introduced earlier as a complete purse frame and the bar from a second were found at Faccombe Netherton in contexts dated *c.*1280-1356 (Goodall 1990, 429, fig. 9.14, 129-30) and an incomplete example of a type without the rigid bar was found in London in a fourteenth century context (Egan and Pritchard 1991, 342 & 356, fig. 237.1707). While the illustration referred to above indicates that purses were used in the same way as modern ones, for keeping money, earlier manuscript illustrations suggest that simple frames like that from London may be from game bags.

Metal purse frames were classified by Ward Perkins (1940, 159-71), who illustrates examples from effigies and brasses dating from 1460 to 1505. Inscriptions, such as that on the first example listed below, are common and would probably have had talismanic significance.

169 Purse frame with a central swivel and a circular suspension ring. There are swivels at each end of the bar to retain the missing loops. The bar has a shield-shaped boss with simple mouldings to either side of it. The boss is pierced vertically for the swivel and flanges project from the arms of the bar, each with three stitch-holes for attaching a fabric purse. The bar and boss carry different inscriptions on each face in Lombardic lettering:
AVE MA[ria] G {IHS} RA[tia] PLEN[a] ('hail Mary, full of grace')

DOMINV {A[ve] M[aria]} S TECVM ('the Lord be with you').
L. 183mm. Drainage coll. *Sal. Mus. Cat.* 1864, 56 no. 235. *SD573; 2008R.628* **Fig 27 & cover**

170 Purse frame of similar type but with an oval suspension loop. The bar and rectangular central boss have incised linear decoration inlaid with a niello-like compound and traced zigzags. The mouldings on either side of the boss are more ornate than on the example above and may represent animal heads. L. 158mm. Found at Shrewton in about 1887. *Sal. Mus. Rep.* 1951-2, 11 and pl. [IIa]; Shortt 1960, fig. 71. *1951.58* **Fig 27**

171 Part of a hoop from a purse frame. It is L-shaped in section with one flange perforated at intervals for attaching the fabric of leather pouch. The frame is inscribed in Lombardic letters and has traces of inlay: DEO HONOR ET GLORIA ('honour and glory to God') with leaf-scrolls between the words. The hoop is broken but at one end there is part of the pierced terminal for attaching it to a bar like Cat 169 and 170 above. Drainage coll. *SD575* **Fig 27**

172 Fragment from the bar of a purse frame. It has one perforated flange for suspension of the pouch. Part of a Lombardic niello-inlaid inscription survives on each side of the bar: […]LAR(?) on one side and […]GO on the other. L. 30mm. From the River Avon, Bridge Street, Salisbury. *1993.1* **Fig 27**

173 Part of the loop from a purse frame. It has incised criss-cross decoration inlaid with niello against a traced background, and a continuous perforated flange for attachment of the pouch. L. 106mm. From Amesbury. *1989.59*

174 Part of the bar from a purse frame similar to above. It has similar decoration. The heavy knop in the centre would have held a swivel loop. L. 103mm. From 2 Meadow Cottages, Laverstock. *1968.76.1*

175 Iron purse frame with remains of two flanged hoops. The bar has linear decoration. It has a swivel loop in the centre and two further swivelling fittings to either side which would have helped to support the pouches. W. 120mm. From the River Avon at Fisherton Bridge, Salisbury. *Sal. Mus. Rep.* 1956-7, 16 and pl. IIb; Shortt 1960, fig. 70. *1957.9* **Fig 28**

176 Iron purse frame similar to above but with a shorter bar, decorated in panels. Possible white metal plating. W. *c.*120mm. Found with Cat 175. From the River Avon at Fisherton Bridge, Salisbury. *Sal. Mus. Rep.* 1956-7, 16 and pl. IIb; Shortt 1960, fig. 70. *1957.9* **Fig 28**

There are two more frames from the same location (*1993.1*).

177 Bar from a purse frame. It has criss-cross decoration inlaid with ?niello and a heavy boss in the centre, pierced to take a swivel loop. The knops at the ends of the bar are of iron. L. 140mm. From King John's House, Tollard Royal. Pitt Rivers 1890, pl. XIX, no. 9. *TR143*

Belt hooks

These large hooks have slots for sliding onto a belt strap and were probably used to suspend a purse. Their date is uncertain: an example in iron from Wharram Percy came from a post-medieval context (Goodall 1979, 123, fig. 65.116) and Ian Goodall has suggested that they may all be post-medieval (Goodall, 1980). The hooks have been included here, however, because they show certain decorative similarities with some of the purse frames above and to which they may be related.

178 Heavy hook with slot for attaching to a belt. Incised hatching and a cross on front of hook. L. 33mm. From Wilton. *1920-21.28* **Fig 29**

179 Belt hook. Heavy casting with a rectangular slot for a *c.*18mm strap to pass through. The hook is not decorated but has a marked keel. L. 42mm. From the River Avon, Bridge Street, Salisbury. *1993.1* **Fig 29**

180 Copper alloy belt hook with slot for a 19mm

strap. The hook is elaborately shaped, terminating in a dragon-like zoomorphic head, and with incised criss-cross lines perhaps suggesting scales. L. 53mm. From Salterton, Durnford. *2002.26*   **Fig 29**

181 Iron belt hook with zoomorphic terminal similar to above. The material and method of manufacture have resulted in a less elegant form than above. L. 64mm. Drainage coll. *SD687*

182 Hinged hook with two perforations in bosses. Hooked end terminates in a rectangular plate. Surfaces gilded. Possibly harness fitting. L. 36mm. From Steeple Langford. *1990.28*   **Fig 29**

Bells

183 Sheet metal bell, made in two parts with a dumbbell-shaped opening in lower half; the loop is made from strip of metal inserted into upper part. L. 29mm. From Great Ridge Wood, Boyton. *1958.2.1*

184 Sheet metal bell, made in two parts with a dumbbell-shaped opening in lower half; the loop is made from strip of metal inserted into upper part. It contains an iron 'pea'. L. 29mm. Found at Old Sarum during the 1909-1915 excavations, castle garderobe pit, *Proc. Soc. Antiq.* 23, 515. *OS.C15*   **Fig 29**

185 Sheet metal bell, damaged, 'pea' missing. L. 19mm. Found at Old Sarum during the 1909-1915 excavations, castle garderobe pit. *Proc. Soc. Antiq.* 23, 515. *OS.C14*   **Fig 29**

186 Sheet metal bell, broken in two halves, 'pea' missing. Found at Old Sarum during the 1909-1915 excavations, castle garderobe pit. *Proc. Soc. Antiq.* 23, 515. *OS.C14*

187 Upper half of large sheet metal bell with strip loop inserted into it. D. 38mm. From the Millstream behind 43 Castle Street, Salisbury. *1957.88.5*

188 Sheet metal bell with damaged loop; 'pea' made of stone or clay. D. 19mm. From the Millstream near St Thomas's Square, Salisbury. *1987.101.8*

Small sheet metal bells, made in two parts, have a long history: indeed, examples dating from the thirteenth century, for instance at Southampton (Harvey et al. 1975, 255, fig. 240.1726), are almost identical to bells which are on sale today. In medieval times they were often attached to the collars of pet dogs, as shown for instance on the memorial brass of Sir Thomas Brook and his wife Joan at Thorncombe, Devon, dated 1437, where a small whippet-like dog with a row of bells on its collar lies at Joan's feet. Bells were, and still are, used in the training of falcons for hunting, attached to the bird's legs to enable the falconer to keep track of it. A row of bells of similar type is also shown suspended from a waist belt in the portrait of Lysbeth van Duvenvoorde of 1430 (Fingerlin 1971, 361, pl. 408).

189 Pear-shaped bell with integral loop. The body of the bell has been made from an almost triangular flat casting with notches cut out of the bottom edge; it has then been wrapped round with the edges butted and the notched edge folded in. Wear on the loop suggests that it was suspended from a metal ring. L. 55mm. From Thruxton, Hampshire. *1957.41*
    Fig 29

190 Small bell similar to above but with solid stem. 'Pea' inside. Attached to a hinged stud mount. L. 22mm. Found at Old Sarum during the 1909-1915 excavations, castle garderobe pit. *Proc. Soc. Antiq.* 23, 515. *OS.C13*
    This bell, with its mount, was illustrated in Cherry 1991, 23 and fig. 4 (Cat 25) as an example of the same type of mount with stud used to attach harness pendants.

A bell of similar form to Cat 189, but less well made, was found at Exeter and dated to the late thirteenth to early fourteenth centuries (Goodall 1984, 341, fig. 191.138). A solid-stemmed bell, like that from Old Sarum (Cat 190), was found at Faccombe Netherton and dated to the late thirteenth to mid-fourteenth century (Goodall 1990, 427, fig. 9.12.11). Pear-shaped bells were sometimes attached to costume or to horse harness; more ornamental bells, with spiral reeding, are shown, for instance, on the trappings of horses in the 1511 Westminster Tournament Roll (Marks and Payne 1978, 82-3, pl. 74).

191 Fragment from a small open-mouthed, cast metal bell. Single moulding wire round the mouth and another pair of wires. Surface is greyish in colour. H. 36mm. Found at Old Sarum, *OS.C152; 1920-1.30.28*   **Fig 30**

The collection also includes a number of rumbler bells of cast copper alloy, which are of post-medieval date.

Pendants

Some twenty five pendants and related fittings have already been published in Part 1 of the Catalogue (Cherry 1991, 17-28), together with a discussion. The following non-heraldic pendants are finds that have come to the Museum or come to light since that volume was published.

192 Quatrefoil shaped pendant showing a forwards-facing human face, apparently wearing some form of head-dress. Loop missing. The pendant was probably not enamelled. L. 26mm. From Amesbury. *1989.1*   **Fig 30**
  Nicholas Griffiths (pers. comm.) has suggested that this may be a thirteenth-century pendant.

193 Circular pendant with incised foliate ornament against a traced zig-zag ground. L. 34mm. From Steeple Langford. *1988.47*   **Fig 30**

194 Square pendant with punched decoration showing a simple saltire in the centre surrounded by a scrolled border. L. 40mm. Found 'near Salisbury'. *1994.50*   **Fig 30**

195 Scallop-shaped pendant and mount of gilded copper alloy. The pendant is enhanced with incised radial lines but the mount is undecorated. The pin that would have held the two parts together and formed the hinge is missing. L. mount 25mm.

L. pendant 25.5mm. From Old Sarum, east suburb. *2006.7.1* and *2006.7.2*   **Fig 30**
  The scallop or cockle shell is well known as a motif in classical art and architecture, but in the medieval period it is most commonly associated with St James the Greater and, in particular, with pilgrimage to Compostela. Pilgrims are depicted wearing a scallop badge on their hat or their cloak. See page 227 and front cover for window glass from Ivychurch Priory, Cat 96, which illustrates this. However, the ubiquity of the scallop as a decorative motif means that we should not necessarily associate these pendants with pilgrimage. Scallop pendants with mounts have been found in possibly twelfth-century contexts at Castle Acre Castle (Goodall 1982, 238-9, fig. 44.36-37) and also at Billingsgate, London (Griffiths 1995, 69, fig. 50.72).

196 Globular copper alloy pendant with mount. The tiny pendant is decorated with stamped circles. L. 26mm. From Old Sarum, east suburb. *2006.7.3*   **Fig 30**

Scabbard Fittings

197 Scabbard chape made from sheet with overlapped edge at back; narrow tapering form with knop at bottom end. Top has a zigzag edge with a row of holes below and a quatrefoil opening outlined by traced lines. L. 68mm. From Clarendon Palace. Goodall et al. 1988, 207 and fig. 70, no.15; *Sal. Mus. Rep.* 1956-7, 15 and pl. IIIa; Shortt 1960, fig. 61(7). *1957.47*   **Fig 30**

198 Scabbard chape made of cast copper alloy. Upper edge has ornamental shaping, bun-shaped knop at bottom. Front decorated with trefoil and quatrefoil shapes in shallow relief, with traces of incised lines between. Hint of gilding. L. 55mm. Found at Old Sarum during the 1909-1915 excavations. *OS.C19*   **Fig 30**

199 Scabbard chape decorated with pairs of horizontal incisions. It tapers to an ornamental knop at the bottom. Two rivet holes near the upper edge to secure it to the scabbard. L. 64mm. From King John's House, Tollard Royal. Pitt Rivers 1890, pl. XIX, no. 8. *TR102*   **Fig 30**

The three chapes described above are from dagger sheaths. There is a similar narrow chape with a knop at the bottom on a scabbard for a rondel dagger of a type associated with late fifteenth-century Burgundy (Peterson 1968, pl. 15). A comparable scabbard chape from Norwich with a knop at the bottom is dated 1500-1580 (Margeson 1993, 227, fig. 175.1856) and another comes from Sandal Castle, where it was similarly dated 1485-1600 (Goodall 1983a, 232, no. 77). Ward Perkins (1940, 287 fig. 88, 3-4) illustrates similar narrow chapes, though without knops, which he dates to *c.*1375, suggesting that chapes of this form appeared in the late medieval period but continued into the post-medieval period.

200   Small scabbard chape made from sheet metal with a double incised line round the upper edge. There is a single rivet hole near the top to attach it to the scabbard. The lower edge has been folded in to close the bottom of the chape. L. 36mm. From Stonehenge. Montague 1995, 433, no. 15. *Stonehenge Cat. 358*

201   Scabbard binding with loop riveted onto back. Edges defined by pairs of incised lines; lower edge scalloped. This mount would have reinforced the top edge of the scabbard and there would have been a chape at the bottom. W. 43mm. From Clarendon Palace. Goodall et al. 1988, 204 and fig. 70, no.14; *Sal. Mus. Rep.* 1956-7, 15 and pl. IIIa; Shortt 1960, fig. 61(3). *1957.47*   **Fig 31**

202   Scabbard binding. It is decorated with pairs of raised ridges, one at the top and another near the bottom: between them is an inscription which appears to read 'findes'. The lower edge has incised geometric decoration. W. 45mm. From the River Avon, Bridge Street, Salisbury. *1993.1*   **Fig 31**

These bindings come from the mouth of the scabbard. The binding from Clarendon Palace

has a loop at the back enabling it to be suspended from a belt or strap. A similar binding but with side loops is attached to an early fourteenth-century sword from the Thames at Westminster (Norman 1972, 74, fig. 98) although an example found at Sandal Castle came from Civil War levels (Goodall 1983a, 232, no. 78). However, the decoration on the binding from the River Avon is consistent with a fourteenth- or fifteenth-century date.

Miscellaneous Mounts and Decorative Fittings

This category includes mounts that are clearly not connected with dress accessories, as well as casket and furniture fittings, and other ornamental fittings, such as gilt binding strips.

203   Large quatrefoil-headed stud. In places reddish metal shows through the patina but there is no gilding. The length of the shank suggests that the stud was used as a decoration on wood, possibly a chest or other item of furniture. W. of head 30mm, L. of shank *c.*27mm. From Old Sarum. *OS.C77; 1920-1.30*   **Fig 31**

Two large gilded quatrefoil studs were found in the bailey area at Goltho Manor in a context dated *c.*1080-1150, with a third found in topsoil (Goodall 1987, 173, fig. 154.13-14). The same context produced large quantities of gilt D-sectioned binding strip and other decorative fittings. A similar stud came from Ludgershall (Ellis 2000, 131-2, fig. 6.10, no. 91).

204   Decorative stud with flat sexfoil head (D. 18.7mm) enhanced by radial incisions which retain what may be traces of gilding. Long shank (*c.*17mm) for inserting into wood. From Stonehenge. Montague 1995, 433, no. 29.

205   Gilt fitting, asymmetrical, possibly from a casket or reliquary. At one end there is a long arm with a pierced lozenge-shaped terminal; other end may be incomplete although there is no obvious fracture. Incised foliate decoration, with infill of traced zigzags.

Two dome-headed rivets in situ. It may have been a mounting for a hasp. L. 134mm. Found at Old Sarum during the 1909-1915 excavations. *OS.C62*

Fig 31

206 Gilt mount possibly from a reliquary, three sided, the longest side being convex and one of the shorter sides concave. Rivet-holes in the corners and two edges down-turned. Foliate decoration, similar to OS.C62, against a ground of traced zigzags. L. 54mm. Found at Old Sarum during the 1909-1915 excavations. *OS.C61*

Fig 31

207 Rectangular mount with domed boss in centre and large round-headed rivet. Boss decorated with openwork sexfoil design; traced ornament on flange. Possible traces of gilding. One corner has been cut away. Possibly from a book. Sides 40mm. Found at Old Sarum during the 1909-1915 excavations. *OS.C60*

Fig 31

208 Large oval plaque with separate U-sectioned binding. Plaque has regularly spaced pins and pin-holes round its edge and there are larger pins which pass through the binding as well. Decorated with an incised barbed quatrefoil motif flanked by the initials 'R' and 'T'. L. 135mm. Found at Old Sarum during the 1909-1915 excavations, from pit 2. *O.S. Diary 1910*, 25. *OS.C59*

Fig 32

209 Gilt mount consisting of a pair of curved arms joined at a vaguely zoomorphic boss. Outer ends of arms appear to have had pierced terminals for attachment; inner ends finished in scallop-shaped terminals. Probably from a casket or furniture, perhaps a keyhole guide. W. 105mm. Found at Old Sarum during the 1909-1915 excavations. *OS.C83*

Fig 32

210 Cast finial in the shape of a dog's head. It has a short stumpy shank. L. (overall) 24mm. Found at Old Sarum during the 1909-1915 excavations. *OS.C82; 1920-1.30*

Fig 32

211 Gilded bar mount with a scallop or foliate cresting in the centre. The bar is D-shaped in section and there are perforated bosses at each end. It is unclear whether the ends of the bar are complete

or have been cut. L. 67mm. From Old Sarum, east suburb. *2006.7.5*

Fig 32

This mount bears certain resemblances to the gilt binding strips discussed below, notably the D-shaped section and the expanded bosses with perforations, probably for attachment.

Gilt binding strips

Excavations at castle and manorial sites with occupation in the twelfth and thirteenth centuries frequently produce a characteristic assemblage of copper alloy finds, including lengths of gilt binding strips, sometimes with large ornamental bosses, and decorative studs and mounts. Examples of these groups of finds have been found at Castle Acre Castle (Goodall 1982), Ludgershall Castle (Ellis 2000) and Goltho Manor (Goodall 1987). At Goltho, some of the fragments of gilt strip seemed to be associated with tiny fragments of wood and what appeared to be bone plates (Goodall 1987, 176), although these were too fragmentary to give any clue to the function of the strips. It is most likely that they embellished items such as caskets or chests and reliquaries, or book bindings. The excavators of the Old Sarum objects suggested that they came from the top or sides of a casket (*Proc. Soc. Antiq.* 23 (1909-11), 515). Ornamental metalwork of this type certainly indicates high status. The fact that many of these objects and fragments in the Museum collection were found in the excavations at Old Sarum is significant in terms of both the date and importance of that site, Old Sarum having been superseded by the new city of Salisbury in the thirteenth century.

An example in iron (Cat 216) shows many similarities of form with the copper alloy pieces, although it has no traces of gilding and is likely to have had a similar use. Traces of wood in the corrosion products suggest that it was mounted on a wooden casket.

212 Narrow D-sectioned strip with transverse mouldings. L. 186mm. One end is intact and terminates in a pierced expansion. At the other end it splits in two and each of the two ends is bent inwards at an acute angle and may originally have joined to form an open triangle; at the split and at the angles there are attachment holes. There is one plain, slightly convex boss in the undivided section of strip. Traces of gilding survive. Found at Old Sarum during the 1909-1915 excavations, from garderobe pit no. 7. *O.S. Diary* 1910, 56. *OS.C2a*   **Fig 32**

213 Y-shaped fragment of narrow strip, very similar to above, with some gilding. L. 180mm. Found at Old Sarum during the 1909-1915 excavations, from garderobe pit no. 7. *O.S. Diary* 1910, 56. *OS.C2b*   **Fig 32**

214 Fragment of narrow strip without transverse mouldings. It has a pierced boss. L. 96mm. Found at Old Sarum during the 1909-1915 excavations, from garderobe pit no. 7. *O.S. Diary* 1910, 56. *OS.C2c*   **Fig 32**

215 Fragment of narrow strip originally forming part of a simple, curved decorative mount. It has pierced terminals and attachment holes wherever the strip divides. There are no transverse mouldings and no gilding survives. L. 110mm. Found at Old Sarum during the 1909-1915 excavations. *OS.C2e; 1920-1.30.36*   **Fig 32**

216 Fragment of similar D-sectioned strip but of iron rather than copper alloy. It is slightly narrower than the copper alloy strips, with a width of just over 3mm. Unlike the copper alloy strips, which have been cast, the iron strip has been forged and the two circular bosses, one of which forms a terminal, are flat and have chiselled notches, with inlay, around their edges. There are traces of non-ferrous plating. Corrosion products on the back of the object contain fragments of wood which may result from the base to which the strip was attached. L. 126mm. Found at Old Sarum during the 1909-1915 excavations. *OS.C2d*   **Fig 32**

Jew's Harps

Jew's harp, jaws harp or Jew's trump are just some of the names given to these instruments, consisting of a frame, usually made of metal,

and a tongue or reed. The origin of the name is uncertain. Jew's harps are known throughout the world and it has been suggested that they originated in China, eventually reaching Europe in the thirteenth century. The form of the instrument has scarcely changed, making them difficult to date.

217 Copper alloy Jew's harp with corrosion indicating missing iron tongue. L. 62mm. From Clarendon Palace, a stray find from the palace area. Goodall et al. 1988, 207 and fig. 70, no. 16. *1974.77*

218 Copper alloy Jew's harp. The iron tongue is missing but there is a depression on one side with ferrous staining where it was attached. L. 38.5mm. From Stonehenge. Montague 1995, 433, no. 30. *Stonehenge Cat. 1078b*   **Fig 33**

There are also two iron Jew's harps recovered from the River Avon (*1993.1*).

Needleworking Equipment

Pins

Pins with heads made from a coil of finer wire, which is either stuck onto the end of the shaft using some form of adhesive or flux or attached by stamping between dies, are commonly found on sites from the sixteenth century onwards. This method of manufacture may have been introduced before the end of the medieval period, but it is possible that most of the examples in the Museum collection are of post-medieval date.

219 Group of globular pin-heads: two appear to be quite large, the other nine are of normal size. All the shafts are broken off and several pins-heads are corroded together. Found at Old Sarum during the 1909-1915 excavations. *OS.C147-150; 1920-21.30.26*

220 Two pins with globular heads and a further two pins which are almost complete but lacking heads. Also four fragments of pins. Found at Old

Sarum during the 1909-1915 excavations. *OS.C20; 2000R.29.1-29.7*

There is a reference in O.S. Diary, 1910, 24 to pins from garderobe pit 2 but it is not clear to which of the two entries above this applies.

221 Two pins, the first with a globular head and being 48mm long, the second with a head made from coiled wire and being 62mm long. From King John's House, Tollard Royal. Pitt Rivers 1890, pl. XIX, no. 11. *TR46A&B*

222 Pin with round head, possibly made in two parts and with the head projecting at the top. L. 48mm, L. of head 5mm. Fenton coll., probably from Oxford. *1940.85.1*

223 Long pin with a globular head, possibly made from coiled wire. L. 133mm. Drainage coll. *SD895; 1999R.49.1*

224 Heavy pin or awl. It has a conical head with a slight indent in the top. L. 77mm. Drainage coll. *SD899; 1999R.49.5*

?Knitting needles

Knitting was known in the medieval period. The tomb of Fernando de la Cerda, who died in 1275 and is buried near Burgos in Spain, contains knitted gloves and a finely knitted silk cushion cover which must have required more slender needles than those generally used in modern hand knitting. There are also illustrations of women knitting, such as on the late fourteenth to early fifteenth-century Buxtehude Altar by Master Bertram of Minden which shows the Virgin Mary knitting a garment in circular fashion, using four double-pointed needles rather than the more common, and perhaps later, backwards and forwards method using a pair of needles with a head and a point at one end only.

225 Possibly a knitting needle. Long pin with a bun-shaped head. L. 165mm. Drainage coll. *SD897; 1999R.49.3*

226 Possibly a knitting needle with a globular head. It is bent in several places. L. *c.*195mm. Drainage coll. *SD896; 1999R.49.2*

Needles

The Museum collection includes only a small number of needles, of which two are netting needles with an eye at each end. They were used in lace making. Of the other three needles, two are too large to have been used in general sewing and must have had some other use such as wool work or furriery. The date of these needles is uncertain and it is possible that some or all of them may be post-medieval.

227 Blunt ended needle with an elongated eye set in a gutter or groove. L. 116mm. Drainage coll. *SD913; 1999R.50.1*

228 Needle with flattened head and an elongated eye set in a gutter. L. 73mm. Drainage coll. *Sal. Mus. Rep.* 1870, 26. *SD826*

229 Needle with circular sectioned stem and a pierced, flattened head. L. 42mm. Found at Old Sarum. *OS.C20*   **Fig 33**

230 Netting needle with an open-ended eye at each end; their planes are at approximately 90° to each other. Large netting needles would have been used for making and repairing nets such as those used in fishing. Smaller needles, like this, were used to make the fine mesh onto which lace was embroidered. L. 172mm. Drainage coll. *SD883; 1996R.13.1*

Fig 33

231 Netting needle similar to the example above. L. 151mm. Drainage coll. *SD884; 1996R.13.2*

Thimbles

The thimbles published here are all likely to be medieval or very early post-medieval. They may be compared with a series from Exeter, with various dates from the thirteenth century to modern (Goodall 1984, 345, fig. 194.211-17).

Medieval thimbles were either cast or hammered into a die and the indentations were punched or drilled. An illustration from Nuremberg dated about 1425 shows a thimble maker supporting a domed thimble on an anvil while he uses a drill to make the indentations (Treue et al. 1965, pl. 13). The finished thimbles on the table at his side include open-topped thimbles and others with domed tops. All have a band around the lower edge without indentations. Medieval thimbles often have an area at the top which has ho indentations. From the sixteenth century, new technologies meant that thimbles could be made in two parts, the cap and sides being made separately and then soldered together (McConnel 1995, 13-22). They also become finer and more decorated. Another study of thimble types and manufacture has been made by Edwin Holmes (Holmes 1988).

232 Large thimble with domed top. There is a fine incised line round the mouth and the somewhat upright indentations are arranged in a spiral. The indentations seem to have been impressed with a multi-toothed tool. H. 20mm. D. 18mm. Drainage coll. *SD809; 2007R.247*   **Fig 33**

233 Small thimble of thin metal, with sugar-loaf profile. The indentations are arranged in vertical rows on the sides of the thimble, and in irregular concentric rings nearer to the top. H. 16mm. From 8 Old Castle Road, Salisbury. *1952.75*

234 Thimble made from thin metal with straight, sloping sides and a shallow conical top. There is an incised line at the mouth and the large, regular indentations are arranged spirally. H. 20mm. From the Millstream near St Thomas's Square, Salisbury. *1987.101.9*

235 Small domed thimble with a hole in the centre of the cap. The indentations are arranged in almost vertical rows on the sides and in concentric rings nearer the top. H. 13mm. From Old Sarum. *OS.C20a; 2000R.29.1*   **Fig 33**

236 Large heavy thimble with a domed top.

The indentations are large and round and have been drilled in an irregular continuous spiral from the top. H. 21mm, D. 23mm. Drainage coll. *SD803; 1999R.1066*   **Fig 33**

237 Small thimble with sloping sides and a shallow conical top with a pit in the centre. There are two grooves running round the mouth and the indentations are arranged in a continuous spiral. H. 16.5mm. Drainage coll. *SD804; 1999R.1066.1*

238 Thimble with sloping sides and domed top with a central pit. There is a plain band with an incised groove round the mouth and the indentations are arranged in a continuous spiral. H. 24mm, D. *c.*25mm. Drainage coll. *SD805; 1999R.1066.2*

239 Tall thimble of thick metal with a domed top. The indentations are large and arranged in a spiral. H. 27mm. D. 22mm. Drainage coll. *SD811; 2007R.251*

240 Thimble of thick metal with domed top. The indentations are rounded in form and arranged in a spiral. H. 22mm. D. 22mm. Drainage coll. *SD814; 2007R.249*

241 Thimble with domed top. It has a moulded or rolled ridge round the mouth and the small indentations are arranged in a spiral. H. 20mm. D. 21mm. Drainage coll. *SD810; 2007R.250*

The three thimbles (Cat 242-4) described below may be later than the others.

242 Thimble of very thin metal with almost straight sides and a domed top. There is a plain, slightly raised band round the mouth. The small indentations, some of which perforate the metal, are arranged in vertical rows on the sides and in a spiral on the top. H. 20mm. D. 18.0-18.5mm. Drainage coll. *SD806; 1999R.1066.3*

243 Small thimble of thin metal with a conical top. There is an incised line round the mouth and the indentations are arranged in a spiral. There is a hole in the centre of the top outlined by four irregular incised lines. H. 17mm, D. 18mm. Drainage coll. *SD807; 1999R.1066.4*

244 Small thimble with shallow conical top. The top has no indentations on it but has a hole in the centre. There is a pair of grooves running round the mouth and the indentations are arranged in vertical rows on the sides and in concentric rings nearer the top. H. 16mm. D. 17mm. Drainage coll. *SD808; 2007R.248*

Domestic and Household Equipment

Kitchen and tableware

245 Tap with an almost rectangular-sectioned spout opening into octagonal-sectioned portion in which the key turns. The key has a perforation through which liquid can flow when the crown or 'M'-shaped handle is correctly aligned. L. 98mm. From 34-36 High Street, Salisbury. *1963.82*   **Fig 34**

246 Similar tap with broken handle, possibly originally trefoil shaped. L. 100mm. Drainage coll. *Sal. Mus. Cat.* 1864, 51 no. 128. *SD930; 1999R.34*

An incomplete tap with an M-shaped handle like the example above, but misidentified as the top of a staff or wand, was found in Dissolution levels at Pontefract Priory (Bellamy 1962-4, 124, fig. 25g) and another came from medieval levels in London (Egan 1998, 242-4, fig. 189.746). Taps with trefoil shaped handles were found in excavations in Amsterdam in contexts dated to the sixteenth and seventeenth centuries (Baart 1977, 352-3, nos. 657 and 658). Taps like these are shown in German illustrations dated between 1425 and 1544: they are inserted into the ends of wooden barrels for drawing off wine (Treue et al. 1965, pls. 39, 215 and 248).

247 Skimmer, missing the socket and handle. The perforations are irregularly spaced. D. 176mm. From the River Avon, Bridge Street, Salisbury. *1993.1*

Fig 33

A skimmer such as this, attached to a long handle, is shown in the fourteenth century *Luttrell Psalter* being used by a cook to remove food from three metal cauldrons. In his other hand the cook holds a long handled flesh-hook. See fig 12.

248 Pair of drop handles, possibly from a chafing dish although their size implies that they could also have been used on furniture. Both have studs for attachment; one is simple, the other is broader and has ornamental grooves. L. 52mm. From the River Avon, Bridge Street, Salisbury. *1993.1*

Fig 34

249 Fragment of heart-shaped drop handle, from a vessel, e.g. chafing dish, or furniture. Rectangular section except for the upper, pivoting bar, which is rounded. Max. W. 55mm. From Old Sarum. *OS.C155*   **Fig 34**

Similar handles were found in fifteenth- and sixteenth-century deposits at Norwich (Margeson 1993, 78-9, fig. 45.489-91) where it was suggested they were from chests or furniture or from chafing dishes.

250 Simple drop handle with splayed ends for suspension. Crudely made; ends may be incomplete. Possibly from a casket. W. 46mm. From Old Sarum. *OS.C154; 1920-1.30.30*   **Fig 34**

251 Plain copper alloy ring with split-pin attachment, possibly a handle. D. 44mm. From the River Avon, Bridge Street, Salisbury. *1993.1*   **Fig 34**

252 Finial probably from a knife handle in the form of a zoomorphic or anthropomorphic head with pointed ears. The collar on which the head sits is decorated with diagonal rows of traced zigzags and it has a slot in the base to take the scale tang of the knife. L. 25mm. ?Drainage coll. *2007R.78*   **Fig 34**

253 Incomplete decorative implement with animal head terminal and traced decoration on one side. There is a large perforation or rivet-hole in the side, indicating that the object was probably originally hinged. L. 48mm. From Netherhampton. *1987.77*

Fig 34

Although this object is smaller, it bears a strong resemblance to a pair of fifteenth-century bronze nut crackers in the British Museum (Cherry 1991, 42-3, fig. 55). It would have been too insubstantial to have been used on nuts, but may have had some other similar use at table, such as for crushing spices or other flavourings.

Candlesticks

254 Candlestick with short stem inserted into a separate base. It has collar and groove mouldings on the socket. The base has concentric markings, possibly the result of being finished by turning. H. *c.*113mm. *1945.118*   **Fig 35 & cover**
    Roger Brownsword (pers. comm. 2005) has commented that this is of 'interesting style, transitional between plain 'bunsen' type of fifteenth century and more elaborate sixteenth century styles' (see Brownsword 1985), and a late fifteenth-century date is thus probable.

255 Socket and stem from a similar, taller candlestick. L. 161mm. From the River Avon, Bridge Street, Salisbury. *1993.1*   **Fig 35**

256 Socket of similar type to above but without the stem. Instead it has a short plug-like end, which would have fitted into a branched candlestick (see Brownsword 1985, fig 3). L. 39mm. From the River Avon, Bridge Street, Salisbury. *1993.1*

The base of the complete candlestick (Cat 254) above bears a resemblance to the English 'trumpet-based' candlesticks of the seventeenth century (Michaelis 1978, 79ff). However, the socket is more like those of earlier sticks. The two sockets from the River Avon are similar to those on candlesticks with skirted bases, a type of base which seems to have evolved in the later fourteenth century (Michaelis 1978, 41ff, figs. 25-6). Similar sockets were excavated in Norwich from deposits dated 1507 (Margeson 1993, 83, fig. 49.537-8). It seems that these candlesticks showed a gradual evolution from the fourteenth to the sixteenth centuries and this

is consistent with a late fifteenth-century date for the examples in the Museum collection.

257 Iron disc with white metal plating and incised concentric lines surrounding a central perforation. Slightly dished profile. Possibly the drip-tray from a candlestick. D. 128mm. From Clarendon Palace, Goodall et al. 1988, 218 and fig. 81, no. 93. *2000R.67*

258 Part of the stem of a folding candlestick. It has three perforated flanges where the hinged legs would have been attached. L. 70mm. From the Laverstock kiln site excavations, found in building 2, a 13th/14th-century context. It was suggested that it may have been scrap metal for use in the preparation of green glaze for pottery. Musty et al. 1969, 149, pl. XVb and fig. 28, no. 3; *Sal. Mus. Rep.* 1959-60, 18 and pl. 3a. *1960.13.1*   **Fig 35**

A complete folding candlestick is illustrated in the London Museum catalogue (Ward Perkins 1940, 179-80, fig. 56.1) and is thought to be early medieval in date.

Writing Implements etc

259 Possibly a stylus. Long tapering object of copper alloy, flattened and slightly hooked at the wider end, pointed acorn-like terminal at the other end. L.105mm. Drainage coll. *SD829 2007R.315*

260 Parchment holder with closing ring and trapeze-shaped expanded ends decorated with traced lines. L. 54mm. Found at Old Sarum during the 1909-1915 excavations. *OS.A 5b*

261 Parchment holder, almost identical to above. L. 59mm. Found at Old Sarum during the 1909-1915 excavations. *OS.A 5a*   **Fig 35 & cover**

A parchment holder very similar to those above was found in excavations at Pleshey Castle (Rahtz 1960, 27, fig. 15.4). Rahtz cites the examples from Old Sarum in his report and states that they were found in a batch in the cathedral

(O. S. Diary 1913, 2). Other examples of comparable type have come from fifteenth-century levels at Winchester (Biddle and Hinton 1990, 758, fig. 215.2326A) and from the medieval lower levels of the reredorter/drain at Bayham Abbey, Sussex (Goodall 1983b, fig. 48.14). It is thought that they were used to hold sheets of manuscript or of music, or to hold the pages of a book, and this identification would be consistent with their being found on monastic or ecclesiastical sites.

Horse Equipment

Bridle bosses

Circular bosses are shown on contemporary illustrations attached to the bridle bit or at the junction of the brow band, headpiece, cheek piece and throat lash of the bridle. An example dated 1328 is on a fresco at the Palazzo Pubblico in Siena; it shows Guidoriccio da Fogliano on horseback (Evans 1966, 138, pl. 9). Bosses are also shown on the bridles of horses in Henry VIII's procession on the Great Westminster Tournament Roll of 1511.

262 Bridle boss with domed centre and broad flange. Decoration of incised concentric lines. Five rivets, one in centre of boss and four in flange, with rosettes on heads; one rivet has been inserted from underside of boss. D. 48mm. From Bilbury Rings, Wylye. *1999R.1058*   **Fig 35**

263 Bridle boss made from thick sheet. Domed centre with pyramidal boss in middle; flange with rolled edge decorated with repoussé cable. Two iron rivets. D. 67mm. Found near Crane Bridge, Salisbury. *1963.26*   **Fig 35**

264 Bridle boss with slightly raised and then countersunk central area; broad scalloped flange with surface gilding and two damaged rivet-holes and a third possibly secondary. Domed rivet in centre. Central area has no gilding and may have been enamelled or held a separate ornamental roundel. D. *c.*85mm. From Clarendon Palace. Goodall et al. 1988, 204 and fig. 70 no. 12; *Sal. Mus. Rep.* 1956-7, 15 and pl. IIIa; Shortt 1960, fig. 61(6). *1957.47*   **Fig 35**

BIBLIOGRAPHY

Baart, J. M. et al. 1977: *Opgravingen in Amsterdam. 20 jaar Stadskernonderzoek*, Dienst der publicke werken / Amsterdams Historich Museum Afdeling Archaeologie (Amsterdam)

Bayley, J., Drury, P. and Spencer, B. 1984: 'Exhibits at Ballots - 2. A medieval mirror from Heybridge, Essex', *Antiq. J.* **64**, 399-402

Bellamy, C. V. 1962-4: 'Pontefract Priory Excavations 1957-1961', *Publ. Thoresby Society* **49**

Biddle, M. and Hinton, D. 1990: 'Book-clasps and page-holder' in M. Biddle (ed.), *Object and Economy in Medieval Winchester*, Winchester Studies **7ii** (Oxford), 755-8

Brownsword, R. 1985: *English Latten Domestic Candlesticks 1400-1700*, Finds Research Group 700-1700 Datasheet **1**

Campbell, M. 2009: *Medieval Jewellery in Europe 1100-1500* (V. & A. Publishing)

Cherry, J. 1991: *Medieval Decorative Art* (British Museum)

Egan, G. 1998: *The Medieval Household*, Medieval Finds from Excavations in London **6**

Egan, G. and Pritchard, F. 1991: *Dress Accessories c. 1150 - c. 1450*, Medieval Finds from Excavations in London **3**

Ellis, P. 2000: *Ludgershall Castle, Wiltshire: a report on the excavations by Peter Addyman, 1964-72*, Wiltshire Archaeol. & Natur. Hist. Soc. Monograph **2**

Evans, J. 1922: *Magical Jewels of the Middle Ages and the Renaissance* (Oxford)

Evans, J. (ed.) 1966: *The Flowering of the Middle Ages*

Evans, J. 1970: *A History of Jewellery 1100 - 1870*

Evans, D. 2000: 'Buried with the Friars' in *British Archaeology* No. 53 (June 2000), 18-23

Fingerlin, I. 1971: *Gürtel des hohen und späten Mittelalters*, Kunstwissenshaftliche Studien **46** (München)

Fowler, P. J. 1963: 'A Rectangular Earthwork Enclosure at Wick Farm, Tisbury', *Antiquity* **37**, 290-3

Goodall, A. R. 1982: 'Objects of Copper Alloy' in J. G. Coad and A. D. F. Streeten, 'Excavations at Castle Acre Castle, Norfolk, 1972-77', *Archaeol. J.* **139**, 235-40

Goodall, A. R. 1983a: 'Non-ferrous metal objects' in P. Mayes and L. A. S. Butler, *Sandal Castle Excavations 1964-1973*, 231-39

Goodall, A.R. 1983b: 'Objects of copper alloy' in A. D. F. Streeten, *Bayham Abbey*. Sussex Archaeol. Soc. Monograph Series **2**

Goodall, A. R. 1984: 'Objects of Non-Ferrous Metal' in J. P. Allan, *Medieval and Post-medieval Finds from Exeter 1971-1980*, Exeter Archaeol. Rep. **3**, 337-348

Goodall, A. R. 1987: 'Medieval copper alloy' in G. Beresford, *Goltho: The development of an early medieval manor c.850-1150*, English Heritage Archaeol. Rep. **4**, 173-6

Goodall, A. R., Hinton, D. A. and James, T. B. 1988: 'Copper-alloy Objects' in T. B. James, and A. M. Robinson, with E. Eames, *Clarendon Palace: The History and Archaeology of a Medieval Palace and Hunting Lodge near Salisbury, Wiltshire*. Soc. Antiq. Res. Rep. **45**, 201-7

Goodall, A. R. 1990: 'Objects of Copper Alloy and Lead' in J. R. Fairbrother, *Faccombe Netherton, Excavations of a Saxon and Medieval Manorial Complex*, Brit. Mus. Occas. Pap. **74**, 424-436

Goodall, A. R. 1993: 'Copper Alloy Objects' in H. K. Murray and J. C. Murray, 'Excavations at Rattray, Aberdeenshire. A Scottish Deserted Burgh', *Medieval Archaeol.* **37**, 188-194

Goodall, A. R. forthcoming a: 'Objects of Copper Alloy' in Evans, D. H., *Excavations at the Austin Friary, Hull, 1994 and 1999*

Goodall, A. R. forthcoming b: Burton Dassett, Warwickshire

Goodall, I. H. 1979: 'Iron Objects' in D. Andrews and G. Milne, *Wharram: A Study of Settlement on the Yorkshire Wolds* Vol. 1. Society for Medieval Archaeology Monograph Series 8

Goodall, I. H. 1980: *Ironwork in Medieval Britain: An Archaeological Study* (unpublished Ph.D. thesis, University College, Cardiff)

Goodall, I. H. 1988: 'Iron Objects' in T. B. James, and A. M. Robinson, with E. Eames, *Clarendon Palace: The History and Archaeology of a Medieval Palace and Hunting Lodge near Salisbury, Wiltshire*. Soc. Antiq. Res. Rep. **45**, 208-223

Griffiths, N, 1995: 'Harness Pendants and Associated Fittings' in J. Clark (ed.), *The Medieval Horse and Its Equipment c.1150-c.1450*, Medieval Finds from Excavations in London **5**

Harvey, Yvonne with Goodall, Ian and Biek, Leo 1975: 'The Small Finds - The Bronze' in C. Platt and R. Coleman-Smith, *Excavations in Medieval Southampton 1953-1969, Vol. 2 - The Finds*, Leicester University Press, 254-268

Hinton, D. 1990: 'Buckles and Buckle-plates' in M. Biddle (ed.), *Object and Economy in Medieval Winchester*, Winchester Studies **7ii** (Oxford), 506-526

Holmes, E. F. [1988]: *Sewing Thimbles*, Finds Research Group 700-1700 Datasheet **9**

Margeson, S. (ed.) 1993: *Norwich Households: Medieval and Post-Medieval Finds from Norwich Survey Excavations 1971-78*, E. Anglian Archaeol. Rep. **58**

Marks, R. and Payne, A. (eds.) 1978: *British Heraldry from its origins to c.1800*

McConnel, B. 1995: *The Collector's Guide to Thimbles*

Mellor, J. E. and Pearce, T. 1981: *The Austin Friars Leicester*. CBA Res. Rep. **35**

Michaelis, R. F. 1978: *Old Domestic Base-Metal Candlesticks* (Woodbridge)

Montague, R. 1995: 'Metalwork' in R. M. J. Cleal, K. E. Walker and R. Montague, *Stonehenge in its landscape: Twentieth-century excavations*, English Heritage Archaeol. Rep. **10**, 432-4

Musty, J. W. G., Algar, D. J. and Ewence, P. F. 1969: 'The Medieval Pottery Kilns at

Laverstock, near Salisbury, Wiltshire, *Archaeologia* **102**, 83-150

Musty, J. W. G. and Algar, D.J. 1986: Excavations at the Deserted Medieval Village of Gomeldon near Salisbury, Wilts', *Wilts. Arch. Mag.* **80**, 127-169

Norman V. 1972: *Arms and Armour* (London)

Ottaway, P. and Rogers, N. 2002: *Craft, Industry and Everyday Life: Finds from Medieval York.* The Archaeology of York: The Small Finds **17/15**

Parrington, M. 1975: 'Excavations at the Old Gaol, Abingdon', *Oxoniensia* **40**, 59- 78 and pl. 3

Peterson, H. L. 1968: *Daggers & Fighting Knives of the Western World from the Stone Age till 1900*

Pitt Rivers, Lt. - Gen. 1890: *King John's House, Tollard Royal, Wilts* (privately printed)

Rahtz, P. 1960: *Pleshey Castle: First Interim Report.* Essex Archaeol. Soc. (1960)

Robinson, P. and Griffiths, N. 2000: 'The Copper Alloy Objects' in P. Ellis (ed.), *Ludgershall Castle, Wiltshire: a report on the excavations by Peter Addyman, 1964-1972,* Wiltshire Archaeol. & Nat. Hist. Soc. Monogr. Ser. **2**, 124-137

Saunders, P. R. 1983: 'An inscribed Medieval Brooch from Amesbury', *Wilts. Arch. Mag.* **77** for 1982, 146-7

Shortt, H. de S. (ed.) 1960: *The Collections Illustrated* (Salisbury)

Treue, W., Goldmann, K., Kellermann, R., Klemm, F., Schneider, K., von Stromer, W., Wissner, A. and Zirnbauer, H. 1965: *Das Hausbuch der Mendelschen Zwölfbrüderstiftung zu Nürnberg: deutscher Handwerkerbilder des 15. und 16. Jahrhunderts* (Munich)

Ward Perkins, J. B. (ed.) 1940: *Medieval Catalogue,* London Museum Catalogues **7**

Whitehead, R. 2003: *Buckles 1250-1800*

Fig 12. Image from the *Luttrell Psalter, c.*1340, f. 207, depicting a cook with a skimmer similar to Cat 247 (page 115) and an iron flesh hook similar to Cat 250 (page 168)

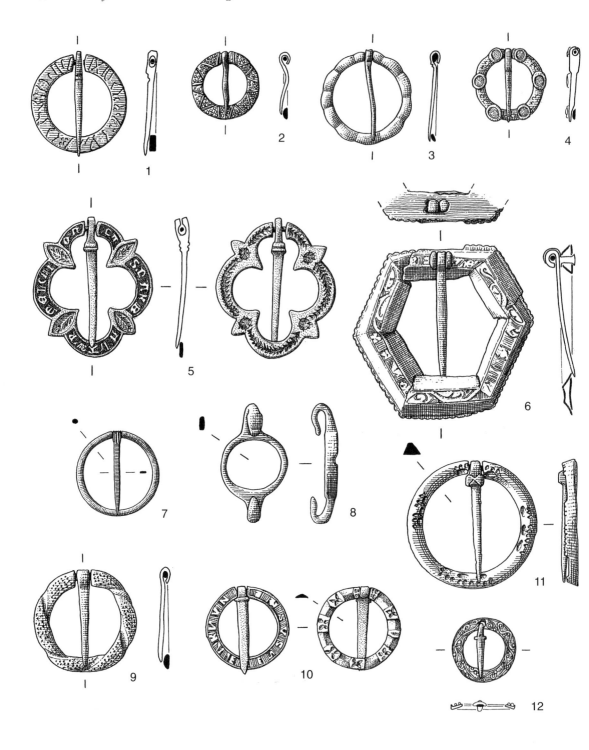

Fig 13. Copper alloy: Cat 1--12, brooches (Cat 10 silver) (1:1)

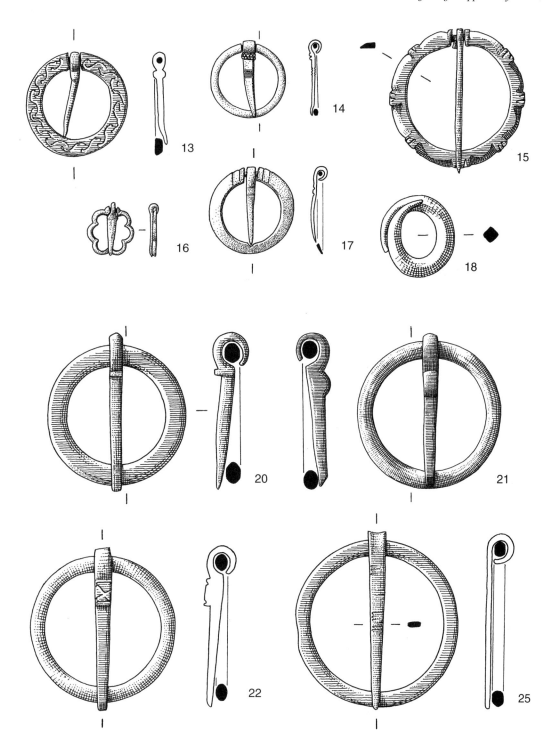

Fig 14. Copper alloy: Cat 13-17, brooches; Cat 18, ear-ring; Cat 20-22, 25, buckles (Cat 14, 16-17 silver) (1:1)

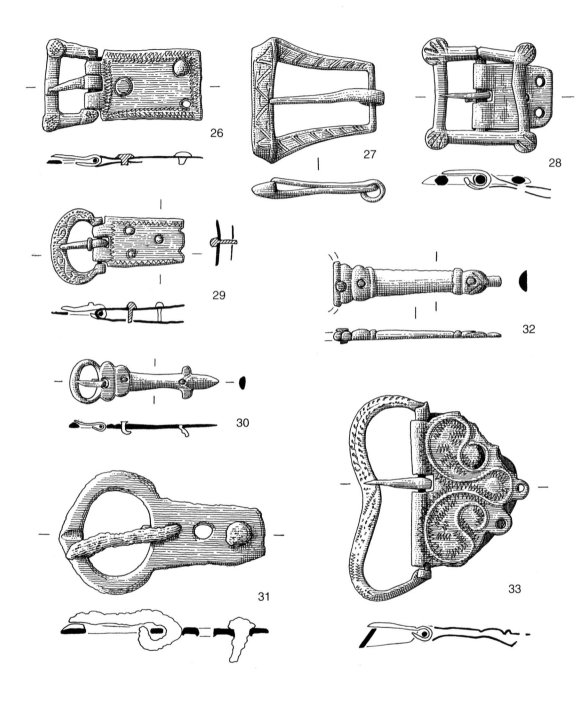

Fig 15. Copper alloy: Cat 26-33, buckles (1:1)

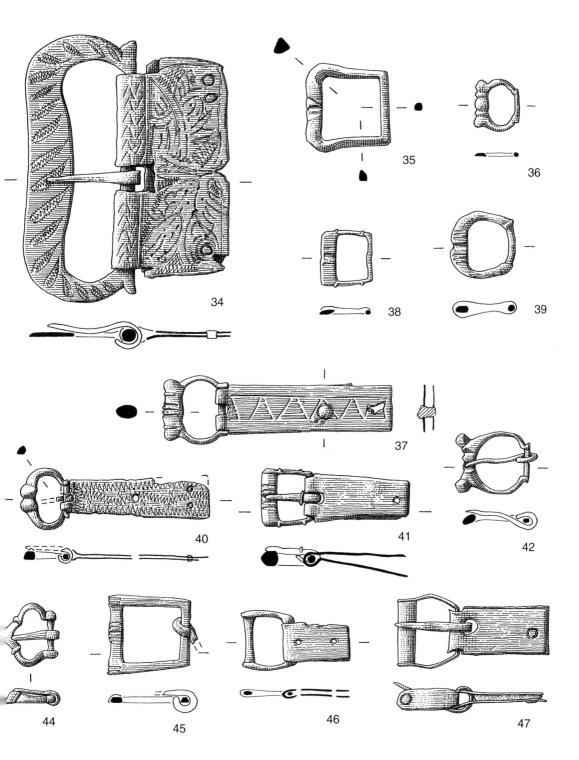

Fig 16. Copper alloy: Cat 34-42, 44-7, buckles (1:1)

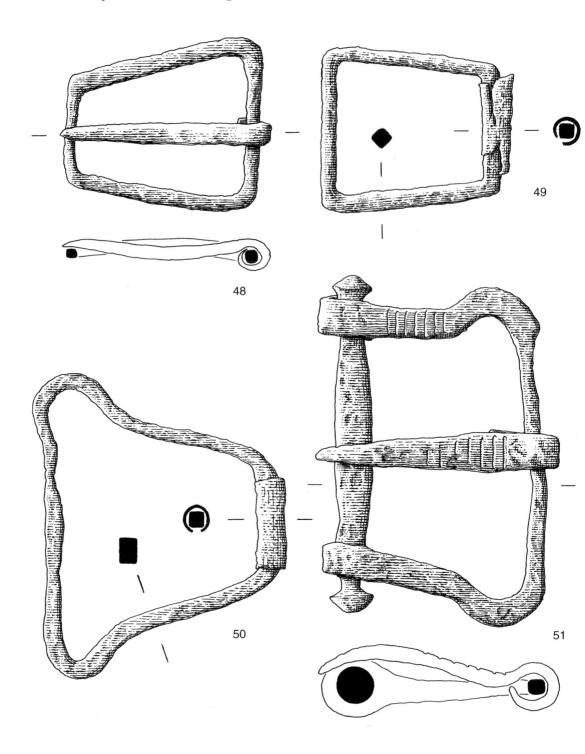

Fig 17. Copper alloy: Cat 48-51, buckles (all iron) (1:1)

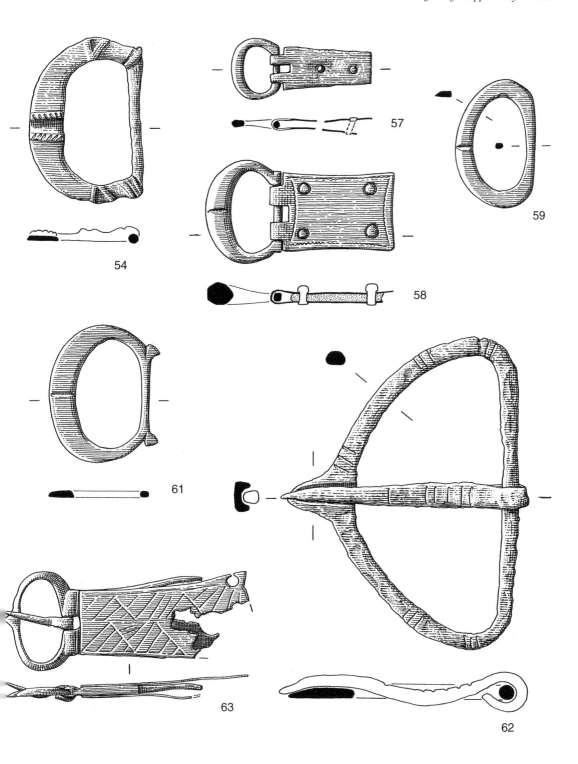

Fig 18. Copper alloy: Cat 54, 57-9, 61-3, buckles (Cat 62 iron) (1:1)

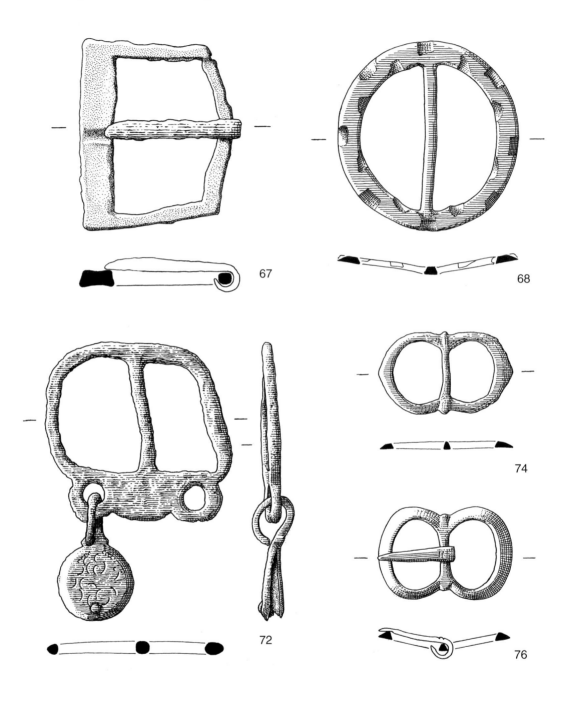

Fig 19. Copper alloy: Cat 67-8, 72, 74, 76, buckles (Cat 67 pewter & iron, Cat 72 iron) (1:1)

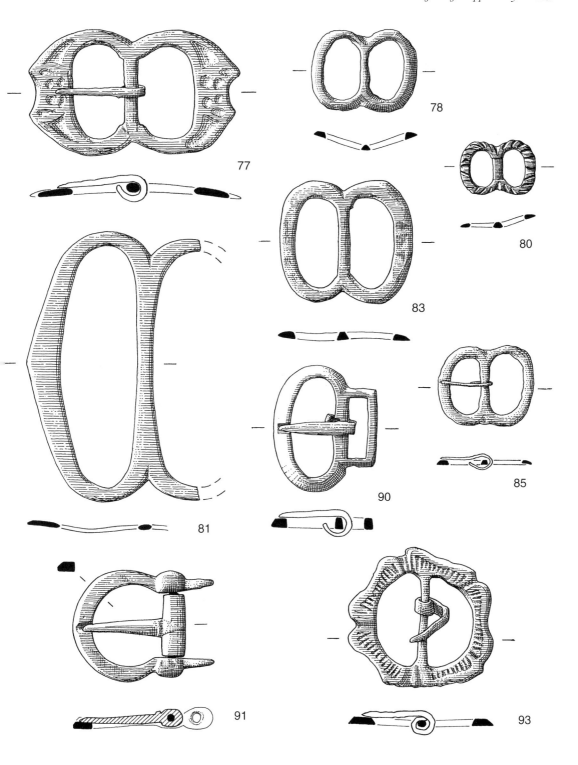

Fig 20. Copper alloy: Cat 77-8, 80-1, 83, 85, 90-1, 93, buckles (Cat 85 with iron) (1:1)

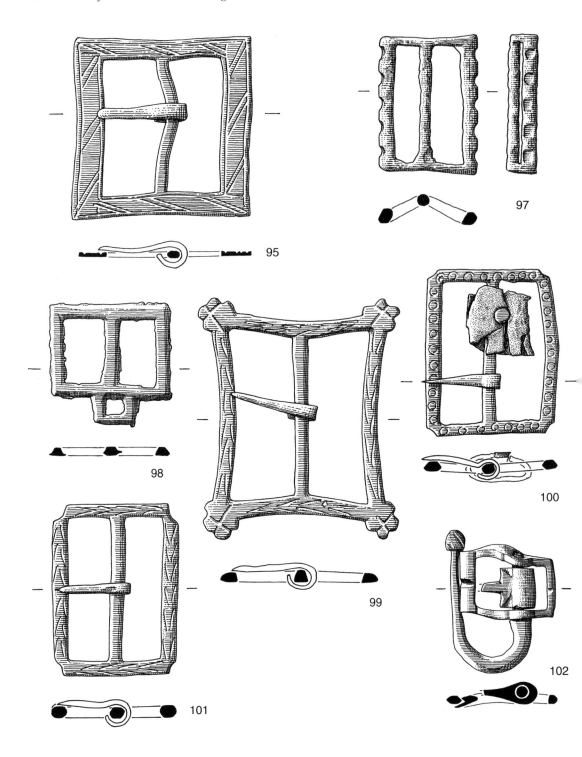

Fig 21. Copper alloy: Cat 95, 97-102, buckles (Cat 97 iron, Cat 100 with leather) (1:1)

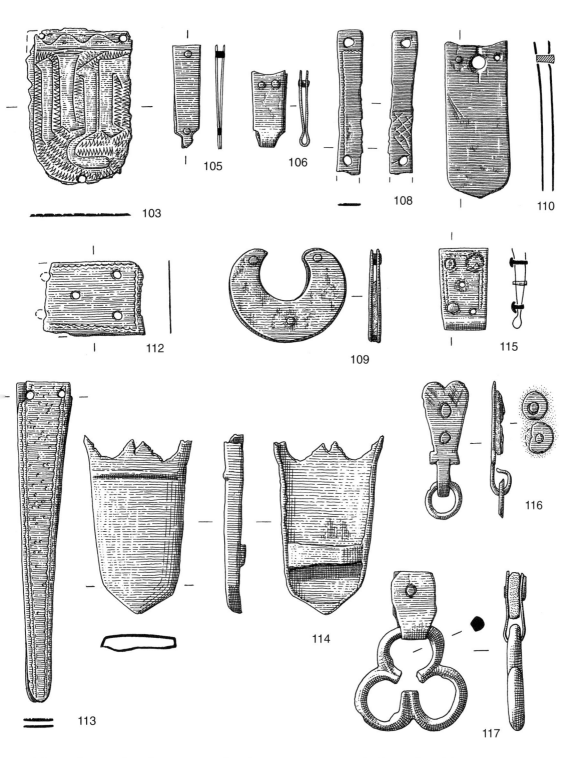

Fig 22. Copper alloy: Cat 103, 105-6, 108-10, 112-7, strap-ends (Cat 116-7 with leather) (1:1)

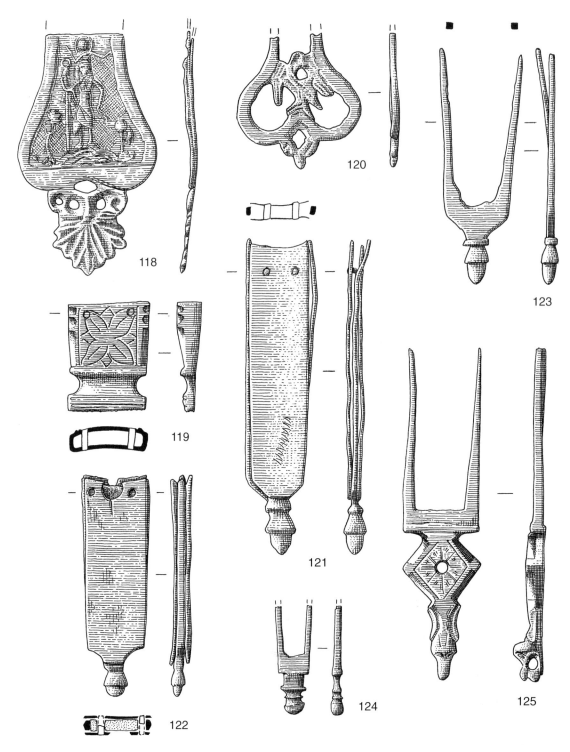

Fig 23. Copper alloy: Cat 118-125, strap-ends (Cat 122 with leather) (1:1)

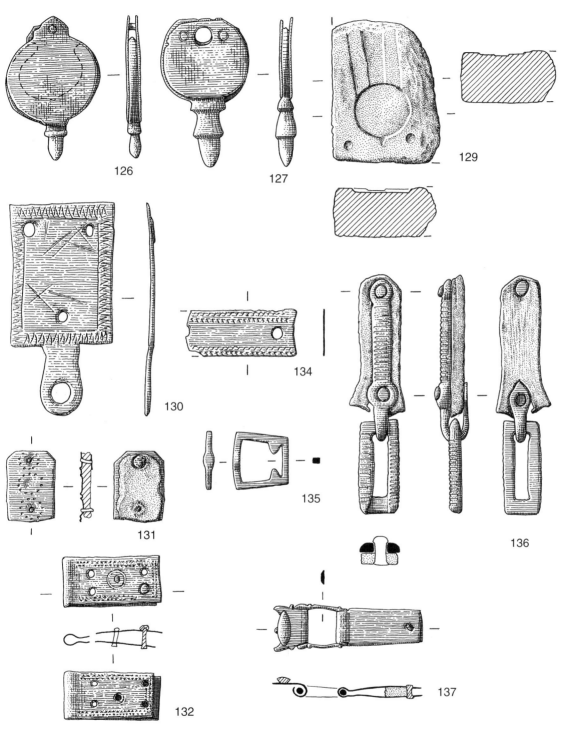

Fig 24. Copper alloy: Cat 126-7, 130-2, strap-ends; Cat 134 buckle plate; Cat 135 belt loop; Cat 136-7, clasps (Cat 131, 136-7 with leather) (1:1); Cat 129, stone mould (1:2)

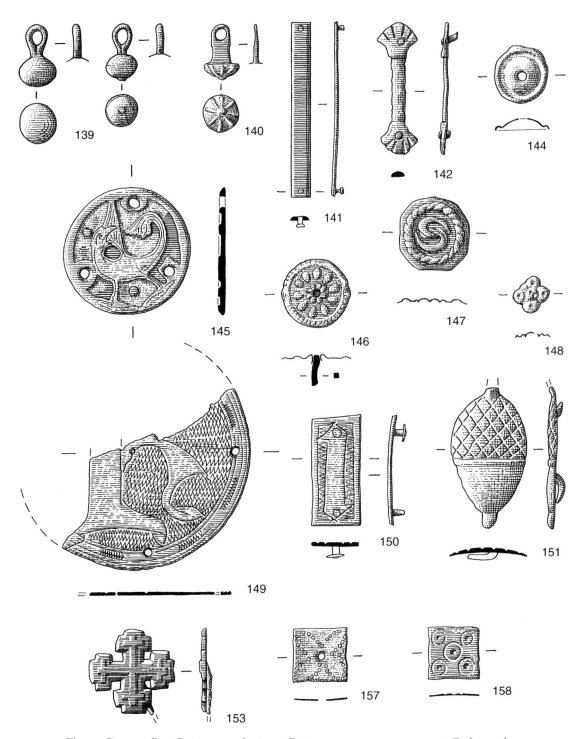

Fig 25. Copper alloy: Cat 139-40, buttons; Cat 141-2, 144-151, 153, 157-8, decorative mounts/ornaments (Cat 145 with enamel, Cat 153 with iron) (1:1)

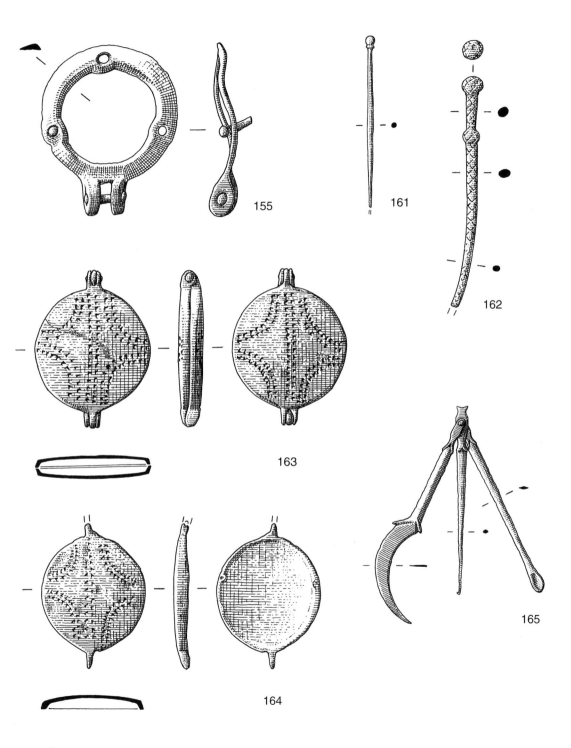

Fig 26. Copper alloy: Cat 155, gilded mount; Cat 161-2, dress pins; Cat 163-4, mirror cases; Cat 165 toilet set (1:1, except Cat 161-2 1:2)

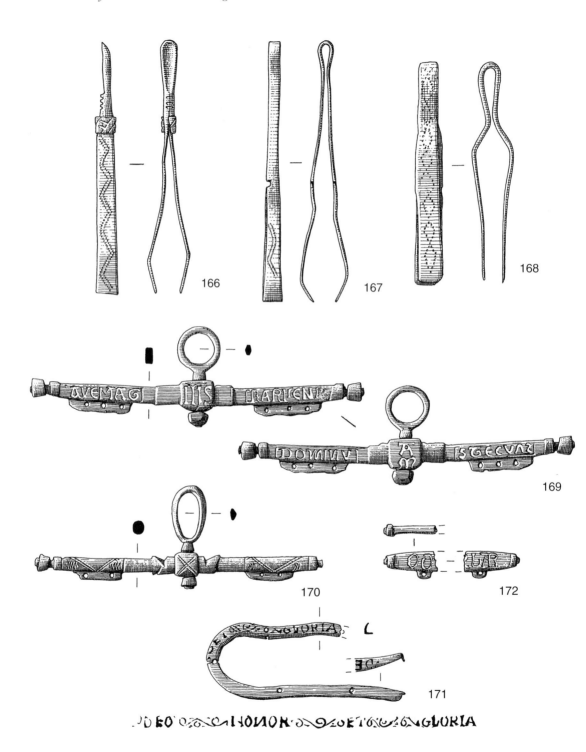

Fig 27. Copper alloy: Cat 166-8, tweezers (1:1); Cat 169-72, purse frames (Cat 171 with niello) (1:2)

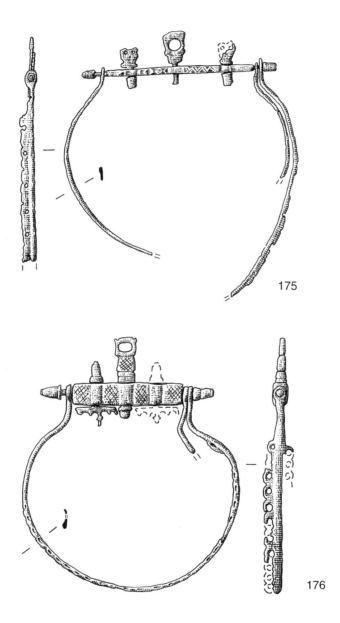

Fig 28. Copper alloy: Cat 175-6, purse frames (both iron) (1:2)

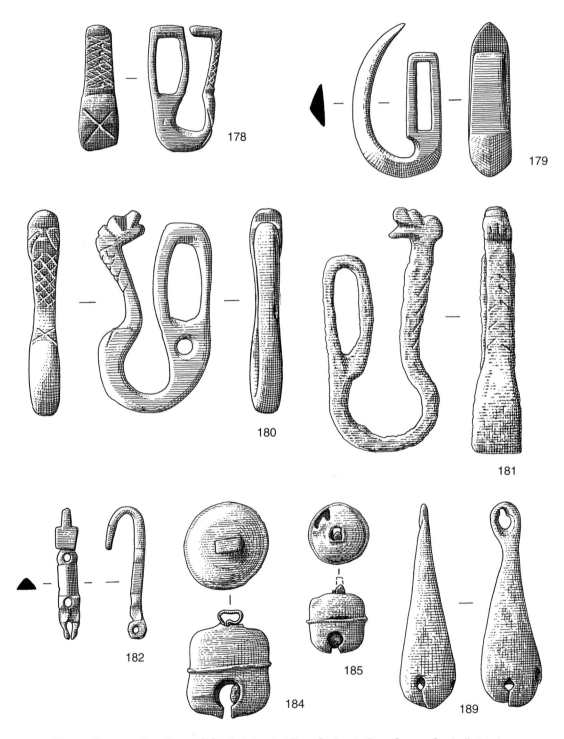

Fig 29. Copper alloy: Cat 178-82, belt hooks (Cat 181 iron); Cat 184-5, 189, bells (1:1)

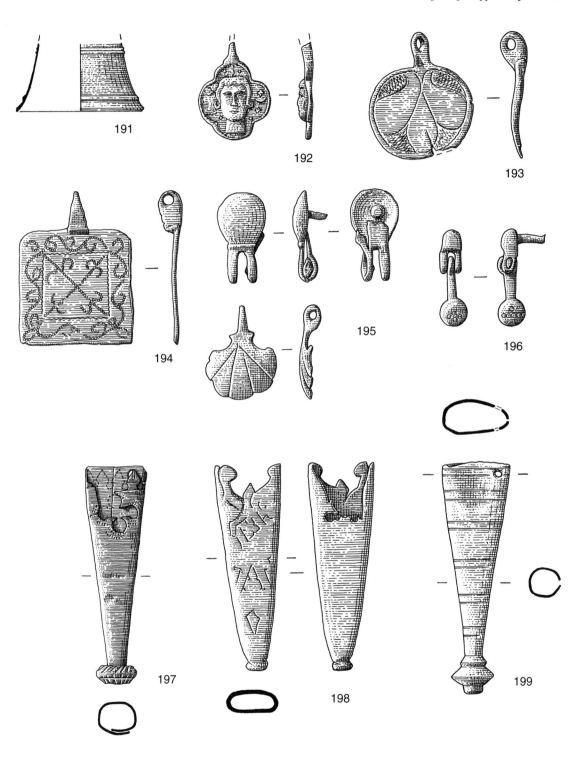

Fig 30. Copper alloy: Cat 191, bell (1:2); Cat 192, 192-6, pendants; Cat 197-9, chapes (1:1)

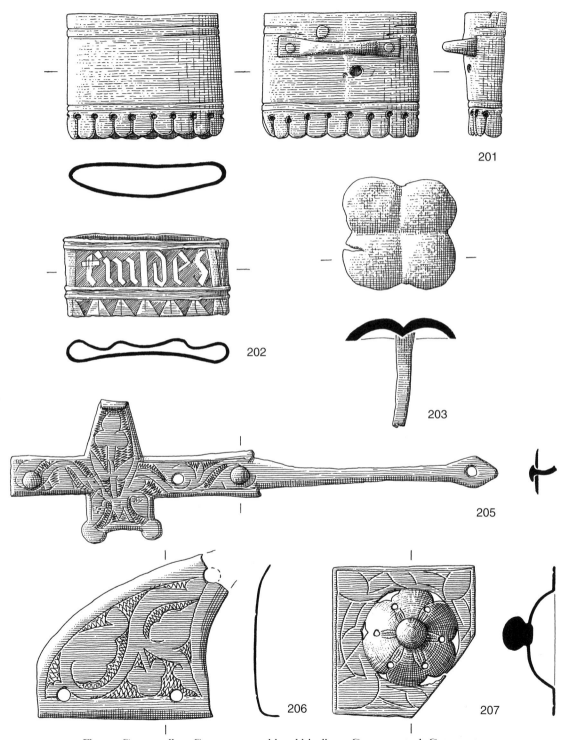

Fig 31. Copper alloy: Cat 201-2, scabbard bindings; Cat 203, stud; Cat 205-7, decorative mounts (Cat 205-6 gilded) (1:1)

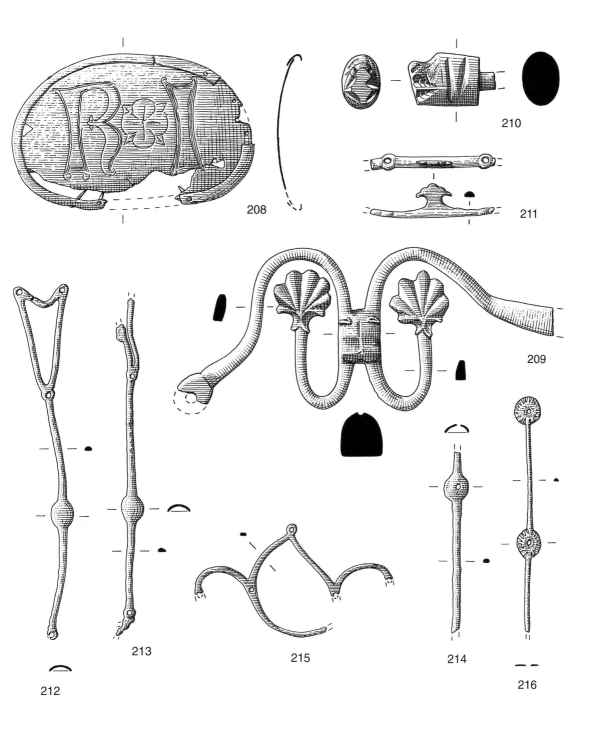

Fig 32. Copper alloy: Cat 208-16, decorative plaque, mounts & bindings (Cat 216 iron, Cat 209, 211-3 gilded) (1:2, except Cat 209-10 1:1)

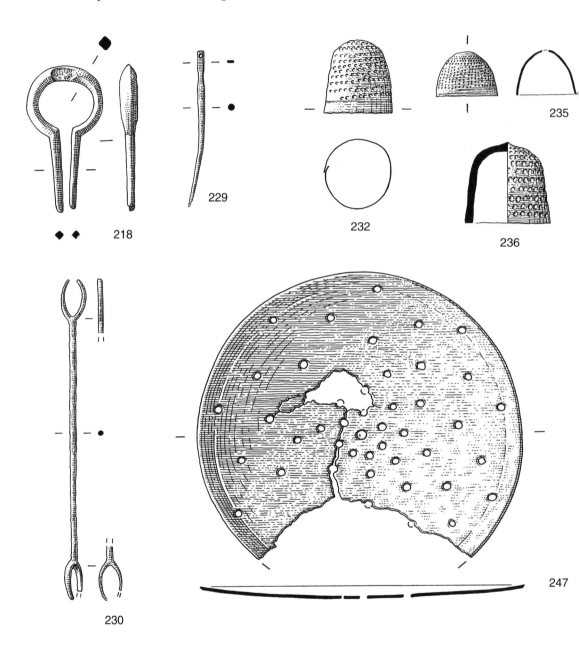

Fig 33. Copper alloy: Cat 218, Jew's harp; Cat 229-30, needles; Cat 232, 235-6, thimbles; Cat 247, skimmer (1:1, except Cat 230, 247 1:2)

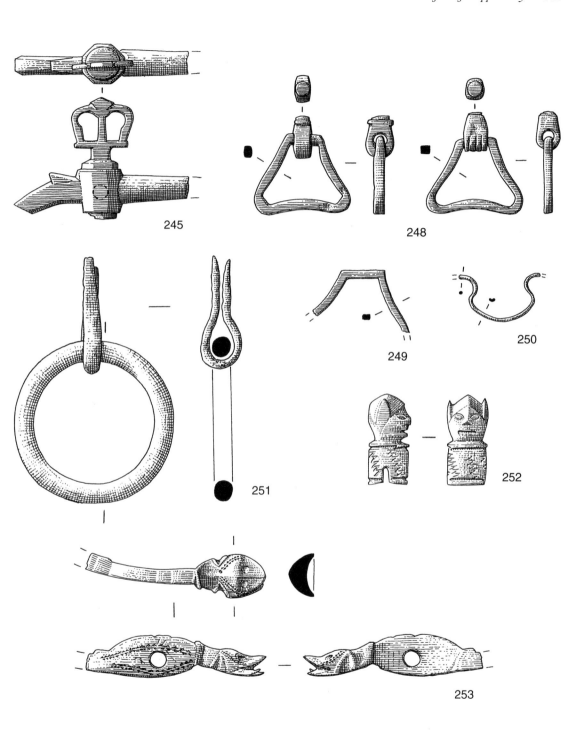

Fig 34. Copper alloy: Cat 245, tap; Cat 248-50, handles; Cat 251, ring; Cat 252, finial; Cat 253, implement (1:2, except Cat 251-3 1:1)

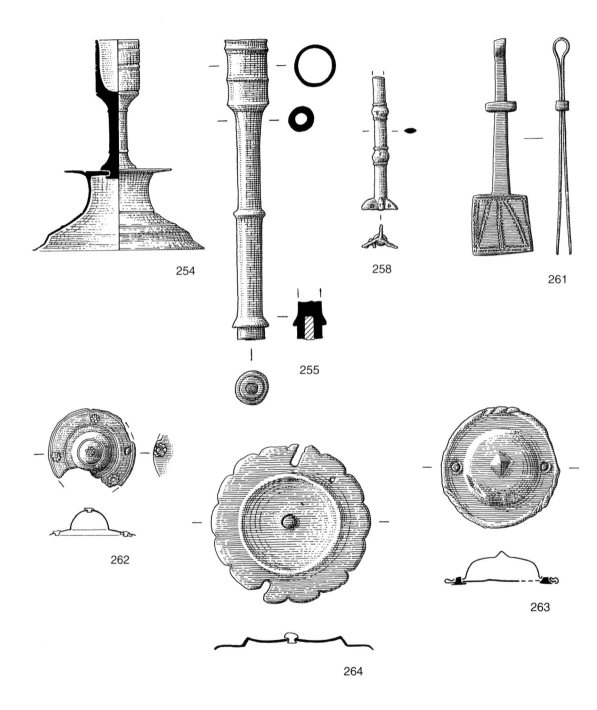

Fig 35. Copper alloy: Cat 254-5, 258, candlesticks; Cat 261, parchment holder; Cat 263-4, bridle bosses
(Cat 263 with iron) (1:2, except Cat 261 1:1)

Objects of Iron

by Jörn Schuster, Peter Saunders and David Algar

INTRODUCTION

The ironwork in the collection is derived essentially from three sources. Firstly, there are objects recovered from dateable contexts, particularly those from excavations at Old Sarum, Clarendon Palace and the deserted medieval village at Gomeldon. Secondly, there are casual finds, notably those from the foundation collection of the Museum, the Drainage Collection, comprising objects recovered from the medieval drainage canals in Salisbury (for an overview of which see Saunders 2009). Thirdly, there are many un-associated finds from the River Avon within the city and from other locations in south Wiltshire. Many of these objects are of forms virtually unchanged from the medieval period until the advent of industrialisation. Of these, emphasis has been given to those that can be dated on typological grounds and are thus most probably of medieval date. There is further south Wiltshire material, much of which may too be of medieval origin but for which direct evidence is lacking and which is thus omitted. This includes some of the iron objects recovered from in and around King John's House, Tollard Royal (Pitt Rivers 1890).

This catalogue follows broadly the order and classification adopted by Ian Goodall in his general survey of the products of the medieval blacksmith (Goodall 1981) and his doctoral thesis, *Ironwork in Medieval Britain: an archaeological survey*, submitted in 1980 and recently published (Goodall 2011). We greatly regret that Ian's untimely death in 2006 prevented him contributing to this catalogue as an author.

Where objects have been made of either iron or copper alloy it has been felt appropriate to catalogue them under the material most commonly used; thus locks and keys of copper alloy are included here, identified by (AE) within the description, while buckles, brooches, belt hooks, purse-frames and jews' harps of iron have been included in the section on copper alloy. For arms and armour and spurs see Part 1 of this catalogue series (Borg 1991, 79-92 and Ellis 1991, 54-78).

Keys, with knives and shears, are particularly numerous. This is perhaps to be expected since very many were recovered from the mid-nineteenth century drainage works (Drainage coll.) at a time when finders would doubtless have been attracted to complete and recognisable objects, whereas today less-appealing fragments would also be collected to enable a broader picture of material culture to be constructed. Given that the wealth of medieval Salisbury was largely founded upon the woollen industry, it is surprising that, apart from shears, so little evidence of textile manufacturing has been collected, perhaps because such items as heckle teeth and tenter hooks have gone unrecognised. Nevertheless, the collection as a whole includes a very wide range of iron objects and its significance as a source of comparison is not to be under-valued.

Of particular note are the exceptionally rare shackles excavated from a grave within the Cathedral at Old Sarum (Cat 238) and a number of pieces of constructional ironwork, including cramps and tie bars, recovered during episodes of restoration on the spire of Salisbury Cathedral (Cat 82-4).

CATALOGUE

Evidence for iron manufacture

1   Seven smithing hearth bottoms. One is plano-convex, D. 100-110mm, Th. 30mm, Wt. *c.*620 g. Half of a second is D. *c.*135mm, Th. 30mm, Wt. *c.*450 g. Found with fragments of slag and iron at Winterbourne Dauntsey, recovered during widening of the A338. *2010.30*

These were associated with seven small thirteenth-century sherds, including two glazed fragments of Laverstock-type fineware. Smithing hearth bottoms form in the blacksmith's hearth during the secondary working of iron and here provide evidence of a medieval roadside smithy at Winterbourne Dauntsey. In the absence of metallurgical analysis the source of the raw material remains uncertain, especially because only very few contemporary primary production sites where ore was smelted are known nationally (Crossley 1981, 30-33). In Wiltshire iron smelting had been carried out at Ramsbury in the Middle Saxon period (Haslam 1980), and only a single medieval, probably twelfth/thirteenth-century, site has been identified, that at Clackers Brook, Melksham (Dungworth 2011). An interesting thirteenth-century roadside smithy at Godmanchester, Cambridgeshire with remains of both furnaces and smithing hearths demonstrates that primary and secondary working did not necessarily have to be spatially separated and that the skills of iron making and blacksmithing could be carried out by the same person (Crossley 1981, 31 and fig. 25).

Metal working tools

2   Hammer-head with two small iron wedges in perforation. L. 85mm. From Old Sarum, east suburb excavations, pit 1. 11th century. Stone and Charlton 1935, 184 and fig. 3, no. 1. *OS.C92; 1934.111; 2000R.7*   **Fig 36**

The head of a claw hammer was also recorded in *O.S. Diary* 1910, 20 as having been found in a garderobe pit within the castle.

3   Square-ended punch; other end has slight burring. L. 100mm. From Gomeldon, building 3. 13th-14th century. Musty and Algar 1986, 154 and fig. 13, no. 29. *1967.148.5.20*   **Fig 36**

There is another iron object from Gomeldon, building 1 that has been described as a punch (Musty and Algar 1986, 154 and fig. 13, no. 30), but this attribution is considered doubtful.

4   Tongs. L. 197mm. One arm has a ball terminal. Casual find from Old Sarum. Goodall 2011, 12 no. A23 and fig. 2.4. *OS.D2; 2000R.34*   **Fig 36**

These are most likely metalworker's tongs but other uses are possible, even tooth extraction. Similar tongs have been found at Degannwy Castle, Gwynedd (Goodall 1981, 51 and fig. 50, no. 1) and at Faccombe Netherton (Fairbrother 1990, 403 and fig. 9.1, no. 10).

Wood working tools

Without a securely dated context utilitarian objects like many woodworking tools have a potentially wide date range: from the Roman to the modern period. While there is a range of tools found in Salisbury, they are not all demonstrably medieval.

5   Carpenter's axe head. L. 192mm. W. of cutting edge 304mm. Found while digging foundations at the Downton tannery. Stevens 1931, 489-90. *1930.176*   **Fig 37**

Comparisons for such T-shaped axe heads from London (Ward-Perkins 1940, 57-8 fig. 12, 3), Milk Street, London (Pritchard in Vince 1991, 137 fig. 3.14) and the Flixborough hoard (Ottaway in Evans and Loveluck 2009, 262-4 figs 7.6-7) illustrate their date range, covering the eighth to thirteenth century.

6   Bearded axe head with winged socket and square hammer butt. There is a maker's mark of three G's on the cheek. L. 203mm. W. of cutting edge 188mm. Found during demolition work at Fisherton Mill, Salisbury. Late medieval. *Sal. Mus. Rep.* 1970-1, 22 and pl. IVA. *1970.94*   **Fig 38**

7   Gimlet. L. 95mm. Head of shaft is split and

ends are forged to form a hollow T-shaped grip. Drainage coll. Egan 1998, 146 and fig. 114. *SD340; 2007R.323*   **Fig 36**

The T-shaped grip was an ideal handle form for use with a rotary tool. There is also a damaged example from the Drainage coll. (*SD343; 1999R.28.3*).

8 Gimlet bit. L. 130mm. From Clarendon Palace. Goodall 1988, 208 and fig. 73, no. 1. *1957.47*   **Fig 36**

9 Auger spoon bit. L. 124mm. Drainage coll. *SD331; 1999R.23.5*   **Fig 36**

This and four others from the Drainage coll. (*1999R.23.2* and *.8-10*) have wedge-shaped narrowing tangs.

Stone working tools

10 Plummet. Circular section, with hook for attachment to a line. L. 172mm. From Clarendon Palace, Goodall 1988, 208 and fig. 73, no. 2. *1957.47*   **Fig 36**

Leather working tools

11 Tanged knife with upturned blade. L. (overall) 99mm. Found on allotments at Great Wishford. *Sal. Mus. Rep.* 1967-8, 18 and pl. IIb. *1968.21*   **Fig 36**

Perhaps fifteenth century. For a comparable example from the Thames at Wandsworth see Ward Perkins 1940, 52 and pl. xi, 4.

12 Currier's knife blade. L. (overall) 135mm. Blade-smith's mark: H. Drainage coll. *SD283; 2007R.314*   **Fig 36**

For a comparable example, dated *c*.1400, see Moore 1999, 77. There is another, similar but much corroded, example (*1999R.12.7*) from the Drainage coll.

There are two currier's knives in material from The Millstream, Salisbury, recovered in 1975, which from the context must be fifteenth century or later (*2005.1*), and fourteen from the Drain-

age coll. of a more elongated form, which are considered to be post-medieval.

Agricultural tools

13 Sickle blade, parallel-sided, tip missing, cutting edge, L. (surviving) *c*.230mm. W. (max) 28mm. Square-sectioned whittle tang, L. *c*.90mm. From Clarendon Palace. Goodall 1988, 208 and fig. 73, no. 3. *1957.47*   **Fig 38**

Knives, shears and scissors

In the eighteenth and nineteenth centuries, the cutlers of Salisbury had their premises around the Market Place or in the streets immediately adjacent to it, a pattern most probably established in the medieval period. Sebode le Cutiller is recorded as holder of a tenement in Brown Street at the end of the thirteenth century (Wordsworth 1903, 146). The 'increased sophistication and self-consciousness of the craftsmen themselves', considered to be an important factor in the development of craft guilds in the thirteenth century (Grew in Cowgill *et al.* 1987, viii-x), led to the appearance of cutlers' marks on the blades of some knives and shears. With regard to the detection of these marks on blades, it should be noted that as a consequence of further analysis by conservators of 25 blades from London, it was found that about a third of these had marks, inlays etc. that were not visible from the x-radiographs (Egan in Cowgill *et al.* 2000, x). Unfortunately, no records of medieval Salisbury cutlers' marks have yet come to light that would link the marks on blades in the collection to named cutlers.

In Salisbury, as early as September 1440, the 'Cotelers' were a part of a guild that included pewterers and saddlers. These trades were referred to in the minutes of a meeting called by the Corporation in connection with raising money to complete the city's defences (Haskins 1912, 59-61). During the reign of Elizabeth I this guild was united with that of the smiths to form one company, which now included all the metal working trades. 'The Companye of Smythes' was the first to be reconstituted under the new Charter of Incorporation given to the City by James I in 1612 (Haskins 1912, 370-1). In the post-medieval period Salisbury cutlery was to be compared favourably with that from London and Sheffield; in an old saying Salisbury had become famed for:

> *The height of its steeple,*
> *The pride of its people,*
> *Its scissors and knives,*
> *And diligent wives.*

Knives

While no chronological assertions can be based on the collection from Salisbury, it is clear from other English sites (see, for example, London: Cowgill *et al.* 1987; 2000, 25) that knife handles before the early fourteenth century were virtually all attached to whittle tangs. After a hiatus since the Roman period, when scale-tang blades were in widespread use throughout the empire, this form of handle attachment becomes increasingly more common again during the fourteenth century, having made its re-appearance around the mid-thirteenth century (see, for example, Winchester: Goodall 1990a, 838–9; compare also Goodall in Margeson 1993, 128). While scale tangs are lacking in the collection from Coppergate, York, where substantial thirteenth to fourteenth-century deposits had been excavated (Ottaway and Rogers 2002, 2751; 2762), London provides the most extensive collection from well-dated contexts (Cowgill *et al.* 1987; 2000), with other important collections for instance from Winchester (Goodall 1990a) and Norwich (Margeson 1993). Ian Goodall developed a typological series for knives based on shape (ten whittle-tang and six scale tang types, see Goodall 2011, 106-8, fig. 8.2-3) but we have relied on description rather than following him since the original outlines of the majority of the knives here are now uncertain.

Whittle-tang blades

The distinguishing feature of the whittle-tanged knife is that it has a handle, typically cylindrical, knocked onto a tang. The latter is tapering and usually of rectangular section and, in the period considered here, is typically central to the blade.

14 Knife. Blade, straight-backed, perhaps with a slight channel. L. (surviving) 150mm. W. (max.) 21mm. Tang central to blade. L. (overall) 189mm. From Clarendon Palace, Goodall 1988, 211 and fig. 73, no. 4. *1957.47*   **Fig 39**

15 Knife. Blade, straight-backed, sloping shoulder, tip broken away. L. (surviving) 96mm. W. (max.) 20mm. Tang set slightly nearer line of back. L. (overall) 139mm. Found in the east suburb of Old Sarum during road construction, 1931-2. *1932.8; OS.C136*

16 Knife. Blade, slightly curved back, with a single swage. L. (surviving) *c.*115mm. W. (max.) 23mm. Tang central to blade. L. (overall) 160mm. From Clarendon Palace, Goodall 1988, 211 and fig. 74, no. 13. *1957.47*   **Fig 39**

17 Knife. Blade, edge curving to straight back. L. 143mm. W. (max.) 20mm. Tang central to blade. L. (overall) 184mm. Found under a medieval pottery kiln at Laverstock. 13th century. *1967.145* **Fig 39**

18 Knife. Blade, with straight back and downward sloping edge, end of blade missing, straight shoulder and choil. Tang, L. 53mm, set slightly nearer line of back. L. (overall surviving) 101mm. Drainage coll. *SD403; 1999R.888*   **Fig 39**
  Compare Cowgill *et al.* 1987, 86 no. 55 and fig. 58 of early-mid fourteenth-century date.

19 Knife. Blade, with slightly curved back. L. 135mm. W. (max) 17mm at about the mid-point. Cutler's mark: ?crescent over an M, impressed twice. Remains of parallel-sided tang, almost aligned with the back of the blade. L. (overall) 156mm. Drainage coll. *SD402; 1999R.889*   **Fig 39**

20 Knife. Blade, curved back, lacking tip. L. (surviving) 103mm. W. 15mm. Tang central to blade. L. (overall) 162mm. From Clarendon Palace, Goodall 1988, 211 and fig. 74, no. 15. *1957.47*   **Fig 39**

21 Knife. Blade, with triangular section and slightly

curved back, Th. (max) 4mm.; sloping shoulder. L. 82mm. W. (max) 11mm. Square tang, central to blade. L. (overall) 100mm. Drainage coll. *SD400; 1999R.886*   **Fig 39**

For a comparable blade of late thirteenth-century date see Cowgill *et al.* 1987, 82 no. 28 and fig. 55.

22 Knife. Blade, slightly curved back. L. (surviving) 92mm. W. (max.) 14mm. Square tang, central to blade. L. (overall) 140mm. From Clarendon Palace, Goodall 1988, 211 and fig. 73, no. 7. *1957.47*   **Fig 39**

23 Knife. Blade, straight-backed, lacking tip, back has a swage on both sides along entire remaining length, sloping shoulder. L. (surviving) 61mm. W. (max) 13mm. Cutler's mark: T, inlaid with copper alloy. Tang central to blade. L. (overall) 125mm. From Clarendon Palace, Goodall 1988, 211 and fig. 74, no. 14. *1957.47.33*   **Fig 39**

This is the only blade from Clarendon Palace with a visible cutler's mark.

There are seven other whittle-tang blades from Clarendon Palace: see Goodall 1988, 211.

24 Knife. Blade, straight-backed, tip broken off, but wear suggests it continued to be used. L. (surviving) 90mm. W. (max) 16mm. Trace of cutler's mark. Copper-alloy hilt plate. Tang extends beyond the end of a bone handle, the end cap of which is missing. The handle, which is set in line with the back of the blade, has its end decorated with 6 ring-and-dot patterns set between 2 transverse lines. L. (overall) 170mm. From the River Avon, Bridge Street, Salisbury. *1993.1*   **Fig 39**

25 Knife. Blade, parallel-sided, the back sloping down to the tip. L. (surviving) 180mm. W. 36mm. Tang central to blade. L. (overall) 231mm. Excavated in Brown Street, Salisbury. 13th to early 14th century. Loader 2000, 29. *2006R.1*   **Fig 40**

X-radiography suggests construction from iron with a steel cutting edge.

26 Knife. Blade, straight-backed. L. 127mm. W. (max.) 36mm. Possible traces of a sheath. The stub of the central tang has traces of a wooden handle. The lack of rivets suggests that this is the remains of a whittle-tang knife. L. (overall) 155mm. From excavations in the east suburb at Old Sarum 1958, bottom of pit 1. 12th-13th century. Musty and Rahtz 1964, 143 and fig. 5, no. 4. *OS.C58; 1963.76*   **Fig 40**

27 Knife. Blade, parallel-sided with the back curving down to the tip. Slight groove, parallel with the back, on both sides; sloping shoulder. L. 105mm. W. (max. surviving) 22mm. Tang central to blade. L. (overall) 150mm. ?Drainage coll. *2007R.230*   **Fig 40**

28 Knife. Blade, back curving down to the tip. Straight cutting-edge. L. 130mm. W. (max.) 24mm. Cutler's mark: irregular X, inlaid with copper alloy. Stub of probable whittle tang aligned with the back of the blade. L. (overall surviving) 142mm. From Old Sarum, possibly the knife found in 1910 near the east end of the 'hall'. ?14th century. *O.S. Diary* 1910, 24. *1920-1.30; OS.C139*   **Fig 40**

29 Knife. Blade, triangular, with straight back sloping down to the tip. L. 82mm. W. (max.) 22mm. Tang central to blade. L. (overall) 133mm. Found in the east suburb of Old Sarum during road construction, 1931-2. *1932.8; OS.C137*   **Fig 40**

30 Knife. Blade, probably parallel-sided. L. (surviving) 20mm. Oval-sectioned horn handle, L. 82mm, rough filing marks from rasp all over surface. From the River Avon, Bridge Street, Salisbury. *1993.1*   **Fig 40**

A similarly-shaped handle comes from Billingsgate Lorry Park, London, but this one is attached to a scale tang (Cowgill *et al.* 1987, 95 no. 133 and fig. 65).

Scale-tang blades

The scale-tanged knife has a handle made using scales or plates, typically of wood, bone or horn, affixed to a flat tang, which extends to the whole length of the handle. More components are required for this type of knife than the whittle-tang and thus greater opportunity exists for decoration.

31 Knife. Blade, straight-backed and with plain copper-alloy shoulder plates extending beyond first rivet. L. 103mm. W. (max) 14mm. Tang is in line with the back of blade and has bone scales held by 3 small iron rivets and top end of scales with at least 4 notches. L. (overall) 194mm. Found in the Mill-stream, Salisbury. *1986.8*   **Fig 40**

Compare a knife from Barentin's Manor, Chalgrove, Oxfordshire, from an early to mid-fourteenth-century context, which has undulating scale ends with one notch but open rivets (Page *et al*. 2005, 94 fig. 3.17, 15), and an example from Swan Lane, London from an early to mid-fifteenth century context, with two grooves at the scale end (Cowgill *et al*. 1987, 102 no. 264 and fig. 66).

32 Knife. Blade, straight-backed and pointed, with decorated copper-alloy shoulder plates. L. 87mm. W. (max) 10mm. Cutler's mark. Flat tang in line with back of blade, scales absent and no rivets apparent. L. (overall) 132mm. Drainage coll. *üC21; 1999R.883*

33 Knife. Blade, straight-backed, incomplete, probably parallel-sided, and with copper-alloy shoulder plates extending beyond first rivet. L. (surviving) 65mm. W. (max) 15mm. Tang in line with back of blade, wooden scales fastened with three remaining iron rivets. L. (surviving) 136mm. From the River Avon, Bridge Street, Salisbury. *1993.1*

See a late fourteenth-century example from London (Cowgill *et al*. 1987, 95 no. 122 and fig. 64).

34 Knife. Blade, back curving down to the tip, with copper-alloy shoulder plates. L. (surviving) 67mm. W. 15mm. Broken parallel-sided tang in line with back of blade, bone/wood scales and single rivet remaining. L. (overall surviving) 110mm. From Clarendon Palace, Goodall 1988, 211 and fig. 74, no. 19. *1957.47*   **Fig 40**

35 Knife. Blade, slightly curved back, tip missing. L. (surviving) 102mm. W. (max) 14mm. Tang in line with back of blade and rounded at the end, 3 tubular copper-alloy rivets. L. (overall) 194mm. From Clarendon Palace, Goodall 1988, 211 and fig. 74, no. 16. *1957.47*   **Fig 40**

36 Knife. Blade, narrow tapering blade, slightly curved, tip missing. L. 143mm. W. (max) 13mm. Tang in line with back of blade, incomplete, with 1 surviving rivet. L. (overall surviving) 172mm. From excavations in the east suburb at Old Sarum 1958. 13th-14th century *Sal. Mus. Rep.* 1962-3, 23 and pl. Ib, Musty and Rahtz 1964, 143 and fig. 5, no. 3. *OS.C56; 1963.75*   **Fig 41**

37 Knife. Blade, parallel-sided, broken tip. L. 95mm. W. 18mm. Tang in line with back of blade and retaining 2 iron rivets. L. (overall surviving) 156mm. From Gomeldon, building 1. Musty and Algar 1986, 154 and fig. 13, no. 26 (where drawing incorrectly shows three holes rather than two rivets). *1967.148.5.19.2*

38 Knife. Blade, straight-backed, parallel-sided, angled down to tip. L. 110mm. W. 17mm. Tang broken away at the first rivet hole. L. (overall surviving) 114mm. From Gomeldon, building 6. Late 13th-14th century. Musty and Algar 1986, 154 and fig. 13, no. 25. *1967.148.5.19.1*

39 Knife. Blade fragment, L. *c*.25mm. Handle-shaped tang, in line with back of blade, 4 iron rivets. L. (overall surviving) 141mm. From Clarendon Palace, Goodall 1988, 211 and fig. 74, no. 17. *1957.47*   **Fig 41**

There is a fragment of one other scale-tang blade from Clarendon Palace: see Goodall 1988, 211 and fig. 74 no. 18.

40 Knife. Blade. L. (surviving) 8mm. Tang with wooden scales held by 3 rivets, probably copper-alloy. L. 81mm. From the site of the Franciscan Friary, Salisbury. *Sal. Mus. Rep.* 1969-70, 19. *1969.81.15*

Compare Cowgill *et al*. 1987, 95 no. 135 and fig. 65. Late fourteenth century.

41 Knife. Blade, straight-backed and slender. L. 70mm. W. (max) 9mm. Tang in line with back of blade with ?bone scales in the shape of the tang, held with 3 iron rivets; small choil still in place when first seen, now missing. L. (overall surviving) 143mm. From the River Avon, Bridge Street, Salisbury. *1993.1*

42 Knife. Blade, straight-backed, tip missing. L. 68mm. W. (max surviving) 12mm. Tang in line with back of blade, with bone scales, expanded and serrated at the end, held by 3 rivets. L. (overall surviving) 138mm. From excavations in the east suburb at Old Sarum 1958. 13th-14th century. *Sal. Mus. Rep.* 1962-3, 23 and pl. Ib, Musty and Rahtz 1964, 143 and fig. 5, no. 2. *OS.C57; 1963.75*   **Fig 41**

43 Knife. Blade, parallel-sided. L. 64mm. W. (max) 11mm. Tang in line with back of blade, with 4 rivet holes and oval copper-alloy end plate. L. (overall) 147mm. Drainage coll. Late medieval. *SD417; 1999R.900*   **Fig 41**
The tip of the blade was probably broken and the blade end subsequently rounded for further use. For a similarly tanged blade compare Cowgill *et al.* 1987, 95 no. 137 and fig. 65.

44 Knife. Blade, straight-backed. L. 65mm. W. (max) 14mm. Cutler's mark, copper-alloy inlaid. Tang in line with back of blade, with 4 rivets and part of a bone scale. L. (overall) 141mm. From Old Sarum excavations 1909-15. 14th-15th century. Goodall 2011, 140 no. G304 and fig. 8.20. *1920-1.30; OS.C142*   **Fig 41**

45 Knife. Blade, straight-backed, pointed. L. 100mm. W. (max) 14mm. Tang in line with back of blade, with 4 rivet holes. L. (overall) 182mm. From Old Sarum excavations 1909-15. 14th-15th century. Goodall 2011, 140 no. G305 and fig. 8.20. *1920-1.30; OS.C141*   **Fig 41**

46 Knife. Blade, straight-backed, cutting edge rises to tip. Copper-alloy shoulder plates. L. 126mm. W. (max) 19mm. Cutler's mark. Tang in line with back of blade. Parts of both scales, of leather, held by 4 rivets, end cap missing. L. (overall) 222mm. ?Drainage coll. *iiC45; 2007R.237*   **Fig 41**
Compare similar tang shapes from late fourteenth-century contexts in London (Cowgill *et al.* 1987, 95 no. 122–3 and fig. 64).

47 Knife. Blade, parallel-sided, broken end. Copper-alloy shoulder plates up to first rivet L. (surviving) 54mm. W. 13mm. Tang in line with back of blade, bone scales with 3 iron rivets and ?copper-alloy lined end hole for suspension, thick copper-alloy oval end plate, tang protruding as end knob. L. (overall) 134mm. Drainage coll. *SD415; 1999R.898*
Compare Cowgill *et al.* 1987, 105 no. 308 and fig. 68 for an undated London example and Goodall in Margeson 1993, 130 fig. 95, 855 for a Norwich tang dated 1550-1700.

48 Knife. Blade, 'scramasax' derivative. Serrated weld line between steel cutting edge and iron back. Groove along one side parallel to and near back of blade. L. 138mm. W. (max) 23mm. Tang in line with back of blade, 3 rivet holes and bone end-pieces held by a single pin. L. (overall) 222mm. Drainage coll. *SD405; 2007R.232*   **Fig 41 & cover**
For shape of blade only, compare Ward Perkins 1940, pl. 11, 5. See Cowgill *et al.* 1987, 95 no. 136 and fig. 65 for a similar two-part welded blade.

49 Knife. Blade, straight-backed and parallel-sided, tip missing. L. (surviving) 117mm. W. (max) 16mm. Tang in line with back of blade, with 3 rivets hold bone/wood scales and a protruding 'rustic' end-piece of copper-alloy. L. (overall) 185mm. Unprovenanced. *iiC26; 2007R.243*   **Fig 42**

50 Knife. Blade, straight-backed triangular. L. 110mm. W. (max) 13mm. Cutler's mark. Shoulder plates. Tang in line with back of blade. Wooden scales held by 3 copper-alloy washered rivets and decorated with copper-alloy pins. L. (overall) 188mm. Drainage coll. *iiC19; 2007R.239*   **Fig 42**

51 Knife. Blade, incomplete, straight-backed. L. (surviving) 69mm. W. (surviving) 18mm Cutler's mark. Copper-alloy shoulder plates, held by first rivet. ?bone scales with 14 decorative tubular iron rivets in line along entire length of handle with 4 set in a lozenge pattern near the end. From the River Avon, Salisbury. Late 14th century. *1987.211.1*   **Fig 42**
Compare knives from Meols (Griffiths *et al.* 2007, 207 pl. 39, 2686) and a late fourteenth-century context at Baynard's Castle Dock, London (Cowgill *et al.* 1987, 95 no. 126 and fig. 64).

52 Knife. Blade, straight-backed   L. 74mm. W. (max) 16mm. Cutler's mark. Decorated copper-alloy shoulder plate. Tang in line with back of blade; 6 rivet holes, two larger ones placed centrally and a pair of smaller ones near each end; 3 rivets survive; large heart-shaped opening below end plate, which is decorated with 2 saltires set in squares; L. (overall) 165mm. Drainage coll. ?Late 15th-16th century. *üC6; 2007R.244*   **Fig 42**

The profile of the back of this knife is noticeable for its gentle curve. Compare Moore 1999, 294 where a tang with a similar heart-shaped perforation is illustrated.

Cat 53-4 come from late in the period considered in this catalogue. Comparable examples include a knife handle with three tubular rivets comes from Old Council House, Bristol, found in a context dated late fifteenth century to 1675 (Jackson 2007, 67 fig. 26, 4). Two handle fragments from Barentin's Manor, Chalgrove, Oxfordshire, come from contexts dated late fourteenth to early fifteenth century and mid to late fifteenth century respectively (Page *et al.* 2005, 94 fig. 3.17. 22–23). A knife with a closely comparable ornamental pattern of similarly arranged tubular rivets was found at Nürings castle near Falkenstein, Taunus, Germany, probably destroyed in 1366, thus corroborating the date range of the Chalgrove knives (Müller 1996, 156 Abb. 2, 7). An undated knife with only one perforated rivet near the end of the handle, probably for suspension from the belt, and a ?tin/lead alloy shoulder plate comes from London (Cowgill *et al.* 1987, 105 no. 308 and fig. 68).

53 Knife. Blade stub. L. 13mm. W. (max) 16mm. Decorated copper-alloy shoulder plates. Tang incomplete with at least 9 cylindrical perforations, 4 of which retain decorative tubular copper-alloy rivets. L. (surviving) 81mm. From the River Avon, Bridge Street, Salisbury. *1993.1*   **Fig 42**

54 Knife. Scale tang, broken away at first of three rivet holes. The end is rounded and has a larger hole containing a tubular copper-alloy rivet, and a U-shaped copper-alloy end plate. L. 100mm. From the River Avon, Bridge Street, Salisbury. Probably late fifteenth century. *1993.1*

Cat 55-62 comprise a group of late medieval knives, all from Salisbury, which are characterised by base-metal fillets soldered around the edges of their tangs. It has been suggested (Moore 1999, 267) that the style belongs to a group of precursors of the Flemish import period and, on the basis of the discovery in Salisbury of knives of a Flemish/Dutch style, that local cutlers may have copied the style or even that possibly a Flemish or Dutch cutler was able to set up in business in Salisbury. No direct evidence, however, has been found to corroborate this. Such knives were popular imports in London in the fifteenth century (Moore 1999, 70-2) and may equally have been so in Salisbury.

55 Knife. Blade, straight-backed, curving down to point. L. 121mm. W. (max) 15mm. Cutler's mark. Tang in line with back of blade, with latten or pewter edging strips creating recesses into which the scales would have fitted; 3 rivet holes and a larger hole (?for suspension) near expanded end. L. (overall) 198mm. Drainage coll. Moore 1999, 267 and first pl. on 269, [no.1]. *üC18*   **Fig 42**

56 Knife. Blade, broken. L. 35mm. Copper-alloy shoulder plates. Tang expands towards a scalloped end, 4 rivet holes, 2 with iron rivets surviving. Sides bound with decorative copper-alloy edging, with separate piece shaped for the end. L. (overall) 110mm. From the River Avon, Bridge Street, Salisbury. Probably late fifteenth century. *1993.1*   **Fig 42**

57 Knife. Blade, straight-backed, edge curves up to point. L. 117mm. W. (max) 14mm. Cutler's mark. Tang with copper-alloy shoulder plates and a scalloped end plate, linked with plain latten or pewter edging strips, which create recesses into which scales would have fitted; 3 rivet holes, one of which contains a tubular rivet and traces of wooden scale on one side. L. (overall) 199mm. Leather sheath, damaged impressed with two opposed plant-like devices. L. (surviving) 117mm. W. *c*.17mm. Drainage coll. *üC31 1999R.905*   **Fig 42**

58 Knife. Blade, broken and parallel-sided. L. 30mm. W. 13mm. Tang in line with back of blade, wooden scales framed within a latten or pewter edging strip; at the flat end the tip of the tang just protrudes. L. (overall surviving) 116mm. From the River Avon, Bridge Street, Salisbury. *1993.1*   **Fig 42**

59 Knife. Blade, straight-backed, cutting edge curves up to tip. L. 79mm. W. (max) 10mm. Tang in line with back of blade, with copper-alloy shoulder plates and an edging, decorated with impressed design reminiscent of wrigglework. L. (overall) 138mm. Drainage coll. *üC17; 2007R.241*   **Fig 43**

60 Knife. Blade, straight-backed and parallel-sided. L. 99mm. W. 13mm. Tang in line with back of blade, copper-alloy shoulder plates, oval end-cap and an edging decorated with impressed design reminiscent of wrigglework; tang end protrudes as a simple 'tenon'. L. (overall) 175mm. Moore 1999, 267 and pl. on 269, [no. 2]. Drainage coll. *SD409; 1999R.892*

61 Knife. Blade, parallel-sided. L. 96mm. W. 11mm. Tang in line with back of blade, copper-alloy shoulder plates; surviving part of copper-alloy edging, decorated with impressed design reminiscent of wrigglework. End cap missing. L. (overall) 169mm. Moore 1999, 267 and pl. on 269, [no. 3]. Drainage coll. *SD411; 1999R.894*

This and Cat 60 may be from the same maker.

62 Knife. Blade, parallel-sided. L. 123mm. W. 15mm. ?Cutler's mark. Tang in line with back of blade, copper-alloy shoulder plates, edging strips decorated with impressed design reminiscent of wrigglework; notched terminal topped by an ovoid finial. Wooden scales. L. (overall) 208mm. Drainage coll. *üC16; 2007R.238*   **Fig 43**

63 Knife-dagger. Blade, symmetrical but with a single cutting edge. L. 90mm. W. (max) 17mm. Cutler's mark. Copper-alloy shoulder plates forming a waisted cylinder, L. 19mm. Tang, slightly tapering, with 4 rivet holes, shaped end. W. (max) 14mm. L. 95mm. ?Drainage coll. *SD406; 2007R.233*   **Fig 43**

See Moore 1999, second pl. on 73, [no. 3], and comparable hilt on knife-dagger from the Thames at Westminster (Ward Perkins 1940, 53 and pl. 12, 5).

64 Knife tang, broken. L. 50mm. One rivet hole visible, copper-alloy end plates with incised linear decoration, different on both sides. From the River Avon, Bridge Street, Salisbury. *1993.1*   **Fig 43**

Fifteenth century. The decoration on the plaques is crude and simple; examples are known with images such as saints, animals and birds. The plaques were probably engraved separately and then applied to the knife. Here the shoulder of the knife has not survived but on such knives found in London and Holland some have their shoulders cut and engraved, often with a row of feathers (see, for example, Moore 1999, 72 and plate on 70).

Knife terminals and finials were to become more ornate or elaborate in the Tudor period and the collection includes some that we have omitted in the absence of secure dateable contexts.

Shears

There are over thirty pairs of shears in the collection. This may in part reflect the importance of Salisbury as a textile production centre in medieval times. Smaller examples were probably used domestically for cutting light-weight fabric, thread and hair while larger ones would have been used in the cloth industry or for sheep-shearing.

Shears comprise two blades, two arms and a sprung bow. The blades taper to points or have angled tips. Once invented, shears display little change over time and their dating often depends upon non-essential features. Thus it can be difficult to determine where, within the medieval/post-medieval continuum, a particular pair, without context, is located. Late fourteenth-century blades frequently have slightly curved backs, often with a cutler's mark on one or both blades, and sometimes multiple cusps. Early to mid fifteenth-century blades tend to become narrower with straighter backs. The backs are occasionally decorated. The arms are plain or have recesses, the latter being cusped and sometimes notched. Bows are characteristic of medieval shears; a central rib becomes a common feature by the early fourteenth century.

65   Shears, one arm broken and blade missing, L. 209mm. Blade, with pointed tip, L. 87mm. W. (max) 17mm. From Old Sarum, east suburb excavations, pit 1. Apparently 11th or 12th century. Stone and Charlton 1935, 184 and fig. 3, no. 2. *OS.C93; 1934.111*   **Fig 43**

Ward Perkins 1940, 153 and fig. 48 no. 2 cited this as one of his dated series of shears because of its association with a coin of William I.

66 Shears, lacking the ends of both blades, L. (max surviving) 92mm. Blade, parallel-sided, L. (surviving) 43mm. W. 10mm. Single cusp. From Old Sarum, found in 1910 in garderobe pit no. 2. *O.S. Diary* 1910, 24. *Proc. Soc. Antiq.* 23, 514. *OS.C28; 2000R.26*   **Fig 43**

A thirteenth to early fourteenth-century date is likely, given their association within the garderobe pit-group.

67 Four fragmentary pairs of shears, all slender. These are L. (overall) *c.*150mm and have blades L. *c.*90mm. W. 10mm, one with tapering tips. From Clarendon Palace. Goodall 1988, 211 and fig. 75, nos. 25-8. *1957.47*

These shears, being small, are likely to have been for domestic or personal use.

68 Shears, tips broken, L. (max surviving) 228mm. Blades taper, L. (surviving) 107mm. W. (max) 25mm. From Gomeldon, in a post-hole of building 2. 12th century. Musty and Algar 1986, 154 and fig. 13, no. 22. *1964.69*

As this is one of the largest shears in the collection, and from a rural context, it is likely to have been used for shearing sheep.

69 Shears, L. 217mm. Blades have slightly curved backs and pointed tips, L. 102mm. W. (max) 23mm. One blade bears two cutler's marks. Concave-sectioned bow and slight trace of a single cusp. Drainage

coll. *SD295; 2007R.288*   **Fig 43**

Compare a smaller pair from an early to mid thirteenth-century context in London (Cowgill *et al.* 1987, 106 no. 312 and fig. 70).

70 Shears, L. 84mm. Blades have pointed tips, L. 42mm. W. (max) 8mm. Single cusp and slight ridge to bow. From Avon Approach, Salisbury. *1957.110.2*
Fig 43

There is another, longer example, from River Avon, Crane Bridge, Salisbury (*1963.26.6*). Compare Cowgill *et al.* 1987, 108 no. 337 and 111 no. 342 and fig. 73. Late fourteenth century.

71 Shears, L. 140mm. Narrow blades, straight-backed with angled tips, L. 78mm. W. (max) 9mm. Cutler's mark: five-point star inlaid with copper alloy on one blade. Single cusp. Drainage coll. *SD292; 2007R.284*   **Fig 44**

There is a similar pair, slightly shorter, from the River Avon, Fisherton Bridge, Salisbury (*1957.9.3*) that has a single surviving blade, the metallurgy of which was examined by R. F. Tylecote in 1981 revealing that 'a very small piece of steel has been welded to the edge' (typescript in Museum). There is another from the Drainage Collection of the same form but 198mm in length (*SD290; 2007R.280*).

72 Shears, ends of both blades snapped off, L. (max) surviving 101mm. Blades parallel-sided, L. (max surviving) 54mm. W. (max) 8mm. There is a complex series of cusps and notches. Bow has central rib. Drainage coll. *SD287; 1999R.16.1*   **Fig 44**

See Cowgill *et al.* 1987, 108 no. 334 and fig. 72 for a late fourteenth-century example with similar multiple notches from London.

73 Shears, L. 130mm. Narrow, slightly tapering blades have angled tips, L. 72mm. W. (max) 9mm. One blade has a partly obliterated cutler's mark, perhaps a letter T. Single cusp. The arms are decorated with a series of notches along the edges. Bow has central rib. Drainage coll. *SD293; 2007R.285*
Fig 44

Compare Cowgill *et al.* 1987, 112 no. 35

and fig. 73, which comes from an early to mid fifteenth-century context in London.

74 Shears, L. 96mm. Blades have slightly curved backs and pointed tips, L. 47mm. W. (max) 11mm. Cutler's mark: X within a circle on one blade. One V-shaped notch. Drainage coll. *SD291; 2007R. 286*   **Fig 44**

75 Shears, incomplete, one arm, broken at the bow, L. (surviving) 132mm. Blade has a very slight curve at the back tapering to a sharp point, L. 74mm. W. (max) 10mm. Cutler's mark: X. Single cusp. Drainage coll. *SD297; 1999R. 16.3*   **Fig 44**

76 Shears, L.106mm. Blades, slender, straight-backed, almost parallel-sided, with angled tips, L. 62mm. W. 7-8mm. Slight ridge to bow. Drainage coll. *SD300; 1999R. 16.6*   **Fig 44**
There is a similar but longer example from Avon Approach, Salisbury (*1957.110.1*).

77 Shears, L. 130mm. Blades, straight-backed, slightly tapering to angled tips, L. 71mm. W. (max) 9mm. Single moulded cusp. There is duck-beak moulding at the junction of the bow with the arm. Drainage coll. *SD288; 2007R.281*   **Fig 44**
A small pair of shears from the Museum of London reserve collection has faint mouldings below the bow and only very faint single cusps (Cowgill *et al.* 1987, 112 no. 366 and fig. 74).

78 Shears, L. 100mm. Blades, straight-backed with angled tips, L. 53mm. W. (max) 11mm. Single cusp. Drainage coll. *SD289; 2007R.283*   **Cover**

Scissors
Compared to shears, scissors are much rarer in the medieval period (Øye 1988, 107-9; Ottaway and Rogers 2002, 2741).

79 Scissors, tips missing, L. (surviving) 128mm. Blades, L. 72mm. Ends of the arms, square-sectioned, are thinned and bent outwards to form looped handles. From Gomeldon, area of building 1. Possibly 16th century. *Sal. Mus. Rep.* 1964-5, 20 and pl. II; Musty and Algar 1986, 154 and fig. 13, no. 23. *1964.78*

80 Scissors, L. 152mm. Blade L. 88mm. Cutler's mark below rivet on both blades. Round looped handles with square-shaped section, and round-sectioned arms, central to blades. Drainage coll. *SD305; 2007R. 298*   **Fig 44**
Compare similar scissors from fourteenth-century contexts in York and London (Ottaway and Rogers 2002, 2740, fig. 1347, 13741; Cowgill *et al.* 1987, 114 no. 370 and fig. 75).

Building ironwork
The construction and fitting out of medieval buildings required the extensive use of iron. The objects catalogued are almost without exception from the excavations at Old Sarum, Clarendon Palace and Gomeldon. They may be used to illustrate the variable types of ironwork peculiar to different classes of site.

Cramps
These were used to secure dressed stones within walls, especially where there was an overhang in the structure, and were sometimes encased in lead to hold them fast and to provide protection from corrosion.

81 Cramp. L. 126mm; section rectangular, 11mm x 4mm. From Clarendon Palace, Goodall 1988, 211 and fig. 75, no. 29. *1957.47*   **Fig 45**

82 Three cramps encased in lead caulking. L. 240mm, 250mm and 265mm; section *c.*20mm square. Removed from the second band of decoration on Salisbury Cathedral spire during its restoration in 1991. *1991.20.1-3*   **Fig 45**
Such cramps were used to join blocks of stone within the spire walls both horizontally and vertically (see Tatton-Brown 1996, 61 and pl. 18b). On the basis that the cramps are original they are most probably dateable to the 1320s (see Tatton-Brown 2009, 95-6).

Tie bars
There are two, both from Salisbury Cathedral spire; each was used in conjunction with a wedge and washers to tie structural ironwork together. See Tatton-Brown 1996, fig. 3 facing 62, stage 10 for the principle of their use.

83 Tie bar. L. 386mm. D. 22mm. Removed from Salisbury Cathedral spire, originally with 5 nails (Cat 108-9) and a section of oak. Early 14th century, probably 1320s. *1945.130*   **Fig 45**

84 Tie bar. Similar to Cat 83. L. 470mm. Recovered from Salisbury Cathedral spire in 1944, together with nail (Cat 107). Early 14th century, probably 1320s. *1952.25*

Wall-hooks

These are all-purpose hooks with tapering shanks driven into timber or into masonry joints.

85 Wall-hook with curved hook arising from the end of the shank. L. 65mm. From Clarendon Palace, Goodall 1988, 211 and fig. 75, no. 32. *1957.47; 2000R.87.4*   **Fig 45**

86 Wall-hook with tip missing and end of shank bent. L. 56mm. From Clarendon Palace. Goodall 1988, 211 and fig. 75, no.31. *2000R.87.3*

87 Wall-hook with pronounced stub; curved hook arising before the end of the shank. L. 120mm. From Clarendon Palace, Goodall 1988, 211 and fig. 75, no. 35. *1957.47*   **Fig 45**

See also Goodall 1988, 211 and fig. 75, no.33-4 for two other examples from Clarendon Palace, and Goodall 2000, 143 fig. 6.20, 38 for one from Ludgershall Castle. An iron gutter support from Fishergate in York is of essentially similar form but larger and with an oval end plate at the wide end to hold the gutter in place (Ottaway and Rogers 2002, 2831-2 fig. 1409 no. 15028; fig. 1411).

88 Wall-hook, very similar to above. L. 143mm. Found in the east suburb of Old Sarum during road construction, 1931-2. *1932.8; OS.C113*   **Fig 45**

Wall anchor

This has a substantial tang, which is driven into a masonry joint to secure a major structural element.

89 Wall anchor. L. 158mm; section rectangular, 18mm x 9mm, blunt point at one end. From Clarendon Palace, Goodall 1988, 211 and fig. 75, no. 30. *1957.47*   **Fig 46**

Staples

Large, rectangular staples (timber dogs) were used to hold adjacent timbers together. Smaller, usually U-shaped, staples were suitable to hold chains or hasps and to support handles on doors and chests.

90 Staple of rectangular form. L. 45mm. From Clarendon Palace 1934, Goodall 1988, 211 and fig. 75, no. 36. *1957.47*   **Fig 46**

There are two other staples from Clarendon Palace (Goodall 1988, 211 and fig. 75, nos. 37-8).

91 Staple of U-shape form. L. 62mm. From Gomeldon, building 7 complex. Musty and Algar 1986, fig. 14, no. 11. *1967.148.5.13.1*   **Fig 46**

There are three other staples from Gomeldon.

Nails

Nails from Old Sarum:

92 Flaring square-headed nail. L. 114mm. Head 20mm x 17mm. Found in the east suburb of Old Sarum during road construction, 1931-2. *1932.8; OS.C118*   **Fig 46**

93 Round-headed nail. L. of shank 74mm. Head D. 33mm. From the east suburb of Old Sarum *1937.74; OS.C102*

94 T-headed nail. L. of shank 77mm. Head 19mm x 8mm. Found in the east suburb of Old Sarum during road construction, 1931-2. *1932.8; OS.C119*   **Fig 46**

95 Headless nail of rectangular section, L. 40mm. From Old Sarum excavations 1909-15 *1920-1.30; OS.C146*   **Fig 46**

There are also five other similar nails, ranging in length from 30mm to 50mm.

96 Coffin nails, many with traces of timber remaining. From Old Sarum, east suburb excavations, grave 2. Stone and Charlton 1935, 183. *2002R.4*

Nails from Clarendon Palace (*1957.47*):

97 Square-headed nail with rectangular shank. L. of shank 68mm. Head 15mm x 15mm. Goodall 1988, 216 and fig. 76, no. 39.   **Fig 46**

98 Square-headed nail with square tapering shank. L. of shank 125mm. Head 22mm x 22mm, flat. Goodall 1988, 216 and fig. 76, no. 40.
Fig 46

99 Slightly-domed circular-headed nail with square tapering shank. L. of shank *c.*65mm, clenched at 40mm. D. of head *c.*25mm. A larger-headed example than Goodall 1988, 216 and fig. 76, no. 41.
Fig 46

100 Flaring rectangular-headed nail with tapering rectangular shank. L. of shank 104mm. Head 20mm x 12mm. Goodall 1988, 216 and fig. 76, no. 42.   **Fig 46**
   See also Cat 243 for an example used through a binding strip.

101 Faceted rectangular-headed nail with rectangular tapering shank. L. of shank 130mm. Head 22mm x 22mm with 4 facets. Goodall 1988, 216 and fig. 76, no. 44.   **Fig 46**

102 Flat-topped diamond-shaped headed nail with square tapering shank. L. of shank 100mm. Head 17mm x 17mm. Goodall 1988, 216 and fig. 76, no. 45.   **Fig 46**

103 Raised faceted circular-headed nail with tapering square shank. L. of shank 143mm. D. of head *c.*35mm. Goodall 1988, 216 and fig. 76, no. 46.   **Fig 46**

Nails from Gomeldon (*1967.148*):

Apart from horseshoe nails (see Cat 286-7 below), three types of nail, all with rectangular or square cross-section shanks, were recovered from the deserted medieval village:

104 Rectangular-headed nails. Shank lengths 36mm - 72mm. Musty and Algar 1986, 154 and fig. 14 (types 1-3).

105 Square-headed nails. Shank lengths 28mm - 72mm. Musty and Algar 1986, 154 and fig. 14 (types 4-7).

106 Round-head nails. Shank lengths 36mm - 40mm. Musty and Algar 1986, 154 and fig. 14 (types 8-10).

Other nails:

107 Nail with multi-faceted, round head (D. 35mm), shank rectangular and tapering. L. (overall) 240mm. Removed from Salisbury Cathedral spire in 1944. Early 14th century, probably 1320s. *1952.25*
Fig 47
   See also Cat 84.

108 Four nails with multi-faceted, round heads (D. 25-30mm), shanks rectangular and tapering. L. (overall) 150-230mm. Removed from Salisbury Cathedral spire. Early 14th century, probably 1320s. *1945.130*

109 Nail with multi-faceted, rectangular head (40mm x 30mm), shank rectangular and tapering from 20mm x 13mm. L. (overall) 310mm, clenched at 265mm. Removed from Salisbury Cathedral spire. Early 14th century, probably 1320s. *1945.130*
Fig 47

110 Three nails. T-headed, with rectangular shank. L. of shank 55-58mm, one clenched at 42mm. Head *c.*13mm x 28mm. Detached from a chest of probably late 15th-century date used by Salisbury Corporation. *1974.63*   **Fig 47**
   See Cat 11, page 205 and plate 21, for the chest.

Studs

111 Rectangular-headed stud with curved top surface and rectangular shank. L. of shank 54mm.

Head 54mm x 51mm. From Clarendon Palace, Goodall 1988, 216 and fig. 76, no. 47. *1957.47*

Fig 47

There is another from Clarendon Palace with a shorter shank, and others, not definitely medieval: two from the Drainage coll. (*2000R. 45. 2-3)* and six from King John's House, Tollard Royal (*TR3-7* and *TR166*). Pitt Rivers described the latter as 'a large door nail' (Pitt Rivers 1890, 19 and pl. 22, 14). However, the group was described in his museum display as 'strike nails for cart-wheels'. Essentially substantial nails, these studs could have served both a structural and a decorative purpose.

Door and window fittings

The majority of the door and window furniture included here comes from Clarendon Palace. There is also a hinge plate tip from Gomeldon and a pivot from Old Sarum east suburb; their medieval date is thus reasonably assured, although the shapes and forms of these items were mainly determined by their function and would thus not have changed significantly in later periods. The lead caulking on a wall loop and a hinge pivot from Clarendon Palace shows they were fitted in stone.

Hinges

112 Shutter hinge. L. 117mm. From Gomeldon, building 3. Musty and Algar 1986, 154 and fig. 13, no. 32. *1967.148.5.21*

113 Strap hinge. L. 213mm. From Clarendon Palace. Goodall 1988, 216 and fig. 77, no. 55. *1957.47*

Fig 48

114 Strap hinge with fleur-de-lis shaped terminal, strap broken. L. 139mm. W. 130mm. From Clarendon Palace. Goodall 1988, 216 and fig. 77, no. 57. *1957.47*

Fig 47

115 Hinge terminal. Part of a ?trefoil. L. 63mm. From Clarendon Palace. Goodall 1988, 216 and fig. 77, no. 58. *1957.47*

Fig 47

116 Pointed tip from end of hinge plate, three

nail-holes surviving in L. 94mm. From Gomeldon, yard area by building 6. Musty and Algar 1986, 154 and fig. 13, no. 33. *1967.148.5.5*

Wall loops

117 Wall loop in lead caulking. L. 65mm. From Clarendon Palace. Goodall 1988, 216 and fig. 76, no. 51. *2000R. 60*

Fig 48

This may be part of a harr-hung door, which pivoted on spindles.

Pivots

118 Hinge pivot in lead caulking. L. 111mm. From Clarendon Palace. Goodall 1988, 216 and fig. 76, no. 54. *1957.47*

Fig 48

119 Hinge pivot with tapering spike. L. 130mm. From Clarendon Palace. Goodall 1988, 216 and fig. 76, no. 53. *1957.47* **Fig 48**

For another, similar, one see Goodall 1988, 216 and fig. 76, no. 52.

120 Hinge pivot with flat tapering spike. L. 76mm. Found associated with Greensand footings in 1957 during a watching brief in the east suburb of Old Sarum. 12th century. Musty 1959, 182 and 191, fig. 6. *1958.38* **Fig 48**

The find spot is identified as part of the 'site of St John's Hospital' on Ordnance Survey maps but the evidence for this is uncertain. There is a similar example (*1964. 70*) from Gomeldon, building 2 (Musty and Algar 1986, 154 and fig. 13, no. 31).

Bolts

121 Hand-operated sliding bolt. L. 206mm. From Clarendon Palace. Goodall 1988, 218 and fig. 79, no. 81. *1957.47*

Fig 48

122 Bolt mount, U-shaped. L. 82mm. From Clarendon Palace. Goodall 1988, 218 and fig. 79, no. 82. *1957.47*

Fig 48

Latch rest

123 Latch rest. L. 96mm. From Clarendon Palace. Goodall 1988, 218 and fig. 78, no. 65. *1957.47*
Fig 48

Roves

Washers, frequently lozenge-shaped, used in conjunction with clench bolts for doors, window shutters and well covers, held together and strengthened with rear ledges. Nails with tips clenched over roves to prevent pulling out.

124 Rove. Lozenge-shaped, with two bevelled edges. L. 71mm. W. 43mm. From Clarendon Palace. Goodall 2011, 188 no. H246 and fig. 9.11. *1957.47*
Fig 48

For this and two others see Goodall 1988, 216 and fig. 76, no. 48-50.

Window bars

125 Window bar with flattened ends. L. 402mm. From Clarendon Palace. Goodall 1988, 216 and fig. 77, no. 61. *1957.47*   **Fig 49**

This is probably from a narrow, possibly lancet, window. Its ends suggest that it was likely to have been set in masonry. Such bars survive *in situ*, as for example in a window at Stokesay Castle, Shropshire (Nicholas Griffiths pers. comm.).

126 Incomplete window bar with flattened offset terminal. L. 208mm. From Clarendon Palace. Goodall 1988, 216 and fig. 77, no. 64. *2000R.82*
Fig 49

This was probably nailed to a timber window-frame through 'perforated' offset terminals. For two other similar ones (*2000R.81* and *1957.47*) see Goodall 1988, 216 and fig. 77, no. 62-3.

127 Fragment of a window bar in lead caulking. L. 93mm. From Clarendon Palace. Goodall 1988, 216 and fig. 77, no. 60. *1957.47*   **Fig 49**

This is possibly from a grille of interlocking horizontal and vertical bars.

Locks and Keys

Security equipment (locks and particularly keys) represents one of the largest groups of objects in the Museum, there being almost 500 keys in the Drainage Collection alone. This catalogue is by necessity selective in the number listed and focuses on keys recovered from excavations and examples of known medieval type. The majority, however, are unfortunately without dateable context, being either from the Salisbury drainage, for which stratigraphic evidence was not recorded, or being casual finds. The Museum's *Catalogue* of 1864 drew particular attention to the quantity and interest of the keys (Stevens 1864, 61). There are many that may be medieval or are post-medieval but medieval in style. These are not catalogued in detail here but an indication is given of their number. They would doubtless repay future specialist study and analysis.

Barrel padlocks

Goodall 1990b, 1001-3 defines four post-Conquest types of barrel padlocks: type A has attached tubes, B has fins and attached tubes, C has L-shaped arms and D has shackles. The majority of the padlock bodies are of type B, which is the most common type.

128 Padlock body with external ribs, with fin broken away. D. 23mm. L. 45mm. T-shaped slot in underside for a padlock key of type C. From Old Sarum, east suburb, found during road construction, 1931-2. *1932.8; OS.C122a*   **Fig 49**

This is the only example where the key is inserted via a slot in the side rather than through the end. For a complete example from a late thirteenth- to early fourteenth-century context, Staple Gardens, Winchester, see Cunliffe 1964, 189, fig. 66, no. 8 & pl. 7, and for a reconstruction of a similar lock in use see Ottaway 2002, 2868-9 fig. 1444.

129 Padlock. Complete, with decoration of twisted copper-alloy wire and possible traces of plating. D. 39mm. L. 159mm (overall). Type B. 13th-14th century. From Fitzgerald's Farm, West Harnham.

Sal. Mus. Rep. 1963-4, 20 and pl. 1b. *1963.155*
                                    Fig 49 & cover

From the x-radiograph the internal mechanism is comparable to one from Coppergate, York (Ottaway and Rogers 2002, 2870-1 and fig. 1447-8 no.12572). For a similar barrel padlock case with longitudinal rods see Goodall 1990b, 1009 and fig. 311 no. 3649).

130 Padlock body, decorated with twisted copper-alloy wire. Lateral pin sheath, only one spring survives, now detached. Type D. D. 34mm. L. 78mm. From Old Sarum excavations 1909-15, probably from the Courtyard House, garderobe pit 1. *O.S. Diary* 1910, 20. *Proc. Soc. Ants.* 23 (1909-11), 514. *1920-1.30; OS.C125*   **Fig 50**

131 Padlock body, similar to Cat 130 but with the springs still inside. Type B. D. *c.*36mm. L. (surviving) 60mm. From Old Sarum excavations 1909-15, probably from the Courtyard House, garderobe pit 1. *O.S. Diary* 1910, 20. *Proc. Soc. Ants.* 23 (1909-11), 514. *1920-1.30; OS.C124*   **Fig 50**

132 Padlock U bolt. L. 64mm. From Clarendon Palace.Goodall 1988, 218 and fig. 78, no. 68. *1957.47*   **Fig 50**

An example from Coppergate, York is dated twelfth/thirteenth century (see Ottaway 2002, 2870-1 figs. 1447-8 no. 12578 and p. 3058).

133 Padlock bolt (AE). L. 33mm. From Old Sarum excavations 1909-15. *1920-1.30.35; OS.C47*   **Fig 50**

This is from a barrel padlock of type C. For one from St. Helens, Isles of Scilly see Dunning 1964, 66 and fig. 7 no. 3 and for an iron example of this type from Winchester see Goodall 1990, 1011 and fig. 313 no. 3667.

134 Padlock spring mechanism. D. 34mm. L. 82mm. 4 springs. From Gomeldon, building 1. Late 13th century. Musty and Algar 1986, 154 and fig. 13, no. 34. *1964.77*   **Fig 50**

This type of mechanism is from a padlock with shackle (type D).

135 Padlock spring mechanism. D. 32mm. L. 82mm. 4 springs. Drainage coll. *SD514; 2007R.150*

Although damaged this appears to be from a padlock of either type A or B.

There are five other spring mechanisms, all from padlocks of type D: two from the east suburb of Old Sarum (*OS.C122-3; 1932.8*), one from Salisbury (*SD 513; 1999R.498*), one from Teffont (*iiE 22; 1999R.665*) and a very small example from Amesbury (*1972.58*).

Padlock keys

The mechanism within a barrel padlock comprises essentially a bar with leaf springs which need to be compressed by a key for the lock to open. In use the key is inserted into the lock with a sliding action and it is thus sometimes known as a 'slide' key. These are typed by the relationship of the bit, which compresses the spring-strips, to the stem of the key.

Type A (bit set laterally to stem)

136 Key. L. 140mm. Stem with looped terminal. ?13th century. Found in the east suburb of Old Sarum during road construction, 1931-2. *1932.8; OS.C126*   **Fig 50**

For a similar key from Winchester see Goodall 1990, 1021, fig. 322 no.3695.

137 Key. L. 179mm. Stem hooked at end. From Clarendon Palace, Goodall 1988, 218 and fig. 78, no. 67. *1957.47*   **Fig 50**

For a similar key from Winchester see Goodall 1990b, 1021, fig. 322 no. 3704-5.

138 Key. L. 180mm. Stem with looped terminal. From Gomeldon, building 6A. Musty and Algar 1986, 154 and fig. 13, no. 35. *1967.148.18*

Type B (bit set centrally to stem)

139 Key. L. 107mm. Stem terminates in a ring. ?13th century. From Clarendon Palace, Goodall 1988, 218 and fig. 78, no. 66. *1957.47*   **Fig 51**

For a similar key from Winchester see

Goodall 1990b, 1022 and fig. 323 no. 3724. Winchester type B.

Type C (bit and stem in line)

These keys, with bits in the same plane as the stem and bow, would have been used with padlocks having a slot running along the length of the barrel enabling the key to be drawn along and over the spring-strips.

140 Key. L. 118mm. Circular bow, decorated stem and bit with central cleft separating symmetrical wards. Drainage coll. *üE242; 1999R.704*   **Fig 51**

For comparable examples from Winchester see Goodall 1990b, 1024 fig. 324.

Padlock keys with shield- or heater-shaped bits occur commonly in iron but also in copper alloy and are often referred to as 'latch keys'. Simpler, more crudely made examples with long stems have been found, for example at Billingsgate and Swan Lane in London, in contexts dating from the later twelfth to the mid-fourteenth centuries (Egan 1998, 100-102, fig. 75.267-8).

Those with short stems are generally better made and would appear to be a later form. They have been found in late medieval or sixteenth-century contexts in Bedford (Baker *et al.* 1979, 281, fig. 176.1425) and Waltham Abbey, Essex (Goodall 1978, 157, fig. 21.2), and two were found in the Baynard House excavations in London in contexts dated to the second half of the fourteenth century (Egan, op. cit. 102-3, fig. 75.269-70).

The following are keys of this later form and demonstrate marked variation.

141 Padlock key. L. 72mm. Circular bow; square stem; round-ended, rectangular bit with trefoil aperture. Drainage coll. Penny 1911, pl. 6 no. 30. *üE249; 1999R.700*   **Fig 51**

Compare Egan 1998, 102, fig. 75 no. 270.

142 Padlock key (AE). L. 62mm. Circular bow, pierced shield-shaped bit and small projecting lugs on the bow. 14th century. Drainage coll. Penny 1911,

14, pl. 6 no. 33. *üE243; 2007R.138*

The bow appears to have been miscast, suggesting that this key may have been made locally.

143 Padlock key (AE). L. 85mm. Thistle-shaped bow and a short stem. Bit is rectangular or trapezoidal rather than shield-shaped and is more elaborate than the example above, ending in a long spike. From Salisbury. Shortt 1960, fig. 59, no. 7. *üE248a*

144 Padlock key (AE). L. 70mm. Round bow and pierced shield-shaped bit. There is incised decoration on the stem. Drainage coll. *üE245; 2007R.139*

145 Padlock key (AE). L. 87mm. Thistle-shaped bow, pierced shield-shaped bit and a long stem. Probably from Salisbury. Penny 1911, 14, pl. 6 no. 34; Shortt 1960, fig.59, no. 8. *üE248; 2007R.147*

The more elaborate form and fine manufacture of this long-stemmed key suggests that it is one of the later examples.

146 Padlock key. L. 86mm. Round bow, shield-shaped bit. ?14th century. From a house near the Old Mill, West Harnham. *Sal. Mus. Rep.* 1964-5, 20 and pl. II. *1965.20*

There are also nine other examples from the Drainage Collection of padlock keys of this type (*1999R.187, 1999R.489.1-2* and *2007R.140-5*).

Mounted locks

Such locks were in common use, mounted on doors, chests, cupboards and the like but few have survived: keys for them, however, are very numerous.

147 Shield-shaped chest lock. H. 93mm. W. 90mm. From the Old Sarum excavations 1909-15. *1920-1.30.15; OS.C128*   **Fig 51**

X-radiography shows this lock possessing a mechanism almost identical to that in an example from Winchester, which is dated to the late fourteenth-?fifteenth century (see Goodall 1990b, 1017 and fig. 321. no. 3691).

148 Shield-shaped chest lock, incomplete. Similar to above. H. 115mm. W. 93mm. From the Old Sarum excavations 1909-15. *1920-1.30.14; OS.C127*

Draw bolts from rotary locks

149 Draw bolt. L. 222mm. From Clarendon Palace. Goodall 1988, 218 and fig. 79, no. 76. *2000R.67*   **Fig 51**

150 Draw bolt. L. 255mm. with slightly turned-up end. From Clarendon Palace, Goodall 1988, 218 and fig. 79, no. 78. *1957.47*

151 Draw bolt. L. 230mm. From Clarendon Palace, most probably from excavations carried out by Sir Thomas Phillips in 1821. Phillips 1833, 151; Goodall 1988, 218 and fig. 79, no. 77. *1932.115*   **Fig 51**

152 Incomplete lock bolt. L. (surviving) 146mm. From Clarendon Palace. *1957.47.17*

For this and another, shorter, fragment (*1957.47.34*) see Goodall 1988, 218 and fig. 79, no. 79-80.

Keys for rotary locks

The classification of rotary keys adopted here follows that used by Ian Goodall at Winchester, where nine types were identified (Goodall 1990b, 1024-5). We acknowledge the work by Ian Goodall in the initial sorting of the keys many years before the preparation of this catalogue, which helped us greatly in applying his classification.

Type 1

Keys of this type have L-section bit and projecting stem tip, and most appear to have a pear-shaped bow.

153 Key with an incomplete pear-shaped bow. Surviving L. (surviving) 43mm. From King John's House, Tollard Royal. Pitt Rivers 1890, pl. XXII, no. 2; Ward Perkins 1940, 134 and 145, fig. 43, no. 1. *1975.12; TR 154*   **Fig 52**

Probably twelfth century. Compare Goodall 1990b, 1024-5, fig. 235.

Type 2

This uncommon type has an L-section bit and hollow stem tip.

154 Key (AE). L. 73mm. Oval bow in the form of a twisted wreath surrounding a bird, possibly a falcon or an eagle. At the top of the bow is a perforated zoomorphic knop; there is another zoomorphic knop at the junction of the stem and the bow. The stem and simple bit are punched all over with ring-and-dot motifs. From Wilton. 11th-12th century. Anon 1871, 248 and fig.; Shortt 1960, fig. 59, no. 1. *iiE201*   **Fig 52**

See Goodall 1990b, 1025 and fig. 326, no. 3739 for a less-complete type 2 key with moulded and in-filled oval bow end loop from Winchester, dated eleventh-?mid twelfth century.

Type 3

These keys are forged by rolling from a single sheet of metal to produce a hollow stem, which does not project beyond the end of the bit. Many exhibit a seam line along the stem and often the bit is offset to the stem. A few of the keys have ring bows but the majority have D- or kidney-shaped bows, some of which are hammered flat. Wards are simple with chisel-cut clefts, sometimes rounded. Some of the keys have unusual angular clefts, which may be peculiar to Salisbury. They range in length from 40mm to 146mm, with a single, heavy example (Cat 156), 188mm. There are some sixty keys of this type. The majority are from the Drainage Collection, some of which were described as being 'found in a layer of bluish clay which occurred at the bottom of the excavations – the lowest point at which relics were discovered – consequently they may be assumed to be the earliest in date' (Penny 1911, 12) and therefore thirteenth century, Salisbury having been founded in 1220. Ward Perkins pointed out, referring to type 3 (his type ll) Salisbury keys with crudely chiselled bits: 'Rough workmanship may be as much due to

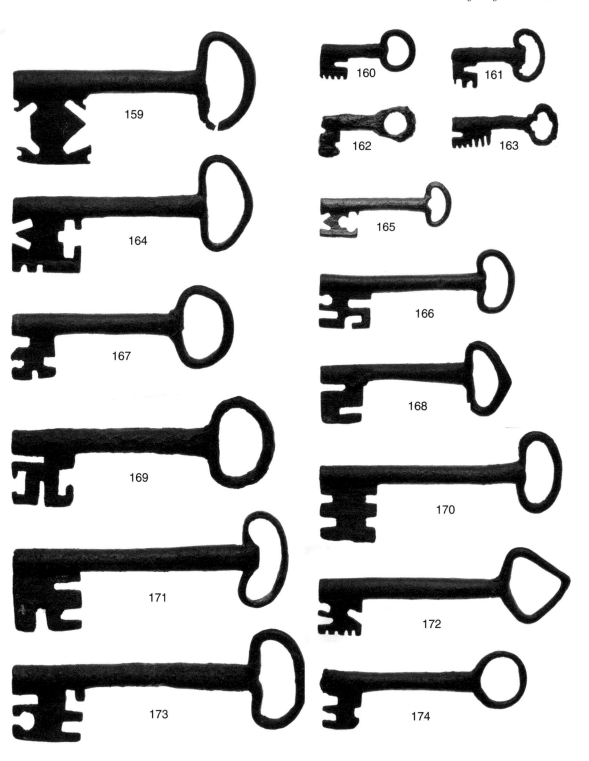

Plate 13. Type 3 keys: Cat 159-174 (1:2)

rusticity as early date' (Ward Perkins 1940, 136). They could therefore date from late eleventh to the thirteenth century, possibly later.

Two keys of this type (Cat 155-6) were found during superficial excavations at Old Sarum cathedral in 1834. The general context suggests a date before the abandonment of the cathedral in the thirteenth century.

155 Key. L. 120mm. D. (stem) 10mm. Flattened D-shaped bow. From Old Sarum cathedral, 'near the site of the high altar' (*Sal. Mus. Cat.* 1870, 28). *OS.C39; 2000R.44*   **Fig 52**

156 Key. L. 188mm. D. (stem) 20mm. Kidney-shaped bow. From Old Sarum cathedral, 'near the site of the west door' (*Sal. Mus. Cat.* 1870, 28). *Gentleman's Magazine* 1835 (ii), 640; Benson and Hatcher 1843, 23-4. *OS.C38; 2000R.5*   **Fig 52**

This key appears in a contemporary coloured drawing by Chevalier J. O. C. Grant (*2011.12*; *Sal. Mus. Rep.* 2010-11, 11 and pl.).

157 Casket key. L. 51mm. From the Old Sarum excavations 1909-15. 14th century. *Proc. Soc. Antiq.* 24, 60. *O.S. Diary* 1910, 20. *OS.C17*   **Fig 52**

Mostly likely a key of type 3 but corrosion prevents certainty.

158 Key. L. 85mm. Stem, moulded at shoulder, with traces of diagonal grooving and non-ferrous plating. Oval bow. Channelled bit. From Crane Bridge, River Avon, Salisbury. 14th century. *1970.125*   **Fig 52**

Similar, though more elaborate, grooving occurs on several keys from Winchester (see Goodall 1990b, 1028-31, nos. 3790 and 3823-4).

159 Key. L. 130mm. D. (stem) 12mm with three faint grooves above and below the bit. Seam visible along length of stem. Welded D-shaped bow. Bit has chisel-cut angular clefts. Drainage coll. Penny 1911, 11, pl. 1, no. 2. *iiE204; 1999R.170*   **Pl 13**

Fifteen keys from the Drainage collection are illustrated photographically (plate 13) to show a typical range in size and designs of bit and bow:

160-74 Fifteen keys of type 3 from the Drainage coll. *SD56, 1999R.272; SD32, 1999R.304; SD17, 1999R.290; iiE295, 1999R.204; iiE220, 2007R.119; SD717, 2007R.124; SD39, 1999R.311; iiE210, 1999R.698.2; SD24, 1999R.296; iiE209, 1999R.173; iiE208, 1999R.698.1; SD34, 1999R.306; SD719, 2007R.120; iiE207, 2007R.121; SD4, 1999R.256*   **Pl 13**

Type 4

These have a hollow stem, separately applied bit and can be difficult to differentiate from type 3.

175 Incomplete key with hollow stem, surviving L. (surviving) 42mm. From Clarendon Palace. Goodall 1988, 218 and fig. 78, no. 69. *1957.47.42*

Type 5

These have a stem, which is solid at the head and then split.

176 Casket key. L. 80mm. Lozenge bow. Drainage coll. 14th century. *iiE218; 2007R.105*   **Fig 52**

177 Key. L. 52mm. Stem 7mm square. Flat-topped bow around a trilobe. From a bunch of keys found in a shed in Culver Street, Salisbury. *1951.28*   **Fig 52**

Type 6

These have a solid stem, the end of which is in line with the bit. For convenience they have been divided into two groups (**a.** and **b.**).

a. This group comprises over fifty small keys, of which the majority are from the Drainage Collection and which are best described as chest or coffer keys. They range in length from 40mm to just over 60mm, most being 45-50mm. The majority have simple bows, round and flat with circular perforation; a few have oval, lozenge, kidney-shaped or thistle-shaped bows. Not only is it the small size but also the form of the bit that define this group. There are usually two offset clefts on the two ends and a series of small clefts on the side.

178 Casket key. L. 45mm. From the Old Sarum excavations 1909-15. 13th century. *Proc. Soc. Antiq.* 24, 60. *O.S. Diary* 1910, 20. *OS.C16*

179 Casket key. L. 51mm. From the Old Sarum excavations 1909-15. 14th century. *Proc. Soc. Antiq.* 24, 60. *O.S. Diary* 1910, 20. *OS.C18*   **Fig 52**

180 Chest key. L. 51mm. Flat, round bow with circular perforation. Drainage coll. *üE212;* *2007R.64*   **Fig 52**

181 Chest key. L. 67mm. Bow with three-lobed piercing surmounted by a crown. Rectangular bit, 18mm x 26mm, with 6 shallow clefts on the side and incised line on both faces. Bow with three-lobed piercing surmounted by a crown. From East Knoyle Church. 14th-15th century. *Sal. Mus. Rep.* 1954-5, 12 and front cover; Shortt 1960, pl. 59, no. 3. *1955.51*   **Fig 52 & cover**

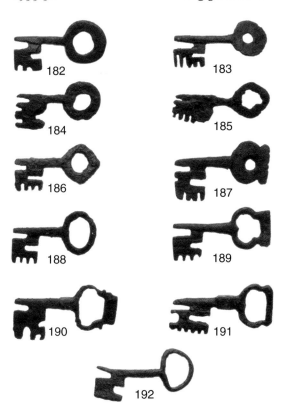

Plate 14. Type 6a keys: Cat 182-192 (1:2)

Eleven keys, from the Drainage collection, are illustrated photographically (plate 14) to show a range of designs of bow and bit within this group:

182-92 Eleven keys of type 6a from the Drainage coll. *üE213, 1999R.174; üE215, 1999R.176; üE216, 1999R.177; üE226, 1999R.181; üE228, 1999R.182; üE293, 2007R.67; üE297, 1999R.205; SD88, 1999R.365.1; SD95, 1999R.365.8; SD96, 1999R.365.9; SD107, 1999R.368.*

          Pl 14

In addition there are four keys, which are different in having channelled bits, the channelling in line with the stem. They include:

193 Casket key. L. 35mm. From the site of the Franciscan Friary, St Ann Street, Salisbury. 14th century. *Sal. Mus. Rep.* 1969-70, 19. *1969.81.6*
          Fig 52

194 Key. L. 67mm. Oval bow. From Crane Bridge, River Avon, Salisbury. 15th century. *1970.126*

b. This group of 47 keys, the majority from the Drainage Collection, comprises larger keys, mostly ranging from 70mm to 100mm in length. Most have oval or D-shaped bows. Many of the bits are larger versions of those seen in casket keys; almost without exception the wards are asymmetrical. Their larger size indicates they were used to secure larger structures such as doors or chests.

195 Key. L. 96mm. Rounded-rectangular stem. D-shaped bow. From Idmiston Manor, Idmiston. ?15th century. *1982.19*   **Fig 53**

196 Key. L. 96mm. Circular stem D. 5mm. Kidney-shaped bow. Complicated bit. Drainage coll. *üE305; 2007R.127*   **Pl 15**

197 Key. L. 92mm. Sub-circular stem with band of decoration on raised band beneath bow. Flat-topped bow. Drainage coll. *üE279; 2007R.108*   **Pl 15**

198 Key. L. 78mm. Incomplete, broken bit. From Sunnyhill Road, Salisbury. *1958.55*

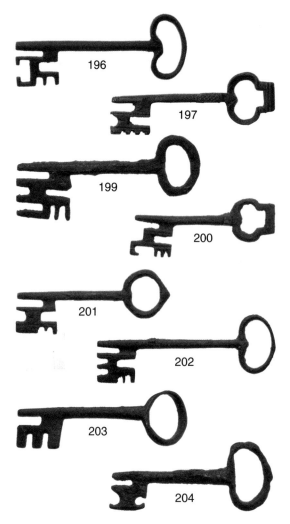

Plate 15. Type 6b keys: Cat 196-7; 199-204 (1:2)

A further six keys of this group, from the Drainage collection, are illustrated photographically (plate 15) to show a typical range of designs of bit and bow:

199-204 Six keys of type 6b from the Drainage coll. *üE237, 2007R.126; üE282, 1999R.196; üE300, 1999R.707; üE304, 1999R.310; SD83, 1999R.361; SD100, 1999R.366.3*   **Pl 15**

There are a further twelve keys, essentially type 6b but characterised by having at least one angular perforation through the bit and usually many narrow clefts in the side. A few have very intricately-cut wards, as Cat 205 below. Cat 206 is apparently an unfinished example.

205 Key. L. 76mm. Bit is rectangular 31mm x 20mm with two angular perforations and 9 deep-cut clefts on the side. Bow is lozenge-shaped with 4 circular perforations. Drainage coll. Penny 1911, pl. 3, no. 12. *üE229; 2007R.102*   **Fig 53**

206 Key. L. 71mm. Stem bent. Flat-topped bow around a two-lobed perforation. Unfinished rectangular bit, 21mm x 29mm, uncut except for two rectangular perforations. Drainage coll. *üE278; 2007R.80*   **Fig 53**

Type 7

These have a solid stem projecting beyond the end of the bit. The ward cuts in the bit are either asymmetrical or arranged symmetrically at both ends of an otherwise solid bit. There are approximately twenty keys of this type, thirteen from the Drainage coll. Many cast, copper-alloy casket keys are of this type.

207 Key (AE). Traces of gilding. L. 45mm. Large collar below annular bow. From Old Sarum 1909-1915 excavations. *OS.C26*   **Fig 53**

A simple casket key from Exeter, with an annular bow and collar between the end of the stem and the head, was found in a context dated *c.*1200-50 (Goodall 1984, 345, fig. 193 no. 181).

208 Key (AE). L. 40mm. Collar below pierced annular bow. From Park Lane, Salisbury. *1972.75*   **Fig 53**

209 Key (AE). L. 43mm. Annular bow, no collar. Drainage coll. *üE202a; 2007R.90*

210 Key (AE). L. 41mm. Pierced annular bow. Noticeably flat. From the Chapel of St John, Harnham Bridge, Salisbury. *üE202; 1999R.697*   **Fig 53**

211 Key (AE). L. 40mm. Pierced annular bow,

no collar. From Radnor/Bartlett Road, Salisbury in material originally from the Southampton Road gravel pits. *OS.C46; 1935.62*

212 Key (AE). L. (surviving) 33mm. with incomplete stem. Pierced annular bow, no collar. From Read's Close, Teffont. *1948.50*

213 Key. L. 163mm. Stem 8mm square. Flattened D-shaped bow. From a Swindon dealer, who described it as having been found by a man who had worked on excavations at Old Sarum. *1946.11; OS.C133*   **Fig 53**

Two keys of this type, from the Drainage Collection, are illustrated photographically (plate 16) to show different designs of bit and bow:
214-5 Two keys of type 7 from the Drainage coll. *üE239, 1999R.701; üE240, 1999R.186.*   **Pl 16**

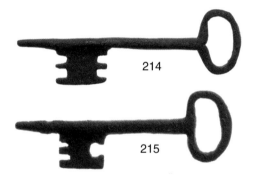

Plate 16. Type 7 keys: Cat 214-5 (1:2)

Type 8
Types 7 and 8 are clearly related forms of key, both having a solid stem projecting beyond the end of the bit. Type 8 differs in having a symmetrically-shaped bit, which incorporates one or more ward cuts running its full depth. This type of bit enabled the key to be used to open a door from either side, a fact which ensured its popularity continued into the post-medieval period. Stems may be decorated and are often stopped over the bit. Most have D-shaped bows. The majority range in length from 110-150mm, with few outside this range, and the need for

large keys for door locks makes them one of the most common in the medieval period. The type occurs from the twelfth century well into the post-medieval period and Goodall 1990b, 1032-3 nos. 3826-37 describes a number of examples from Winchester ranging in date from the twelfth to the sixteenth century. There are ten keys from Old Sarum and Clarendon Palace, 66 in the Drainage Collection and a further nine are recorded as casual finds from other locations.

216 Key. L. 152mm with flat, D-shaped bow. From the Old Sarum excavations 1909-15, Courtyard House. 13th century or later. *O.S. Diary 1910, 11 or 1911, 24. 1945.312; OS.C132*   **Fig 53**

217 Key. L. 165mm. Stem, stopped over bit, with knobbed tip. D-shaped bow. From Old Sarum, east suburb, during road construction, 1931-2. *OS.C130; 2000R.40*

There is another (*OS.C131; 2000R.41*) from the same source. Both are undated but are included because they are of medieval form and provenance.

There are six keys of this type from Clarendon Palace (Cat 218-23). From their context they should all be of medieval date.

218 Key. L. 61mm with round stem and oval bow. From Clarendon Palace, Goodall 1988, 218 and fig. 78, no. 70. *1957.47*

219 Key. L. 68mm with hexagonal stem and D-shaped bow. From Clarendon Palace, found in 1844 when Sir Frederick Bathurst restored the east wall of the Great Hall and affixed an inscribed commemorative plaque. Goodall 1988, 218 and fig. 78, no. 71. *üE367; 1932.114*   **Fig 53**

220 Key. L. 77mm with a decorated stem of diamond-shaped cross-section and D-shaped bow. From Clarendon Palace, Goodall 1988, 218 and fig. 78, no. 73. *1957.47.39*

221-3 Three keys. L. 68mm, 73mm and 80mm. with rectangular or square cross-section stems and D-shaped bows. From Clarendon Palace, Goodall 1988,

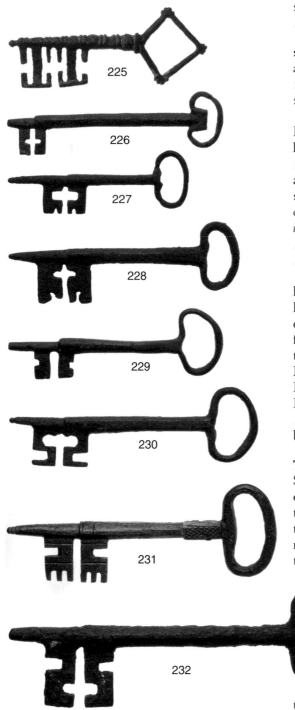

218 and fig. 78, nos. 75, 72 and 74. *1957.47.40-41; 1950.63*

224 Key. L. 130mm. with heart-shaped bow. 'Found at Old Sarum'. In the Museum since 1883. Possibly 15th or 16th century. Penny 1911, 13 and pl. V no. 25. *OS.C44; 2000R.6*

Eight keys of this type, from the Drainage Collection, are illustrated photographically (plate 17) to show a typical range of designs of bit and bow:

225-32 Eight keys of type 8 from the Drainage coll. *iiE219, 2007R.104; iiE241, 1999R.702; iiE258, 1999R.705; iiE259, 1999R.189; iiE264, 1999R.192; iiE266, 1999R.699; iiE277a, 1999R.195; iiE303a, 1999R.209*   **Pl 17**

A further nine casual finds of this type of key within Salisbury and district are noted here to provide a record of their geographical distribution represented within the collection; further description would be superfluous: Castle Street, *1957.57*; Endless Street, *1939.27*; Macklin Road, *1999R.683*; River Avon, Bridge Street, *1962.65*; River Avon, Crane Bridge, *1970.122.1* and .2; Cathedral Close, *1957.106*; West Harnham, *1966.42*; Winterbourne Stoke, *1971.20*.

Type 9

Stem is hollow at the tip, solid above; the end of stem and the bit are in line. Iron keys of this type are usually post-medieval and none of those in the Drainage Collection is convincingly medieval in character. Copper-alloy keys of this type, usually cast, occur in medieval contexts and there are several in the collection. A particularly good series, dated 1235-80, was recovered from the Priory and Hospital of St Mary Spital, London, see Egan 1997, fig. 26, S12-20.

233 Key (AE). L. 39mm. Round pierced bow. From the Old Sarum excavations 1909-1915. *OS.C27*   **Fig 53**

Cat 234-6 are of the same form, dated to the

Plate 17. Type 8 keys: Cat 225-32 (1:2)

late twelfth to late fourteenth century; see Egan 1998, 111.

234 Two similar keys (AE). L. 40 and 39.5mm. Annular bows, moulded stem heads and channelled bits. Drainage coll. *SD712; 2007R.92* and *SD713; 2007.93*

These compare closely with a key from Winchester, which is described as fifteenth century (Goodall 1990b, 1035, no. 3852), and one from Billingsgate, London (Egan 1998, 111 and fig. 86 no. 298).

235 Key (AE). L. 36.5mm. Annular bow and collar. Simple bit. Noticeably flat. Drainage coll. *iiE238; 2007R.91*

236 Key (AE). L. 36mm. Annular bow. Simple bit. Noticeably flat. Drainage coll. *iiE221; 1999R.178*

Escutcheon plate

237 Part of a triangular escutcheon plate. 82mm x 62mm. From the Old Sarum excavations 1909-15. ?15th century. *1920-1.30; OS.C129*

Fig 53

There is a larger example from Billingsgate, London, which is dated *c.*1350-*c.*1400 (Egan 1998, 120 and fig. 92 no.334).

Shackles

238 Shackles. Two ankle cuffs (max. internal D. 98mm) joined together by a short chain of three links, two elongated, and a smaller central ring, which would have allowed movement of only 140mm. between legs. Each cuff is made up of two C-shaped pieces of iron rod (D. 8-9mm) expanded, flattened and riveted at their ends. Found around the ankles of a (presumed) male interred north east of the Choir in the Cathedral at Old Sarum. Skeleton showed signs of decapitation. *O.S. Diary* 1913, 4; *Proc. Soc. Ants.* xxvi (1914),116. *OS.C55*   **Fig 54 and cover**

Hawley (*O.S. Diary,* 1913, 4) questioned whether the human remains might have been those of the king's cousin, William d'Eu, who died in 1096. For similar riveted shackles in the Musée Municipal, Louviers see Halbout *et al.* 1987, 111, no. 207, for which no dating is given. Several complete barrel padlocks with shackles come from Winchester; three were found at Cathedral Green from a late tenth- to eleventh-century context, one from Brook Street and one from Wolvesey Palace, loosely dated from the early eleventh to early fifteenth century (Goodall 1990b, 1011-4 and fig. 314-5 nos.3671-5). See also Thompson 1986 for iron shackles, probably associated with a barrel padlock, from the River Tyne at Corbridge.

The Salisbury shackles are important evidence for the use of shackles on humans; firstly, because they were found *in situ*, and, secondly, because they represent a particularly severe form of restraint that could not be taken off as quickly and easily as the more common types of shackles that are secured with the help of chains and/or padlocks. The latter have often been interpreted as animal hobbles only, a distinction which according to Henning (1992, 405-6) and Gustafsson (2009) is not necessary and would not have been made by their original users as they would have worked perfectly on both men and livestock.

Household fittings

Furniture

The drop handle and strip bindings listed here are all likely to come from chests, attesting to the importance of these items of furniture as containers for storage, an importance kept in rural households well into the twentieth century.

239 Binding strip. L. 173mm. Shaped fragment probably from a casket. From Clarendon Palace. Goodall 1988, 218 and fig. 80, no. 84. *2000R.58*

Fig 54

For two other fragments (*1957.47*) see Goodall 1988, 218 and fig. 80, no. 86-7.

240 Binding strip with end widened, flattened and perforated. L. 77mm. From Clarendon Palace. Goodall 1988, 218 and fig. 80, no. 85. *2000R.84*

Fig 54

241 Corner binding. L. 52mm; 58mm. From Clarendon Palace. Goodall 1988, 218 and fig. 80, no. 88. *2000R.64*   **Fig 54**

There is another much narrower strip (*2000R.61*): see Goodall 1988, 218 and fig. 80, no. 89.

242 Fragment of binding. L. 115mm. W. 22mm. Th. 2mm. Pierced by a flat-headed, rectangular nail. L. of shank 94mm. Head 16mm x 3mm. From Clarendon Palace. Goodall 1988, 218 and fig. 80, no. 90. *2000R.63*   **Fig 54**

243 Strap fragment with single rivet, probably from a chest. L. 92mm. W. 35mm. From Clarendon Palace. Goodall 1988, 216 and fig. 77, no. 59. *2000R.83*

244 Rectangular drop handle perhaps from a chest. L. 192mm. From Clarendon Palace. Goodall 1988, 218 and fig. 80, no. 92. *1957.47*   **Fig 54**

For another example see Goodall 1988, 218 and fig. 80, no. 91.

Lighting

245 Wax-pan from candlestick. Tinned surface, concentric engraved lines. D. 130mm. From Clarendon Palace. Goodall 1988, 218 and fig. 81, no. 93. *2000R.67*   **Fig 55**

For a complete thirteenth-century candlestick with wax-pan from Winchester see Goodall 1990c, 981-3, fig. 306 no. 3530.

246 Single cup candle holder. Cup is poorly preserved, D. 22mm and H. 20mm. Stub of angled stem surviving. From excavations on the site of the Franciscan Friary, St Ann Street, Salisbury. *Sal. Mus. Rep.* 1969-70, 19. *1969.81*

Candle holders, as below, cannot be closely dated as the form is a basic one, which spans the medieval and post-medieval periods.

247 Single cup candle holder with spike at right angle. Cup D. 20mm. Drainage coll. *SD341; 1999R.28.1*   **Fig 55**

248 Single cup candle holder with spirally twisted stem. Cup D. 15mm. H. 92mm. Drainage coll. *SD342; 1999R.28.2*   **Fig 55**

249 Two cup candle holder with a pricket. Downward spike or bracket broken off. Cups D. *c.*15mm. H. 70mm. Drainage coll. *SD344; 1999R.28.4*   **Fig 55**

For a similar fourteenth-century example from Swan Lane, London see Egan 1998, 144 no. 416.

Hooks

250 Flesh hook with triple prongs and a bent whittle tang. From the Old Sarum excavations 1909-15. Goodall 2011, 308 no. J22 and fig. 11.4. *1920-1.30; OS.C144*   **Fig 55**

For a three-pronged flesh-hook from Winchester see Goodall 1990d, 820 and fig. 242, no. 2548. A simpler, two-pronged, hook comes from Fishergate, York. The type originates in the late Anglo-Saxon period and continues in use into the thirteenth century (Rogers 1993, 1330-1 fig. 643).

251 Hook with nailed flanged arm. L. 175mm. From Clarendon Palace. Goodall 1988, 218 and fig. 81, no. 94. *1957.47*   **Fig 55**

Designed to be attached to a pole, this could have been used as a boat, fire or general purpose draghook.

Chain fittings

252 Three links, 2 parallel-sided (L. 58mm. W. 13mm), separated by a circular one (D. 31mm). From Clarendon Palace. Goodall 1988, 218 and fig. 81, no. 95. *1957.47*   **Fig 56**

253 Figure-of-eight link. L. 56mm. W. 14mm. From Clarendon Palace. Goodall 1988, 218 and fig. 81, no. 96. *2009R.43*   **Fig 56**

254 Chain with swivel ring. Found in the east suburb of Old Sarum during road construction, 1931-2. *1932.8; OS.C110*   **Fig 56**

255 Swivel fitting. L. 63mm. From Clarendon Palace. Goodall 1988, 218 and fig. 81, no. 97. *1957.47*   **Fig 56**

Rings and collars

256 Ring. D. 40mm. From Clarendon Palace. Goodall 1988, 218 and fig. 81, no. 98. *1957.47*
                                                            Fig 56
For another from Clarendon Palace see Goodall 1988, 218 and fig. 81, no. 99.

257 Collar. D. 40mm. W. 10mm. From Clarendon Palace. Goodall 1988, 218 and fig. 81, no. 100. *1957.47*   **Fig 56**
There is another from Clarendon Palace. Goodall 1988, 218 and fig. 81, no. 101.

Book chains

The value of books painstakingly produced and illuminated by hand before the printing press made multiple-production possible was so great that they were often stored in locked chests. As libraries became established, particularly from the thirteenth century onwards, books were made more accessible by securing them to bookcases and desks by chains, which were attached by rings to rods, themselves secured by lock and key. The chains varied in length, being sufficient to allow the books to be taken down to be read. Libraries continued to chain books well beyond the medieval period. The Bodleian Library in Oxford, for example, paid £25 10s (£25.50) in 1660 to chain the books in one bequest alone, though by 1761 it was unchaining 1448 books at a cost of one halfpenny each (Fletcher 1914, 14-5). The chains here may be, but cannot be proven to be, medieval.

258 Chain of 14 forged parallel-sided 60mm-long links (7 and 7 linked by a swivel ring) with a circular ringlet at each end. L. (overall) 905mm. From Salisbury Cathedral Library. *Sal. Mus. Cat.* 1864, 52 no. 201. *1999R.26*   **Fig 56**
The Museum has another similar chain, of 5 and 7 links (*1934.131*), L. 880mm, possibly from Salisbury and there is also a fragment of two links (60mm long) with part of a swivel fitting at one end in the Drainage Collection (*SD361; 1999R.25.1*).

There are 110 chains of this design and similar in length in Salisbury Cathedral Library where they hang as a reminder of the security they once offered precious medieval books and manuscripts. The library building dates from the mid-fifteenth century and it is interesting to note that when, at that time, a canon gave some books there was written inside two of them the stipulation that they be chained (Cox and Harvey, 1907, 331).

259 Chain of three 70mm-long links and a swivel ring at one end. L. (overall) 225mm. Drainage coll. *SD367; 2007R.198*
This is different in design from the above but possibly from a book.

Horse equipment

Horseshoes

We are particularly grateful to Ken Smith for his comments on the shoes and help with their dating, which in the case of the casual finds is tentative given the absence of context and the conservative nature of the blacksmith's craft. All the Petersfinger Farm shoes are from his collection and were found on land north of the River Avon at the boundary of the parishes of Laverstock and Ford and that of Clarendon Park. The terminology and typology used here is that adopted by John Clark (see Clark 1995, 81-91), where four basic types of shoe are defined:

Type 1 is crude, has a broad, thin (2-3mm) web, usually with three round nail-holes cut in each branch. A wavy edge is created by the countersinking for nail-heads, which are typically T-shaped. Rarely do they have calkins.

Type 2 is similar but usually well-made, has a narrower and thicker (>5mm) web, and usually has three nail-holes (round in type 2A, rectangular in 2B) cut in each branch. Deep countersunk slots for, typically fiddle-key form, nail-heads result in a wavy edge to the shoe. It normally has calkins in one or both heels.

Type 3 is a heavier shoe. At over 200g, it is generally about twice as heavy as type 2. It has a broader web with more nail-holes, four in each branch being not uncommon. The nail-holes are rectangular and have narrow rectangular countersunk slots, which generally do not deform the shoe edge. Calkins are less common than on type 2.

Type 4 is similar, with a broad web, sometimes tapering towards the heel. The distinguishing feature is the form of the nail-holes and nails. The holes have no separate countersunk slot for the nail-head but are square or, less commonly, rectangular, and taper inwards. Calkins may be present.

The dating of horseshoes without secure archaeological context is notoriously difficult. This series is chronological within the period eleventh-fifteenth century but there is considerable overlap between the occurrence of the types and it is essential to be cautious of using type alone as a means of dating. See Clark 1995, 91-7 for a chronological assessment of 360 horseshoes from London.

260 Shoe with hint of wavy edge, one calkin and 6 countersunk round nail-holes, one nail in situ. L. 111mm. W. 97mm. Type 1. From Petersfinger Farm. *2010.43.24* **Fig 57**

261 Wavy edge shoe, with two calkins and two of six T-shaped nails present. L. 104mm. W. 90m. Type 2. From the Pembroke Estate, Wilton. Probably 12th century. *1996R.2084*

262 Wavy edge shoe, with two calkins and one of six nails present. L. 105mm. W. (max) 92mm. Type 2. From the River Test at Fullerton, Hampshire. Probably 12th century. *1999R.830* **Fig 57**

263 Wavy edge shoe with angular inner profile, 'swept-back' calkins and 6 countersunk, round/oval nail-holes. L. 111mm. W. (max) 90mm. Type 2.?Drainage coll. Probably 12th-13th century. *1996R.2085.9*

264 Wavy edge shoe with two calkins and 6 countersunk oval nail-holes (one corroded away). L. 107mm. W. 94mm. Type 2B. From Petersfinger Farm. Late 12th century. *2010.43.2* **Fig 57**

For a similar shoe, from a dateable context in London see Clark 1995, 104 and 116, fig. 82 no.125.

265 Arm of a shoe with a calkin and countersunk nail-holes. Type 3. L. 103mm. From Clarendon Palace, 13th century or earlier. Goodall 1988, 222 and fig. 82, no. 111. *1957.47* **Fig 57**

266 Shoe, much corroded, with one calkin surviving, apparently 6 nail-holes, with one fiddle-headed/T-shaped nail in situ. L. 107mm. W. 94mm. Type 3. Dug up in the graveyard of Britford Church in 1930 (Ward 1941, 13). Probably late 12th-13th century. *1996R.2083*

This is the only medieval shoe in the collection from south of the River Avon at Britford. To the north of the river, on land to the north and east of the Salisbury sewage works near Petersfinger Farm, many shoes have been located (Smith, 1984, 337-9). These are mostly post-medieval but four are medieval (Cat 267-8 and 279-80, ex K. Smith coll.).

267 Shoe with 2 small, worn but still prominent, calkins, 6 square countersunk nail-holes and distinct wavy-edge bulging of the outer perimeter. L. 97mm. W. (max) 95mm. Type 3. From Petersfinger Farm. Probably 13th century. *2010.43.4*

This well-preserved shoe is smaller than average and shows visible thickening of the toe to compensate for additional wear.

268 Shoe with 2 broad and somewhat worn calkins, 6 square nail-holes and a distinctly arched inner profile. L. 113mm. W. 94mm. Type 3. From Petersfinger Farm. Probably 13th century. *2010.43.5* **Fig 57**

This well-preserved shoe has a very noticeably thickened toe to allow for wear caused by the relatively high calkins and is clearly intended for a rear hoof.

269 Shoe without calkins and with 6 square nail-holes. L. 101mm. W. 98mm. Type 3/4. Drainage coll. Probably 12th/13th century. *1999R.812.1*

270 Shoe, incomplete, with four square nail-holes on each side. L. 113mm. W. 112mm. Type 4. From Clarendon Palace, Late medieval. Goodall 1988, 222 and fig. 82, no. 112. *1957.47*   **Fig 57**

There are four other shoe fragments from Clarendon Palace. Goodall 1988, 222 and fig. 82, no. 113-16.

271 Shoe with single calkin and 3 nail-holes each side, 3 nails surviving. L. 122mm. W. 114mm. Type 4. Drainage coll. 14th century. *SD604; 2007R.219*   **Fig 58**

272 Shoe with 2 calkins and 4 rectangular nail-holes each side. L. (surviving) 115mm. W. 124mm. Type 4. Drainage coll. 15th century. *SD 608; 2007R.220*

273 Shoe with pointed arch internal profile. Heels have a wedge and a calkin; 6 nail-holes, 3 of which have nails in situ. L. 117mm. W. 114mm. Type 4.?Drainage coll. 14th or early 15th century. *1996R.2081.1*

One of the nails might possibly be the remains of a spiral clench, which theoretically allowed a loose shoe to be tightened without the need to replace the nail.

274 Shoe with arched inner profile. The heels have a calkin and a worn wedge; 6 square nail-holes, 1 corroded through. L. 124mm. W. 112mm. Type 4.?Drainage coll. 14th century. *1996R.2081.3*

275 Shoe with a worn, broad calkin on one heel (other heel broken) and 6 large, square nail-holes. L. 117mm. W. 106mm. Type 4. ?Drainage coll. 14th15th century. *1996R.2085.10*   **Fig 58**

This well-preserved and very solid shoe is bent as though possibly wrenched from the hoof.

276 Shoe with prominent arched inner profile; heels have a wedge and calkin; 7 square nail-holes (4 and 3). L. 131mm. W. 119mm. Type 4. ?Drainage coll. Late medieval. *1996R.2085.1*

277 Shoe with no visible calkins or wedges, 6 large square nail-holes and well-rounded shape. L.

112mm. W. 99mm. Type 4. ?Drainage coll. 13th-14th century. *1996R.2085.3*   **Fig 58**

Almost certainly a fore-shoe. It has slight distortion and damage to one branch that may have occurred during loss from the hoof.

278 Shoe with rounded inner profile, worn and shallow calkins and 8 square nail-holes (3 nails in situ). L. 127mm. W. 115mm. Type 4. ?Drainage coll. Late medieval. *1996R.2085.4*   **Fig 58**

The calkins are shaped almost to a point, which may indicate the shoe was for winter use. Another example probably from the Drainage coll. (*1996R.2085.8*) has calkins shaped to 'chisel points' that also suggest modification to winter conditions (pers. comm. Ken Smith).

279 Shoe with worn wedge/calkin on the heels and 6 square nail-holes. Wide web, almost flat, slightly dished, with rounded inner profile. L. 123mm. W. 119mm. Type 4. From Petersfinger Farm. Late medieval. *2010.43.1*

280 Shoe with one broad low calkin on one branch but no wedge on the other, 6 square nail-holes, distinctly arched profile and a dished form. Some wear evident at toe. L. (surviving) 106mm. W. 107mm. Type 4. From Petersfinger Farm. Probably 14th-15th century. *2010.43.3*

281 Plain edge shoe with one calkin and two of the six nails present. L. 111mm. W. 107mm. Type 4. From Gomeldon, building 1. 13th-14th century. Musty and Algar 1986, 154 and fig. 14, no. 40. *1964.74*

282 Plain edge shoe with two calkins and five of the six nails present. L. 116mm. W.112mm. Type 4. From Gomeldon, building 1. 13th-14th century. Musty and Algar 1986, 154 and fig. 14, no. 41. *1964.74*   **Fig 58**

Since Cat 281-2 retained some of their nails and were found in the same building the excavators suggested that it may be evidence for farriery. Clark cites these as early examples of his type 4 (Clark 1995, 97).

283 Shoe, much corroded, with one calkin and

a wedge, 6 nail-holes and prominent arched inner profile. L. 114mm. W. 112mm. Type 4. Casual find from the deserted village at Gomeldon. Probably 14th century. *1974.20*

284 Shoe with single relatively high calkin and 6 square nail-holes. L. 132mm. W. 112mm. Type 4. Found 1932 in Exeter Terrace, Salisbury. Probably 14th-15th century. *1996R.2082*

285 Shoe with one calkin and wedge, both worn, and probably 6 square nail-holes. L. 120mm. W. 122mm. Type 4. From Milford Street, Salisbury. Probably late 15th-16th century. *1999R.801*
Fig 59

Found at the bottom of a bell-founding pit below a bell cope fragment (see Cat 21, page 75).

There are a further six medieval shoes from the Drainage coll. (*1999R.804, 806-8, 811 and 812.2-4*) and one from Petersfinger Farm (*2010.43.25*).

Horseshoe nails

There are many horseshoe nails, of two types, from Gomeldon deserted medieval village:

286 Nails of 'fiddle-key' type. L. 27mm. Musty and Algar 1986, 154 and fig. 14 (types 7c-d). *1967.148*
Fig 59

These nails were common until the thirteenth century. See Cat 262 for a horse shoe that would have taken nails of this type.

287 Nails of rectangular-headed type. L. 24mm. Musty and Algar 1986, 154 and fig. 14 (types 7a-b). *1967.148*
Fig 59

Probably thirteenth century or later. The nail illustrated is from the horseshoe Cat 282 (fig. 58).

Stirrups

The stirrups here are typical of so many found in that unfortunately they lack a good archaeologically dateable context but they do have features in common with stirrups accepted

as medieval. We are most grateful to John Clark for commenting on the stirrups, the discussion of which is essentially his.

288 Stirrup. Trapezoidal form, with rounded lower corners; asymmetrical; oval foot-rest with irregular lozenge-shaped central cut; wide rectangular loop for suspension from strap. H. 163mm. W. 128mm. Drainage coll. *SD615; 2007R.229*   **Fig 59**

For the type see Ward Perkins 1940, 91 fig. 25 nos. 2 and 3. Although these are un-stratified stray finds (possibly from the Thames), Ward Perkins's mid thirteenth-century dating is acceptable (see also Clark 1995, 72-3 no. 83). A 'split' foot-rest is also found on an otherwise differently shaped example, illustrated in Ward Perkins (1940, fig. 25 no. 1), found in a thirteenth-century storage jar (see Andrews and Dunning 1939, 303-6).

The stirrup is asymmetrical rather than just bent out of shape (that is right and left stirrups differ), which Ward Perkins considered typical of the fourteenth century (see his fig. 23 no. 9); however, the ones he cites, and similar examples from London (Clark 1995, 73-4 no. 85) and Winchester (Goodall 1990e, 1042-3, no. 3879, fig. 332) all have 'boxes' or cover plates in front of the suspension bar (possibly a later development), so are not directly comparable. An asymmetrical stirrup without a 'box' is capable of being used on either foot as it allows the leathers to be fastened as required.

Based on a recent survey of the types and dating of post-medieval and modern horse equipment, John Clark (pers. comm.) is not aware of stirrups similar to the Salisbury example that can be firmly dated later. The nineteenth century did see lighter, more curvilinear stirrups replacing or alongside, the chunky, D-shaped stirrups typical of the sixteenth to eighteenth centuries, but these are usually readily identifiable as factory products, lacking the hand-crafted irregularitie of medieval times. Equally, the stirrup form does not seem to feature in nineteenth-century catalogues or illustrations. Thus on balance a late thirteenth/fourteenth-century date for this stirrup appears most likely.

289 Stirrup (AE). Trapezoidal form, with curved foot-rest, oval, with turned down edges at front and rear; rectangular-sectioned suspension bar for stirrup leather, protected by plain cover plate at front. H. 125mm. W. 102mm. Drainage coll. *SD613; 2007R.228*   **Fig 59**

This form is known both in cast copper alloy and wrought iron. For copper-alloy examples see Clark 1995, 73 fig. 55 - an example from the River Thames in the Museum of London (O2587) - and other parallels quoted (ibid 74), and for wrought iron see Ward Perkins 1940, 94 fig. 26 no. 2 (MoL 7321). The type is probably fourteenth- to fifteenth-century in date; Clark (ibid 74) suggests a date in the second half of the fourteenth century on the basis of a fragment from a well-dated London archaeological context.

BIBLIOGRAPHY

Andrews, H. C. and Dunning, G. C. 1939: 'A Thirteenth-Century Stirrup and Storage-Jar from Rabley Heath, Herts', *Antiq. J.* **19**, 303-12

Anon 1871: 'Antiquities and Works of Art Exhibited: by J. E. Nightingale, a brass key', *Archaeol. J.* **28**, 248

Baker, D., Baker, E., Hassall, J. and Simco, A. 1979: 'Excavations in Bedford 1967-1977', *Beds. Archaeol. J.* **13**, 7-307

Bayley, J., Drury, P. and Spencer, B. 1984: 'Exhibits at Ballots - 2. A medieval mirror from Heybridge, Essex', *Antiq. J.* **64**, 399-402

Benson, R. and Hatcher, H. 1843: *The History of Old and New Sarum* (vol. 6 of R. C. Hoare, *The History of Modern Wiltshire*)

Biddle, M. (ed.) 1990: *Artefacts from Medieval Winchester Parts i & ii: Object and Economy in Medieval Winchester*, Winchester Stud. **7** (Oxford)

Blair, J. and Ramsay, N. (eds.) 1991: *English Medieval Industries: Craftsmen, Techniques, Products* (London and Rio Grande, Ohio)

Borg, A. 1991: 'Arms & Armour' in P. and E. Saunders (eds.), *Salisbury Museum Medieval Catalogue Part 1*

Clark, J. (ed.) 1995: *The Medieval Horse and its Equipment c. 1150-c. 1450*, Medieval Finds from Excavations in London **5**

Coad, J. G. and Streeten, A. D. F. 1982: 'Excavations at Castle Acre Castle, Norfolk, 1972-77', *Archaeol. J.* **139**, 138-301

Cowgill, J., de Neergaard, M. and Griffiths, N. 1987: *Knives and Scabbards*, Medieval Finds from Excavations in London **1**

Cowgill, J., de Neergaard, M. and Griffiths, N. 2000: *Knives and Scabbards (new ed.)*, Medieval Finds from Excavations in London **1** (Woodbridge)

Cox, J. C. and Harvey, A. 1907: *English Church Furniture*

Crossley, D. W. 1981: 'Medieval iron smelting' in D. W. Crossley (ed.), *Medieval Industry*, CBA Res. Rep. **40**, 29-41

Cunliffe, B. 1964: *Winchester Excavations 1949-1960*, **1** (Winchester)

Dungworth, D. 2011: 'Appendix 6: metallurgical residues' in P. Davenport and J. Schuster, *Land at Clackers Brook, East Melksham, Wiltshire*, Cotswold Archaeology unpubl. client report no. 11034, 42-7

Dunning, G. C. 1964: 'Objects of Metal, Stone and Bone' in H. E. O'Neil, 'Excavation of a Celtic Hermitage on St. Helens, Isles of Scilly, 1956-58', *Archaeol. J.* **121,** 66-69

Egan, G. 1997: 'Non-ceramic finds' in C. Thomas, B. Sloane and C. Phillpotts, '*Excavations at the Priory and Hospital of St Mary Spital, London*', MoLAS Monogr. **1**, 201-10

Egan, G. 1998: *The Medieval Household: Daily Living c. 1150-c. 1450*, Medieval Finds from Excavations in London **6**

Ellis, B. 1991: 'Spurs' in P. and E. Saunders (eds.), *Salisbury Museum Medieval Catalogue Part 1*, 54-78

Evans, D. H. and Loveluck, C. 2009: *Life and economy at early medieval Flixborough, c. AD 600-1000: the artefact evidence.* Excavations at Flixborough 2 (Oxford)

Fairbrother, J. R. 1990: *Faccombe Netherton: Excavations of a Saxon and Medieval Manorial Complex*, Brit. Mus. Occas. Pap. **74**

Fletcher, J. M. J. 1914: 'Chained Books in Dorset and Elsewhere', *Proc. Dorset Natur. Hist. & Antiq. Field Club*, **30**, 8-26

Goodall, A. R. 1984: 'Objects of non-ferrous metal' in J. P. Allan, *Medieval and Post-Medieval Finds from Exeter, 1971-80*, Exeter Archaeol. Rep. 3, 337-48

Goodall, I. H. 1978: 'Appendix 6: Iron Objects' in A. E. S. Musty 'Exploratory Excavation within the Monastic Precinct, Waltham Abbey, 1972', *Essex Archaeol. Hist.* **10**, 157-60

Goodall, I. H. 1981: 'The medieval blacksmith and his products' in D. W. Crossley (ed.), *Medieval Industry*, CBA Res. Rep. **40**, 51-62

Goodall, I. H. 1988: 'Iron Objects' in T. B. James and A. M. Robinson with E. Eames, 208-223

Goodall, I. H. 1990a: 'Knives' in Biddle, M. (ed.) 1990, 835-60

Goodall, I. H. 1990b: 'Locks and keys' in Biddle, M. (ed.) 1990, 1001-36

Goodall, I. H. 1990c: 'Iron fittings for lights' in Biddle, M. (ed.) 1990, 981-3

Goodall, I. H. 1990d: 'Iron domestic implements' in Biddle, M. (ed.) 1990, 818-28

Goodall, I. H. 1990e: 'Stirrups' in Biddle, M. (ed.) 1990, 1042-3

Goodall, I. H. 2000: 'Iron objects' in Ellis, P. (ed.), *Ludgershall Castle. Excavations by Peter Addyman 1964-1972*, Wiltshire Archaeological and Natural History Society Monograph Ser. 2 (Devizes). 143-156

Goodall, I. H. 2011: *Ironwork in Medieval Britain: an archaeological study*, Soc. Medieval Archaeol. Monogr. **31**

Griffiths, D., Philpott, R. A. and Egan, G. (eds.) 2007: *Meols: The Archaeology of the North Wirral Coast. Discoveries and observations in the 19th and 20th centuries, with a catalogue of collections*, Oxford University School of Archaeology Monogr. **68**

Gustafsson, N. B. 2009: 'För folk och fä: om vikingatida fjättrar och deras användning', *Fornvännen* **104**, 89-96

Halbout, P., Pilet, C. and Vaudour, C. (eds.) 1987: *Corpus des objets domestiques et des armes en fer de Normandie: Du 1ᵉʳ au XVᵉ siècle*, Cahier des Annales de Normandie **20** (Caen)

Haslam, J. 1980: 'A Middle Saxon iron smelting site at Ramsbury, Wiltshire', *Medieval Archaeol.* **24**, 1-68

Henning, J. 1992: 'Gefangenenfesseln im slawischen Siedlungsraum und der europäische Sklavenhandel im 6. bis 12. Jahrhundert', *Germania* **70**, 403-26

Jackson, R. 2007: 'Excavations at the Old Council House, Corn Street, Bristol, 2005', *Bristol and Avon Archaeology* **22**, 47-78

James, T. B. and Robinson, A. M. with Eames, E. 1988: *Clarendon Palace: the History and Archaeology of a Medieval Palace and Hunting Lodge near Salisbury, Wiltshire.* Soc. Antiq. Res. Rep. **45**

Loader, E. 2000: 'The Metalwork' in M. Rawlings, 'Excavations at Ivy Street and Brown Street, Salisbury, 1994', *Wilts. Arch. Mag.* **93**, 29

Margeson, S. 1993: *Norwich Households: The Medieval and Post-medieval Finds from Norwich Survey Excavations 1971-1978*, E. Anglian Archaeol. Rep. **58** (Norwich)

Moore, S. 1999: *Cutlery for the table: a history of British table and pocket cutlery* (Sheffield)

Müller, M. 1996: 'Die Turmburg Nürings bei Falkenstein im Taunus' in B. Schroth, (ed.), *Burgenforschung in Hessen*, Kleine Schriften aus dem Vorgeschichtlichen Seminar der Philipps-Universität Marburg **46**, 161-176 (Marburg)

Musty, J. W. G. 1959: 'A Pipe-line near Old Sarum: Prehistoric, Roman and Medieval Finds including Two Twelfth Century Lime Kilns', *Wilts. Arch. Mag.* **57**, 179-91

Musty, J. and Rahtz, P. 1964: 'The Suburbs of Old Sarum', *Wilts. Arch. Mag.* **59**, 130-54

Musty, J. W. G. and Algar, D. J. 1986: 'Excavations at the Deserted Medieval Village of Gomeldon near Salisbury, Wilts', *Wilts. Arch. Mag.* **80**, 127-69

Ottaway, P. 1992: *Anglo-Scandinavian Ironwork from Coppergate,* The Archaeology of York **17/6** The Small Finds (York)

Ottaway, P. and Rogers, N. 2002: *Craft, Industry and Everyday Life: Finds from Medieval York,* The Archaeology of York: **17/15** The Small Finds (York)

Øye, I. 1988: *Textile Equipment and its Working Environment, Bryggen in Bergen c. 1150–1500,* Bryggen Papers **2** (Oslo)

Page, P., Atherton, K. and Hardy, A. 2005: *Barentin's Manor: Excavations of the moated manor at Harding's Field, Chalgrove, Oxfordshire 1976-9.* Thames Valley Landscapes Monograph **24**

Penny, W. E. W. 1911: 'The Medieval keys in Salisbury Museum', *Connoisseur* **29**, 11-16

Phillips, T. 1833: 'Survey of the manor and forest of Clarendon, Wiltshire in 1272', *Arch.* **25**, 151-8

Pitt Rivers, Lt.-Gen. 1883: *On the Development of Primitive Locks and Keys*

Pitt Rivers, Lt.-Gen. 1890: *King John's House, Tollard Royal, Wiltshire* (privately printed)

Rogers, N. S. H. 1993: *Anglian and other finds from Fishergate.* The Archaeology of York **17/9** The Small Finds (York)

Saunders, P. 2009: *Channels to the Past: the Salisbury Drainage Collection* (Salisbury, 2nd, revised edition)

Shortt, H. de S. (ed.) 1960: *The Collections Illustrated* (Salisbury)

Shortt, H. de S. (ed.) 1973: *Salisbury Heritage* (Salisbury)

Smith, K. 1984: 'Ancient horseshoes: their value as indicators', *The Hatcher Review,* **2** (no. 17), 335-42

Stevens, F. 1931: 'Three axes found at Downton', *Wilts. Arch. Mag.* **45**, 489-490

Stone, J. F. S. and Charlton, J. 1935: 'Trial excavations in the E. Suburbs of Old Sarum', *Antiq. J.* **15**, 174-90

Tandy, W. A. 2007: *The Chained Library in Wimborne Minster* (Wimborne)

Tatton-Brown, T. 1996: 'The Archaeology of the Spire of Salisbury Cathedral' in L. Keen and T. Cocke (eds.), *Medieval Art and Architecture at Salisbury Cathedral,* Brit. Archaeol. Assoc. Conf. Trans. **17**, 59-67

Tatton-Brown, T. and Crook, J. 2009: *Salisbury Cathedral: The Making of a Medieval Masterpiece*

Thompson, F. H. 1986: 'Exhibits at Ballots: Iron shackles with barrel padlock and chain from the R. Tyne at Corbridge', *Antiq. J.* **68**, 311 and pl. L

Tylecote, R. F. 1981: 'The medieval smith and his methods' in D. W. Crossley (ed.), *Medieval Industry,* CBA Res. Rep. **20**, 42-50

Vince, A. G. (ed.) 1991: *Aspects of Saxo-Norman London. 2, Finds and environmental evidence.* London & Middlesex Archaeol. Soc. Spec. Pap. **12**

Ward, G. 1941: 'The Iron Age Horseshoe and its Derivatives', *Antiq. J.* **21**, 9-27

Ward Perkins, J. B. 1940: *Medieval Catalogue,* London Museum Catalogues **7**

Wordsworth, C. 1903: *Cartulary of St. Nicholas Hospital* (Wiltshire Record Society)

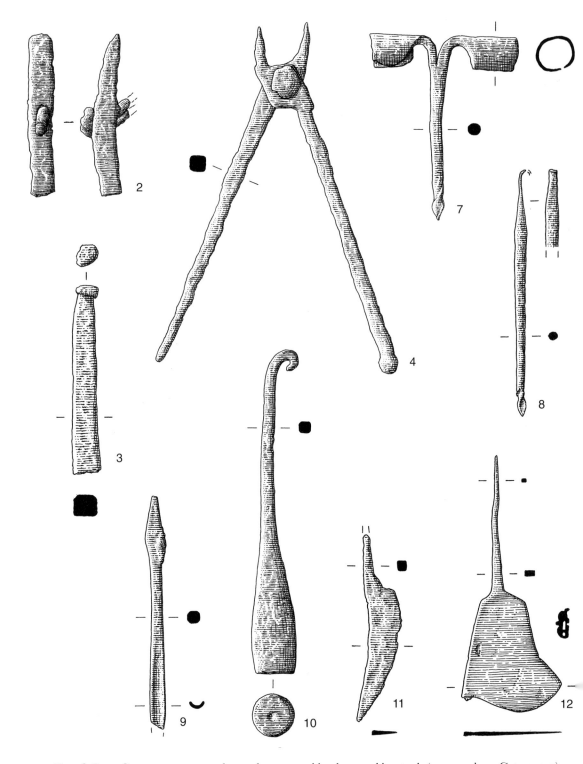

Fig 36. Iron: Cat 2-4, 7-12, metal, wood, stone and leather working tools (1:2, mark on Cat 12 1:1)

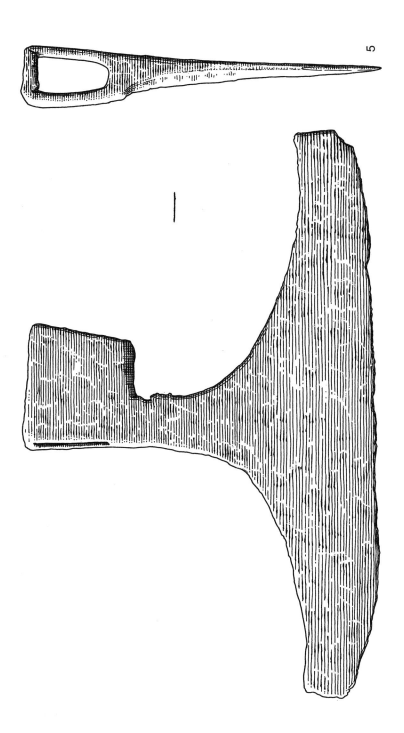

Fig 37. Iron: Cat 5, carpenter's axe head (1:2)

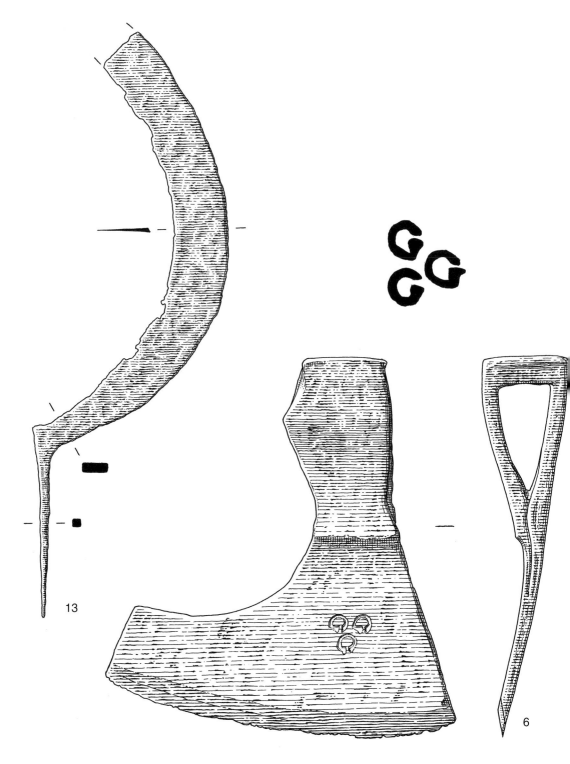

Fig 38. Iron: Cat 6, axe head; Cat 13, sickle blade (1:2, mark on Cat 6 1:1)

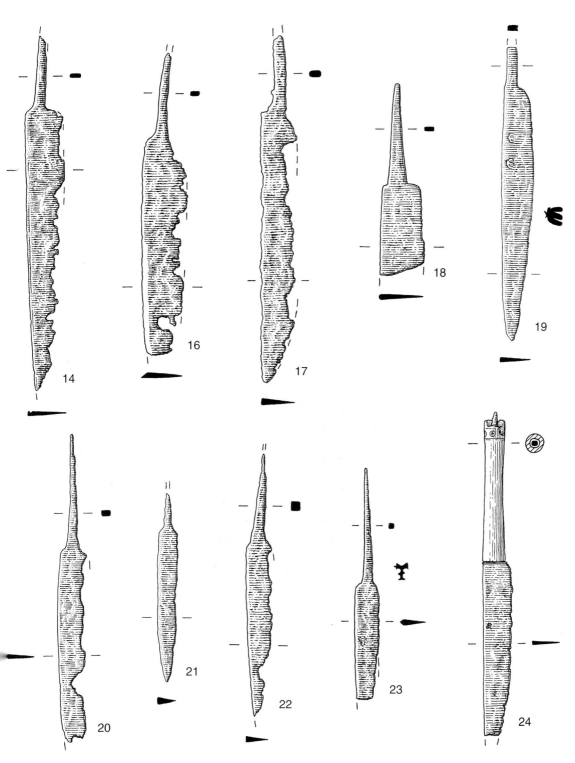

Fig 39. Iron: Cat 14, 16-24, knives (Cat 24 with bone handle) (1:2, marks on Cat 19, 23 1:1)

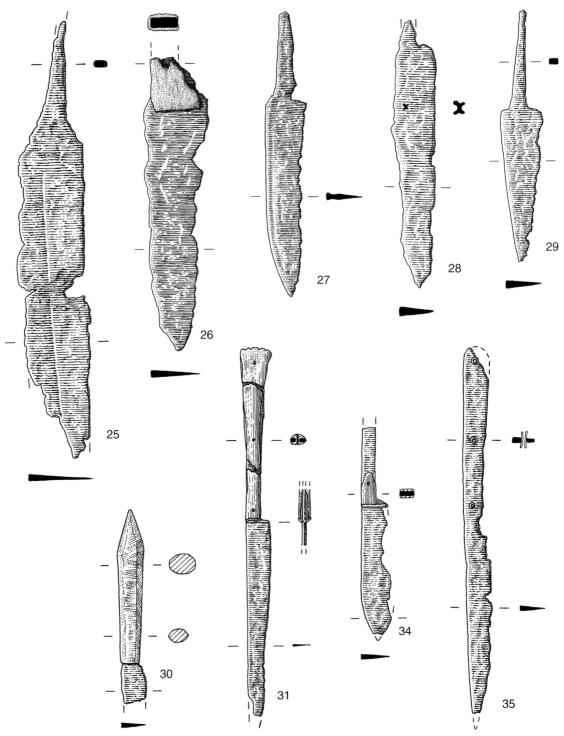

Fig 40. Iron: Cat 25-31, 34-5, knives (Cat 26 with wood, Cat 30 with horn handle, Cat 31, 34 with bone handles) (1:2, mark on Cat 28 1:1)

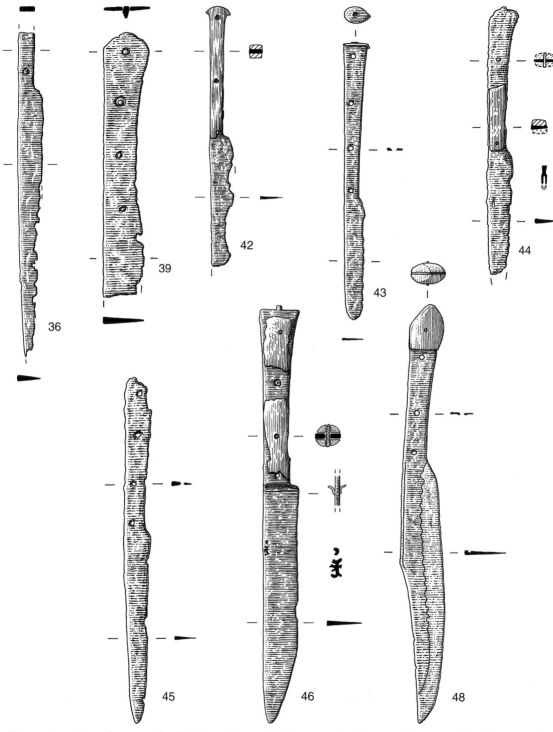

Fig 41. Iron: Cat 36, 39, 42-6, 48, knives (Cat 42 with bone scales, Cat 43 with copper alloy, Cat 44 and 48 with bone, Cat 46 with leather) (1:2, marks on Cat 44, 46 1:1)

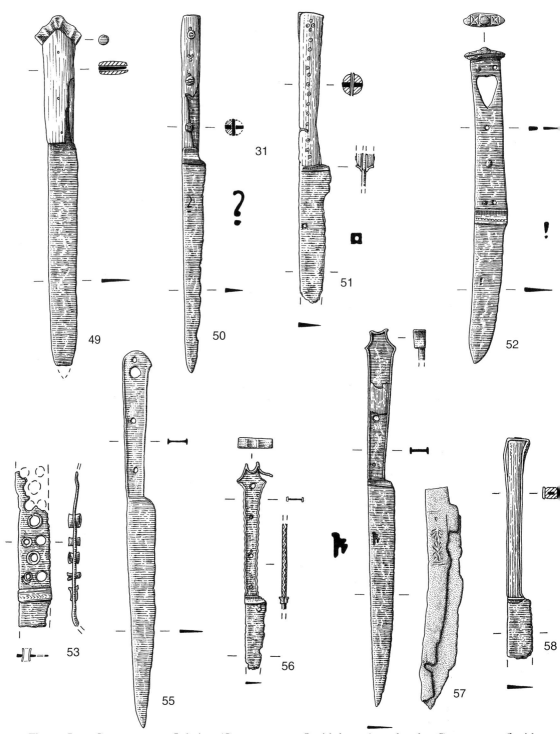

Fig 42. Iron: Cat 49-53, 55-8, knives (Cat 49, 51, 57-8 with bone/wood scales, Cat 49, 53, 56 with copper alloy, Cat 57 with leather sheath) (1:2, marks on Cat 50-2, 57 1:1)

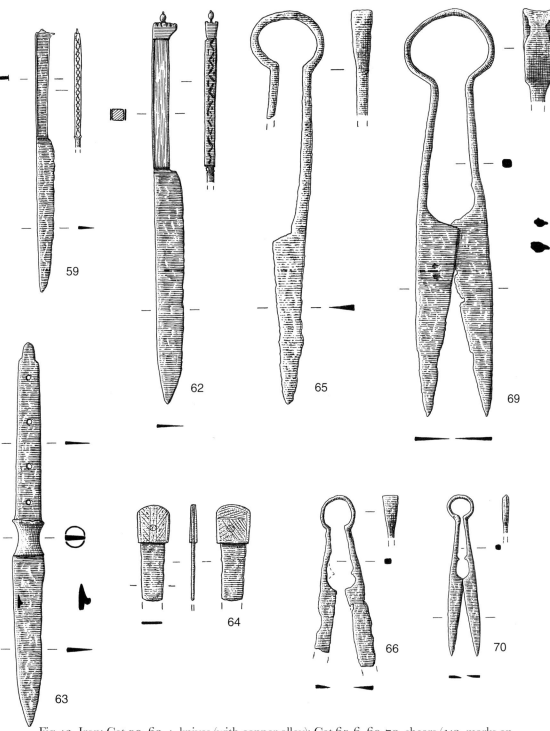

Fig 43. Iron: Cat 59, 62-4, knives (with copper alloy); Cat 65-6, 69-70, shears (1:2, marks on Cat 63, 69 1:1)

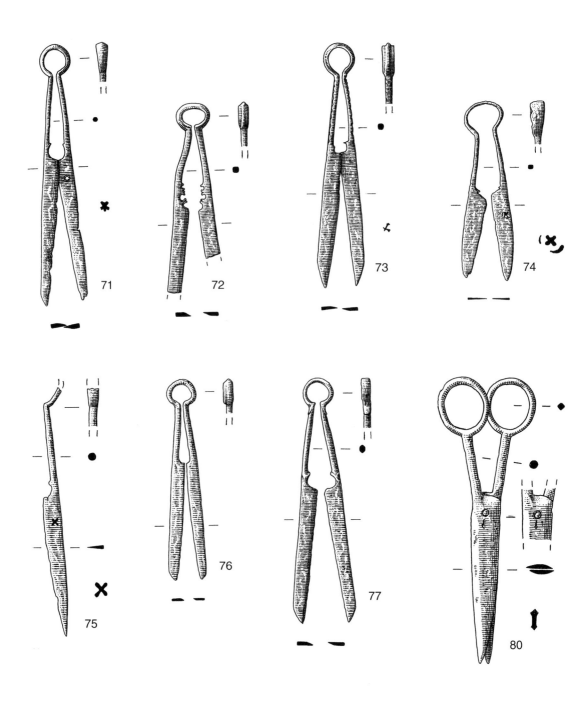

Fig 44. Iron: Cat 71-7, shears: Cat 80, scissors (1:2, marks on Cat 71, 73-5, 80 1:1)

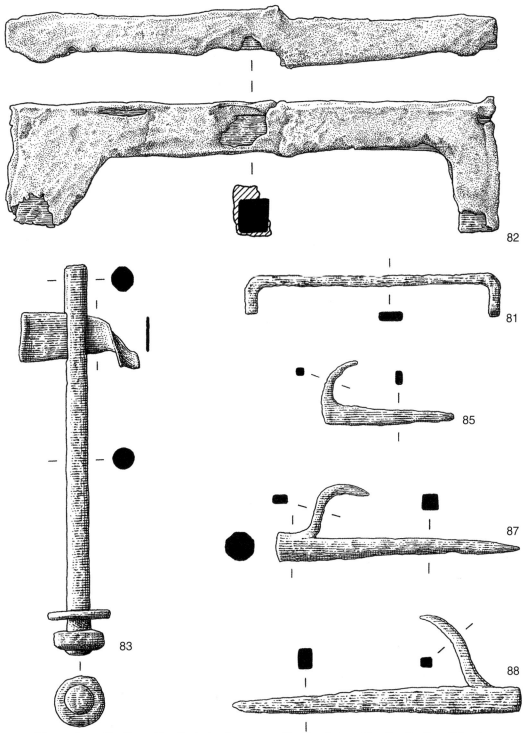

Fig 45. Iron: Cat 81-2 (Cat 82 in lead), cramps; Cat 83, tie bar; Cat 85, 87-8, wall-hooks
(1:2, except Cat 83 1:4)

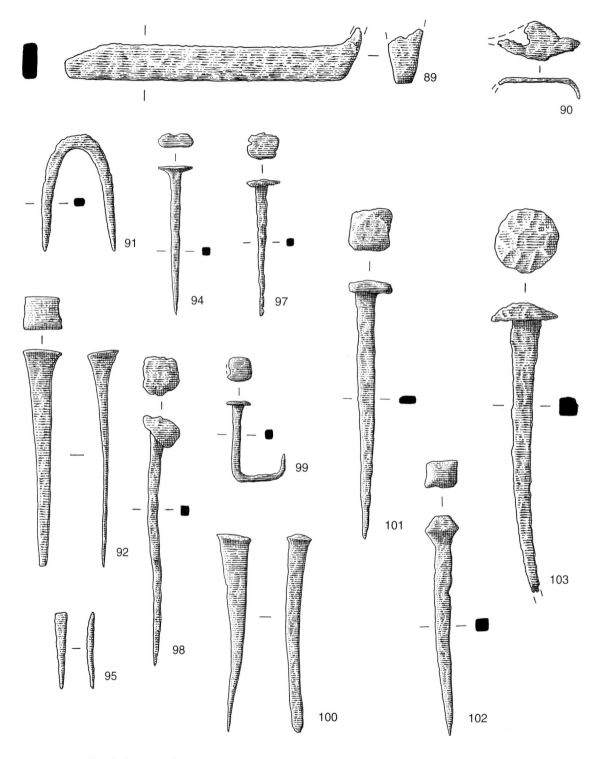

Fig 46. Iron: Cat 89, wall anchor; Cat 90-1, staples; Cat 92, 94-5, 97-103, nails (1:2)

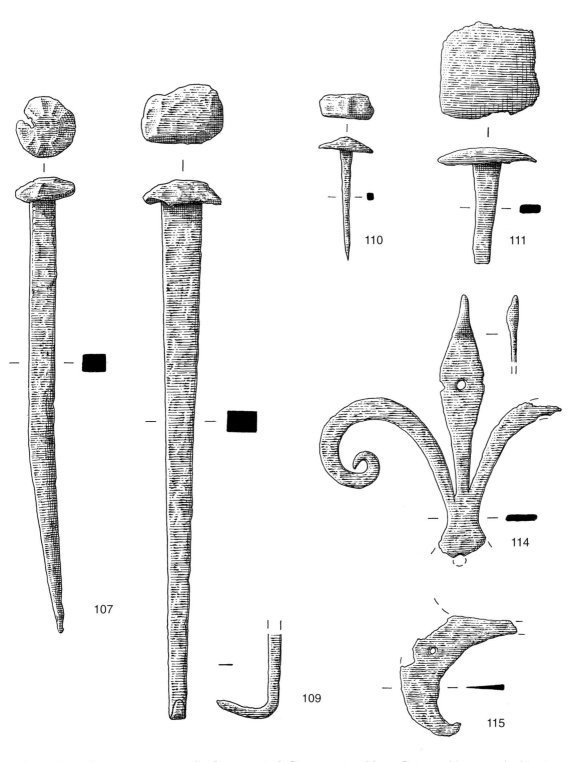

Fig 47. Iron: Cat 107, 109-10, nails; Cat 111, stud; Cat 114, strap hinge; Cat 115, hinge terminal (1:2)

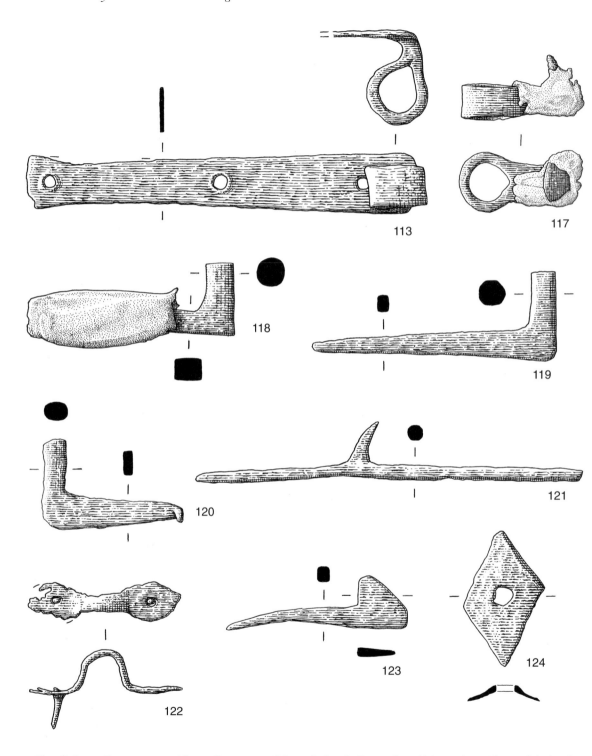

Fig 48. Iron: Cat 113, strap hinge; Cat 117, wall loop (in lead); Cat 118-20, hinge pivots (Cat 118 in lead);
Cat 121-2, bolts; cat 123, latch rest; Cat 124, rove (1:2)

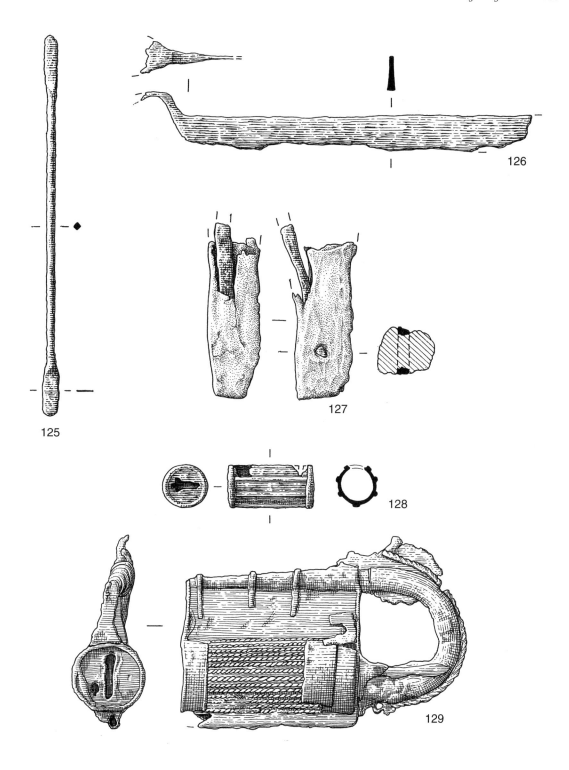

Fig 49. Iron: Cat 125-7 (Cat 127 in lead), window bars; Cat 128-9, padlocks (1:2, except Cat 125 1:4)

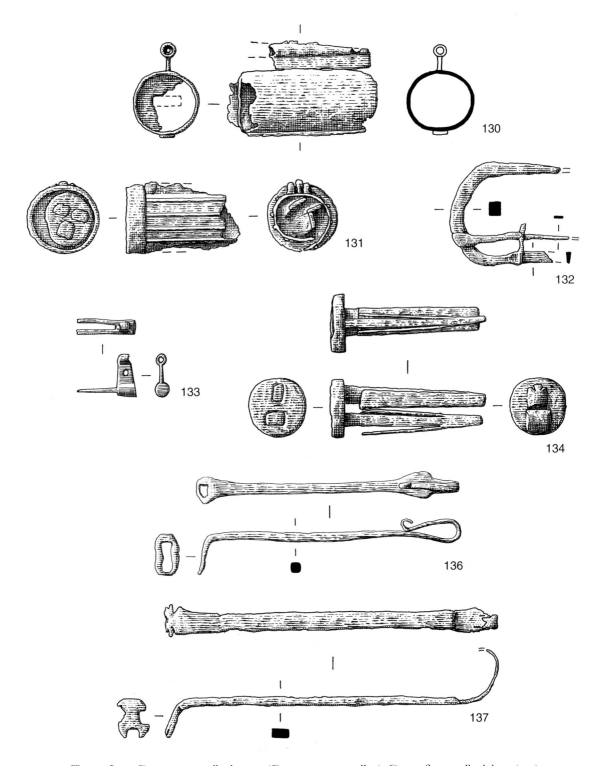

Fig 50. Iron: Cat 130-4, padlock parts (Cat 133 copper alloy); Cat 136-7, padlock keys (1:2)

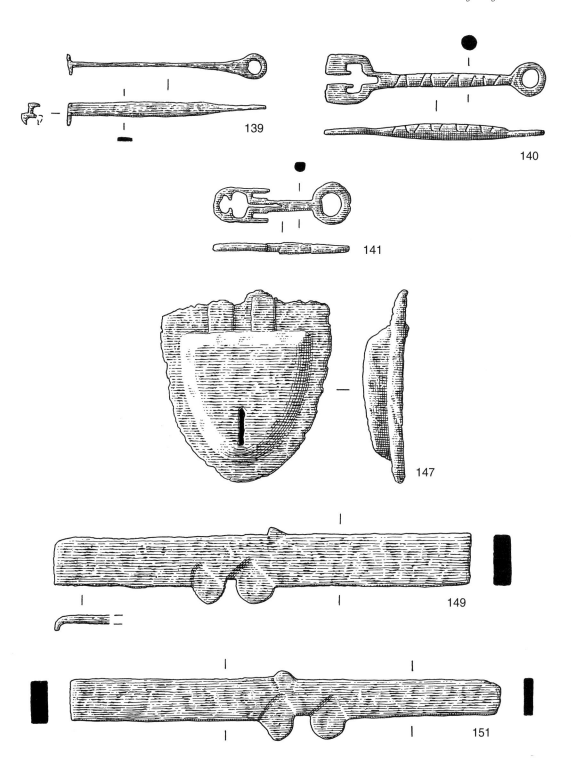

Fig 51. Iron: Cat 139-41, padlock keys; Cat 147, chest lock; Cat 149, 151, draw bolts (1:2)

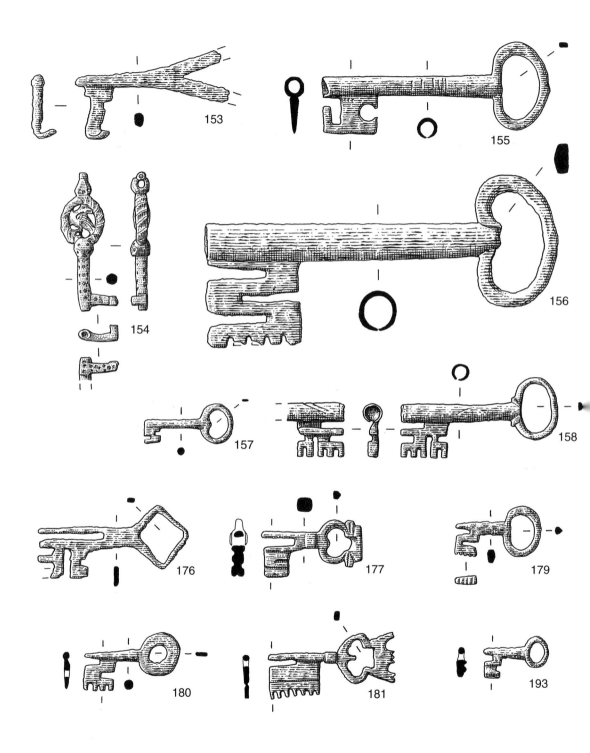

Fig 52. Iron: Cat 153-8 (Cat 154 copper alloy), 176-7, 179-81, 193, keys (1:2)

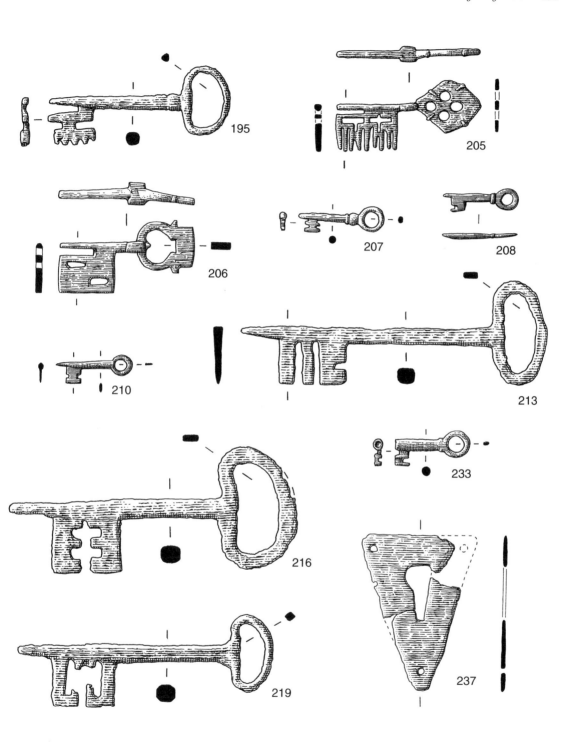

Fig 53. Iron: Cat 195, 205-8, 210, 213, 216, 219, 233 (Cat 233 copper alloy), keys; Cat 237, escutcheon plate (1:2)

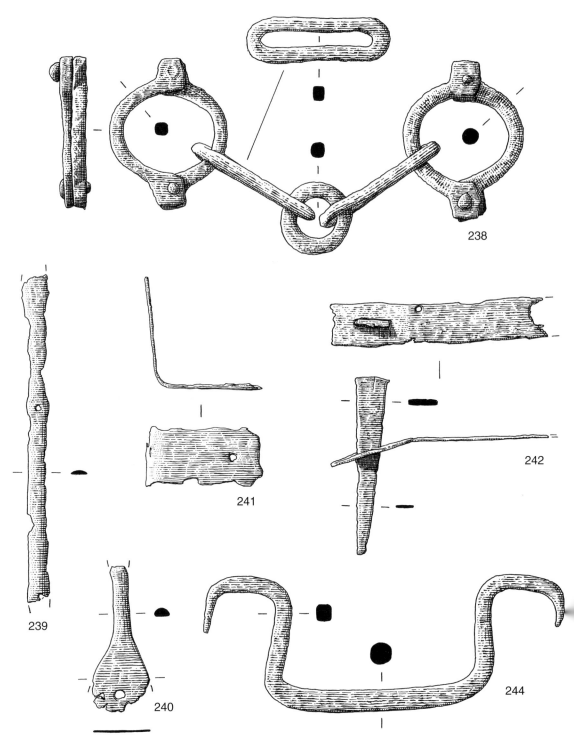

Fig 54. Iron: Cat 238, shackles; Cat 239-42, bindings; Cat 244, drop handle (1:2, except Cat 238 1:4)

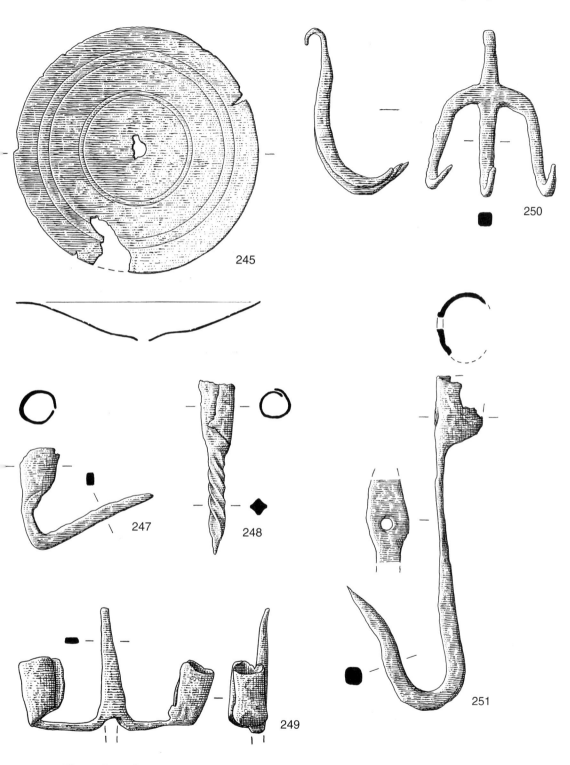

Fig 55. Iron: Cat 245, wax-pan; Cat 247-9, candle holders; Cat 250-1, hooks (1:2)

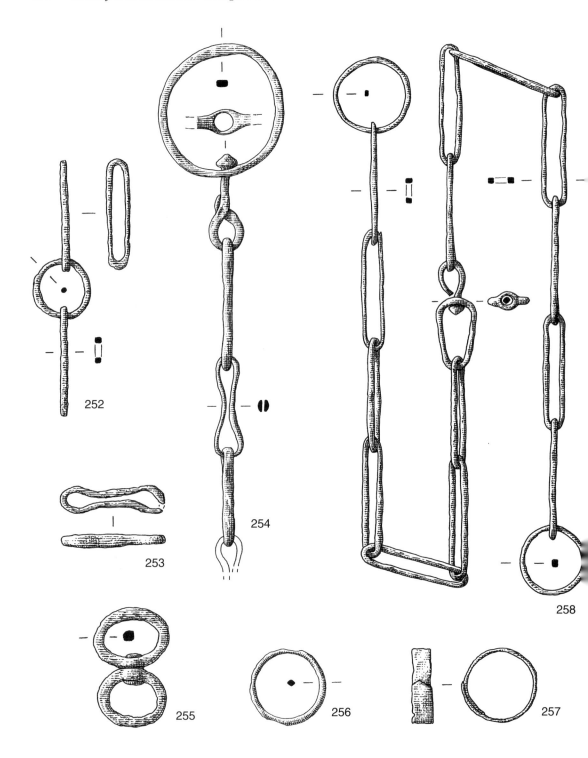

Fig 56. Iron: Cat 252-4, chains; Cat 255-8, swivel fitting, ring, collar (1:2)

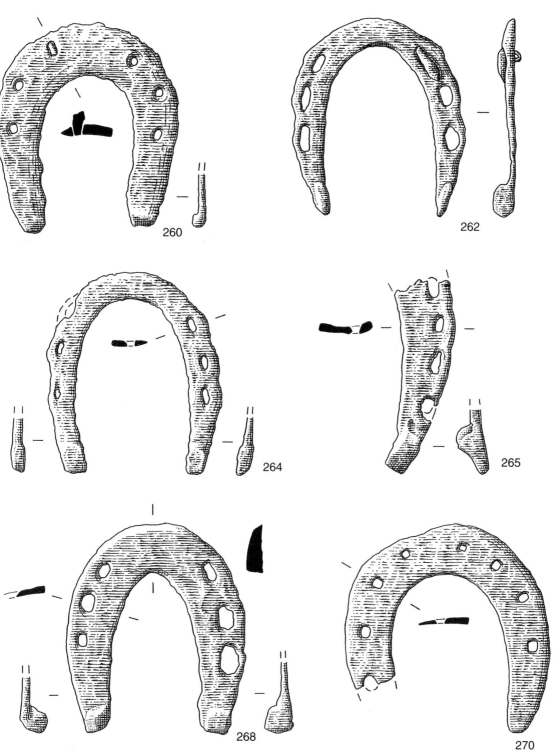

Fig 57. Iron: Cat 260, 262, 264-5, 268, 270, horseshoes (1:2)

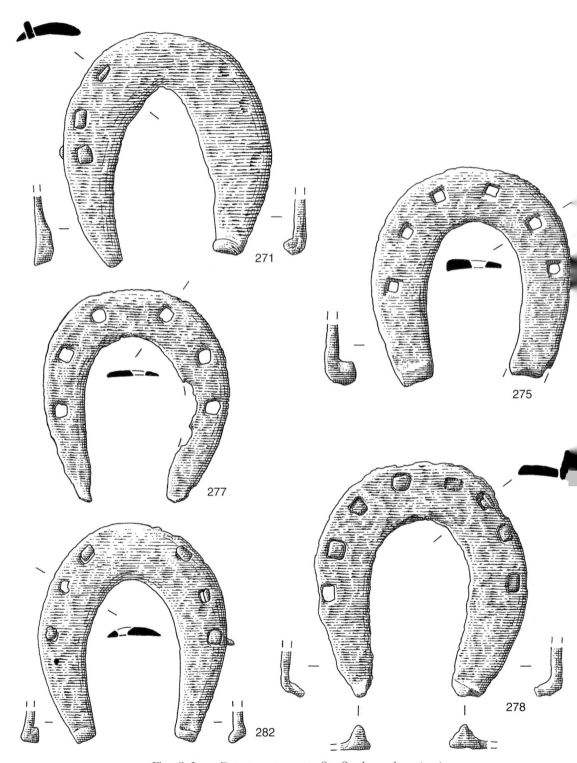

Fig 58. Iron: Cat 271, 275, 277-8, 282, horseshoes (1:2)

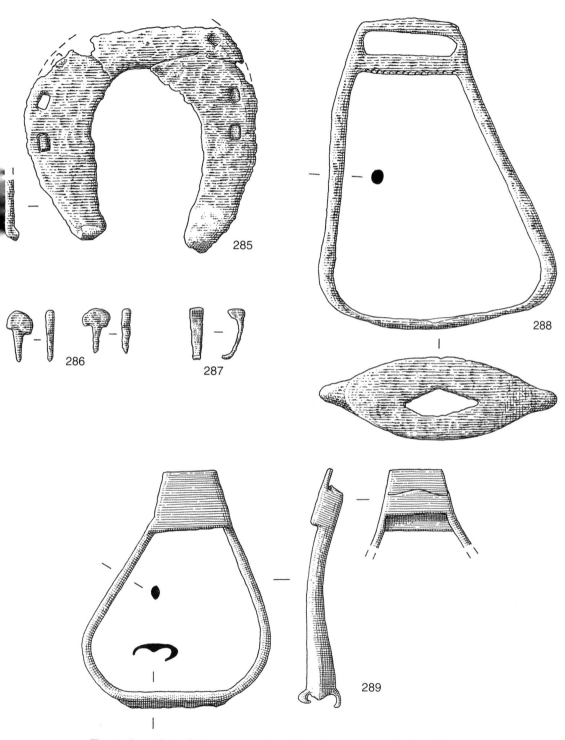

Fig 59. Iron: Cat 285, horseshoe; Cat 286-7, horseshoe nails; Cat 288-9,
stirrups (Cat 289 copper alloy) (1:2)

Objects of Wood

by John McNeill
with Peter Saunders and David Algar

INTRODUCTION

The collection comprises a number of miscellaneous fragments of architectural woodwork of oak, the most notable being four roof bosses from Ivychurch Priory, an early fifteenth-century beam end; two city chests; and a bowl from the site of Salisbury's Dominican Friary. Three oak trusses that supported the bells in the church at North Wootton in Dorset are catalogued in the more appropriate section on bells and copper alloy vessels (pages 76 and 84-5). Excepting the chests and the Ivychurch bosses, individual items are unrelated, but though there are instances in which the provenance is uncertain it is likely all the architectural woodwork was manufactured locally, with the possible exception of a pair of brackets (Cat 7). None of the pieces has been sampled dendrochronologically, and the dates suggested in the catalogue are largely stylistic.

For much needed help and many kindnesses the author wishes to thank David Cousins, the Reverend and Mrs Hugh Hoskins, and Dr Charles Tracy.

CATALOGUE

Architectural Woodwork

IVYCHURCH PRIORY

Four wooden bosses from the roof of the former refectory at Ivychurch Priory were acquired by the Museum in 1890, following the demolition of a substantial house occupying the site of the former claustral precinct. Their immediate context was described by J. E. Nightingale, who witnessed the demolition of the post-medieval house at Ivychurch in 1889 and reported his findings in a paper read to the Society of Antiquaries in 1891 (Nightingale 1891). Nightingale makes it clear that the cloister at Ivychurch was built to the north of the church, and that when its north range 'was divested of its casing of later buildings and its two floors' a 50 feet by 20 feet hall was revealed. Nightingale identified this as the monastic refectory, and went on to describe the remains of an important wall-painting depicting the Last Supper occupying the width

of the lower east wall. The roof was discovered above an inserted plaster ceiling, 'a fine open timber roof in excellent condition'. Indeed, so good was the condition of the refectory roof timbers that the fourth Earl of Radnor handed them over to his son, Canon Bertrand Pleydell-Bouverie, then rector of Pewsey, who instructed the architect, Charles Ponting, to redeploy them in the roof over the vestry and organ chamber of the church of St John the Baptist, Pewsey (pl. 18). Although Nightingale is infuriatingly unspecific in his description of the roof's discovery, given the size of the refectory it seems most likely the Museum's bosses would have covered the intersection between the ridge and its principal rafters.

The date of the bosses is arguable and depends, in part, on what is known of the history of Ivychurch Priory. Ivychurch Priory was an Augustinian house, said to have been founded by King Stephen, and certainly in existence by the early years of the reign of Henry II. It lie ust to the north of Alderbury, at the edge of Clarendon Park, and, in addition to functioning as a parish church for the inhabitants of Clarendon Forest, canons from Ivychurch were bound to serve in the king's chapel at Clarendon Palace. Indeed, it is likely it was initially founded to provide a pool of priests for the royal chapel at Clarendon. The priory was never particularly well endowed, and came perilously close to complete impoverishment between *c.*1350 and the 1420s, before Henry VI's grant of the alien priory of Upavon in 1423 effectively re-located the Augustinian house, bringing with it a prebendal stall at Salisbury. Ivychurch priory was dissolved in 1536, at which time it was financially stable and its church and other buildings were reported to be in good condition 'with moch newe buylding of stone and breke'. (VCH Wilts.1956, 289-295). The greater part of the church was destroyed soon after the Dissolution, but the north nave aisle, cloister and three surrounding ranges were transformed into a house, a plan of which was made some time before the redevelopment of this house *c.*1680 (reproduced in RCHM(E) 1987, 150). Prior to the *c.*1680 remodelling, the former monastic refectory acted as a great hall to the house. Inserted into a niche in its north wall (presumably the site of the refectory pulpit) was a fireplace bearing the arms of Edward Thatcham, prior of Ivychurch from 1467-1493. Although the fireplace could have been introduced into the refectory when it was transformed into a great hall in the late 1530s, the subdivision and transformation of monastic ranges into prioral lodgings and halls was commonplace in the late fifteenth century, and the possibility that the fireplace was site-specific and formed part of a larger remodelling of the refectory initiated by Edward Thatcham should not be discounted.

The four roof bosses form a group and have been carved to a similar specification, each being approximately 230mm square, with a cruciform recess on the underside which enabled them to be fitted across a beam intersection. These recesses or channels are of truncated triangular section, 70-80mm deep (pl. 19). The longevity of English late medieval foliage styles makes it difficult to date the bosses with any precision, but a date towards the end of the fifteenth century seems more likely than a date in the early sixteenth century. The Museum contains three panels of early sixteenth-century glass from Ivychurch, attributed to the priorate of Richard Page (1493-1536). The bosses should probably be associated with his predecessor as prior, Edward Thatcham (1467-1493), and testify to the significant investment in new building work that marked the later stages of Ivychurch as an Augustinian priory, an investment that probably extended across half a century and was recognised in the report of the 1536 chantry certificate, that there was 'moch newe buylding of stone and breke'.

Pl. 18. Timbers from the refectory roof of Ivychurch Priory redeployed in the vestry roof of St John the Baptist Church, Pewsey

1 Roof boss. Approximately 230mm square and 150mm deep. Carved with a four-petal design, primrose-like though highly simplified. Three fixing holes cut through the boss to coincide with the centre of channels cut into the underside of the boss. From the former refectory at Ivychurch Priory, Alderbury. *c*.1470-1490. *1890-1.2.1*   **Pl 19**

2 Roof boss. Approximately 230mm square and 150mm deep; four fixing holes. Carved with a double rose. From the former refectory at Ivychurch Priory, Alderbury. *c*.1470-1490. *1890-1.2.2*   **Pl 19**

3 Roof boss. Approximately 230mm square and 160mm deep; four fixing holes, one of which retains its apparently-original iron nail. Carved with four oak leaves emerging from a spiral stem, the leaf tips pointing outwards. From the former refectory at Ivychurch Priory, Alderbury. *c*.1470-1490. *1890-1.2.3*   **Pl 19**

4 Roof boss. Approximately 230mm square and 150mm deep; four fixing holes. Carved with four stylised oak leaves, the leaf tips pointing inwards at the centre of the boss. From the former refectory at Ivychurch Priory, Alderbury. *c*.1470-1490. *1890-1.2.4*   **Pl 19**

MISCELLANEOUS

5 Small panel depicting the head of a creature eating grapes. W. 100mm. H. 95mm. Th. (max) 30mm. The panel is said to have come from a roof in the church of St Mary and St Mellor, Amesbury. It depicts a demonic head, with cat-like ears and a broad mouth, devouring a stem from which protrude two berry-like seed clusters. There is a small secondary perforation above the nose. Probably 15th century. *1999R.1112*   **Pl 21 & cover**
The chancel of St Mary and St Mellor at Amesbury was re-roofed in the late fifteenth century, but as part of William Butterfield's radical restoration of 1852-53 the late medieval roof was removed, and replaced by the present steeply-pitched roof. The relief panel presumably came from this chancel roof, and may have been intended as a satire: the demon chewing on a grape stalk poking fun at the priest taking communion wine at the altar below. Shorn of its context it is now impossible to say. The carving is rough, and intended to be finished in paint. Its one notable feature is the presence of a thick central lock of hair, a feature associated with Romanesque corbels, and perhaps inspired by the existence of a Romanesque corbel table embellishing the exterior of Amesbury's twelfth-century nave.

6 Beam end with female head in twin-horned headdress. H. 245mm. W. 185mm. The beam has been cut down, and its surviving length is a maximum of 360mm, with a depth of carving of around 140mm. It is the truncated section of a substantial structural wooden beam. The beam is morticed to take a vertical post, and is decorated by the head of a woman wearing an elaborate headdress, known as a split or heart-shaped hennin. The heart-shaped hennin was often worn with the hair coiled into two buns, or cauls, held in place at the side of the head by nets, which seem to have been cut away from the carving. The figure would have been seen from below as if gazing down upon the observer, and the bulbous protrusions to either side of the neck are intended to represent the type of shawl opening away from the collar fashionable in early 15th-century womens' dress. First half of the 15th century. *2008R.1712*   **Pl 21**
The piece's original provenance in unknown, as is the date of its original accession into the Museum. However, the form and dimensions of the beam end are virtually identical to surviving examples at the Old George Inn, Salisbury, as is the detailing (one of the George beam-end figures (RCHM(E), 97-99 and pl. 84) similarly does not occupy the full height of the beam end and is outlined by a discrete hollow chamfer). As such, it seems likely that the George was its original setting. The greater part of the medieval George Inn is assumed to have been constructed under its first owner, William Teynturer the Younger, in the third quarter of the fourteenth century, though this is too early for the beam under discussion here, and if it did indeed come from the George it must have been part of an

extension or remodelling undertaken after the George Inn was made over to the Corporation of Salisbury in 1413 (RCHM(E), 1980, 97-100). The heart-shaped hennin as worn by the woman seems to have been introduced at the beginning of the fifteenth century and enjoys a great vogue between *c.*1415 and *c.*1460. The most splendid, and earliest, representations of the headwear are French, as in the donor page of a copy of the work of Christine de Pizan of *c.*1413, but good parallels can be found in the Devonshire Hunting Tapestries of the early 1430s or the Neville Hours of a decade later.

7a and 7b Pair of brackets. L. 1120mm (1170mm originally, before notch cut out). W. 535mm (585mm before notch cut out). Bracket 7a is 80mm thick (max) and the length of its arc is 1030mm. Bracket 7b is 73mm thick (max) with an arc 1040mm long. Both brackets have been sawn vertically in modern times to form a decorative gothic arch which was then affixed to an internal wall at the Crown Hotel (a largely early 19th-century building occupying an L-shaped site between High Street and Crane Street, Salisbury, demolished in 1969). Bracket 7a is embellished with an encircled triple mouchette and bracket 7b with an encircled four-petal rosette with additional loops on the diagonals. The brackets are not symmetrical, and both have been cut down. Subsidiary roundels have been cut in two in both brackets, and elements of a traceried border have been partially pared away from the intrados of bracket 7a. They have also been sawn vertically, so as to remove at least some of their original weight 7b is the lightest, being the thinner of the two). The joinery is very similar, however, and both are made up of planks of oak, three for 7a and two for 7b, the planks having been joined originally on the rear by long dowels. The dowelling channels show appreciable distortion as the result of load-bearing. The original dowels (three in 7a, two in 7b), no longer survive, and the planks are now held together by modern battens.

The outer faces of the two brackets are decorated with blind tracery, expertly cut with a squared outer profile, and a hollow chamfer employed for the cusping. The repertoire is English curvilinear, and, in the particular combination used here, most likely to date from the second quarter of the 14th century; *c.*1330-1350. *1970.51*   **Pl 20**

The original provenance of the brackets is unknown. Since the trajectory of the arch in both cases would have continued to join the outer frame, they must originally have formed spandrels. This makes it far more likely that they were designed to act as decorative panels, affixed to structural timbers, rather than that they were structural brackets in themselves. An example of a blind-traceried structural bracket survives at the Old George Inn, Salisbury, where one can see how the vertical post and bracket are necessarily continuous, which can never have been the case with the Museum brackets. Prior to their acquisition the brackets were in an early nineteenth-century wing of the Crown Hotel, and though a medieval inn variously known as La Rose or La Hotecorner is known to have occupied a part of the site, this is only first recorded in 1410 (RCHM(E), 1980, 68, 72). As such, there is nothing to connect the site and the brackets from an archaeological perspective.

There is also nothing in the types of blind tracery used that suggests a specifically local provenance. If anything the forms would be more at home in eastern England, though since very little early fourteenth-century building survives in Salisbury, and Decorated was an architectural style that travelled easily across southern England, this isn't saying much. Most of the motifs are staples of English early-to-mid-fourteenth-century tracery design; the encircled triple mouchettes, daggers, and types of cusping are pretty much ubiquitous. Even the windmill-like four-petal rosette was used in the West Country, at St Augustine's, Bristol (now Bristol Cathedral). The loops that are added to the diagonals of this four-petal rosette are unusual, however, and much more readily paralleled in East Anglia than further west, turning up in the early fourteenth-century choir clerestory at Ely Cathedral and the parish churches of Snettisham (Norfolk) and Grantchester (Cambs) (Fawcett, 2008, figs. 5b, 5g and 5h). It is, of course, entirely possible that this rather fastidious design was widely adopted by wood carvers, given its absolute symmetry and the ease with which it could be drawn out, and was therefore more widely distributed than now seems the case. However, in our existing state of knowledge, their regional accent seems slightly out of place. They are, in their way, the great puzzle piece in the architectural woodwork collection here catalogued.

8 Window head. H. 410mm. W. 635mm (including two lateral tenons, each with two holes for 17mm diameter dowels). Th. 110mm. Window head carved with a trefoiled ogee arch for a window opening 425mm wide. The arch is articulated by a hollow chamfer on both the inner and outer faces, while the area between the shouldered insets of the trefoil and the notional containing arch has been excavated, in the manner of high quality curvilinear tracery in stone. There are traces of ochre paint surviving on the inner chamfer. Nailed on the outer face is a post-medieval bronzed disc impressed with the letters R W H above I. The window head came from the first storey of 49 New Canal, Salisbury, a subdivided property that before its demolition contained remnants of a substantial 14th-century hall with a two-storey cross wing. The window head came from the cross wing, and was drawn out and illustrated prior to demolition. Second quarter 14th century. See RCHM(E) 1980, 101-02 and *Sal. Mus. Rep.* 1966-67, 18 and pl. 1b. *1967.6*   **Pl 20**

9 Lintel. H. 353mm. W. 1110mm. Triangular-headed lintel designed for an opening 940mm wide. The lintel is carved on one side only, with a simple concave moulding articulating the underside. The spandrels are decorated with double roses over leaves in low relief, the relief carving set in broadly symmetrical triangular fields outlined by single concave mouldings. There are traces of original paint and gilding. Fixing was originally provided via two channels 80mm. wide cut to the rear, which formed a lap joint with two vertical timbers; *c.*1510-1525. *1947.8*
Pl 20

The lintel was accessioned in 1947, when Hugh Shortt, the museum curator responsible for the accession, recorded that it was said to

have been removed from the Bishop's Palace, Salisbury *c.*1900. Shortt evidently entertained doubts as to this provenance. The early sixteenth-century character of the lintel's carving is too late to have formed any part of the last major late medieval reconstruction of the Bishop's Palace under bishop Richard Beauchamp (1450-1481). Nor is there an obvious context for its removal *c.*1900, though J. Arthur Reeve restored the under-croft of the Bishop's Palace between 1885 and 1890 during which time he removed a wooden partition 'considered to be medieval' (RCHM(E) 1993, 72). If the lintel did originate from the Bishop's Palace, this is most likely to have been its position, part of a secondary screen inserted into earlier fabric in the first quarter of the sixteenth century.

The type of wooden lintel of which the Salisbury example is representative was ubiquitous in late medieval England. It was used in screens, partitions, corridors, pentices, and porches - and is particularly common as a lintel above doors in screens passages. Margaret Wood cites innumerable examples, one being Rufford Old Hall of *c.*1500 illustrating exactly how such a lintel would most likely be set (Wood, 1965, 135). The rather soft, crumpled angularity of the outer petals of the roses suggests the lintel was carved in the first quarter of the sixteenth century, though the serrated triangular leaves look somewhat old-fashioned alongside the roses.

10 Panel. H. 390mm. W. 360-380mm. Th. (max) 90mm. The panel is carved with an encircled quatrefoil set within a square, the quatrefoil being set diagonally. It has been cut down on one side and damage to the panel from cracking on this same side has been repaired with a post-medieval metal plate. The opposite side has also been repaired using dowelling pegs. The base of the panel is square-cut, while the upper edge has a very slight moulding. The panel came from a stone-fronted two-storey 15th-century house known as 'The Barracks' on Brown Street, Salisbury, which was demolished between *c.*1860 and *c.*1880 (RCHM(E) 1980, 118); second half of the 15th century. *1936.75*   **Pl 20**

The panel is most likely to have been cut

down from a wooden fireplace lintel. Wooden fireplace lintels are effectively square-headed as a matter of course, for the lintel is simply a wooden beam. Square-headed fireplace lintels in stone, however, were not developed before the late fourteenth century, and are frequently decorated with a quatrefoil frieze. It is this motif which has been adopted in the panel from 'The Barracks'. There is now no evidence of paint on the surviving fragment, but late medieval quatrefoil friezes were frequently used as fields for displays of heraldry, or were embellished with initials or emblems associated with the owner of the house. The quatrefoil, either simple or cusped, becomes immensely popular above fireplaces in the last third of the fifteenth century, and is well represented in Salisbury by fireplaces in the Hall of John Halle of *c*.1470 and at Church House of *c*.1500 (RCHM(E) 1980, pl. 90). It is notable that the quatrefoil described here is set diagonally, as the late medieval stone examples are invariably set square.

Chests
by Peter Saunders

Chests are one of the commonest forms of furniture to have survived from the medieval period. Churches often provide good, accessible examples, and notable amongst these locally are the five medieval chests in Salisbury Cathedral (see Brown 1999, 62-4 and figs. 42-4 and Geddes 1999, 367-8) and a fine fifteenth- or early sixteenth-century example in St Thomas's Church, Salisbury made of oak and with distinctive lock plates (paralleled on a chest in St Michael's Church, Coombe Bissett and St Mary's, Mendlesham, Suffolk (Simpson 2008, 55 fig. 2).

For an overview of the construction of chests see Eames 1977, 108-180; Geddes 1999, 31-4; and Tate 1960, 35-42.

I am particularly indebted to Dr Jane Geddes, Gavin Simpson and Will Hobbs for helpful comment on Cat 11-12 and advice on chests generally.

11 Chest of wood, iron-bound. Thick pine board construction, almost completely held by a lattice of massive iron straps, nine overlying four on the front and back; three over three on the ends and bottom; and eleven overlying four on the domed lid. L. 1330 mm. W. 510 mm. H. (max) 550 mm. All the iron on the body is held by prominent nails with rose heads. The bands on the domed lid are secured by prominent, and larger, T-headed nails, three of which, from the right-hand end band, are now detached (see Cat 110, page 155) and stored separately from the chest, which is normally on public display. All of the bars on the lid widen near to each of the nine hinges, and those with hasps, of which there are five, also widen towards the hasp end. Where these expansions occur there are five nails instead of three, giving added strength. The chest was secured by the five hasps (each with curled tip), the centre hasp of which is longer than the others and covers a central lock plate; the staple for this hasp is no longer extant. One padlock, which appears not to be contemporary with the chest, survives of perhaps originally five. The hasps could also have once been secured by a draw bar (not present) that passed through eight staples (the right-hand one now missing), though it is difficult to see how a bar and padlocks could have been used simultaneously; a bar may have been employed to enhance security when the central lock only was in use. The lid ends have gable overhangs protected by curved iron plates. On each end is a pair of large carrying ring handles. There are internal wooden divisions of comparatively modern date, including a small storage compartment of oak. 15th century. *Sal. Mus. Rep.* 1973-4, 19 and pl. IIIC. *1974.63*

Pl 21

This type of chest is known as a 'standard', i.e. of box form with a domed or canted lid (Eames 1977, 172-7 and fig. 17). It would have been suitable for travelling, being very robust and with a lid well-suited to throwing off rain water. Eames 1977, 173-4 cites examples of comparable chests that are of mid-late fifteenth-century date, and Geddes 1999, 230-32 notes the tendency towards the very heavy strapping of chests and doors in the fifteenth and sixteenth centuries. A date of *c*.1440-1500 is thus suggested.

Prior to its acquisition by the Museum in 1974 this impressive chest was used by Salisbury Corporation as a muniment chest to store archives of the City of New Sarum. Its origin is not known, but it was certainly one of those noted by Rathbone as being in the Council House in 1951 (Rathbone 1951, 67), and it may have been in the Corporation's possession when the latter occupied the Old Council House. A minute book relating to 1387-1452, salvaged from the fire there in 1780, frequently mentions 'the common chest' (noting that in 1414 it was in St Thomas's Church), a 'smaller chest' and 'mayor's chest', and records that in 1440 the Assembly ordered 'the common seal to be placed under six locks and six keys in a chest', though in 1447 this was reduced to four (Carr 2001, 179 and 213). This chest may be secured by a maximum of five padlocks and would thus have been suitable for such use from 1447. Its immense strength also supports the suggestion that the city may have used it to store money and valuables other than muniments in earlier times.

12   Chest of wood, iron-bound. Thin elm board construction; lid is hipped, made of planks. The chest is held together by thin gauge iron straps of average 50mm width (seven under two horizontal bands around the box; and five under three, with additional end bands wrapped over gabled ends on lid). There are five hinges. Three of the bands over the lid are expanded to support hasps which drop to two (not original) lock plates (locks no longer extant) and one central staple, which took a padlock (not extant) to secure the chest. The hasps are oval, are flanked by vertical struts each ending in a square head with incised diamond design (apparently secondary) and have pendent pear-shaped rings. There are cranked drop handles of angular section iron rod on all four sides, those on the longer sides set asymmetrically to avoid the central staple and allow balanced carriage. L. 1350 mm. W. 585 mm. H. (max) 630mm. The lid is 1410mm. x 610mm. There is 'recent' repair to both wood and metal around the base, which is now supported on three battens, giving the impression that the original base may have rotted away; additionally

there are repairs/alterations to the lid and former lock plates. In modern times the inside has been lined with fabric, two internal partitions have been added and the whole has been painted black externally. *1974.64*   **Pl 21**

Prior to 1974 this chest, like Cat 11 a 'standard', was used by Salisbury Corporation as a muniment chest to store archives of the City of New Sarum. In shape this chest has some resemblance to one in the Public Record Office associated with Lady Margaret Beaufort (Eames, 177 and pl. 52), which would suggest possibly a late fifteenth-century date but on the basis of the hasps and rings, which are distinctly renaissance in character, its date is probably later: sixteenth century and possibly even later. A chest in the church of St Giles, Great Wishford is somewhat similar in size, shape and ironwork detailing but possesses ball feet and ornately-carved woodwork, and is described by Pevsner (1975, 593-4) as Jacobean.

There is also an iron-bound chest of post-medieval date in the collection from the Salisbury Tailors' Hall, where it had been used for the safe-keeping of the archives of the medieval Guild of Tailors (acc. no. *1996R.2160*).

Box type. L. 920 mm. W. 485 mm. H. (max) 630mm. The lid is 960mm x 513mm. The chest is bound by wide bands of iron attached by nails and rivets, circular and flat-headed (those on the lid *c*.35mm in diameter). The bottom front edge is repaired in wood. There are five hinges and single drop handles at either end with grips of twisted design. The chest is secured by two hasps (hinged upwards from the central strap band on the front), which engage with staples descending from the lid, and two padlocks, one of which is perhaps original, the other later in date. There is a key hole in the centre of the lid, simple and with a modest cover plate, and another in the centre of the front of the chest. The latter is surrounded by an ornate star-shaped escutcheon with a raised centre. Within the chest is a complicated lock mechanism.

The key to the lock (acc. no. *1999R.353*) in the lid survives but the key to the lock in the front of the chest is un-located, believed stolen.

Domestic
By David Algar

13 Fragments of a lathe-turned bowl. These have been restored yielding the greater part of a shallow bowl with a plain rim, D. 220mm and 40mm deep, standing on a solid foot, 88mm in diameter and 7mm high. The flat base has two shallow grooves near to the edge. The wood is ash. Pre-Dissolution. From a burial on the site of the Dominican Friary, Fisherton Street, Salisbury. *1983.111*   **Fig 60**

During the medieval period and indeed later, lathe-turned wooden bowls of many shapes and sizes must have existed in vast numbers. From the early thirteenth century ash became increasingly popular as a wood for the production of turned vessels and by the second half of the fourteenth century was the most favoured wood for bowls and dishes. Not only was ash easily turned and water resistant but also had an attractive decorative grain. This solitary bowl from Salisbury is a rare survivor, having been deposited in anaerobic waterlogged conditions, and falls within a group of small bowls, which were most probably used as containers in the consumption of food and drink. For a series of similar bowls from London see Keys 1998, 203-6, no. 563-73. Three leather shoes (see page 87) and fragments of rope (see page 330) were found at the same site.

I am grateful to Jan Lister for the identification of the wood.

BIBLIOGRAPHY

Brown, S. 1999: *Sumptuous and Richly Adorn'd; The Decoration of Salisbury Cathedral* (RCHM(E))

Carr, D. R. 2001: *The First General Entry Book of the City of Salisbury 1387-1452,* Wiltshire Record Society **54** (Trowbridge)

Eames, P. 1977: *Furniture in England, France and the Netherlands from the twelfth to the fifteenth century*

Fawcett, R. 2008: 'Snettisham Church' in J. McNeill (ed.), *King's Lynn and the Fens: Medieval Art, Architecture and Archaeology*, Brit. Archaeol. Assoc. Conf. Trans. (Leeds), **31, **134-147

Geddes, J. 1999: *Medieval Decorative Ironwork in England*

Keys, L. 1998: 'Wooden Vessels' in G. Egan (ed.), *The Medieval Household, Daily Living c.1150-c.1450*, Medieval Finds from Excavations in London **6**, 196-217

Nightingale, J. E. 1891: 'The priory of Ivychurch and the remains of wall-paintings lately discovered there', *Proc. Soc. Antiq.* **13**, 352-5

Pevsner, N. 1975: *Wiltshire*. The Buildings of England (2nd ed., revised by B. Cherry, Harmondsworth)

Rathbone, M. G. 1951: *List of Wiltshire Borough Records earlier in date than 1836*, Wiltshire Archaeological and Natural History Society Records Branch **5** (for 1949, Devizes)

RCHM(E) 1980: *Ancient and Historical Monuments in the City of Salisbury* **1** (HMSO)

RCHM(E) 1987: *The Churches of South-East Wiltshire* (HMSO),149-153

RCHM(E) 1993: *Salisbury: The Houses of the Close* (HMSO)

Simpson, G. 2008: 'The Pine Standard Chest in St Margaret's Church, King's Lynn, and the Social and Economic Significance of the Type' in J. McNeil (ed.), *King's Lynn and the Fens: Medieval Art, Architecture and Archaeology*, Brit. Archaeol. Assoc. Conf. Trans. (Leeds), **31**, 53-65

Tate, W. E. 1960: *The Parish Chest* (Cambridge)

VCH Wilts. 1956: R.B. Pugh and E. Crittall (eds.), 'The Religious Houses of Wiltshire' in *A History of Wiltshire* (Victoria History of the Counties of England) **3**, 289-95

Wood, M. 1965: *The English Medieval House*

Pl 19. Wood: Cat 1-4 roof bosses from Ivychurch Priory, *c.* 1470-90 (principal faces of 1-4, side view of 1 and back view of 3)

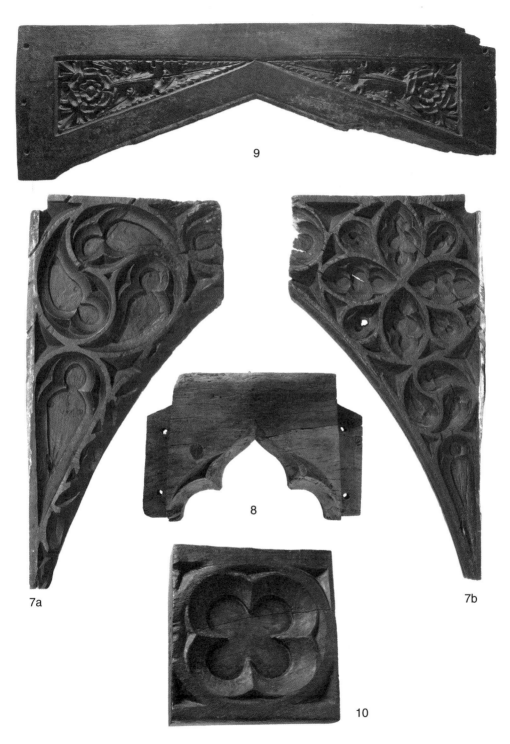

Pl. 20. Wood: Cat 7a-b, brackets, *c.*1330-50; Cat 8, window head, second quarter 14th century;
Cat 9, lintel, *c.*1510-25; Cat 10, quatrefoil probably from fireplace lintel, late 15th century

5

6

11

12

Pl 21. Wood: Cat 5, panel, probably 15th century; Cat 6, figurative beam end, early 15th century; Cat 11-12, chests

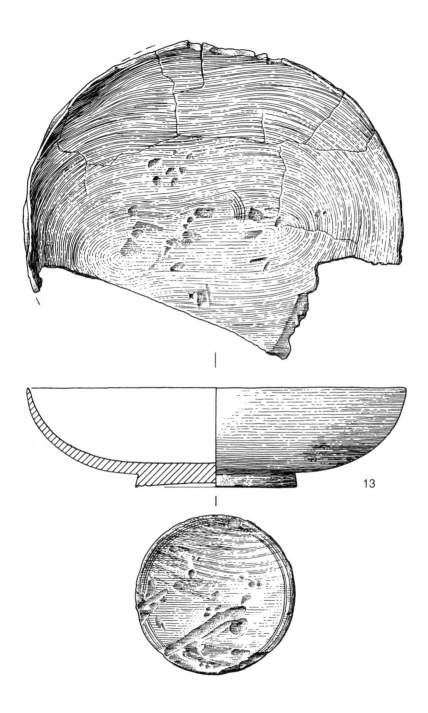

Fig 60. Wood: Cat 13, wooden bowl (1:3)

Porphyry

by Tim Tatton-Brown

INTRODUCTION

Porphyry, a rare and exotic material, takes its name, *lapis porphyrites*, from a very hard igneous rock, of a rich purple colour, that was first discovered on a mountain-top site, early in the first century A.D., in the very remote eastern desert of Egypt (Malgouyres 2003). It was transported overland to the Nile at Qena some 120 km. away, and then floated down the river to the Mediterranean, where it was much used for columns, statuary etc., particularly in Imperial contexts in the later Roman period. The most famous example is the sculpture of the four tetrarchs from Constantinople, now a trophy on the corner of St. Mark's basilica in Venice. The quarries were abandoned in the early fifth century, and the site was not rediscovered until the nineteenth century, so all medieval porphyry is reused from Roman contexts (Peacock and Maxfield 2001). This, the 'original' form of porphyry, is now called 'purple' (or sometimes 'red') porphyry to distinguish it from a second type of porphyry, 'green' porphyry'. This form is anciently called *lapis lacedaemonius* (and more recently *verde-antico* or *serpentino*, though it should not be confused with serpentine, a different material) and comes from Krokeai in the southern Greek Peloponnese. The quarries are in porphyritic andesite domes, some 30 km. south-south east of Sparta, and not far from the Gulf of Laconia (Higgins and Higgins 1996, 54-5). Green porphyry was also extracted between the early first and early fifth centuries A.D., and it too was much reused in the medieval period, particularly for paving and wall-veneering (*opus sectile*).

From the eleventh century onwards purple and green porphyry was much used in Rome and the surrounding areas of central Italy for elaborate geometric pavements, and by the thirteenth century this had reached a peak, particularly under a group of craftsmen, known collectively as the Cosmati (Hutton 1950). They used the purple and green porphyry, along with some other materials, as beautifully cut inlay in tombs, shrines, sedilia and other church furnishings (like screens and pulpits), as well as in many fine pavements. Purple porphyry was also used magnificently in the very fine twelfth and thirteenth century Imperial tombs that can still be seen in Palermo Cathedral.

In England, the remarkable late twelfth century pavement of so-called '*opus Alexandrinum*' work, immediately to the west of the great shrine of St. Thomas Becket in Canterbury Cathedral is full of inlaid purple and green porphyry. These materials may have been used in other twelfth and early thirteenth century pavements in England (like St. Augustine's Abbey in Canterbury, where porphyry fragments were found in the excavations), but none have survived *in situ*. However, the wonderful new eastern arm of Westminster Abbey received two magnificent Cosmati pavements in *c*.1269 (in front of the high altar, and around the new shrine of St. Edward the Confessor), where large amounts of purple and green porphyry were inlayed into the Purbeck marble paving (Tatton-Brown 1998b). The porphyry was also used in other places, most splendidly on the shrine of St. Edward itself. It should also be noted that the two largest surviving rectangular slabs of purple porphyry from medieval England are fixed to the front and back faces of Henry III's tomb chest, which is almost adjacent to the shrine of St. Edward in Westminster Abbey.

Porphyry in the Cathedral at Old Sarum

When the Society of Antiquaries of London instigated new excavations at Old Sarum in 1909, they started by clearing out the castle at the centre of the hilltop site. In 1912 they moved to the northwest quadrant and were soon uncovering the outer faces of the outer walls of the cathedral, particularly its earlier, western half. Remarkably, by the end of the following year, they had almost completely stripped out the interior of the whole of the 235 feet long Romanesque cathedral. They had also discovered the two main phases, late eleventh century nave and short eastern arm with apsidal terminations to the chapels, and the very large new aisled transepts and presbytery of the early twelfth century. As the workmen cleared down to the floor levels, in the summer of 1913, they discovered that most of the evidence for the original floors (and its bedding make-up) was still there. The work was organised by Lt. Col. William Hawley and D.H. Montgomerie; the overall director, William St. John Hope, who only visited the site periodically, wrote the annual report for the Society. This is his description of the newly discovered flooring in his February 1914 report (Hope 1914, 107):

> 'The whole of the new work, except in one or two places, was paved throughout with squared blocks of stone, either of white Chilmark or the delicate green from Hurdcote. These blocks were faced on one side only, leaving the other side rough; in order, therefore, to obtain a level surface, the blocks were laid in a very thick bed of mortar. When the church was dismantled these blocks were taken up, leaving the mortar bed exposed, with here and there embedded chips of disturbed stones. By diligent brushing of the dust and rubbish out of the hollows we have been able to recover from these beds the disposition of the blocks, and Lt. Col. Hawley noticed one damp day the alternating colours of the stone chips. Mr Montgomerie and I have accordingly been able to measure and lay down on paper the patterns, with the colouring, of a large extent of the floor, and so to recover what may at present be looked upon as a unique feature of a twelfth-century English church.'

The Hurdcote stone is the nearest source of building stone to Old Sarum. It is found in the Upper Greensand, just to the southwest of Barford St. Martin, and was used for most of the ashlar work at Old Sarum as well as for half the paving. The much harder Chilmark or Tisbury stone was not much used at Old Sarum. For the new cathedral in New Salisbury, by contrast, only Chilmark/Tisbury stone was used (Tatton-Brown 1998b).

Montgomerie's (and Hope's) original coloured plan of the cathedral at Old Sarum was never published, but survives in Salisbury Museum (pl. 22). It is still the most important record of Romanesque paving in an English cathedral. The nave paving is probably of the late eleventh century, and a very small fragment of it is still visible on the site. All the rest of the paving (in the eastern arm) must date from the early twelfth century, and it is not known how much of it, or its bedding, survives *in situ* below the turf.

Although the eastern arm of the cathedral was built under bishop Roger le Poer (1107-39), there was some evidence from the excavations that the chapels at the extreme eastern end of the building were rebuilt later, probably in the later twelfth century (RCHM(E) 1980, 18-19). Here an axially-placed altar was discovered that was probably in the chapel of All Saints. It was flanked by two other chapels, all with their floors one step up from the ambulatory in the presbytery. In the central chapel, the altar platform was raised up two further steps, and in front of it traces of the bedding for an elaborate geometric pavement were found, which were described by Hope as follows:

> 'The altar platform was paved with rows of stone blocks, alternately white and green [i.e. Chilmark and Hurdcote stone again], and some of the mortar beds remained in part in front of and to the north of the altar. The chapel floor also retained the mortar bed of a curious pavement of interlacing circles, but not of the same material as the altar platform, the stones composing it having been flat and not rough underneath.'

Hope goes on to mention fragments of 'black marble or touch' that were scattered about the altar and may have formed the altar slab, but he does not say anything further about the 'curious pavement of interlacing circles', though they and the blocks of the steps in front of the altar are clearly shown on the plan, with a gap between the two areas (pl. 22). The 'pavement of interlacing circles' is also shown in a contemporary photograph (pl. 23), which has, in the fore-ground, the worn Hurdcote stone step leading up to the chapel from the eastern ambulatory.

Towards the end of his 1913 report, Hope does mention the green and purple porphyry fragments which must have been found in the loose spoil overlying the cathedral floors. Unfortunately he does not say exactly where they were found, and it is unlikely, at that time, that they would have been plotted out on the plan. This is his description (Hope 1914, 116):

'A more remarkable discovery is that of quite a considerable quantity of pieces of *verde-antico* [i.e. green porphyry] and red porphyry of various sizes [12 pieces were recorded by Col. Hawley - see below]. These materials are so rare in this country, Westminster and Canterbury (both at Christchurch and St. Augustine's Abbey) being the only known places of their occurrence, that it would be very important to say how they could have been used here. They were however, so scattered about that this is impossible. There was, moreover, no shrine or important tomb here that we are aware of, yet these precious materials were used in a church that was destroyed before the Canterbury and Westminster works were begun.'

It is surprising that Hope did not know that a 'tomb of St. Osmund', in Old Sarum cathedral, is mentioned in the 'Sarum Consuetudinary' which Hope himself later discussed in print (Hope 1917). This 'tomb of St. Osmund' is almost certainly the still surviving Purbeck marble tomb-shrine of Blessed Osmund, which was taken down to the new cathedral, with the tombs of bishops Roger and Jocelyn in 1226 (Tatton-Brown 1999). As well as this, Hope probably did not examine the fragments of porphyry very closely, or he would have seen that the porphyry fragments were flat on both their top and undersides, and hence that they are highly likely to have come from the 'curious pavement of interlacing circles' in the eastern chapel. Osmund's tomb-shrine was perhaps placed at the centre of this chapel, between the pavement and the eastern altar, in the later twelfth century, at a time when the cult of 'Blessed Osmund', as he was then called, was beginning. This tomb-shrine was very similar to that placed over the original burial place of St. Thomas Becket in the crypt of Canterbury Cathedral soon after his very rapid canonisation in 1173. The Purbeck marble tomb-shrine and the geometric pavement at Old Sarum cathedral are most likely to have been put in place in the 1180s, when an increasing number of miracles are recorded, and the cathedral itself was becoming a place of local pilgrimage (Tatton-Brown 1999).

The eight fragments of green and purple porphyry in the collections from Old Sarum, are almost certainly all that now survives of a very fine late Romanesque geometric pavement in the cathedral. Its only English surviving parallel is the magnificent *in situ*, but worn and restored, *opus Alexandrinum* pavement in the Trinity Chapel in Canterbury Cathedral, which was once immediately to the west of the shrine of St. Thomas Becket.

CATALOGUE

All dimensions are for the probable upper surfaces, on most pieces the cut faces have a slight chamfer so that the under surfaces are slightly smaller than the upper ones. Incomplete measurements are indicated with +.

Green Porphyry

Col. Hawley records the finding of ten pieces of green porphyry, all in the Cathedral area, one in 1912 and nine in 1913. *OS. Diary 1912*, 28; *ibid. 1913*, 8 (two), 11 (two), 12, 14, 15, 39 and 44 (cloister); *Proc. Soc. Antiq.* (1913) 25, 99; *ibid.*

(1914) 26, 116. All the fragments are smooth on both the upper and under surfaces.

Polygonal piece

1 The largest surviving fragment. A polygonal, approximately D-shaped piece with one long cut edge of *c*.115mm, and three other edges of *c*.45mm. at an angle of very approximately 135 degrees to each other. There are diagonal tooling marks on the probable under surface. They are parallel to one side, which is possibly an original edge. Upper and under surfaces are polished. Traces of lime mortar cement remain on one side. L. 123mm. W. 50mm (max). Th. just over 20mm. Found in the Cathedral area in 1912/13. *1945.311*; *OS.C165*   **Pl 23**

Rectangular pieces

2 Corner fragment from a rectangular piece. The cut edges have a slight chamfer so that the lower surface of the piece would have been slightly smaller than the upper one. Original tooling on the probable under surface. L. 85mm+. W. 53mm+. Th. very slightly more than 10mm. Found in the Cathedral area in 1912/13. *1945.311*; *OS.C166*

3 Small fragment probably as above. There is evidence of two cut edges at right angles with traces of bedding mortar. Polished on upper and lower surfaces. L. 23mm+. W. 19mm+. Th. 15mm. Picked up at Old Sarum Cathedral between 1910-20. *1956.62*; *OS.C168a*

Narrow pieces

4 Small length of very narrow piece, broken at both ends. Traces of bedding mortar on the two long sides. L. 33mm+. W. 11mm. Th. 9mm. From the 1909-15 excavations. *1959.58*; *OS.C168b*

5 Rectangular fragment, broken at one end. Polished probable upper and tooled under surface. L. 58mm+. W. 27mm. Th. 11mm. Found in the Cathedral area in 1912/13. *1945.311*; *OS.C168*   **Pl 23**

6 Rectangular fragment broken at both ends. The longitudinal edges are slightly undercut. Polished both sides. White lime mortar cement adhering to one edge. L. 66mm+. W. 33mm. Th. 11mm. From the 1909-15 excavations. *1920-1.30*; *OS.C164*

Narrow curved piece

7 Rectangular fragment, broken at one end. L. 85mm+. W. 38mm. Th. 19mm. Although the sides are parallel, this piece does show a very slight curvature of the long axis, which would make it a part of a circle of the order of 300mm. diameter. Polished probable upper surface and tooled under surface. Found in the Cathedral area in 1912/13. *1945.311*; *OS.C167*   **Pl 23**

This is the only surviving piece with a curvature on it.

Purple Porphyry

Only two pieces of purple porphyry were found, one in the north transept, the other in the cloister. *O.S. Diary* 1913, 2 and 45. *Proc. Soc. Antiq.* (1914) 26, 116.

Narrow piece

8 Rectangular fragment, broken at one end. This is smooth on both the upper and lower surface. L. 64mm+. W. 27mm. Th. 15mm. Found at Old Sarum in the Cathedral area in 1913. *1920-1.30*; *OS.C163*   **Pl 23 & cover**

BIBLIOGRAPHY

Higgins, M. and R. 1996: *A Geological Companion to Greece and the Aegean*

Hope, W. H. St. John 1914: 'Report of the Excavation of the Cathedral Church of Old Sarum 1913', *Proc. Soc. Antiq.* **26**, 100-119

Hope, W. H. St. John 1917: 'The Sarum Consuetudinary and its relation to the Cathedral Church of Old Sarum', *Archaeologia* **68**, 111-126

Hutton, E. 1950: *The Cosmati: the Roman marble workers of the XIIth and XIIIth centuries*

Malgouyres, P. 2003: *Porphyre, la pierre pourpre des Ptolémées aux Bonaparte* (catalogue of 2003-4 exposition, Louvre, Paris)

Peacock, D. and Maxfield, V. 2001: *The Roman Imperial Porphyry Quarries: Survey and Excavation at Mons Porphyrites 1994-1998, 1 Topography and Quarries* (Egypt Exploration Society)

RCHM(E) 1980: *Ancient and Historical Monuments in the City of Salisbury 1* (HMSO)

Tatton-Brown, T. 1998a: 'Purple and green Porphyry at Old Sarum Cathedral', *Hatcher Review* **5**, no. 45 (Salisbury), 33-38

Tatton-Brown, T. 1998b: 'The Building Stone for Salisbury Cathedral', *Hatcher Review* **5**, no. 45 (Salisbury), 39-47

Tatton-Brown, T. 1998c: 'The two great marble pavements in the sanctuary and shrine areas of Canterbury Cathedral and Westminster Abbey' in J. Fawcett (ed.), *Historic Floors: their History and Conservation*, 53-62

Tatton-Brown, T. 1999: 'The burial places of St. Osmund', *Spire 1999* (Salisbury), 19-25

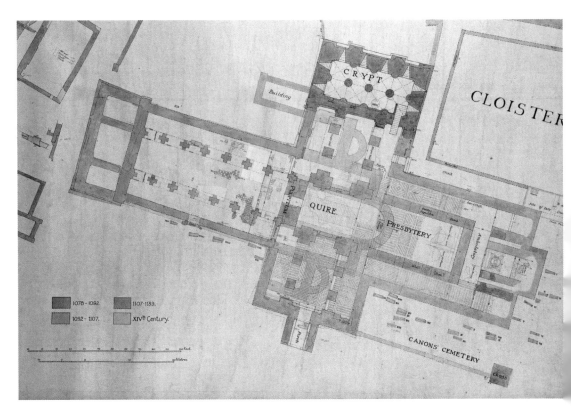

Pl 22. Porphyry: Plan of Cathedral at Old Sarum by D. H. Montgomerie

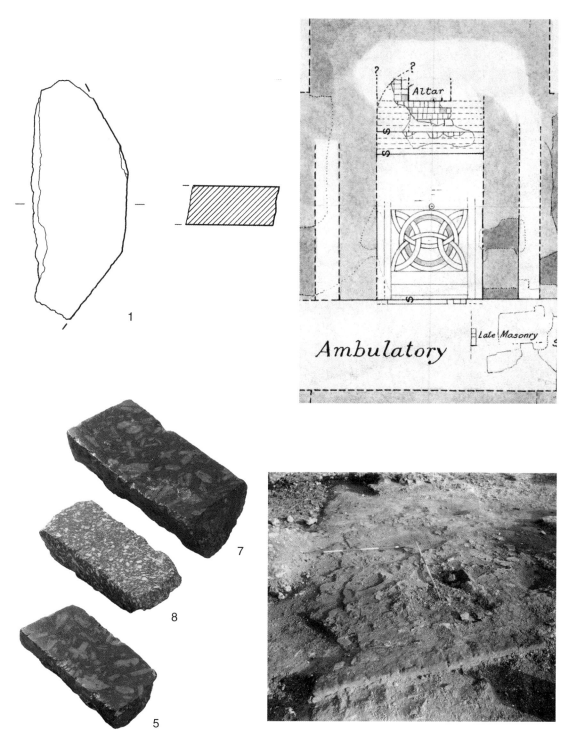

Pl 23. Porphyry: Cat 1 (1:1), 5, 7-8; detail from Montgomerie's plan (pl. 22) showing pavement of interlacing circles in central chapel and photograph showing its mortar bedding

Window Glass

by Anna Eavis

INTRODUCTION

The Museum collection of window glass is principally composed of the fragmentary material recovered during the excavations at Old Sarum and at Clarendon Palace. The Old Sarum glass, which originated in the castle and cathedral, dates largely from the twelfth century. The Clarendon Palace fragments, dating from the thirteenth century, are among the earliest examples of English domestic painted glazing. The Museum also holds two late medieval panels from the Tailors' Hall in Salisbury and four sixteenth-century fragments from Ivychurch Priory, Wiltshire.

CATALOGUE

Editorial note: The glass from Old Sarum is catalogued by colour and that from other sites by provenance.

Old Sarum

The 1909-15 excavations yielded large quantities of window glass from the castle at Old Sarum, of which at least seventy-three pieces survive in the museum collection. The majority was recovered from a latrine, subsequently a rubbish pit, within the courtyard house. Only a few pieces can be more precisely located, four from the site of St Margaret's Chapel and one from the Great Hall, both also part of the Courtyard House.

As the twelfth-century remodelling of the cathedral east end must have included an impressive glazing scheme, it is surprising that so little glass appears to have been recovered from the cathedral site. This suggests the wholesale removal and possible destruction of the glass, perhaps with the departure of the cathedral community in 1226 or as part of further demolitions in 1237. The 'few fragments of window glass' from the cathedral church (tentatively identified as Cat 19-22, 36, 40-42, 43) were found in an area known to have been used for breaking up the cathedral fabric from 1226 (McNeill 2006, 35). It is possible that panels of particular importance were removed for installation in the new cathedral, as at York and Canterbury cathedrals, for example. Although the new building preserved intrinsic proportional aspects of the old cathedral's design there is, however, no record of any earlier glass in its windows. Indeed, the community's whole-hearted investment in a virgin site and completely new architectural aesthetic – including larger windows than at Old Sarum – may have precluded a practice adopted elsewhere. Further excavation at Old Sarum might, of course, reveal more.

The absence of stratigraphical data and the fragmentary nature of the glass itself constrain identification of date and original location. The form and painted decoration of some pieces, however, supports some tentative analysis. Almost half of the glass is blue, one third is white and the remainder is green, red or amber. The blue glass, of an average thickness of 3mm is, as noted by the excavators, extraordinarily well-preserved, a fact probably explained by the high proportion of soda it contains (Newton 1977). Although soda-rich window glass was not commonly used in the late medieval period, the discovery of similar glass at the Abbey of St Denis,

Chartres Cathedral, Dover Castle, York Minster and a number of sites in Winchester suggests that it was available to the glaziers of prestigious North French and Anglo-Norman buildings. In Winchester soda-rich glass may have been used in windows as early as the tenth century and was certainly a feature of late eleventh- and twelfth-century glazing at Wolvesey Palace and Winchester Castle (Biddle and Hunter 1990, 377-380). At York too it appears to have been used in the late eleventh and twelfth centuries (Phillips 1985, 159). Although not scientifically analysed, the mid twelfth-century blue glass excavated at Glastonbury Abbey is so well-preserved as to suggest that it may also be of this type (Lewis 1991).

It is not possible to offer a date for the remainder of the glass apart from those pieces retaining identifiable painted decoration. At least seventeen pieces appear to have been painted. With the exception of a few small fragments of putative drapery designs, no figural painting survives, although it must have formed part of the glazing scheme in the chapel and cathedral windows at least. The most common designs are stylised foliate and petal patterns, each leaf or petal decorated with varying numbers of radiating lines; part of the repertoire of border and background ornament common throughout the second half of the twelfth century, similar designs can be found at St Denis (*c.*1140-44), Chartres Cathedral (*c.*1145), Arnstein an der Lahn Abbey (*c.*1160), York Minster (*c.*1180) and Canterbury Cathedral (*c.*1190-1205). Eleven pieces survive intact, their edges grozed in the manner described by Theophilus in his twelfth-century treatise on the arts (Dodwell 1961, 36-60). Generally small in size, the range of shapes – circular, semi-circular, segmental, teardrop, lobed and triangular – is consistent with their use in a decorative border or background, as in the twelfth-century work at St-Denis, York Minster and Canterbury Cathedral.

Although the majority of the painted glass may be ascribed to the twelfth century, the limited nature of the evidence means that a more precise dating should be treated with caution.

As the stylistic parallels date from the mid to late twelfth century, it is possible that the glass excavated from the castle is associated with extensive building work carried out during the late 1170s, perhaps when Eleanor of Aquitaine was imprisoned there (Colvin 1963, 826; Vincent 2004). It is most likely to have come from the castle chapels, as extensive use of painted and coloured glass in domestic windows appears not to have preceded Henry III's reign (see below). The occasional excavation of coloured glass in tenth- and eleventh-century domestic contexts, however, suggests that its use for secular glazing was not unknown (Harden 1961, 46; Biddle and Hunter 1990, 354).

Blue Glass

Cat 1-17 found in 1910 in garderobe pit 2. *O.S. Diary* 1910, 27. *Proc. Soc. Antiq.* 23 (1909-11), 514.

1 Segment-shaped piece. All edges grozed acutely away from the painted surface. Thick, well-preserved brown paint. Stylised petal design, each petal painted with three lines of varying thickness and separated by a series of u-shaped flourishes. From decorative border or ground. Excellent condition, despite slight iridescence. *c.*35mm x 65mm. Th. 3-4mm. Mid-late 12th century. *1934.51; 1920-21.30; OS.C170*
Fig 61

2 Segment-shaped piece. All edges grozed acutely away from the painted surface. Thick, well-preserved brown paint. Stylised petal design, each petal painted with three lines of varying thickness and separated by a series of u-shaped flourishes. From decorative border or ground. Excellent condition. Mild pitting is likely to be due to manufacture rather than corrosion. *c.*35mm x 65mm. Th. 3-4mm. Mid-late 12th century. *1934.51; 1920-21.30; OS.C170* **Fig 61**
Similar painted flourishes occur in mid-twelfth century glass excavated from Glastonbury Abbey and Wolvesey Palace, Winchester.

3 Lobe-shaped piece. All edges grozed. Paint shadow. Stylised foliate spray, each of three leaves painted with

a pair of lines. From decorative border or ground. Slight iridescence. *c.*30mm x 55mm. Th. 3mm. Mid-late 12th century. *1934.51; 1920-21.30; OS.C170*
Fig 61

Similar border designs occur for example in windows at Canterbury Cathedral (*c.*1190-1205).

4 Light blue segment-shaped piece. All edges curved and grozed. Paint shadow. Stylised petal design, each of three petals painted with a cluster of radiating lines. From decorative border or ground. Slight iridescence and pitting on both surfaces. *c.*51mm x 55mm. Th. 3mm. Mid-late 12th century. *1934.51; 1920-21.30; OS.C170*
Fig 61

5 Deep blue irregular-shaped piece. All edges grozed. Paint shadow. Hand-like design. Slight iridescence and pitting on both surfaces. *c.*64mm x 84mm. Th. 4mm. Mid-late 12th century. *1934.51; 1920-21.30; OS.C170*
Fig 61

6 Fragment. Two grozed edges. Paint shadow. Remains of simple foliate spray with three circles perhaps representing vine stem and bunch of grapes. From decorative border or ground. Good condition, although the painted surface has a number of deep scratches. *c.*42mm x 80mm. Th. 3-4mm. Mid-late 12th century. *1934.51; 1920-21.30; OS.C170*
Fig 61

7 Unpainted square fragment (all edges grozed). Slight iridescence. 40mm x 46mm. Th. 3mm. *1934.51; 1920-21.30; OS.C170*
Fig 61

8 Unpainted triangular fragment (two edges grozed, one damaged). Slight iridescence. *c.*40mm x 45mm. Th. 3mm. *1934.51; 1920-21.30; OS.C170*
Fig 61

9 Unpainted rectangular strip (two edges grozed). Slight iridescence. W.23mm. L.38mm (min), Th. 4mm. *1934.51; 1920-21.30; OS.C170* **Fig 61**

10 Unpainted rectangular-shaped fragment. One grozed edge. Surface has one deep scratch and some iridescence. *c.*21mm x 34mm. Th. 2mm. *1934.51; 1920-21.30; OS.C170*
Fig 61

11 Tear-shaped piece with grozed edge. Paint shadow. Stylised foliate spray, each of three leaves painted with three lines. From decorative border or ground. Almost opaque due to heavy iridescence. *c.*80mm x 40mm. Th. 6-7mm. Mid-late 12th century. *1949.75; OS.C176*
Fig 61

12 Fragment. One grozed edge. Paint shadow. Beaded design, perhaps from the edge of a garment. Some iridescence. *c.*12mm x 27mm. Th. 3mm. 12th century? *1949.75; OS.C176*
Fig 61

13 Light blue semi-circular piece. Grozed edges (straight edge damaged). Indecipherable paint shadow. Possibly from decorative border or ground. Slight iridescence. *c.*29mm x 50mm. Th. 2-3mm. 12th century? *1949.75; OS.C176*
Fig 61

14 Semi-circular piece. Grozed edges. Paint shadow. Stylised foliage design. From decorative border or ground. Slight iridescence. *c.*17mm x 39mm. Th. 3-4mm. 12th century? *1949.75; OS.C176*
Fig 61

15 Lozenge-shaped piece. Grozed edges. Paint shadow. Two bands of curved lines at right angles to a cluster of straight lines. Slight iridescence. *c.*36mm x 88mm. Th. 3-4mm. *1949.75; OS.C176* **Fig 61**

16 Irregular, triangular-shaped piece, grozed edges one corner damaged. *c.*25mm x 70mm. Th. 2-3mm. *1949.75; OS.C176* **Fig 61**

17 Twelve fragments of various shapes and sizes. Some evidence of grozing and paint shadow. Most are iridescent. Th. ranges from 1-5mm. *1949.75; OS.C176*

Cat 18 found in 1911 on the site of the Great Hall. *O.S. Diary* 1911, 26.

18 Fragment. Three grozed edges, the other damaged. Very faint paint shadow. Condition good. *c.*40mm x 55mm. Th. 4mm. *1934.51; OS.C169* **Fig 62**

Cat 19-22 probably found in 1912 on the cathedral site in a trench SW of the transept. *O.S. Diary* 1912, 15.

19 Unpainted circular piece with grozed edge. Slight iridescence. One surface is scratched. From decorative border or ground. D. 42mm. Th. 3-4mm. 12th century? *1956.62; OS.C198a*   **Fig 62**

20 Unpainted semi-circular piece with grozed edges. From decorative border or ground. One corner removed for analysis (Newton 1977, no. 517). Slight iridescence. *c.*18mm x 35mm. Th. 3mm. 12th century? *1956.62; OS.C198b*   **Fig 62**

21 Unpainted triangular piece with one grozed edge. One corner removed for analysis (Newton 1977, no. 516). *c.*19mm x 30mm. Th. 3mm. *1956.62; OS.C198c*

22 Six fragments of varying shapes and sizes. Some pieces have grozed edges and very faint traces of paint. Th. ranges from 0.5-3mm.

Cat 23-24 Found on the site of St Margaret's Chapel during the 1909-15 excavations.

23-24 Two small fragments, the larger of which has three grozed edges. Th. ranges from 2-3mm. *1937.170; OS.C175*

White Glass

Cat 25-32 found in 1910 in garderobe pit 2. *O.S. Diary* 1910, 27. *Proc. Soc. Antiq.* 23 (1909-11), 514.

25 Semi-circular fragment. Grozed edge, one edge damaged. Painted stylised petal design. From decorative border or ground. Cement-like deposit and iridescence on painted surface. Unpainted surface is almost opaque. *c.*50mm x 90mm. Th. 3mm. Mid-late 12th century. *1949.75; OS.C179*   **Fig 62**

26 Fragment with greenish tinge. One grozed edge. Painted stylised petal design. From decorative border or ground. Thin deposit on painted surface. Unpainted surface is slightly pitted and almost opaque. *c.*32mm x 55mm. Th. 2-3mm. Mid-late 12th century. *1949.75; OS.C179*   **Fig 62**

27 Sixteen fragments of various shapes and sizes. Most have a greenish tinge. Some grozed edges and faint traces of paint. Most are almost opaque. Th. ranges from 0.5-4mm. *1949.75; OS.C179*

28 Fragment, possibly from a semi-circular piece. Greenish tinge. Two grozed edges. Painted stylised foliage design, each leaf painted with a pair of thick lines, stem painted with one thick line. From decorative border or ground. Surface deposit, pitting and iridescence. *c.*41mm x 45mm. Th. 3mm. Mid-late 12th century. *1934.51; 1920-21.30; OS.C173*   **Fig 62**

Similar border designs occur, for example, in Canterbury Cathedral, *c.*1190-1205.

29 Rectangular-shaped fragment with greenish tinge. Two grozed edges and traces of paint. Opaque, with surface deposit and pitting. W. 47mm. L. (min) 70mm. Th. 2-4mm. *1934.51; 1920-21.30; OS.C173*   **Fig 62**

30 Rectangular-shaped fragment with greenish tinge. Three grozed edges. Opaque, with surface deposit and pitting. W. 44mm. L. (min) 84mm. Th. 3-4mm. *1934.51; 1920-21.30; OS.C173*   **Fig 62**

31 Irregular-shaped fragment with greenish tinge. Grozed edges and traces of paint. Opaque, with surface deposit and pitting. *c.*44mm x 70mm. Th. 2-3mm. *1934.51; 1920-21.30; OS.C173)*   **Fig 62**

32 Irregular-shaped fragment with greenish tinge. Two grozed edges and traces of paint. Opaque, with surface deposit and pitting. *c.*24mm x 40mm. Th. 2-3mm. *1934.51; 1920-21.30; OS.C173*   **Fig 62**

Cat 33 probably from garderobe pit no. 2.

33 Fragment, once rectangular or square. Two grozed edges. Surface deposit. Th. 2-3mm. *1920-21.30; OS.C186*

Cat 34 probably found in 1912 on the cathedral site in a trench SW of the transept. *O.S. Diary* 1912, 15.

34 Five fragments, all with a greenish tinge. Apparently unpainted. Surface deposits, pitting and iridescence. Th. ranges from 2-4mm. *1956.62; OS.C198k, l, p, q and r*

Green Glass

Cat 35 found in 1910 in garderobe pit 2. *O.S. Diary* 1910, 27. *Proc. Soc. Antiq.* 23 (1909-11), 514.

35 Twelve fragments. Some grozed edges and traces of paint. Poor condition. Surface deposits, pitting and iridescence. Th. ranges from 1-3mm. *1934.51; OS.C171; 1949.75; OS.C177 and 1920-21.30*

Cat 36 Probably found in 1912 on the cathedral site in a trench SW of the transept. *O.S. Diary* 1912, 15.

36 Two fragments, one light green, one dark green. The dark green piece appears to have been rectangular in shape and has grozing marks on three of its edges. The other has traces of paint. Very poor condition. Severe surface flaking and iridescence. Th. 2mm. *1956.62; OS.C198i and j*

Ruby Glass

Cat 37 found on the site of St Margaret's Chapel during the 1909-15 excavations.

37 One narrow strip broken in two. W. 13mm. L. (min) 23mm. Th. 2mm. *1937.170; OS.C175*
                                                        Fig 62

Cat 38-39 found in 1910 in garderobe pit 2. *O.S. Diary* 1910, 27. *Proc. Soc. Antiq.* 23 (1909-11), 514.

38 Two fragments, one so streaky that it is largely white. Both are pitted. The streaky piece is iridescent. Th. 2mm. *1949.75; OS.C178*

39 Squarish fragment. Lacquered. Original surfaces have flaked away. Th. 2mm. *1934.51; 1920-21.30; OS.C172*

Amber Glass

Cat 40-42 probably found in 1912 on the cathedral site in a trench SW of the transept. *O.S. Diary* 1912, 15.

40 Painted fragment. Stylised petal design. From decorative border or ground. Slight pitting. Almost opaque. *c.*30mm x 32mm. Th. 3mm. 12th century? *1956.62; OS.C198n*   **Fig 62**

41 Painted fragment. Painted lines of varying thickness. Poor condition. Unpainted surfaces pitted and partly eroded and pitted. *c.*26mm x 33mm. Th. 3mm. *1956.62; OS.C198m*   **Fig 62**

42 Painted fragment. Painted lines of varying thickness. Poor condition. Unpainted surfaces pitted and partly eroded and pitted. *c.*16mm x 38mm. Th. 3-4mm. *1956.62; OS.C198o*   **Fig 62**

Miscellaneous

Cat 43 probably found in 1912 on the cathedral site in a trench SW of the transept. *O.S. Diary* 1912, 15

43 Three tiny fragments, two with traces of paint. Opaque. Th. 2-3mm. *1956.62; OS.C198t, u and v*

Clarendon Palace

This section is based, by kind permission of the Society of Antiquaries and Richard Marks, on the report written by the latter and published in 1988 (Marks 1988).

The Museum collection contains about 240 fragments of window glass found during the 1933-39 excavations, all are accessioned as *1957.47*, except where otherwise stated. Many are quite small, all have become opaque through de-vitrification in the soil and many are also pitted on the reverse, the result of atmospheric corrosion caused by exposure to the elements whilst still in the window openings. None is coloured; all are of white glass with decoration applied in black paint and fired.

The artistic merit of the Clarendon fragments is transcended by their historical importance. Traces of English medieval domestic glass prior to the fourteenth century are few and far between; that it was uncommon before then is suggested by the sparse documentary evidence, which mainly concerns, as might be expected, royal residences. Henry III seems to have been the first English monarch to make widespread use of window glass, which was but one aspect of his lavish embellishment of his palaces and castles (Borenius 1943, 40-50). As at Henry's other residences, the Clarendon windows included figural glass (Pettigrew 1859, 234, 254 and 256), but no traces of these historiated windows have come to light on the site. Most of the references to glazing at Clarendon do not specify the subject matter and it is likely that the majority of the windows would have been of white or *grisaille* glass. The fragments catalogued here are sufficiently large to give an impression of the *grisaille* windows. They appear, with two exceptions (Cat 69 and 70), to date from Henry III's reign and the designs do not differ from those found in contemporary ecclesiastical glazing in England.

A number of the motifs can be paralleled in the *grisaille* windows of Salisbury Cathedral although it should be noted that they are not exactly the same (Winston 1865, 106-121). Curving stems and trefoil leaves, both with and without bunches of grapes, on cross-hatched grounds form the basis of the Salisbury windows and are very similar to the patterns found at Clarendon (Cat 53, 56, 58 and 78). The original contexts of the strip with the pointed quatrefoil and a cinquefoil (Cat 44) and the curving piece with trefoil sprays (Cat 46) can be reconstructed from their counterparts in Salisbury, where they act as framing and encircling motifs for the trefoils and stems; the curved bead pattern (Cat 71) also occurs in the Salisbury glazing as an encircling motif. The cinquefoil flower on a cross-hatched ground and enclosed within a border (Cat 47 and 48) is another motif common to both Salisbury and Clarendon.

The two pieces with stylized leaves on clear as opposed to cross-hatched grounds (Cat 69 and 70) do not find a parallel in the glazing of the cathedral proper, but do in the remains of the chapter house windows, which are to be seen in the south transept and in the lady chapel. The chapter house, begun in 1279, was probably glazed in the 1280s, so it is possible that these two fragments may post-date Henry III's reign by a few years. All the others may with confidence be assigned to the period of his occupancy of the throne.

From the accounts it is clear that all the principal apartments in the palace received glass windows in this period. For a summary of the references to the provision of window glass which occur in the Liberate Rolls and the Pipe Rolls see Pettigrew 1859. It is not possible to identify the surviving fragments with any specific location, but they at least remain as one aspect of Henry III's artistic patronage and amongst the earliest examples of English domestic glazing with painted decoration.

From North of the Antioch Chamber

44 Complete rectangular quarry with four grozed edges. Painted quatrefoil on a cross-hatched ground and bordered by parallel lines. W. 50mm. L. 79mm. Th. 2.5-3mm. Marks 1988, no. 1. From widening trench N. of buttress. **Fig 63**

45 Irregular-shaped fragment. Painted trefoil on a cross-hatched ground. *c.*28mm x 50mm. Th. 2mm. Mid-13th century. N. buttress. **Fig 63**

46 Curved fragment. Two painted trefoil sprays on a cross-hatched ground and set within a border. W. 42mm. L. (min) 43mm. Th. 2.5-3mm. Marks 1988, no. 2. From widening trench N. of buttress.

Fig 63

47 Fragment. Three grozed edges. Part of a painted cinquefoil on a cross-hatched ground and bordered on three sides. W. 87mm. L. (min) 53mm. Th. 2.5mm. Marks 1988, no. 12. N. buttress. **Fig 63**

48 Fragment. ?Two grozed edges. Part of a painted cinquefoil on a cross-hatched ground with a border on two sides. *c.*40mm x 60mm. Th. 3mm. Marks 1988, no. 4. From widening trench N. of buttress.
Fig 63

49 Fragment. Part of a painted cinquefoil on a cross-hatched ground and touched by two stems. *c.*31mm x 55mm. Th. 2.5mm. Marks 1988, no. 3. From widening trench N. of buttress.   **Fig 63**

50 Fragment. Part of a painted cinquefoil and curving stem on a cross-hatched ground. *c.*30mm x 35mm. Th. 3mm. Marks 1988, no. 13. N. buttress.
Fig 63

51 Fragment. Two grozed edges. Painted curving stems on a cross-hatched ground with border on two sides. *c.*32mm x 50mm. Th. 3mm. Marks 1988, no. 14. N. buttress.   **Fig 63**

52 Fragment. Two grozed edges. Painted curving stem on a cross-hatched ground with border on two sides. *c.*27mm x 36mm. Th. 2mm. Marks 1988, no. 15. N. buttress.   **Fig 63**

53 Fragment. Three grozed edges. Painted curling stem terminating in a trefoil leaf and bunch of grapes on a cross-hatched ground. W. 77mm. L. (min) 60mm. Th. 3-4mm. Marks 1988, no. 9. Found between buttresses.   **Fig 63**

54 Irregular-shaped fragment. Painted bunch of grapes. *c.*20mm x 30mm. Th. 3mm. Mid-13th century. N. buttress.   **Fig 63**

55 Irregular-shaped fragment. One grozed edge. Painted foliate spray on a cross-hatched ground. Lacquered. *c.*18mm x 60mm. Th. 2.5mm. Mid-13th century. From widening trench N. of buttress.
Fig 63

56 Fragment. Painted trefoil leaf and intertwining stems on a cross-hatched ground. *c.*44mm x 60mm. Th. 3mm. Marks 1988, no. 10. Found between buttresses.   **Fig 63**

57 Fragment. ?Three grozed edges. Elaborate painted curving stem and leaves on a cross-hatched ground with a border along one edge. W. 77mm. L. (min) 77mm. Th. 2.5-4mm. Marks 1988, no. 16. N. buttress.   **Fig 63**

58 Fragment. Two grozed edges. Painted trefoil and stem on a cross-hatched ground. *c.*34mm x 36mm. Th. 3-4mm. Marks 1988, no. 5. From widening trench N. of buttress.   **Fig 63**

59 Irregular-shaped fragment. Painted foliate spray on a cross-hatched ground. Lacquered. *c.*29mm x 68mm. Th. 2.5mm. Mid-13th century. From widening trench N. of buttress.   **Fig 64**

60 Irregular-shaped fragment. ?One grozed edge. Painted stem on a cross-hatched ground. Lacquered and opaque. *c.*29mm x 48mm. Th. 2.5mm. Mid-13th century. From widening trench N. of buttress.
Fig 64

61 Irregular-shaped fragment. One grozed edge. Painted foliate spray. Lacquered. *c.* 28mm x 40mm. Th. 2.5mm. Mid-13th century. From widening trench N. of buttress.   **Fig 64**

62 Irregular-shaped fragment. Painted foliate spray. *c.*31mm x 42mm. Th. 2.5mm. Mid-13th century. N. buttress.   **Fig 64**

63 Rectangular-shaped fragment. Two grozed edges. Three painted circles. Part of a border. Opaque. W. 10mm. L. 29mm. Th. 2mm. Mid-13th century. From ?tile gulley east side of buttress.   **Fig 64**

64 Fragment, originally a rectangular strip. Three grozed edges. Paint traces. Lacquered and opaque. W. 36mm. L. (min) 39mm. Th. 2.5mm. From ?tile gulley east side of buttress.

65 Fragment. One grozed edge. Paint traces. Lacquered and opaque. *c.*20mm x 35mm. Th. 2.5mm. From ?tile gulley east side of buttress.

66 Twelve fragments of varying shapes and sizes. Most bear traces of painted foliate stems with cross hatching. All lacquered and opaque. Mid-13th century. From widening trench N. of buttress.

67 21 fragments of varying shapes and sizes. Most bear traces of paint, including foliate sprays and stems on a cross-hatched ground. All lacquered and opaque. N. buttress.

68 14 fragments of varying shapes and sizes. Some bear paint traces. All lacquered and opaque.

Perhaps from the Antioch Chamber

69 Fragment. Painted trefoil and curving stem on a plain ground. *c.*35mm x 45mm. Th. 3mm. Marks 1988, no. 17. Late 13th century.   **Fig 64**

Unprovenanced: possibly from the Antioch Chamber

70 Fragment. Two grozed edges. Painted curving stems on a plain ground with a border on one edge. *c.*57mm x 80mm. Th. 3mm. Marks 1988, no. 18. Late 13th century.   **Fig 64**

71 Curved fragment. Three grozed edges. Beading and slightly curving parallel lines framing cross-hatching. W. 57mm. L. (min) 96mm. Th. 3-4mm. Marks 1988, no. 19.   **Fig 64**

72 Irregular-shaped fragment. ?Two grozed edges. Painted foliate design on a cross-hatched ground. Lacquered and opaque. *c.*50mm x 60mm. Th. 3mm.   **Fig 64**

73 Eight fragments of varying shapes and sizes. Some bear paint traces. All lacquered and opaque.

From the King's Apartments

74 Fragment. Part of a painted stem and leaf on a cross-hatched ground. *c.*40mm x 32mm. Th. 3.5mm. Marks 1988, no. 6. From 'humus North of S.D'.   **Fig 64**

75 Fragment. Two grozed edges. Painted foliate spray on a cross-hatched ground with a border on two sides. W. (min) 83mm. L. (min) 57mm. Th. 2-3mm. Marks 1988, no. 8. From 'S.C.'   **Fig 64**

76 Fragment. One grozed edge. Painted foliate spray on a cross-hatched ground with part of a stem. *c.*33mm x 46mm. Th. 2mm. Marks 1988, no.11. From 'Sb-1.'   **Fig 64**

77 Irregular-shaped fragment. One grozed edge. Painted foliate spray on a cross-hatched ground. Lacquered and opaque. *c.*50mm x 56mm. Th. 2.5mm. Mid-13th century. From 'humus north of S.D.'   **Fig 65**

78 Fragment. One grozed edge. Painted palmette leaf on a cross-hatched ground. *c.*30mm x 50mm. Th. 3mm. Marks 1988, no. 7. From 'humus North of S.D.'   **Fig 65**

79 Irregular-shaped fragment. One grozed edge. Painted rectangular pattern with cross-hatching. Opaque. *c.*34mm x 48mm. Th. 2.5mm. Mid-13th century. From North Annex.   **Fig 65**

80 Irregular-shaped fragment. Painted stem with arching branches. Lacquered and opaque. *c.*43mm x 30mm. Th. 3mm. Mid-13th century. From North Annex.   **Fig 65**

81 Irregular-shaped fragment. Painted traces. Lacquered. *c.*45mm x 55mm. Th. 3-4.5mm. Mid-13th century. From North Annex.   **Fig 65**

82 Rectangular fragment 40mm x 22mm in its original leading, which certainly came from the King's Apartments, has been recorded previously. This was labelled '1933, site 2'. Marks 1988, 225 and pl. LIXa. *1957.10*

83 Rectangular quarry with four grozed edges, no trace of paint, lacquered and opaque, W. 35-38mm. L. 69mm. Th. 4.5mm. Now in two fragments. From Solar B.

84 Nine fragments of varying shapes and sizes. Some

bear traces of paint. All lacquered and opaque. From 'humus north of S.D.'.

85 16 fragments of varying shapes and sizes. A small number may be painted. All opaque. With label 'CL P 36 A/C Glass T-I'.

86 Seven fragments. All either opaque or so severely eroded that surface has flaked away to reveal translucent green-white core. With label 'CL P 36 AC Beauchamps Glass C 36 Oct'.

87 Six fragments. All opaque, except one very thin (*c.*1mm) clear green-white piece. With labels 'CL P 36 Solar AA' and 'Solar + C 34'.

88 23 fragments of varying shapes and sizes. May be coloured. All opaque. With label 'Solar sealed II'.

89 Three fragments of varying shapes and sizes. Some bear traces of paint. All are lacquered and opaque. With label 'CL P 39 SA+'.

Unprovenanced: possibly from the King's Apartments

90 Kidney-shaped unpainted piece in its original leading. The glass is extremely fragile, opaque and cracked. *c.*30mm x 18mm. Unprovenanced. *1957.10*
Fig 65

Unprovenanced

91 Irregular-shaped fragment (originally a rectangular strip?). Painted foliate stem on a cross-hatched ground. W. 28-30mm. L. (min) 60mm. Th. *c.*4mm. Mid-13th century. Neighbourhood of Clarendon Palace. *2000R.48.2*   **Fig 65**

92 48 fragments of varying shapes and sizes. A small number painted and some may be coloured. Most have a cement-like surface deposit and are opaque. Unprovenanced.

93 15 fragments of varying shapes and sizes. Some bear traces of painted foliate sprays, stems on a cross-

hatched ground. All lacquered. Mid-13th century. Unprovenanced.

The Tailors' Guild, Salisbury

Two figurative stained glass panels belonging to the Tailors' Guild are likely to have come to the Museum during the 1870s-1880s along with other objects, including the Guild figures of the Giant and Hob Nob. The figures, of the Virgin and Child, and of St Christopher carrying the Christ Child, were made to fit tracery lights and date from the late fifteenth century.

Established early in the fifteenth century, the Tailors' Guild was one of the wealthiest of Salisbury's guilds (Haskins 1912; 98-219; VCH Wilts. 1962, 134-5). In 1449 it founded a chantry at St Thomas' church in William Swayne's newly built south chancel aisle (Tatton-Brown 1997, 107). In 1534 it built Tailors' Hall in Swaynes Chequer, (RCHM(E) 1980, 93-4), holding all its meetings there until 1880, when the Guild was disbanded. The upper floor of the hall was given over to an assembly room, lit by three windows originally filled with fifteenth-century stained glass (Haskins 1912, 217).

Frank Stevens, a former Curator of Salisbury Museum, suggested that the two panels may have been transferred to the Tailors' Hall from the Guild chantry in St Thomas' church after the chantry's suppression in 1548. The evidence for this is inconclusive. The location of the Tailors' chantry within the chancel aisle is unknown, although it was presumably not under the east window which retains its original glazing. The style of these figures shows affinities with stained glass produced in the south west (e.g. Cheddar, Langport, Winscombe, Trull and Exeter) and is different from that remaining at St Thomas'. This need not preclude a provenance in the chancel aisle, however, where decorative work continued into the 1470s and may have involved a number of different stained glass workshops.

94 Virgin and Child
Panel. H. 315mm. W. 85mm, originally made for a

tracery light. The Virgin Mary, shown as Queen of Heaven, is crowned and holds a sceptre in her right hand. The Christ Child sits on her left arm. Both are nimbed. White glass, black paint, yellow stain. Little evidence of modelling washes or smear shading, save for drapery folds. The scene is incomplete. The Virgin's right side and the top half of her sceptre are lost, as well as the original background. To the right of the child is a fragment which may be all that is left of the sceptre or a throne. Late 15th century.

Missing portions are made up with pieces of later glass, including plain blue and red quarries. Fragment of medieval white glass with traces of yellow stain, slightly pitted. Fragment of a square or rectangular piece depicting part of a rose bush. Probably a (royal?) heraldic device or badge. White glass, with paint and yellow stain. 16th century? *1996R.2169.2*   **Pl 24**

95 St Christopher and Christ Child

Panel. H. 350mm. W. 130mm, originally made for a tracery light. St Christopher carries the nimbed Christ Child on his shoulder. St Christopher has no nimbus. His staff is a plain branch, conforming to the Golden Legend. The Christ Child holds an orb and raises his left hand in blessing. White glass, black paint, yellow stain. Little evidence of modelling washes or smear shading, save for drapery folds. The scene is incomplete. Some paint and stain loss. Late 15th century.

The remainder of the panel is a composite of different pieces including much later plain blue, orange and white quarries. Three pieces of medieval white glass with traces of paint and yellow stain. *1996R.2169.1*   **Pl 24**

Ivychurch Priory

Four panels of stained glass, including a head of St James Major and part of a motto '*ou bien dire*', and described as being from Ivychurch Priory, were acquired by the Museum in 1946.

This former Augustinian house founded by King Stephen declined almost to extinction in the late fourteenth century but revived in the sixteenth century. On the eve of the Reformation the priory was financially stable and its church and other buildings in good condition 'with moch newe buylding of stone and breke' (VCH Wilts.1956, 289-93). Much of the church was destroyed soon after the Dissolution, but the north aisle, cloister and three surrounding ranges were transformed into a house which was itself almost completely demolished in 1889. A small part of the remaining north aisle was incorporated in a farmhouse, whose ground floor windows were altered in the 1950s (RCHM(E) 1987, 149-153).

The stained glass, which dates from the early sixteenth century, was probably installed as part of improvements to the fabric of the priory made during the 1530s under the well-connected Prior Richard Page. Technically accomplished, it bears comparison with Flemish glass of the period and was probably influenced by it.

96 St James Major

Panel. H. 130mm. W. 95mm. Head of St James Major, nimbed, wearing a pilgrim's hat with scallop shell. The upper part of his staff is visible. White glass, paint and yellow stain. Expert application of brown wash, modelled to highlight facial features. Confident and free application of black paint (eyes, nose, mouth, beard, hair and hat fabric). There is a large crack across the lower left corner of the piece. Some stain loss and pitting. The rest of what was presumably a full-length figure has been lost. Early 16th century. *1946.182*   **Fig 65 & cover**

Stylistically, the head of St James is similar to a fragmentary figure in the west window of Winchester Cathedral which probably originated in Bishop Fox's choir glazing (1501-28). The flowing hair and open mouth are also paralleled in the figure of Herod (dated *c.*1510-15) at St Mary's, Fairford (Wayment 1984, pl. XL). Similarly textured hats are worn by early sixteenth-century figures of St James in Netherlandish-type glass at King's College, Cambridge and in wood at the Musée Vleehuis in Antwerp. (Ayre 2002, 10; Santiago 1985, 341).

97 Heraldic motto

Panel. H. 100mm. W. 85mm. Scroll bearing in blackletter the inscription *ou bien dire* set within an oval Renaissance decorative border. White glass completely covered in brown wash on which some details (scroll outline, inscription, border 'jewels') are painted, either in black paint or yellow stain. Other elements (the border foliate pattern, for example,) are scratched out, showing the white glass beneath. The panel has been cut down from an oval or larger rectangular piece. Otherwise, its condition is good. It has been leaded within four later triangular pieces, each painted with a different, relatively crude foliate design in paint and yellow stain. Early 16th century. *1946.182*   **Fig 65**

First recorded in 1401 at Eltham Palace, mottoes on scrolls became popular subjects for stained glass throughout the fifteenth and sixteenth centuries, particularly in domestic settings like Ockwells Manor House (*c.*1460), the passage windows at St Cross, Winchester (*c.*1490s) and Hampton Court Palace (1532-3). Bishop Fox's motto *'Est Deo Gratia'* appears on scrolls in the east window of Winchester Cathedral, glazed by Flemish craftsmen *c.*1501-1515 (Marks 1993, 213). The Ivychurch motto cannot be assigned to a particular family or individual but probably belongs to a patron of the early sixteenth-century glazing scheme.

98-9 Two hearts
Each heart H. 40mm. W. 40mm. Probably from a heraldic design. Each is of white glass covered in brown wash and modelled by scratching out. Good condition. Early 16th century. *1946.182*   **Fig 65**

I should like like to thank, for various sorts of help, Heather Gilderdale Scott, Richard Marks and David Park. I am also grateful to David Algar and Peter Saunders for all their help and forbearance during the preparation of this catalogue.

BIBLIOGRAPHY

Ayre, K. 2002: *Medieval English Figurative Roundels* (British Academy, OUP)

Biddle, M. and Hunter, J. 1990: 'Window Glass, 1. Early Medieval Window Glass' in M. Biddle, *Object and Economy in Medieval Winchester,* Winchester Stud. **7i** (Oxford) 350-386

Borenius, T. 1943: 'The cycle of images in the palaces and castles of Henry III', *Journal of the Warburg and Courtauld Institutes* **vi**, 40-50

Colvin, H. 1963: *The History of the King's Works,* Vol. 2: *The Middle Ages,* 826

Dodwell, C. 1961: *Theophilus, De Diversis Artibus*

Harden, D. B. 1961: 'Domestic Window Glass: Roman, Saxon and Medieval' in E.M. Jope, S*tudies in Building History: Essays in Recognition of the Work of B.H. St. J. O'Neil,* 39-63

Haskins, C. 1912: *The Ancient Trade Guilds and Companies of Salisbury* (Bennett, Salisbury)

James, T. B. and Robinson, A. M with E. Eames. 1988: *Clarendon Palace: the History and Archaeology of a Medieval Palace and Hunting Lodge near Salisbury, Wiltshire.* Soc. Antiq. Res. Rep. **45**.

Lewis, A. R. 1991: *The Stained and Painted glass of Glastonbury Abbey* (unpublished report for the trustees of Glastonbury Abbey)

McNeill, J. 2006: *Old Sarum,* English Heritage

Marks, R. 1988: 'Window Glass' in T. B. James and A. M. Robinson with E. Eames, 229-233

Marks, R. 1993: *Stained Glass in England during the Middle Ages* (Univ. of Toronto Press, Toronto and Buffalo), 213

Newton, R. 1977: 'More 12th century Blue Soda Glass', *Corpus Vitrearum Newsletter* **24** (18th Feb 1977), 3-4

Pettigrew T. J. 1859: 'On the ancient royal palace of Clarendon', *JBAA,* **15**, 246-64

Phillips, D. 1985: *Excavations at York Minster,* Vol. 2: *The Cathedral of Archbishop Thomas of Bayeux,* RCHM(E)

RCHM(E) 1980: *Ancient and Historical Monuments in the City of Salisbury* **1** (HMSO)

RCHM(E) 1987: *The Churches of South-East Wiltshire* (HMSO)

Santiago de Compostela 1985: *1000 ans de Pèlerinage Européen.* Exhibition Catalogue, Centrum voor Kunst en Cultur, Abbaye Sainte-Pierre, Ghent

Tatton-Brown, T. 1997: 'The Church of St Thomas of Canterbury, Salisbury', *Wilts. Arch. Mag.* **90**, 101-109

VCH Wilts. 1956: R. B. Pugh and E. Crittall (eds.), 'The Religious Houses of Wiltshire' in *A History of Wiltshire* **3** (Victoria County Histories of England)

VCH Wilts. 1962: E. Crittall (ed.), 'The Guild Merchant and Craft Guilds before 1612' in *A History of Wiltshire* **6** (Victoria County Histories of England)

Vincent, N. 2004: 'Aliénor, Reine d'Angleterre' in Martin Aurell (ed.), *Aliénor d'Aquitaine*, Revue 303, Arts, Recherches et Creations, numero 81 (hors series), Nantes, 60-61

Wayment, H. 1984: *The Stained Glass of the Church of St Mary, Fairford, Gloucestershire*, Soc. Antiq. London Occas. Pap. new series vol. 5

Winston C. 1865: *Memoirs Illustrative of the Art of Glass-Painting*

94   95

Pl 24. Window glass: Tailors' Guild Cat 94-5

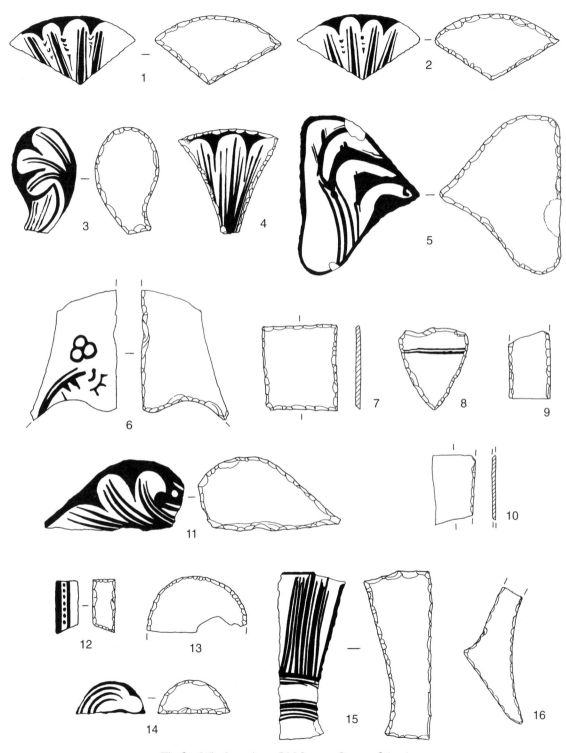

Fig 61. Window glass: Old Sarum Cat 1-16 (1:2)

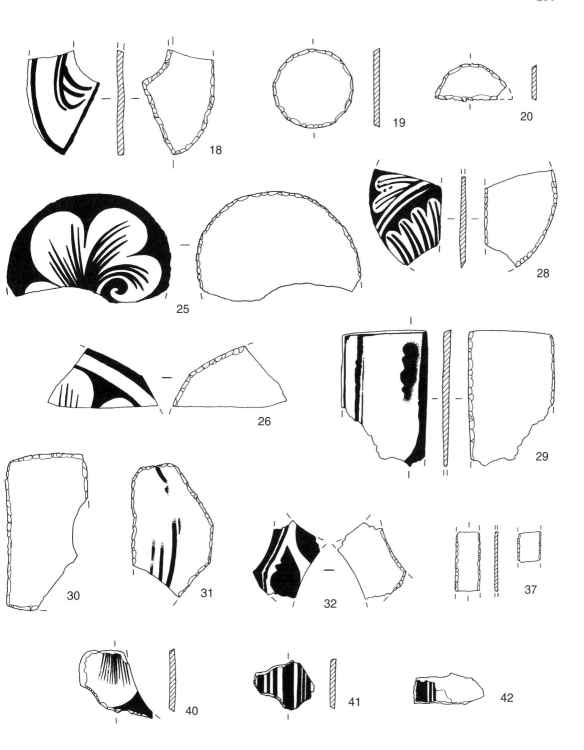

Fig 62. Window glass: Old Sarum Cat 18- 20, 25-6, 28-32, 37, 40-2 (1:2)

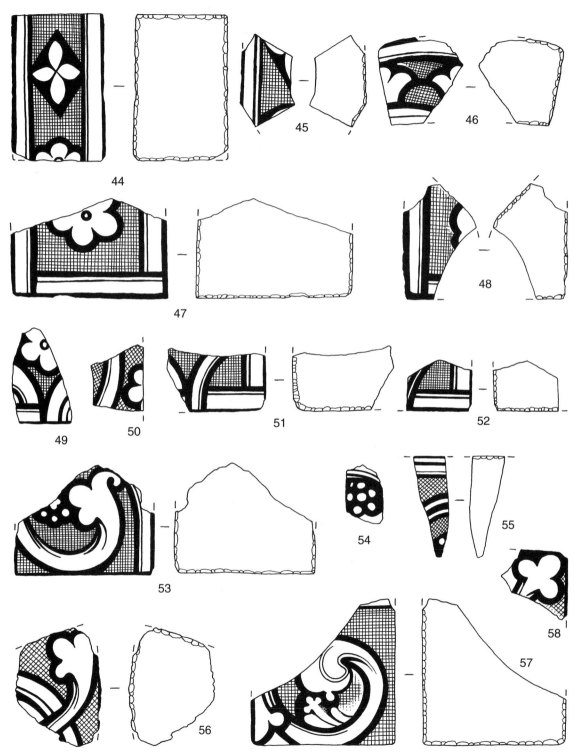

Fig 63. Window glass: Clarendon Palace Cat 44-58 (1:2)

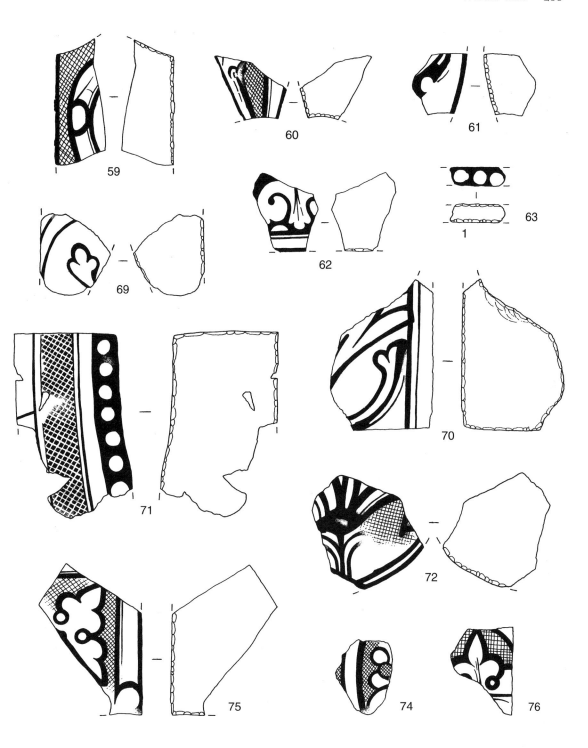

Fig 64. Window glass: Clarendon Palace Cat 59-63, 69-72, 74-6 (1:2)

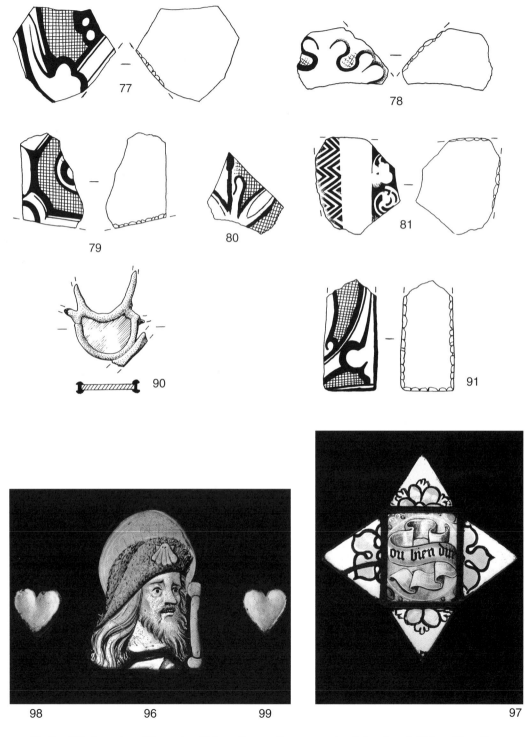

Fig 65. Window glass: Clarendon Palace Cat 77-81, 90, 91 (1:2); Ivychurch Priory Cat 96-9

Addenda to Parts 1-3

Arms and Armour

by Nicholas Griffiths

INTRODUCTION

Since publication of Part 1 of this catalogue two further fragments of mail have been acquired.

CATALOGUE

Editor's note:
In order to avoid possible confusion in future citation the catalogue here commences at Cat 115, which is sequentially the next catalogue number in the series for this class of object in Part 1 of the Catalogue (Borg 1991).

Armour

115 Mail fragment consisting of 10 copper-alloy rings. Each ring is about 10mm in diameter and is closed with an iron rivet. From the River Avon, Bridge Street, Salisbury. *1993.1*   **Fig 66**

116 Mail fragment consisting of 4 copper-alloy rings. Each ring is about 10mm in diameter and has ends flattened to hold an iron rivet. From the River Avon, Bridge Street, Salisbury. *1993.1*   **Fig 66**

From the earliest use of mail, perhaps in the third century BC, shirts were constructed of iron rings. Iron proved its defensive worth but copper-alloy rings (as here) were also used. Being softer, however, they were reserved for decorative additions to iron mail, as, for example, on a complete shirt of the fourteenth century in the Royal Armouries (Burgess 1958, 197-204 and pl. 21), which has two rows of copper-alloy rings on the lower edge of the body and three rows edging the sleeves. On occasion, such edging occurs in the form of vandykes (that is, triangles), as on a fourteenth-century shirt of Italian provenance (the Sinigaglia shirt - see Burgess 1957, 199-205 and pl. 24). A fourteenth century date for these fragments, as for Cat 1-3 (Borg 1991, 80-1), seems likely.

BIBLIOGRAPHY

Borg, A. 1991: 'Arms and armour' in Peter and Eleanor Saunders (eds.), *Salisbury Museum Medieval Catalogue Part 1* (Salisbury), 79-92

Burgess, E. Martin 1957: 'The mail shirt from Sinigaglia', *Antiq. J.* **37**, 199-205

Burgess, E. Martin 1958: 'A mail shirt from the Hearst Collection', *Antiq. J.* **38**, 197-204

115   116

Fig 66. Arms and armour: Cat 115-6 mail fragments (1:1), detail of Cat 115 (2:1)

Bone and Antler

by David Algar

INTRODUCTION

Since the publication of Part 3 of this Catalogue (MacGregor 2001), a few more objects of bone or antler have come to light or been added to the collection. Most of these are of classes of object not represented in the earlier publication. There is also a short note on the manufacture of pins in Salisbury prompted by the pinner's bone, Cat 22. I am grateful to Geoff Egan for help with parts of this text.

CATALOGUE

Editor's note:

In order to avoid possible confusion in future citation the catalogue here commences at Cat 18, which is sequentially the next catalogue number in the series for this class of object in Part 3 of the Catalogue (MacGregor 2001).

18 Awl, made from a piece of sawn antler, shaft length 65mm, with a sharpened tine at right angles to shaft, length 70mm. The antler is of deer. A practical tool easily made from perhaps otherwise waste material. From the site of the Franciscan Friary, Salisbury. *1969.81* **Fig 67**

19 Pen, made from the right radius of a domestic goose. L. 133mm. D. 5-6mm. The distal end has been cut obliquely to a point. Early 15th century. From a well containing bronze founder's waste at the rear of 35 Guilder Lane. *2008.21* **Fig 67**

Similar implements recovered from thirteenth- and fourteenth-century contexts have been tentatively described as 'medieval pens'. See MacGregor, 1985, 125 and fig. 67h-l, where examples from Coventry and Cambridge are illustrated.

The site of the well lay within property associated with the bell-founder John Barbur who died in 1404 (Tyssen 1908, 351). See pages 70-1 for foundry waste from this well. An arcaded jug from the same well has been published by Musty 2001, 160, no. 178 and fig. 63.

20 Needle. Fragment from the end of a bone needle, surviving L. 26mm with eye, D. 3.5mm, flanked by a shallow longitudinal groove. From the site of the Franciscan Friary, Salisbury. *1969.81*

21 Stylus of bone, lathe-turned, slightly tapering shank with oval knop, total L. 86mm. Tipped with an iron pin which protrudes 3.5mm. This is a relatively long example. From the River Avon below Fisherton Bridge, Bridge Street. *1993.1* **Fig 67**

Such implements are late medieval and are now interpreted as styli for use with wax tablets (having formerly been described as parchment prickers). See Egan 1998, 272-3 and fig. 210, nos. 899-911; Biddle and Brown 1990, 743-7; MacGregor 1985, 174-5 and fig. 67d-e.

Pin-making

In Salisbury, as early as September 1440, the 'Pynners' (pin-makers) were a part of the guild which included pewterers and saddlers referred to in the minutes of a meeting called by the Corporation of the City in connection with raising money to pay for the completion of the great ditch (Haskins 1912, 60-1). During the reign of Elizabeth I this guild was united with that of the smiths to form one company, which now included all the metal working trades. 'The Companye of Smythes' was the first to be reconstituted under the new Charter of Incorporation given to the City by James I in 1612 (ibid. 371).

During the medieval period brass pins were made individually from lengths of drawn wire. Methods of forming the bulbous heads were quickly developed but the efficient production of sharp points proved more difficult until the late eighteenth century by which time the process had become mechanised (Tylecote, 1972). In the sixteenth and probably the late fifteenth centuries it was usual to file the points using a bone rest in order to improve the grip and avoid bending the pin during sharpening. Metapodials of horses and cattle were the bones of choice with horse bones much preferred because of their greater density. Usually the distal end was trimmed flat on four faces, perhaps to be held firm in a vice or similar arrangement. Four flat surfaces were cut into the proximal end of the bone, and two or three narrow grooves were made lengthwise into this surface probably with a saw. The pins were held and rotated in these grooves while the points were being filed, sometimes resulting in the bone being scored with diagonal file marks (Macgregor 1985, 171 and fig. 89).

Much of the physical evidence for pin-mak-ing in Salisbury has been recovered from near the Town Mill and from the River Avon downstream from it, suggesting that pin-making was established by the end of the medieval period in the vicinity of Bridge Street. See also page 112 where pins are described in the section on copper alloy.

22 Pinner's (pin-maker's) bone made from a horse metapodial. L. 168mm, roughly sawn to the required shape, the proximal end cut to a lozenge *c.*21x18mm, the four flat surfaces so formed having longitudinal grooves to hold wire shafts, while their ends were pointed by filing. Found among material, largely pottery of the 16th century, salvaged from a bank of the River Avon during revetment improvements near Crane Bridge, Salisbury. *2008.1*

Fig 67

This object may date from just into the post-medieval period. It is comparable with pinners' bones from London (e.g. Egan 2005, nos. 722-3 fig. 129). For another example see MacGregor 1991, 370 and fig. 187c. There are three other pinners' bones in the Museum collection that are very similar to this piece in both form and colouration, all found on the site of the Town Mill late in the nineteenth century.

BIBLIOGRAPHY

Biddle, M. and Brown, D. 1990: 'Writing Equipment' in M. Biddle (ed.), *Object and Economy in Medieval Winchester,* Winchester Stud. **7ii**, Oxford, 729-53

Egan, G. 1998: *The Medieval Household: Daily Living c.1150-c.1450,* Medieval Finds from Excavations in London **6**

Egan, G. 2005: *Material Culture in London in an Age of Transition: Selected Tudor and Stuart Period Finds c.1450-c.1700 from Excavations at Riverside Sites in Southwark, South London,* Museum of London Archaeology Monograph **19** (Museum of London)

Haskins, C. 1912: *The Ancient Trade Guilds and Companies of Salisbury* (Salisbury)

MacGregor, A. 1985: *Bone, Antler, Ivory and Horn. The Technology of Skeletal Materials since the Roman Period* (London and Sydney)

MacGregor, A. 1991: 'Antler, Bone and Horn' in J. Blair and N. Ramsay (eds.), *English Medieval Industries,* 355-78

MacGregor, A. 2001: 'Objects of bone, antler and ivory' in Peter Saunders (ed.), *Salisbury Museum Medieval Catalogue Part 3* (Salisbury), 14-25

Musty, J. 2001: 'Pottery, Tile and Brick' in Peter Saunders (ed.), *Salisbury Museum Medieval Catalogue Part 3* (Salisbury), 132-212

Tyssen, A. D. 1908: 'John Barbor of Salisbury, Brasier', *Wilts Arch. Mag.* **35**, 351

Tylecote, R. F. 1972: 'A Contribution to the Metallurgy of Eighteenth and Nineteenth Century Brass Pins', *Post-Medieval Archaeology* **6**, 183-90

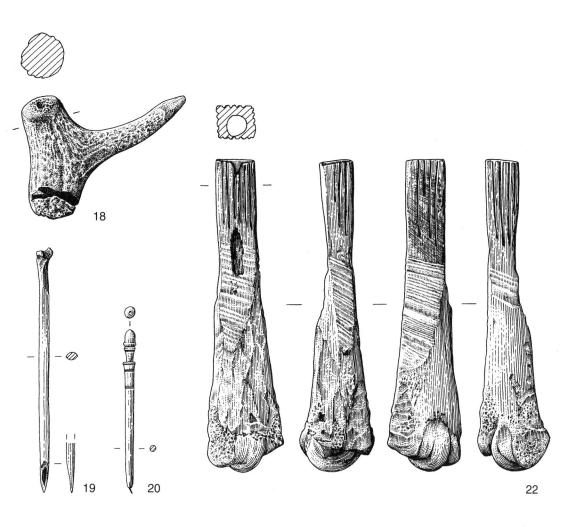

Fig 67. Bone: Cat 18, awl; Cat 19, needle; Cat 21, stylus; Cat 22, pinner's bone (1:2)

Cloth Seal

by Geoff Egan

INTRODUCTION

One seal has been added to the collection since the publication of Part 3 of this Catalogue (Egan 2001).

CATALOGUE

Editor's note:
In order to avoid possible confusion in future citation the catalogue here commences at Cat 178, which is sequentially the next catalogue number in the series for this class of object in Part 3 of the Catalogue (Egan 2001). The convention // separates obverse and reverse descriptions.

Low Countries

Leiden (Netherlands)

178 Lead; D. 50mm. // 47mm, corroded.
ornate shield with saltire keys, letter G to each side (from 3 o'clock) (illegible device) .·. LEY .·. DEN... LEY .·. DEN around (blackletter) // (incomplete flan; stamp as on first side but letter to either side of shield appears to be I, incomplete flan)
From the garden of Marshmead, Clarendon Road, Alderbury. *2001.40* **Fig 68**

The arms are those of the city. The letters to each side of the arms may refer to the year of issue of the die or to individual searchers, or they may indicate different grades etc. of textile. This substantial official seal would have been applied to heavyweight woollens. (?)sixteenth-century.

Leiden's textile industry experienced a variety of fortunes during the 1500s. Production there, following a slack period early in the century, rallied around 1515, peaking in 1521 with nearly 29,000 cloths, but falling from the 1530s to less than 1,100 in 1573; after the siege of the city in 1574, which effectively saw the end of traditional woollens, the textile industry was rebuilt, the turning point from 'old' to 'new' draperies being seen by contemporaries as 1580, to flourish until threatened by rival, rural production after 1635 (Noordegraaf 1997, 177-8 & 183-5). This seal probably dates from the first three quarters of the century.

Compare MOL acc. no. 87.131/4 with ?l and ?t to the sides of the arms and acc. no. 95.236/8 with e to the right and the imprint of a very coarse textile (four to five threads per 10mm in the most legible system) and Mitchiner 1991, 963 nos. 3002a and b, found in London and assigned to the sixteenth/seventeenth centuries. The letters flanking the arms are D // G on no. 3002a and A on the surviving side of no. 3002b. Mitchiner suggests these may have stood for varieties or finishing treatments for the cloth rather than to have been officers' initials (the use of different pairs of letters on respective sides presents an unresolved difficulty - the parallel cited by Mitchiner from Sabatier is later than the present variety).

BIBLIOGRAPHY

Egan, G. 2001: 'Cloth Seals' in Peter Saunders (ed.), *Salisbury Museum Medieval Catalogue, Part 3* (Salisbury), 43-86

Mitchiner, M. 1991: *Jetons, Medalets and Tokens, vol. 2: the Low Countries and France*

Noordegraaf, L. 1997: 'The New Draperies in the North Netherlands, 1500-1800' in N. B. Harte (ed.), *The New Draperies in the Low Countries and England*, Pasold Studies in Textile History **10** (Oxford), 173-95

Fig 68. Cloth seal: Cat 178 (1:1)

Coins

by Paul Robinson and David Algar

INTRODUCTION

In Part 1 of this catalogue 329 coins were published by Christopher Blunt, David Algar and Eleanor Saunders (Blunt 1991). Here are catalogued (using the format adopted by Christopher Blunt) a further 114 coins acquired by the Museum, and for ease of future reference these are numbered from 330. They comprise coins found in the city of Salisbury, the majority being from the River Avon and a few from south Wiltshire. The most notable addition is the Grahame C. Moody Collection of sixty five silver pennies minted in Wilton. These are published here for the first time.

CATALOGUE

References to North 1975 and 1980 are given as 'North' followed by the number. BMC is British Museum Catalogue.

The Grahame C. Moody Collection

Grahame Charles Moody was born in Bristol in 1909. He qualified as a pharmacist and moved to Wilton in 1934 having purchased the long established pharmacy in the town. He took an active part in local affairs, served as mayor of Wilton in 1951 and was a leading member of the Congregational Church. For many years he was also part owner of a pharmacy in Castle Street, Salisbury and was a keen Rotarian and Freemason in the City.

He had a keen interest in the history of Wilton and in the 1950s began collecting coins minted there, which he acquired from London coin dealers, notably B.A. Seaby Ltd. and A.H. Baldwin and Sons Ltd. He also purchased Wilton coins from the auction sales of some of the leading collections sold at that time, such as the R.C. Lockett collection, at which Baldwins bid on his behalf. His aim was to form a collection of the finest coins of the Wilton mint with examples of the coins of as many individual moneyers as possible.

He died in 1979 and, following the death of his widow, his children Robert and Anne generously presented in 1991 sixty two coins from this collection to the Museum in memory of their father (acc. no. 1991.60), *Sal. Mus. Rep.* 1991-2, 22 and pl. on 21. Three duplicates, Cat 335, 375 and 388, which were once on loan to the Wilton Town Museum, have been acquired (acc. no. 2009R.122.1-3) so that it is now possible to publish the whole of the Moody Collection together.

The Grahame C. Moody Collection is an important one and is now published for the first time. It is extensive and includes a number of rarities, for example the two coins of Edgar (Cat 330-1) which are the earliest recorded coins to have been struck at Wilton. Only eight of the coins were previously represented in the Museum. The collection may be summarised as follows:

King		Moneyers
Eadgar	2	Eadstan, Leofsige
Æthelred II	9	Leofwold, Sæwine
		Wulfgar
Cnut	2	Ælfred, Ælfstan
Harold I	1	Ælfstan
Edward		
the Confessor	17	Ælfwine, Ælfwold
		Hærred, Sæwine, Swetric
		Thurcil, Winus

Harold II	2	Centwine, Winus
William I	13	Ælfwine, Godric, Owi
		Sefara, Sewine
William II	1	Sefara
Henry I	1	Ailward
Stephen	4	Eller, Falche, Tomas
		(Tumas)
Henry II	3	Osber, Rodbert
Henry III	10	Huge, Ion, Willem

Unfortunately there was no record with the collection giving the pedigree or source of any of the coins and to date it has been possible to identify their sources in only a few cases. The help of Bill Lean in this regard is gratefully acknowledged.

The Wilton 'Mint'

Coins were minted at Wilton for longer and in greater quantities than at any other Wiltshire town. Its history in this respect is closely linked to that of Salisbury: some moneyers were active at different times in each town and the economy of each town, as indicated by the number of moneyers active there at any one time, was affected by that of the other – invariably adversely. For the relationship between Wilton and other Wiltshire mints see Shortt, 1948.

The minting of coins at Wilton began at an uncertain date prior to 973 with two moneyers (Eadstan and Leofsige) striking coins there. Following a major reform of the currency by Eadgar in 973, the number of moneyers was increased to five (Ælfsige, Boi(g)a, Eadwine, Leofwold and Osbern), which, while fewer than at Winchester and London, nevertheless ranks with towns such as Lincoln and Chester, showing the particular importance of Wilton. Under Æthelred II (978-1016) the number of moneyers was at first maintained, with between four and six active there at any one time. In 1003, however, Swein sacked Wilton and the striking of coins there ceased for a while (Dolley 1954). The minting of coins was transferred to Old Sarum, where the strong defences of the hill fort had prevented Swein from overrunning that town. Three of the former Wilton moneyers were among those who now struck coins at this new mint. At the beginning of the reign of Cnut (1016-35), the striking of coins was resumed at Wilton, but its output was very small in comparison with Old Sarum. Not until the reign of Edward the Confessor (1042-66), over forty years after its sack by Swein, did the economy of Wilton revive. In this period the number of moneyers striking coins at Wilton at any one time steadily increased while the number at Old Sarum declined and was in fact almost negligible after 1050.

During the brief reign of Harold II (1066) there was a short interlude when the quantity of coin struck at Wilton may have been second only to London (Pagan 1990). The purpose of this may have been to build up a war chest to help oppose the Danish and Norman invasions in that year. Coins continued to be minted at Wilton after the Norman Conquest but under new moneyers. Initially under William I (1066-87) four were active at any one time. This number declined to three and then, in the middle of the reign of William Rufus (1087-1100), to two only. Coins of Henry I (1100-35) and Stephen (1135-54) minted at Wilton are scarce but suggest that this pattern continued in these reigns. In the early part of the reign of Henry II (1154-89), three moneyers (Aschetil, Lantier and William) struck coins at Wilton as opposed to two at Salisbury. Then, as part of the steady process of centralisation of the production of the coins of England, in about 1180 the minting of coins at Salisbury ceased, leaving Wilton as the only town in Wiltshire where coins were still being struck, now under two moneyers (Osber and Rodbert). This may be explained by the fact that Wilton was a royal borough and struck coinage for the King's own convenience (Stewartby 2009, 15). This was, however, a brief respite and in 1189 the striking of coins at Wilton ceased. It resumed in 1248 for a brief period with four moneyers (Huge, John and two moneyers with the name William, whose coins cannot be distinguished), but in 1250 ceased for good.

Of the moneyers themselves we can say very little. In the Saxon period most, as would be expected, have Saxon names. Boia is an Irish name, while Thurcil is Danish but may reflect the fashion in the Saxon upper classes, after the accession of Cnut, of adopting Danish names. After the Norman Conquest, while some Saxon names continue, we see the appearance of new Norman-French names such as Ricard, Willem and Tomas. With regard to their identities, Boia, who struck coins at Wilton in the reigns of Eadgar, Edward the Martyr and Æthelred II, may possibly be the same person as the moneyer(s?) of this name who struck coins at a number of other towns throughout Britain. He may also be the same person as the landowner who gave his name to Boyton in Wiltshire. Brixi, who struck coins at Wilton briefly under Edward the Confessor, is possibly to be equated with the Brixi, who was recorded in Domesday Book as a holder of land in Wiltshire, Somerset and Dorset. It is not until the middle of the thirteenth century, for the recoinage of 1248-50, that more specific names for Wilton moneyers are recorded (Stewartby 2009, 85 and 87), and for the first time it is possible to identify the moneyers as specific individuals in Wilton. *Huge* is Hugh Goldrun, whose probable descendant John Goldron is recorded as a burgess and goldsmith in Wilton in about 1300 (VCH Wilts.1962, 18). *Ion* is Iohannes Berte, who was a witness at the Post Mortem Inquisition of William Isemberd in 1259-60 (Fry 1908, 28). The two moneyers called *William* are Willelmus filius Radulfi and Willelmus Manger. William Manger or Mauger came from a family important in Wilton in the thirteenth century and appears in Feet of Fines as a tenant of part of lands at Fugheliston (Fugglestone) and a messuage at Wilton in 1236, and in 1241 as the plaintiff in a case concerning part of a messuage there (Fry 1930, 25, 50 and 33, 48).

EADGAR, 959-975

330 *BMC* type iii (circumscription - cross). North

749. Moneyer Eadstan. Rev: +EADSTAN MONETA ÞILTVN

Wt. 1.42g (22.0gr.). Die axis 6. *Ex* Lockett (1955) lot 625.   **Pl 25**

331 *BMC* type iii North 749. Moneyer Leofsige. Rev: +LEOFSIGE M⁻O ÞILTVNE·⁙

Wt. 1.17g (18.0gr.). Die axis 6.   **Pl 25**

ÆTHELRED II, 978-1016

332 *BMC* type iid (second hand). North 768. Moneyer Sæwine. Rev: +SÆÞINE M⁻O ÞILTV

Wt. 1.68g (25.9gr.). Die axis 3.   **Pl 25**

The only other published example of this coin appears to be a cut halfpenny with the same obverse in Stockholm (CNS 1.2.4. 1000), Jonsson, 1987, 97.

333 *BMC* type iiia (crux). North 770. Moneyer Leofwold. Rev: +LEOFÞOLD M⁻O ÞILT

Wt. 1.60g (24.7gr.). Die axis 12.   **Pl 25**

334 *BMC* type iiia. North 770. Moneyer Wulfgar. Rev: +ÞVLFGAR M⁻O ÞILT

Wt. 1.65g (25.4gr.). Die axis 3.   **Pl 25**

From the same obverse die as Cat 14 (Blunt 1991) and Cat 335 but all have different reverses.

335 *BMC* type iiia. North 770. Moneyer Wulfgar. Rev: +ÞVLFGAR M⁻O ÞILT

Wt. 1.51g (23.3gr.). Die axis 12. Slight split. *2009R. 122.1*   **Pl 25**

Compare Cat 14 (Blunt 1991).

336 *BMC* type iiia North 770. Moneyer Sæwine. Rev: +SÆÞINE M⁻O ÞILTV

Wt. 1.65g (25.4gr.). Die axis 12.   **Pl 25**

337 *BMC* type i (intermediate small cross). North 773. Moneyer Wulfgar. Rev: +ÞVLFGAR M⁻⊙ ÞILTV

Wt. 1.68g (25.9gr.). Die axis 3. Pecked on reverse.   **Pl 25**

For comment on the intermediate small cross issues at Wilton see Blunt and Lyon 1990, 28.

338 *BMC* type iva (long cross). North 774. Moneyer Leofwine. Rev: +LEO FÞIN E M'O ÞILT
Wt. 1.67g (25.6gr.). Die axis 10.   **Pl 25**

339 *BMC* type iva. North 774. Moneyer Sæwine. Rev: +SÆ ÞINE MΩO ÞILT   (NE ligated)
Wt. 1.76g (27.0gr.). Die axis 4.   **Pl 25**

340 *BMC* type iva. North 774. With pellet at nape of neck. Moneyer Sæwine. Rev: +SÆ ÞINE MΩ☉ ÞILT (NE ligated)
Wt. 1.68g (25.9gr.). Die axis 4. Pecked on reverse.
                                                    Pl 25

The same obverse die was also used by the London moneyers Æthelwerd and Godwine.

CNUT, 1016-1035

341 *BMC* type xvi (short cross). North 790. Moneyer Ælfred. Rev: +[Æ]LFRED ON ÞILTV
Wt. 0.83g (12.8gr.). Die axis 3.   **Pl 25**

The low weight of this coin may be noted, although it falls within the recorded weight limits of the type (Petersson, 1969, table 23).

342 *BMC* type xvi. North 790. Moneyer Ælfstan. Rev: +Æ LFSTAN ON ÞIL
Wt. 1.07g (16.5gr.). Die axis 5.   **Pl 25**

HAROLD I, 1035-1040

343 *BMC* type v (long cross and fleur-de-lis). North 803. Moneyer Ælfstan. Rev: ÆLF STA N ON ÞILT
Wt. 1.12g (17.3gr.). Die axis 12. *Ex* Lockett (1960) lot 3785; *ex* Bliss (1916) lot 113.   **Pl 25**

EDWARD THE CONFESSOR, 1042-1066

344 *BMC* type v (expanding cross - heavy coinage). North 823. With annulet in second quarter. Moneyer Ælfwine. Rev: +ÆL'FÞINE ON ÞILTVN:
Wt. 1.36g (21.0gr.). D. 19mm. Die axis 3.   **Pl 25**

345 *BMC* type v. North 823. Moneyer Ælfwine. Rev: +ÆLFÞINE ON ÞILTV:

Wt. 1.68g (25.9gr.). D. 20mm. Die axis 12. *Ex* SCMB (Nov. 1966, no. H3754).   **Pl 25**

346 *BMC* type v. North 823. Moneyer Ælfwine. Rev: +ÆLFÞINE ON ÞILTVNEE   (first NE probably ligated)
Wt. 1.63g (25.1gr.). D. 19mm. Die axis 9.   **Pl 25**

347 *BMC* type vii (pointed helmet). North 825. Moneyer Ælfwine. Rev: +Æ LFÞINE ONN ÞILTVN
Wt. 1.27g (19.5gr.). Die axis 12.   **Pl 25**

348 *BMC* type vii. North 825. Moneyer Thurcil. Rev: +ÐVRECIL ON ÞILT
Wt. 1.29g (19.9gr.). Die axis 12.   **Pl 26**
From the same dies as Mack 1973 no. 1220.

349 *BMC* type ix (sovereign/eagles). North 827. Moneyer Thurcil. Rev: +ÐVRCIL' ON ÞILT[ ]
Wt. 1.29g (19.9gr.). Die axis 9.   **Pl 26**
This is a better example from the same dies as Cat 21 (Blunt 1991).

350 *BMC* type ix. North 827. Moneyer Thurcil. Rev: +ÐVRCIL ON ÞIL
Wt. 1.33g (20.5gr.). Die axis 3.   **Pl 26**
Compare Cat 21 (Blunt 1991).

351 *BMC* type ix. North 827. Moneyer Ælfwold. Rev: +ΛLFÞOLD ON ÞIL[T]
Wt. 1.20g (18.5gr.), slight chip. Die axis 6. *Ex* Lockett (1955) lot 839.   **Pl 26**
From the same dies as *BMC* 1337.

352 *BMC* type ix. North 827. Moneyer Swetric. Rev: +[S]ÞETRIC ON RIL
Wt. 1.27g (19.6gr.), broken and rejoined. Die axis 3. *Ex* Lockett (1955) lot 839.   **Pl 26**

353 *BMC* type ix. North 827. Moneyer Hærred. Rev: +HÆRRED' ON ÞILTVNE   (NE ligated)
Wt. 1.22g (18.8gr.). Die axis 12. *Ex* Lockett (1955) lot 839.   **Pl 26**

354 *BMC* type xi (hammer cross 'EADÞEARD' variety with legend starting at 8 o'clock, see Robinson

1983). North 828. Moneyer Sæwine.
Obv: EADÞEARD REX Rev: +SÆÞINE· ON ÞILTV
Wt. 1.22g (18.8gr.). Die axis 12.   **Pl 26**

355 *BMC* type xi. North 828. Moneyer Hærred.
Rev: +HÆRRD: ON ÞILTVN
Wt. 1.22g (18.8gr.). Die axis 12. Purchased Spink, *ex*
Lockett (1955) lot 849.   **Pl 26**
Compare Cat 23 and 24 (Blunt 1991).

356 *BMC* type xi. North 828. Moneyer Thurcil.
Rev: +ÐVRCIL ON ÞILTVNE   (NE ligated)
Wt. 1.32g (20.3gr.). Die axis 9. 138 written on re-
verse. Purchased Spink, *ex* Lockett (1955) lot 849.
          Pl 26
This is a better example than Cat 25 (Blunt
1991).

357 *BMC* type xiii (facing bust/small cross). North
830. Moneyer Ælfwine. Rev: +ÆLFÞINE ON ÞILTV
Wt. 0.70g (11gr.). Die axis 9.   **Pl 26**
This is among the lightest recorded coins of
this type (Petersson 1969, table 36).

358 *BMC* type xiii. North 830. Moneyer Leofwine.
Rev: +LEOFÞINE ON ÞIVN
Wt. 1.05g (16.2gr.). Die axis 12. *Ex* Elmore Jones
(1971) lot 914.   **Pl 26**

359 *BMC* type xiii. North 830. Moneyer Ælfwold.
Rev: +ÆLFÞOLD · ON ÞILTV
Wt. 1.03g (15.9gr.). Die axis 6.   **Pl 26**
Different obverse die to both Cat 27 and 28
(Blunt 1991).

360 *BMC* type xv (pyramids). North 831. Moneyer
Winus. Rev: +ÞINVS ON ÞILT
Wt. 1.16g (17.9gr.). Die axis 12.   **Pl 26**

HAROLD II, 1066

361 *BMC* type i (PAX). North 836. Moneyer Winus.
Obv: +HAROLD REX ANGOL Rev: +ÞINVS ON ÞILTVN
(VN ligated)
Wt. 1.32g (20.3gr.). Die axis 3.   **Pl 26**

362 *BMC* type i. North 836. Moneyer Cen-

twine. Rev: +CENTÞINE ON ÞI   Legend starts at 6
o'clock.
Wt. 1.29g (19.9gr.). Die axis 6. *Ex* SCMB (March
1965, no. H2736).   **Pl 26**

WILLIAM I, 1066-1087

363 *BMC* type i (profile/cross fleury). North 839.
Moneyer Owi. Rev: +OÞI ON ÞILTVN
Wt. 1.22g (18.8gr.). Die axis 11.   **Pl 26**

364 *BMC* type ii (bonnet). North 842. Moneyer
Godric. Rev: +GODRIC ON ÞILTVN
Wt. 1.09g (16.8gr.). Die axis 12. *Ex* Lockett (1955)
lot 898.   **Pl 26**

365 *BMC* type ii. North 842. Moneyer Godric. Rev:
+GODRIC ON ÞILTVN
Wt. 1.26g (19.4gr.). Die axis 6.   **Pl 26**
The same reverse die as Cat 363.

366 *BMC* type iii (canopy). North 843. Moneyer
Godric. Rev: +GODRIC ON ÞILTVEN
Wt. 1.19g (18.3gr.). Die axis 12. *Ex* Carlyon-Britton
(1916) lot 1220.   **Pl 27**

367 *BMC* type iv (two sceptres). North 844. Moneyer
Sewine. Rev: +SÆÞI ON ÞILTVNEO
Wt. 1.33g (20.4gr.). Die axis 6.   **Pl 27**

368 *BMC* type v (two stars). North 845. Moneyer
Ælfwine. Rev: +ÆLFÞINE ON ÞILTV
Wt. 1.34g (20.7gr.). Die axis 7. *Ex* Lockett (1960) lot
3859; ex Roth (1917) lot 102.   **Pl 27**

369 *BMC* type v. North 845. Moneyer Sewine. Rev:
+SEÞINE ON ÞILTV
Wt. 1.38g (21.3gr.). Die axis 10.   **Pl 27**

WILLIAM I or II

370 *BMC* type viii (PAXS). North 848. Moneyer
Ælfwine. Rev: +Æ LFÞINE ON ÞITII
Wt. 1.39g (21.4gr.). Die axis 6.   **Pl 27**

371 *BMC* type viii. North 848. Moneyer Sewine.

Rev: +SEÐINE ON ÞILTII

Wt. 1.40g (21.6gr.). Die axis 9.   **Pl 27**

This is a better example than Cat 41 (Blunt 1991).

372 *BMC* type viii. North 850. Moneyer Sewine. Rev: +SEÐINE ON ÞILTV

Wt. 1.39g (21.4gr.). Die axis 6.   **Pl 27**

Same obverse die as the Sefara pennies Cat 373-5.

373 *BMC* type viii. North 850. Moneyer Sefara. Rev: +SEFAROI ON ÞITI

Wt. 1.40g (21.6gr.). Die axis 6.   **Pl 27**

374 *BMC* type viii. North 850. Moneyer Sefara. Rev: +SEFAROI ON ÞITI

Wt. 1.39g (21.4gr.). Die axis 12.   **Pl 27**

375 *BMC* type viii. North 850. Moneyer Sefara. Rev: +SEFAROI ON ÞI[ ]

Wt. 1.39g (21.4gr.). Die axis 4. *2009R.122.2*
    Pl 27

Cat 373-5 are die duplicates and are struck from the same obverse die as the Sewine penny Cat 372.

WILLIAM II, 1087-1100

376 *BMC* type iii (cross voided). North 853. Moneyer Sefara. Rev: +SEF[ ]N ÞLTIINE

Wt. 1.42g (21.9gr.). Die axis 12. *Ex* Lockett (1960) lot 3892; *ex* Wills (1938) lot 368.   **Pl 27**

HENRY I, 1100-1135

377 *BMC* type xiv (pellets in quatrefoil). North 870. Moneyer Ailward. Rev: [+A]ILÞA[R]D: ON: ÞILTV

Wt. 1.07g (16.5gr.). Die axis 5.   **Pl 27**

STEPHEN, 1135-1154

378 *BMC* type i ('Watford'). North 873. Moneyer Falche. Rev: +FAL[CHE:ON: Þ]ILT :

Wt. 1.07g (16.5gr.). Die axis 1.   **Pl 27**

379 *BMC* type i. North 873. Moneyer Tomas. Rev: [ ]MAS:ON: ÞILTVN

Wt. 1.23g (19.0gr.). Die axis 12. Octagonal flan.
    Pl 27

Better portrait than Cat 46 (Blunt 1991).

380 *BMC* type i. North 873. Moneyer Tomas. Rev: +TOMA[S:]ON: ÞILTVN   (VN probably ligated)

Wt. 1.26g (19.4gr.). Die axis 6. *Ex* Lockett (1960) lot 3930; *ex* Rashleigh (possibly by private sale); *ex* Carlyon-Britton (1918) lot 1964.   **Pl 27**

381 *BMC* type vii ('Awbridge'). North 881. Moneyer Eller. Rev: +E[LLER:ON: Þ]ILT

Wt. 1.14g (17.6gr.). Die axis 5. *Ex* Carlyon-Britton (1918) lot 1479).   **Pl 27**

This coin is from the same dies as a coin in the British Museum, *BMC* 223, *ex* Awbridge hoard, and another in the Portsdown Hill hoard found in 1995. See Allen 2006, 284-5, no 274.

HENRY II, 1154-1189

Short cross coinage

382 Type Ib. North 963. Moneyer Osber. Rev: +OSBER · ON ·WILTV

Wt. 1.41g (21.7gr.). Die axis 9.   **Pl 27**

383 Type Ib. North 963. Moneyer Osber. Rev: +OSBER · ON ·WILT[?]

Wt. 1.46g (22.5gr.). Die axis 11.   **Pl 27**

384 Type Ib. North 963. Moneyer Rodbert. Rev: +RODBERT · ON ·WILT

Wt. 1.42g (21.8gr.). Die axis 7.   **Pl 28**

HENRY III, 1216-1272

Long cross coinage

385 Type IIIa. North 986. Moneyer Ion. Rev: ION ONW ILT ONE   (ON, NW and ON ligated)

Wt. 1.31g (20.2gr.). Die axis 5.   **Pl 28**

386 Type IIIb. North 987. Moneyer Huge. Rev:

HVG EON WIL TON   (first ON ligated)
Wt. 1.34g (20.7gr.). Die axis 3.   **Pl 28**

387 Type IIIb. North 987. Moneyer Huge. Rev:
HVG EON WIL TON   (both ON ligated)
Wt. 1.61g (24.8gr.). Die axis 5.   **Pl 28**

The weight is heavier than the standard weight for the period (22.5gr.) and the average for the regular coins (21.5gr.) but not significantly so.

388 Type IIIb. North 987. Moneyer Huge. Rev:
HVG EON WIL TON   (both ON ligated)
Wt. 1.49g (23.0gr.). Die axis 12. Bent edge. *2009R. 1 22.3*   **Pl 28**

389 Type IIIb. North 987. Moneyer Ion. Rev: ION ONW ILT ONE   (all ON ligated)
Wt. 1.37g (21.1gr.). Die axis 3. Double struck.   **Pl 28**

A better example than Cat 65 (Blunt 1991).

390 Type IIIb. North 987. Moneyer Willem. Rev:
WIL LEM ON WIL   (EM ligated)
Wt. 1.33g (20.5gr.). Die axis 7.   **Pl 28**

391 Type IIIb. North 987. Moneyer Willem. Rev:
WIL LEM ONW ILT   (EM and ON ligated)
Wt. 1.48g (22.8gr.). Die axis 9.   **Pl 28**

A better example than Cat 66 (Blunt 1991).

392 Type IIIc. North 988. Moneyer Huge. Rev:
HVG EON WIL TON   (first ON ligated)
Wt. 1.34g (20.7gr.). Die axis 4.   **Pl 28**

393 Type IIIc. North 988. Moneyer Willem. Rev:
WIL LEM ONW ILT   (EM and ON ligated)
Wt. 1.42g (21.9gr.). Die axis 6.   **Pl 28**

394 Type Vc. North 993. Moneyer Ion. Rev: ION ONW ILT ONE   (both ON ligated)
Wt. 1.37g (21.1gr.). Die axis 9.   **Pl 28**

Other miscellaneous coins

Included here are coins recovered by metal detectorists in 1992 from the River Avon south of Fisherton Bridge (acc. no. 1993.1) and from the Millstream, Salisbury. This group should be viewed as complementary to the jettons from the River and already published in Part 3 (Mernick and Algar 2001). Most of these coins are in very poor condition, being variously worn, clipped and corroded. This is partially due to the environmental conditions of where they were lost, that is in a fast-moving, shallow river. However, it is possible that worn and clipped coins were deliberately discarded, perhaps because they were no longer usable as change.

Other coins catalogued here include a few pieces of note: a primary sceatta (Cat 395), a cut halfpenny of Harold I (Cat 397) and a cut farthing of Edward the Confessor (Cat 398).

ANGLO-SAXON

Primary Sceatta Coinage, c.690-710

395 AR *Sceat*. 'Runic' type, series C2. *BMC* type 2b. North 161; Metcalf 1994, 108, pl. 6 (no. 124). Obv: diademed bust right [T]æpa to right and A flanked by annulets to left. Rev: standard, inscribed TT//II around central annulet, crossed above, below and to each side, with T projecting from each corner.
D. 11mm. Wt. 1.14g (17.6gr.). Die axis 3. Found at Salterton, Durnford. *2001.63*   **Pl 28**

Thanks to Laura Burnett for help with this identification.

ENGLISH

CNUT, 1016-1035

396 Penny. *BMC* type xiv (pointed helmet). North 787. Mint Salisbury. Moneyer Ælfwine. Rev: +Æ L·FÞINE: ⊙N SERE
Wt. 0.97g (14.9gr.). Die axis 3. Purchased Spink sale 27.3.2002, lot 320. *2002.29*   **Pl 28**

The two coins below (Cat 397 and 398), with Cat 241 and 242, are the only examples in the Museum of cut fractional pennies.

HAROLD I, 1035-1040

397 Cut halfpenny. *BMC* type i (jewel cross). North 802. Mint Lincoln. Moneyer Osferth.
Wt. 0.54g (8.3gr.). Die axis 6. Found at Salterton, Durnford. *2007.4* **Pl 28**

Cut fractions, which begin in the tenth century, are, with only a few exceptions, under represented in coin hoards from Britain and Scandinavia, the chief source for museums and collectors of Saxon and Norman coins. Site finds in recent years from excavations, and discoveries made by metal detectorists (as here), have shown that cut halfpennies and cut farthings were much more common in use, particularly in the twelfth century.

EDWARD THE CONFESSOR, 1042-1066

398 Cut farthing. *BMC* type i (radiate/small cross). North 816. Mint probably London.
Wt. 0.18g (2.8gr.). Die axis 2. Found at Stapleford. *2004.41* **Pl 28**

See comment on Cat 397.

HENRY III, 1216-1272

Long cross coinage

399 Penny. Type III. North 986-988. Mint London, Canterbury or Winchester. Moneyer [Nic]ole.
Wt. 0.49g (7.5gr.). Die axis uncertain. Fragment only. From the Millstream near Tesco, Salisbury. *2005.1.170*

400 Penny. Type Va. North 991. Mint London. Moneyer Henri.
Wt. 1.33g (20.5gr.). Die axis 3. Found at Custom Bottom, Great Wishford. *2004.47*

EDWARD I, 1272-1307

401 Penny. Type 3b. North 1017. London.
Wt. 0.97g (14.9gr.). From Amesbury. *1989.54*

402 Penny. Type 3d. North 1019. London.
Wt. 0.86g (13.2gr.). From River Avon, Bridge Street, Salisbury. *1993.1*

403 Penny. Type 3e. North 1020. Newcastle.
Wt. 1.33g (20.5gr.). Found in North Field, Ebbesbourne Wake in 1924. *1983.141*

404 Halfpenny. Type 3c. North 1045/1. London.
Wt. 0.39g (6.0gr.). Corroded on one edge. From River Avon, Bridge Street, Salisbury. *1993.1*

405 Unidentified voided long cross penny, post 1279. Rev: CIVI TAS [   ]
Wt. 0.81g (12.5gr.). Corroded. From excavations at 39 Brown Street, Salisbury. *1990.1*

EDWARD III, 1327-1377

Third ('Florin') coinage 1344-1351

406 Penny. North 1123. Canterbury.
Wt. 0.60g (9.2gr.). Incomplete. From River Avon, Bridge Street, Salisbury. *1993.1*

Fourth coinage 1351-1369

407 Half groat. North 1148. Pre-treaty period, series C, 1351-2.
Wt. 1.78g (27.4gr.). From River Avon, Bridge Street, Salisbury. *1993.1*

408 Half noble. North 1223. Treaty period, transitional series, 1361-63.
Wt. 3.86g (59.5gr.). Found at Laverstock. *2001.1* **Pl 28**

409 Penny. North 1228. York. Archbishop Thoresby. Treaty period, transitional series, 1361-63.
Wt. 0.74g (11.4gr.). Incomplete. From River Avon, Bridge Street, Salisbury. *1993.1*

410 Penny. North 1268. York. Archbishop Thoresby. Treaty period, treaty series, 1363-69.
Wt. 0.73g (11.2gr.). Worn and split. From River Avon, Bridge Street, Salisbury. *1993.1*

411 Penny. North 1295. York. Post Treaty period, 1369-77.

Wt. 0.93g (14.3gr.). In the process of being clipped. From River Avon, Bridge Street, Salisbury. *1993.1*
Pl 28

RICHARD II, 1377-1399

412 Quarter noble. North 1319. London. Escallop over shield.
Wt. 1.47g (22.7gr.). Slight evidence that mount has been removed from edge. Purchased locally but perhaps not a local find. *2001.2*   **Pl 28**

413 Penny. North 1329 York.
Rev: +CIVI TAS [   ]CI
Wt. 0.59g (9.1gr.). Very worn and clipped. From excavations at 18 Gigant Street, Salisbury *1991.53*

HENRY V or VI

414 Penny. Probably Durham. Mullet to left of crown.
Wt. 0.60g (9.2gr.). Very worn and clipped. From River Avon, Bridge Street, Salisbury. *1993.1*

415 Penny. York. Mullet to left of crown.
Wt. 0.70g (10.8gr.). Double struck, worn and clipped. From River Avon, Bridge Street, Salisbury. *1993.1*

HENRY VI, first reign, 1422-1461

416 Penny. North 1432. Calais. Annulet coinage.
Wt. 0.62g (9.5gr.).
From River Avon, Bridge Street, Salisbury. *1993.1*

417 Halfpenny. North 1434. London. Annulet coinage.
Wt. 0.43g (6.6gr.). From the Millstream near Tesco, Salisbury. *2005.1.172*   **Pl 29**

418 Halfpenny. North 1434. London. Annulet coinage.
Wt. 0.29g (4.4gr.). Clipped. From River Avon, Bridge Street, Salisbury. *1993.1*

419 Halfpenny. North 1453. London. Rosette-mascle coinage.

Wt. 0.38g (5.8gr.). From the Millstream near Tesco, Salisbury. *2005.1.173*   **Pl 29**

420 Halfpenny. North 1454. Calais. Rosette-mascle coinage.
Wt. 0.31g (4.8gr.). Worn and split. From River Avon, Bridge Street, Salisbury. *1993.1*

421 Halfpenny. North 1468. London. Pinecone-mascle coinage.
Wt. 0.38g (5.8gr.). From River Avon, Bridge Street, Salisbury. *1993.1*

422 Halfpenny. North 1512. London. Leaf-pellet coinage.
Wt. 0.39g (6.0gr.). Edge corroded. From River Avon, Bridge Street, Salisbury. *1993.1*

EDWARD IV, first reign, 1461-1470

423 Penny. North 1598. York. Archbishop George Neville. Trefoils by bust. 1467-68.
Wt. 0.68g (10.5gr.). Clipped. From River Avon, Bridge Street, Salisbury. *1993.1*

424 Halfpenny. North 1608. London. Trefoils by bust. Initial mark unclear.
Wt. 0.24g (3.7gr.). Edge corroded. From the Millstream near Tesco, Salisbury. *2005.1.175*   **Pl 29**

EDWARD IV, second reign, 1471-1483

425 Penny. North 1648. York, sede vacante. E and rose by bust. 1476.
Wt. 0.52g (8.1gr.). Clipped. From the Millstream near Tesco, Salisbury. *2005.1.174*   **Pl 29**

426 Penny. York. Unidentified letter and key by bust.
Wt. 0.67g (10.4gr.). Worn and clipped. From River Avon, Bridge Street, Salisbury. *1993.1*

427 Halfpenny. North 1667. London. Initial mark pierced cross. 1473-77.
Wt. 0.29g (4.4gr.). From River Avon, Bridge Street, Salisbury. *1993.1*   **Pl 29**

There are four other unidentified pennies all most probably of Edward IV.

428 Penny. London.
Wt. 0.49g (7.5gr.). Clipped. From River Avon, Bridge Street, Salisbury. *1993.1*

429 Penny. Probably London or Canterbury.
Wt. 0.32g (5.0gr.). Very worn and clipped. From the Millstream near Tesco, Salisbury. *2005.1.171*

430 Penny. York.
Wt. 0.75g (11.5gr.). Worn, corroded and clipped. From the Millstream near St Thomas's Square, Salisbury. *1987.101.16*

431 Penny. Perhaps Durham.
Wt. 0.41g (6.3gr.). Worn fragment. From River Avon, Bridge Street, Salisbury. *1993.1*

HENRY VII, 1485-1509

432 Penny. 'Sovereign' type. North 1727-9. York. Archbishop Thomas Rotherham.
Wt. 0.49g (7.5gr.). Worn.
From River Avon, Bridge Street, Salisbury. *1993.1*

433 Penny. Probably as Cat 432. North 1727-9. York.
Wt. 0.40g (6.1gr.). Very worn. From River Avon, Bridge Street, Salisbury. *1993.1*

434 Halfgroat. Third (profile) coinage. North 1750, Canterbury. Initial mark on obv. and ?rev. martlet. 1507-9.
Wt. 1.59g (24.6gr.). Found at Fonthill Gifford in 1861 in a small hoard of late 15th- and early 16th-century coins. See Blunt 1978. *2006R.147* **Pl 29**
This currency hoard originally consisted of nine coins. The six fifteenth-century pieces were published by Blunt in Part 1 of this catalogue (see Cat 197-201 and 207). Details of this sixteenth-century coin and a soldino (see Cat 443 below) now complete its publication. The ninth coin was apparently another Canterbury halfgroat of Henry VII and remains un-located as it was in 1978.

CONTINENTAL

ANGLO-GALLIC

HENRY VI

435 Denier tournois. cf. Elias nos. 307-316. Mint uncertain. After 1423.
D. 20mm. Wt. 0.35g (5.4gr.). Corroded and incomplete. From River Avon, Bridge Street, Salisbury. *1993.1*
Thanks to Barrie Cook for help with the identification of this coin.

FRANCE

CHARLES VIII, 1483-98

436 Denier. cf. Duplessy no. 615. *c.*1490.
Rev: cross pattée in quatrefoil.
D. 14mm. Wt. 0.58g (8.9gr.). Worn. From River Avon, Bridge Street, Salisbury. *1993.1* **Pl 29**

LOUIS XII, 1498-1514

437 Douzain. cf. Duplessy no. 664. Mint Paris (pellet below R of REX).
Rev: cross pattée alternate crowns and lis in the angles, all within a quatrefoil.
D. 28mm. Wt. 2.08g (32.1gr.). Clipped. From River Avon, Bridge Street, Salisbury. *1993.1* **Pl 29**

SPAIN

FERDINAND AND ISABELLA, 1474-1504

438 Four maravedis. cf. Cayon and Castan 1983, 380, type 7. *c.*1500
D. 28mm. Wt. 4.77g (73.6gr.). Very worn and pierced. From River Avon, Bridge Street, Salisbury. *1993.1*

PORTUGAL

JOHN I, 1385-1433

439 Real de 10 soldos. cf. Vaz and Saldago 1984,

116ff. *c.* 1390.
D. 23mm. Wt. 2.05g (31.6gr.). Very worn. From River Avon, Bridge Street, Salisbury. *1993.1*

VENICE

There are four soldini in the collection, those of the sixteenth century being included here to complete the listing of these Venetian pieces. Popularly known as 'galley halfpence', soldini circulated in England in two periods – in the early fifteenth century, *c.*1400-15, and in the early sixteenth century, *c.*1501-26. These debased silver pieces passed as halfpennies though their intrinsic value was much less. Venetian records state that in the first period up to 100,000 ducats worth of soldini, that is about ten million coins, were sent each year to England. Even allowing for exaggeration, they must have been extremely common in use and were banned in turn by Henry IV, V and VI. Their use resumed at the end of the fifteenth century and they were finally banned by Henry VIII in 1519/20. See Blunt 1978, 131; Spufford 1963, 137 and Stahl 1996, 299ff.

MICHELE STENO, 1400-1413

440 Soldino. cf. Paolucci 1990, 38.
Obv: Doge standing left holding banner.
Rev: Winged lion of St Mark holding Gospels.
D. 16mm. Wt. 0.19g (2.9gr.). Approximately one half of the coin only. From River Avon, Bridge Street, Salisbury. *1993.1*

TOMASO MOCENIGO, 1414-1423

441 Soldino. cf. Paolucci 1990, 39.
Same type as Cat 440.
D. 11mm. Wt. 0.16g (2.4gr.). Worn. From River Avon, Bridge Street, Salisbury. *1993.1*

Of the seventy two soldini from England listed in Stahl 1996, only one is of Doge Mocenigo, while more recently the Portable Antiquities Scheme has recorded four of his soldini from England (Daubney 2009, 187) as opposed to seventy five of Doge Steno.

LEONARDO LAUREDAN, 1501-21

442 Soldino. cf. Paolucci 1990, 55.
Obv: Doge right, kneeling left before St Mark ·LEO LAV ·S ·M ·V·
In exergue: XAO
Rev: Figure of Christ standing, haloed and holding cross ·IAVS ·TI BI ·SOLI·
D. 12mm. Wt. 0.20g (3.1gr.). From River Avon, Bridge Street, Salisbury. *1993.1*

443 Soldino. cf. Paolucci 1990, 55.
Obv: Doge right, kneeling left before St Mark ·LEO LAV ·S ·M ·V·
In exergue: XAO
Rev: Figure of Christ standing, haloed and holding cross ·IAVS ·TI BI ·SOLI·
D. 12mm. Wt. 0.33g (5.2gr.). Found at Fonthill Gifford in 1861 in a small hoard of late 15th- and early 16th-century coins. See Blunt 1978; Shortt 1964, 53. *2006R.148*   **Pl 29**
See Cat 434 above.

BIBLIOGRAPHY

Allen, M.R. 2006: 'The English coinage of 1153/4-1158', *British Numismatic J.* **76**, 242-302

Blunt, C.E. 1978: 'Coins found at Fonthill Gifford in 1861', *Wilts. Arch. Mag.* **70/71** (for 1975-6), 131

Blunt, C. E. and Lyon, C. S. S. 1990: 'Some notes on the mints of Wilton and Salisbury' in K. Jonsson (ed.) *Studies in Late Anglo-Saxon Coinage in memory of Bror Emil Hildebrand*, Numismatiska Meddelanden, **35** (Stockholm), 25-34

Blunt, C. E. 1991: 'Coins' in P. and E. Saunders (eds), *Salisbury Museum Medieval Catalogue Part 1* (Salisbury), 140-168

BMC: *A Catalogue of English Coins in the British Museum: Anglo-Saxon series,* 2 vol., 1887 and 1893 (by C. F. Keary and H. A. Grueber) and *The Norman Kings,* 2 vol., 1916 (by G. C. Brooke)

Cayon, Juan R. and Castan, Carlos 1983: *Las Monedas Españolas desde los Reyes Visigodos año 406 a Juan Carlos* (Madrid)

Daubney, Adam 2009: 'The Circulation and Prohibition of the Venetian soldini in Late Medieval England', Brit. Numis. J. **79**, 186-98

Dolley, R. H. M. 1954: 'The sack of Wilton in 1003 and the chronology of the "Long Cross" and "Helmet" types of Æthelræd II', *Nordisk Numismatisk Unions Medlemsblad,* May 1954, 152-6

Duplessy, J. 1988: *Les Monnaies Françaises Royales de Hugues Capet à Louis XVI (987-1793) -* Tome 1 Hugues Capet - Louis XII (Paris)

Elias, E. R. Duncan 1984: The Anglo-Gallic Coins (Les Monnaies Anglo-françaises) (Paris and London)

Fry, E. A. (ed.) 1908: *Abstracts of Wiltshire Inquisitiones Post Mortem Henry III -Edward II (1242-1326),* British Record Society **37**

Fry, E. A. (ed.) 1930: *A Calendar of the Feet of Fines relating to the County of Wiltshire Richard I - Henry III (1195-1272)* (Wiltshire Archaeo-logical and Natural History Society, Devizes)

Jonsson, Kenneth 1987: *Viking-age hoards and Late Anglo-Saxon coins: a study in honour of Bror Emil Hildebrand's Anglosachsiska mynt* (Stockholm)

Mack, R. P. 1973: *Sylloge of Coins of the British Isles 20: R. P. Mack Collection - Ancient British, Anglo-Saxon and Norman Coins*

Mernick, P. and Algar, D. J. 2001: 'Jettons or Casting Counters' in P. Saunders (ed.), *Salisbury Museum Medieval Catalogue Part 3* (Salisbury), 213-260

Metcalf, D. M. 1994: *Thrymsas and Sceattas in the Ashmolean Museum,* vol. 1

North, J. J. 1975: *English Hammered Coinage* vol. 2, 2nd ed.

North, J. J. 1980: *English Hammered Coinage* vol. 1, 2nd ed.

Pagan, H. 1990: 'The coinage of Harold II' in Kenneth Jonsson (ed.), *Studies in late Anglo-Saxon coinage in memory of Bror Emil Hildebrand,* Svenska Numismatiska Foreningen Numismatiska Meddelanden **35** (Stockholm), 177-205

Paolucci, Raffaele 1990: *Le Monete dei Dogi di Venezia* (Padova)

Petersson, H. B. A. 1969: *Anglo-Saxon Currency – King Edward's Reform to the Norman Conquest,* Bibliotheca Historica Lundensis **22** (Lund)

Robinson, P. 1983: 'The EADPEARD variety of the Hammer Cross type of Edward the Confessor', *Brit. Numis. J.* **52**, 123-31

SCMB: *Seaby's Coin and Medal Bulletin*

Shortt, H. de S. 1948: 'The mints of Wiltshire', *Archaeol. J.* **104**, 112-128

Shortt, H. de S. 1969: 'A denier of Charles the Bald from Preshute', *Wilts. Arch. Mag.* **64**, 51-5

Spufford, P. 1963: 'Continental coins in late medieval England', *Brit. Numis. J.* **32**, 127-39

Stewartby, Lord 2009: *English Coins 1180 -1551*

Stahl, A. M. 1996: 'The Deathbed Oration of Doge Mocenigo and the Mint of Venice' in B. Arbel (ed.), *Intercultural Contacts in the Medieval Mediterranean: Studies in Honour of David Jacoby*

Vaz, J. Ferraro and Saldago, Javier 1984: *Livro das Monadas de Portugal* (Braga)

VCH Wilts. 1962: 'The Borough of Wilton' by Margery K. James in *A History of Wiltshire 6* (Victoria History of the Counties of England)

Plate 25

G. C. Moody Collection of pennies of the Wilton mint.

Cat 330 Edgar. Circumscription – cross. Eadstan.
331 Edgar. Circumscription – cross. Leofsige.
332 Æthelred II. Second hand. Sæwine.
333 Æthelred II. Crux. Leofwold.
334 Æthelred II. Crux. Wulfgar.
335 Æthelred II. Crux. Wulfgar.
336 Æthelred II. Crux. Sæwine.
337 Æthelred II. Intermediate small cross. Wulfgar.
338 Æthelred II. Long cross. Leofwine.
339 Æthelred II. Long cross. Sæwine.
340 Æthelred II. Long cross. Sæwine.
341 Cnut. Short cross. Ælfred.
342 Cnut. Short cross. Ælfstan.
343 Harold I. Long cross and fleur-de-lis. Ælfstan.
344 Edward the Confessor. Expanding cross. Ælfwine.
345 Edward the Confessor. Expanding cross. Ælfwine.
346 Edward the Confessor. Expanding cross. Ælfwine.
347 Edward the Confessor. Pointed helmet. Ælfwine.

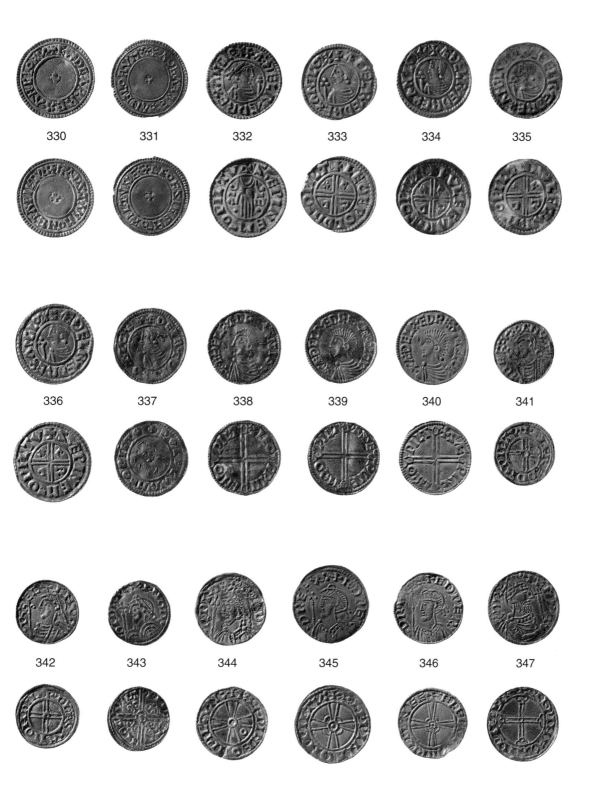

330 331 332 333 334 335

336 337 338 339 340 341

342 343 344 345 346 347

Plate 26

G. C. Moody Collection of pennies of the Wilton mint.

Cat 348   Edward the Confessor. Pointed helmet. Thurcil.
349   Edward the Confessor. Sovereign/eagles. Thurcil.
350   Edward the Confessor. Sovereign/eagles. Thurcil.
351   Edward the Confessor. Sovereign/eagles. Thurcil.
352   Edward the Confessor. Sovereign/eagles. Swetric.
353   Edward the Confessor. Sovereign/eagles. Hærred.
354   Edward the Confessor. Hammer cross. Sæwine.
355   Edward the Confessor. Hammer cross. Hærred.
356   Edward the Confessor. Hammer cross. Thurcil.
357   Edward the Confessor. Facing bust/small cross. Ælfwine.
358   Edward the Confessor. Facing bust/small cross. Leofwine.
359   Edward the Confessor. Facing bust/small cross. Ælfwold.
360   Edward the Confessor. Pyramids. Winus.
361   Harold II. PAX. Winus.
362   Harold II. PAX. Centwine.
363   William I. Profile/cross fleury. Owi.
364   William I. Bonnet. Godric.
365   William I. Bonnet. Godric.

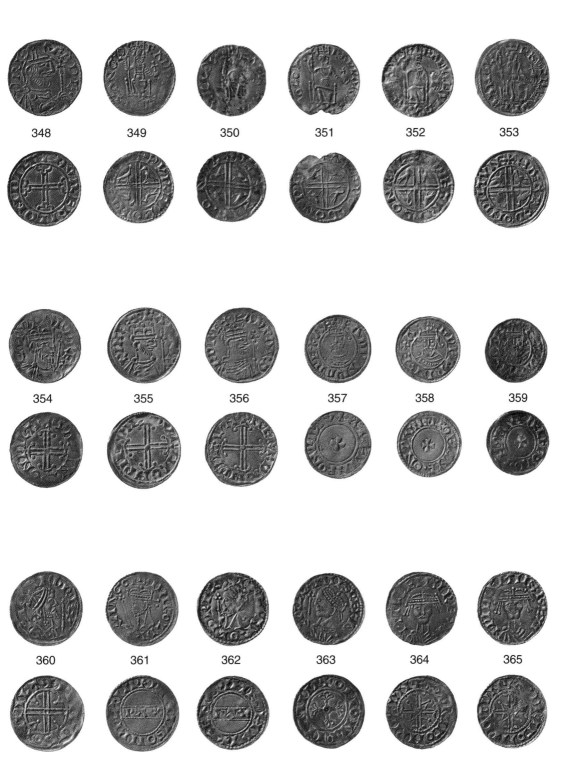

348 349 350 351 352 353

354 355 356 357 358 359

360 361 362 363 364 365

Plate 27

G. C. Moody Collection of pennies of the Wilton mint.

Cat 366 William I. Canopy. Godric.
 367 William I. Two sceptres. Sewine.
 368 William I. Two stars. Ælfwine.
 369 William I. Two stars. Sewine.
 370 William I or II. PAXS. Ælfwine.
 371 William I or II. PAXS. Sewine.
 372 William I or II. PAXS. Sewine.
 373 William I or II. PAXS. Sefara.
 374 William I or II. PAXS. Sefara.
 375 William I or II. PAXS. Sefara.
 376 William II. Cross voided. Sefara.
 377 Henry I. Pellets in quatrefoil. Ailward.
 378 Stephen. Watford. Falche.
 379 Stephen. Watford. Tumas.
 380 Stephen. Watford. Tumas.
 381 Stephen. Awbridge. Eller.
 382 Henry II. Short cross. Osber.
 383 Henry II. Short cross. Osber.

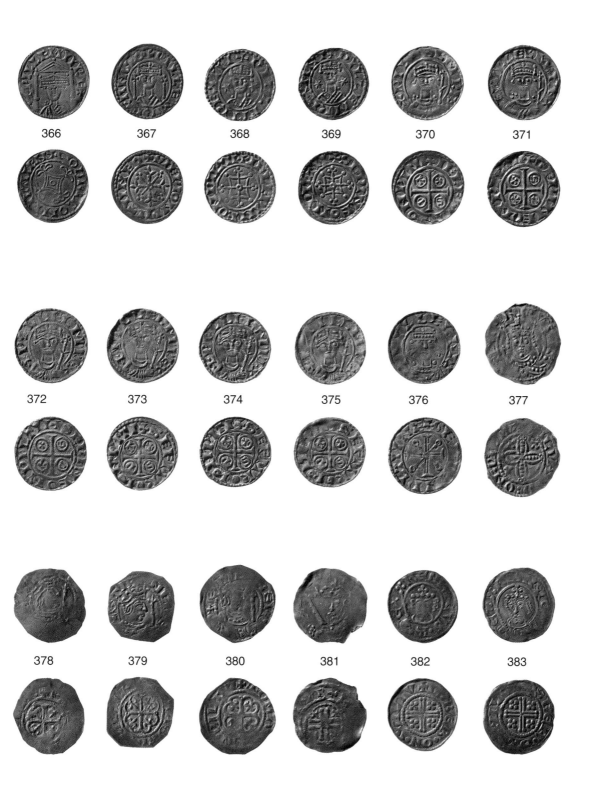

366   367   368   369   370   371

372   373   374   375   376   377

378   379   380   381   382   383

Plate 28

G. C. Moody Collection of pennies of the Wilton mint.

Cat 384 Henry II. Short cross. Rodbert.
385 Henry III. Long cross. Ion.
386 Henry III. Long cross. Huge.
387 Henry III. Long cross. Huge.
388 Henry III. Long cross. Huge.
389 Henry III. Long cross. Ion.
390 Henry III. Long cross. Willem.
391 Henry III. Long cross. Willem.
392 Henry III. Long cross. Huge.
393 Henry III. Long cross. Willem.
394 Henry III. Long cross. Ion.

Other coins.

395 Anonymous sceat.
396 Cnut. Penny. Pointed helmet. Salisbury. Aelfwine.
397 Harold I. Cut halfpenny. Jewel cross. Lincoln. Osferth.
398 Edward the Confessor. Cut farthing. Radiate/small cross. Probably London.
408 Edward III. Fourth coinage, treaty period. Half noble.
411 Edward III. Fourth coinage, post treaty. Penny. York.
412 Richard II. Quarter noble. London.

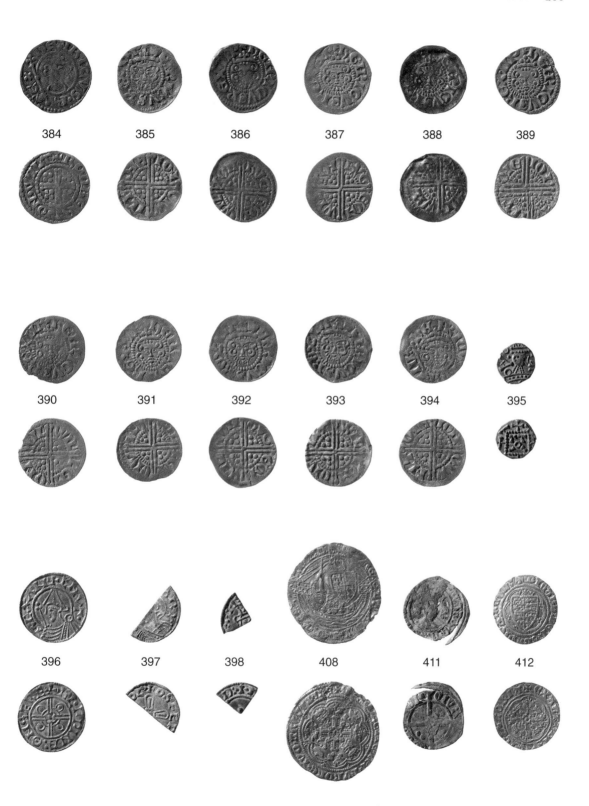

384 385 386 387 388 389

390 391 392 393 394 395

396 397 398 408 411 412

Plate 29

Cat 417 Henry VI. Annulet coinage. Halfpenny. London.
419 Henry VI. Rosette-mascle coinage. Halfpenny. London.
424 Edward IV. Halfpenny. London.
425 Edward IV (second reign). Penny. York.
427 Edward IV (second reign). Halfpenny. London.
434 Henry VII. Third (profile) coinage. Halfgroat. Canterbury.
436 France. Charles VIII. Denier.
437 France. Louis XII. Douzain. Paris.
443 Venice. Leonardo Lauredan. Soldino.

417   419   424   425   427   434

436   437   443

Domestic Stonework

by David Algar

INTRODUCTION

This section extends the record of objects of domestic stonework published in Part 1 of this Catalogue (Drinkwater 1991). The help of Justin Delair with the identification and possible sources of the stone types is gratefully acknowledged. His comments have been incorporated into the descriptions.

Two parts of bivalve moulds for the casting of strap-ends and annular buckles are recorded in the copper alloy and lead/tin sections of this Catalogue.

CATALOGUE

Editor's note:

In order to avoid possible confusion in future citation the catalogue here commences at Cat 58, which is sequentially the next catalogue number in the series for this class of object in Part 1 of the Catalogue (Drinkwater 1991).

Mortars

58 Large ?limestone mortar. The greater part of a shelly limestone mortar. D. (overall) 475mm. H. 255mm. Depth of bowl (max) 180mm. Wall thickness 70mm. There are the remains of four rounded lugs. The upper part of the wall is polished from use but the base of the bowl is damaged probably by pounding. A rather neat section, 150mm wide x 108mm, is missing from the centre of one side. Found in *c*.1984 beneath the Old Town Hall, now the Baptist Church, Wilton. *2005.84*   **Fig 69**

59 Purbeck marble mortar fragment. This has one dressed and polished hollow moulded face. 60mm x 30mm. The fragment is of shelly limestone which comes from one of the shell beds within the Middle Purbeck series. Ashurst and James 1988, 249, no. 91. From Clarendon Palace. *1957.47*

60 Purbeck stone mortar fragment. Wall thickness 46mm; its slight curve would indicate an external diameter of about 320mm. The piece has a smooth inner face and rough outer face with pecking marks. It is of a fine-grained micaceous limestone, contain-

ing fossil bivalve fragments. Its origin is uncertain but it very probably comes from the Greensand of the Middle Cretaceous. From excavations in 1969 on the site of the Franciscan Friary, Salisbury. *1969.81*

61 Limestone mortar or basin fragment. This is a small irregular piece, 120mm high and 50-80mm wide, of mortar wall with a flat-topped rim. Th. *c*.45mm. It has an external rim moulding, 33mm deep and *c*.5mm thick. The outer surface of the fragment is rough, the inner smooth. The piece, which shows a very slight curvature, appears to be a fragment from a very large mortar or possibly a lavabo that, when complete, would have had an internal diameter of about 340mm and a depth in excess of 120mm. The material is a fine-grained limestone with occasional calcitic crystals, possibly derived from the Portland series. From Clarendon Palace. *1957.47*   **Fig 69**

Ashurst and James published this as a possible quern fragment (Ashurst and James 1988, 249, fig. 95, no. 90. See Drinkwater 1991, 170, no. 8 and fig. 45 for a mortar of similar proportions found near the site of the Franciscan Friary in Salisbury.

Hones

62 Hone stone fragment of pale grey, fine-grained sandstone of rectangular section 45mm x 23mm surviving length 70mm. All faces are smooth. The stone tapers laterally towards the end and both broad faces bear traces of slight grooves. 13th century. Recovered from an area of occupation beneath the city rampart, Rampart Road, Salisbury. *2008.19* **Fig 69**

63 Hone stone of fine black stone, slate grey in section. L. 153mm; irregular section very approximately 21mm x 15mm. From the garden of Vine Cottage, Swallowcliffe. *1997.8* **Fig 69**

The garden of Vine Cottage, Swallowcliffe has yielded a scatter of medieval finds; see Cat 55 and 254 in Musty 2001, 147 and 169. This material includes fragments of five hones. However, only this fragment is considered to be most probably of medieval date.

The stone shows signs of having been sampled, perhaps for petrological examination. The comments on the stone are from a note with the fragment, which is probably based on a specialist report (not extant). Stated to be transitional between schist and black phyllite and probably imported from Southern Norway. Geoff Egan described this as Norwegian 'rag'. It is a ferriferous stone, an ironstone; one formed from a very fine-grained, densely-compacted sediment containing a high content of iron-based compounds, and not directly igneous. Almost certainly foreign to Wiltshire and could come from deposits anywhere from Silurian to Tertiary.

Roofing coverings

Cat 64-5 were among material originally deposited in Devizes (now Wiltshire Heritage) Museum by the Old Sarum Excavation Committee of the Society of Antiquaries in 1913 (*Wilts. Arch. Mag.*, 38, 540).

64 Two irregular pieces of Kimmeridge shale tile. The largest piece gives minimum tile dimensions of 176mm for the width and 250mm for the length. There is a roughly circular nail hole 10mm in diameter, 35mm from the top edge of the tile. The one good sawn edge which survives shows the tile to be, at most, *c.*15mm thick. A second less complete tile is at least 160mm wide and between 10-15mm thick. The nail hole is *c.*15mm in diameter, 60mm from the top edge of the tile. From the excavations at Old Sarum before 1913. Possibly from the bakery south of the main castle gate. *O.S. Diary* 1911, 65 and 70. *2008.17*

65 Tile of Cornish or Devonian slate. An almost complete tile. W. 118mm. L. (surviving) 187mm. Th. 6-7mm. The top edge is rounded and there is an oval perforation 13mm x 9mm, 55mm from the top edge. The slate may be from N. Devon or W. Cornwall, but similar micaceous slate-stone is known from the Mendips area. From the excavations at Old Sarum before 1913, possibly from the site of the Great Hall. *O.S.Diary* 1911, 22. *2008.17* **Fig 69**

See Drinkwater 1991, 174.

Cat 66-8 are roof tiles from Clarendon Palace and are made of shelly Purbeck limestone, known locally as Chilmark stone, found to the west of Salisbury (Lady Down Quarry, Tisbury, pers. comm. Tom Beaumont James). Tiles of this stone were not common at Clarendon Palace and these may be of material re-used from the Roman period, when it was commonly used for roofing. The range of widths recorded suggests that the tiles may have come from graded courses.

66 Stone roofing tile, almost complete. W. 125mm. L. 190mm. Th. 18mm (max), with peg hole, D. 5mm. From the Musty 1961 excavations. Ashurst and James 1988, 249 no. 86, fig. 95. *1990.24*

67 Fragment of stone roofing tile. W. 160mm. L. (surviving) 140mm. Th. 19mm (max). From the Musty 1961 excavations. Ashurst and James 1988, 249 no. 87. *1990.24*

68 Fragment of stone roofing tile. W. 145mm. L. (surviving) 115mm. Th. 18mm (max). From the Musty 1961 excavations. Ashurst and James 1988, 249 no. 88, fig. 95. *1990.24*

BIBLIOGRAPHY

Ashurst, J. and James T. B. 1988: 'Stone-work and Plasterwork' in T. B. James and A. M. Robinson with E. Eames, *Clarendon Palace: the History and Archaeology of a Medieval Palace and Hunting Lodge near Salisbury, Wiltshire.* Soc. Antiq. Res. Rep. **45,** 234-258

Drinkwater, N. 1991: 'Domestic stonework' in Peter and Eleanor Saunders (eds.), *Salisbury Museum Medieval Catalogue Part 1* (Salisbury), 169-183

Musty, J. 2001: 'Pottery, Tile and Brick' in Peter Saunders (ed.), *Salisbury Museum Medieval Catalogue Part 3* (Salisbury), 132-212

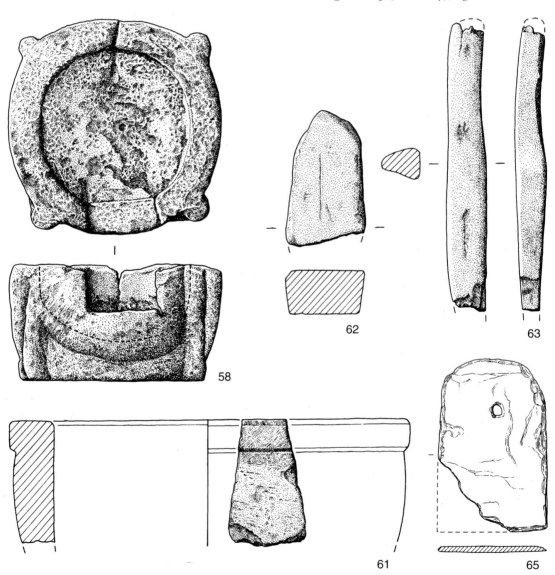

Fig 69. Domestic stonework: Cat 58 (1:8), 61 (1:4) mortars; Cat 62-3 hone stones (1:2);
Cat 65 roof tile (1:4)

Enamels

by Peter Saunders

INTRODUCTION

Two Limoges enamelled objects of twelfth or early thirteenth-century date were catalogued in Part 3 of this Catalogue (Cherry 2001, 39-42). They are good examples of enamelling in the champlevé technique, that is, where copper surfaces are cut with engraving tools and the resulting sunken fields take fine powdered glasses, fired so that they flow and bond with the copper. The bright colours of the enamel stand out against the remaining copper, which is often gilded, a process that enhances the contrast.

A further enamelled object is recorded here for the first time (as Cat 3) and is of interest in being of earlier date and being made using the cloisonné technique. This is a more delicate process than champlevé and involves thin strips of metal being laid edge-on to the surface of the metal object, often finely beaten gold, and soldered on to form cells or compartments (*cloisons* in French), which are filled with enamel and fired, leaving the edges visible to outline the overall pattern. Very little cloisonné occurs in England, perhaps the most well-known being from the Anglo-Saxon period (for example the Alfred and Minster Lovell jewels). At a later date (in the late tenth and eleventh centuries), its use on copper alloy brooches is well-documented (see Buxton 1986, 8-18). Cloisonné was especially suited to gold or silver, which is softer and more receptive than base metal, and gold cloisonné, as might be expected and in this case, is most commonly seen used on small objects, notably jewellery, which reflect their owners' wealth. However, cloisonné enamel on gold in the eleventh and twelfth centuries is very rare in England.

CATALOGUE

3 Gold plaque/pendant with cloisonné enamel (green, red, blue and white). Gold base plaque is approximately 10mm x 10mm. White enamel is used to create a design incorporating what may loosely be interpreted as a Gothic 'M' within a roundel, D. 6mm, which is impressed centrally on the plaque, thus creating two layers of gold. There are 4 holes, asymmetrically placed around the edge, one of which has been punched through from the back, and a loop. The top edge has been folded over and either end is broken away. Two of the holes were subsequently pierced through the fold. There is a mark suggestive of a guide intended for the punching or drilling of another hole through this fold, aborted perhaps because the loop attachment underneath made this impractical. The loop itself is probably contemporary with the plaque since completion of the fold appears to have been hindered by its presence. Less plausibly, if the loop originally projected at an angle from the back, damage that bent it flat may have been the cause of the crumpling in the edge of the fold. Alternatively the loop may be tertiary. There is a faint suggestion on the surface of the back of the gold that a second loop may once have been positioned behind the opposing 'ear' (which is where one might be expected if the plaque were to hang or be attached to show the 'M' device clearly). The two further complete holes, like the others, are secondary and have been formed with less finesse than might be expected, given the quality of the object, and there is the suggestion of a fifth, though this is obscured by later damage. 11th-early 12th century. From the River Avon, just downstream of Fisherton Bridge, Salisbury. *1988.22*

Fig 70 & cover

The small size of this object belies its significance as an unusual example of a high-status possession lost within Salisbury, reflecting something of the city's wealth in medieval times. Its original use was possibly as a plaque to decorate a book cover (see below) or a portable altar, but in its present form it may have acted as a pendant. Thus a precious fragment seems to have been converted, albeit crudely, to new uses over time, thereby escaping the melting pot.

A date range of early eleventh to early twelfth century is suggested for the production of this object on the grounds of style and because cloisonné production tended to give way to champlevé after this time. A near parallel for it is to be found on an early twelfth-century book at Trier, which has various shapes of enamels, all with borders like this one (see Steenbock 1965, no. 79, pl. 107). Others are found on a book cover at Aachen of earlier date (first quarter of the eleventh century) but they are less comparable (ibid. no. 51, pl. 72).

Interpretation of the design is unclear. Viewed as drawn it is possible to see an elaborate 'M' with a trefoil above. Other suggestions have been made, including an arrow piercing a heart, but all are less than convincing.

In a city whose cathedral is dedicated to the Blessed Virgin Mary it is tempting to imagine that the 'M', a common motif in the medieval period used symbolically to represent Maria, the Virgin, may have possessed special significance to its owner. How it came to be in the River Avon is unknown but the find-spot has produced many pilgrim souvenirs (including most of those described on pages 290-8): these may have been placed there as propitiatory gifts by returning pilgrims (Spencer 1990, 11). Could this trinket too have served its last purpose, many years after its manufacture, as a thank-offering, the more significant because of its value?

I am grateful to the late Brian Spencer both for facilitating the Museum's acquisition of this object and for suggesting parallels for it.

BIBLIOGRAPHY

Buxton, D. 1986: 'Late 10th- and 11th-century *cloisonné* enamel brooches', *Medieval Archaeol.* **30**, 8-18

Campbell, M. 1983: *An Introduction to Medieval Enamels*

Cherry, J. 2001: 'Enamels' in Peter Saunders (ed.), *Salisbury Museum Medieval Catalogue Part 3* (Salisbury)

Spencer, B. 1990: 'Pilgrim Souvenirs and Secular Badges' in *Salisbury Museum Medieval Catalogue Part 2* (Salisbury)

Steenbock, F. 1965: *Der Kirchliche Prachteinband im frühen Mittelalter* (Berlin, Deutscher verlag fur Kunstwissenschaft)

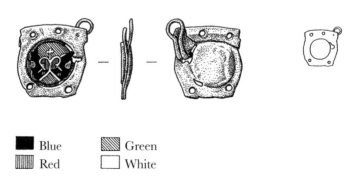

Blue   Green
Red   White

Fig 70. Enamels: Cat 3 pendant (2:1, outline at 1:1)

Floor Tiles

by Beverley Nenk

INTRODUCTION

Since the publication of the medieval floor tile collection in Part 1 of this Catalogue (Eames 1991), additional fragments have been acquired: eighty six decorated and twenty plain. These augment the known material from Ivychurch Priory, the Franciscan Friary in Salisbury and Clarendon Palace. There are also two collections of fragments associated with Salisbury Cathedral. In addition there are some stray pieces recovered from the River Avon in Salisbury, from excavations in Brown Street, Salisbury and isolated fragments from the King's House garden in Salisbury Cathedral Close, the churchyard at Britford and from the deserted medieval village at Gomeldon.

For the decorated tile fragments the design numbers used in Eames 1991 are retained in this catalogue for the sake of compatibility. Where Eames 1980 illustrates more of a given design, the British Museum design number is also given.

The plain tiles in this additional material are fragmentary and consist of square, triangular and oblong shapes. The majority of the plain tiles were probably products either of Clarendon kiln 1 or of the Salisbury/Wessex school. None has been identified as Netherlandish imports (Eames 1991, 100).

Only one tile, Cat 768 from Clarendon Palace, appears to be a waster (from Clarendon kiln 1).

CATALOGUE

Editor's note:
In order to avoid possible confusion in future citation the catalogue here commences at Cat 733, which is sequentially the next catalogue number in the series for this class of object in Part 1 of the Catalogue (Eames 1991).

In addition to the standard abbreviations used elsewhere in this volume, the following are specific to tiles:

BM design number: Eames 1980, vol. 2.
Cl 1: The products of kiln 1 at Clarendon Palace, *c.*1244-45. Eames 1991, 94-6; Norton 1996, 93.
Cl 2: Clarendon kiln 2. Eames 1991, 96; Norton 1996, 98 and note 22.
Sc: scooped key + number present.
W: Wessex school of tiles. Tiles derived from the Salisbury group are usually referred to as belonging to the Wessex school of manufacture, and are widespread in Wiltshire, Dorset and Hampshire. Eames 1980, ch.10; 1991, 98; Norton 1996, 98.
W/S: Tiles of the Salisbury group of the Wessex school, *c.*1250-52, related to the pavement found *in situ* in one of the Queen's chambers at Clarendon Palace, which is dated from orders in the Liberate Rolls issued between 1250 and 1252 (Eames 1958; 1980, ch 10; 1991, 96), and to a series present in Salisbury Cathedral which probably dates to the 1250s and 1260s (Norton 1996, 93-8, 100-101).
*: incomplete dimension.

Ivychurch Priory

The former Augustinian Priory of Ivychurch (or Ederose) was founded in the reign of King Stephen. Throughout the medieval period it was intimately connected with the royal palace of Clarendon, being responsible for saying offices in the chapels there. Although Ivychurch Priory passed into secular hands after the Reformation, major parts of the fabric of the buildings survived until the final destruction of the house in 1889. No formal excavations have taken place on the site. See RCHM(E) 1987, 19, 148-153. For further description see page 200 in the section devoted to wood.

During the construction of a drive into the Ivychurch Priory site in 1986, seventeen tile fragments were recovered (acc. no. *1989.7*):

Decorated tiles

733 Design 106. Fragment. Sc1 surviving. Th. 19mm. W/S.

734 Design 112. Fragment. Sc2 surviving. L. 138mm. Th. 23mm. Cl 2.

735 A variant of designs 121-22. Sc1. Th. 22mm. Cl 2/W?.   **Fig 71**

736 Design 122. Fragment. Sc1. Th. 20mm. W.   **Fig 71**

737 Similar (but not identical) to design 130. Fragment. Sc1. Th. 22mm.   **Pl 30 & Fig 71**
Same design as Cat 738. See below for comment on slip decoration.

738 Similar (but not identical) to design 130. Fragment. Sc1. Th. 22mm.   **Fig 71**
Same design as Cat 737. See below for comment on slip decoration.

739 Unidentified design. Fragment. Th. 23mm.   **Fig 71**
See below for comment on slip decoration.

740 Design 186. Fragment, scored for cutting. Sco. Th. 25mm. Cl 2.

741 Unidentified design. Corner fragment. Sco. Th. 22mm. W/S?   **Fig 71**

742 Unidentified design. Corner fragment. Sc1. Th. 23mm. Cl 2.   **Fig 71**

743 Unidentified ?lozenge design. Fragment. Sco. Th. 24mm.   **Fig 71**
See below for comment on slip decoration.

744 Unidentified design with large area of cream inlay. Fragment. Sco. Th. 23mm. W/S?   **Fig 71**

Plain tiles

745 Dark green glaze. Sco. Th. 26mm.

746 Dark green glaze. Sco. Th. 22mm.

747 Dark green glaze. Sco. Th. 25mm.

748 Greenish yellow glaze. Fragment. Not a waster, but a small area of glaze running into surface crack; base sheared off with small area of glaze over broken edge. Sco. Th. 30*+mm.

749 Worn green glaze. Sco. Th. 24mm.

Designs, 107, 123, 130, 161, 184, 197 were recorded for this site in part 1 of this catalogue series (Eames 1991). Designs 106, 112, and 186 are recorded here for the first time. These were intended to make up four-tile panels, designs 106 and 112 being decorated with addorsed birds; and design 186 a four-tile design incorporating fleur-de-lis and addorsed birds. Design 186 is a product of Clarendon tile kiln 2 which may also be the source of the other designs.

Slip-decorated tiles

Two fragments (Cat 737-8) are decorated with designs which are closely comparable to Eames 1991, design 130. The latter is one of a group of largely complete tiles from Ivychurch and other sites which were described as having been decorated in a stencilled slip-painted technique (Eames 1991, 99-100). However, examination of that group along with the more fragmentary tiles (Cat 737-8) suggests that the designs were in fact probably stamped onto the surface of the tile, as the slip sits in a shallow depression in the surface of the tile, rather than on the surface of the tile, as would be the case were it painted on through a stencil. The designs were therefore probably either lightly stamped into the surface of the tile, and the resulting impression slipped, or possibly the stamps were dipped in slip prior to being impressed into the surface of the tile. The slip is thicker around the outlines of each design and patchier over the internal areas of the design displaying what appear to be brush-strokes, suggesting that the slip may have been finished by hand with a brush dipped in a thin slip (Eames 1991, designs 123, 161, 184 and 197). Cat 737-8 both have part of a knife-cut scoop, while those from Eames 1991 have a single key made with a round ended implement or finger, but not knife-cut. Cat 739 and 743 may also be part of this group. The designs suggest a fourteenth- or fifteenth-century date range for the group. Eames suggested a local source for this group of tiles, as all the Wiltshire examples have been found in or near Salisbury (Eames 1991, 99-100).

Franciscan Friary, Salisbury

The Franciscans or Grey Friars established themselves in Salisbury in about 1230 south of St Ann Street on a low-lying site most probably given to them by the Bishop of Salisbury and still known today as The Friary. Numerous gifts of timber for the construction of the house indicate that initially the conventual buildings were of wooden construction and roofed with shingles. That some of these buildings were subsequently replaced in stone became clear from the results of very small scale excavations and salvage during redevelopment of the site in the 1960s. This work exposed quite substantial flint and ashlar foundations together with evidence for the use of stone and ceramic roof tiles, green-glazed ball finials and crested ridge tiles. Some walls had been plastered and painted with red lines perhaps to represent stone work and, as indi-

cated here, a range of inlaid and plain tiles was used to pave the floors. The house was dissolved in 1538 and in 1545 passed from the king into secular hands.

Twelve fragments of floor tile were found during excavations within the Friary precinct in 1966 and 1969 and during subsequent re-development of the site (see Moore 1969). Cat 750-8 and 760-1 are accessioned *1969.81*, and Cat 759 *1966.46*.

All the designs recorded here (35, 127 and 136 and designs similar to 82, 83, 155 and 185/186) are new for the site. Designs 82 (not the same stamp?) and 127 are known from the Chapter House of Salisbury Cathedral and, with 35, all occur at Clarendon Palace. Designs 155 and 185 occur at Wilton. Two designs (90 and 92, both Wessex tiles) have been previously recorded (see Eames 1991, 118 and fig. 34).

Decorated tiles

750 Probably design 35. Small fragment of border tile. Cl 1 or W/S.

751 Design as 82/83. Fragment. Sc4. 137mm Th. 21mm. W/S.

752 Design 127.Small fragment. Sc1. W/S.
This design occurs in Salisbury Cathedral Chapter House, where it is thought to date to the 1260s (Norton 1996, fig. 3, no. 14).

753 Design 136. Fragment. Sc1. Th. 24mm. ?Cl 2.

754 Design as 185/186. Fragment. Sc1. Th. 21mm. ?Cl 2.

755 Design as 155; four-tile design. Sco. Th. 18mm. ?Cl 2 or W

756 Similar to designs 153-157. Sc1. Th. 22mm. ?Cl 2 or W.

757 Unidentified design; possibly border tile with fleur-de-lis design (compare design 38-40). Corner fragment. Sc1. Th. 21mm. W/S.   **Fig 71**

Plain tiles

758 Buff/brown glaze. Triangular tile; scored before firing. Sco. 80mm x 80mm x 115mm. Th. 20mm.

759 Buff/brown glaze. Triangular tile; scored before firing; dished during firing. Sco. 80mm x 80mm x 109*mm. Th. 21mm.

760 Streaked yellow slip. Fragment of triangular tile; scored before firing. Sco. Th. 29mm.

761 Dark green glaze. Fragment. Sc1. Th. 22mm.

Clarendon Palace

Previously un-catalogued tile fragments come from four sources:
a. the site of the pre-war excavation finds hut from which material was recovered in 1952 by members of the Bishop Wordsworth School Archaeological Society
b. excavations conducted by John Musty in 1961
c. material recovered by Winchester University during survey and management of the site between 1998 and 2004
d. casual finds.

No new designs are recorded, except perhaps for Cat 764, a riser, and Cat 767. Cat 762-3 (and tile Cat 836 from Brown Street, Salisbury) and Cat 765 represent two of the decorated segmental bands which made up the circular pavement in the King's Chapel at Clarendon. The segmental tiles from group a, the excavations carried out in the 1930s by Borenius and Charlton, probably came from the neighbourhood of the building in which the King's private chapel was situated, and are assumed to have fallen from the first floor when the building collapsed; they were probably part of the chapel pavement (Eames 1965, 63). The King's new chapel was built for Henry III by Elias of Dereham between about 1234 and 1237; Henry issued the order for a pavement for the chapel on 14 March 1244. The tiles for the pavement were made in the tile-kiln at Clarendon which

was excavated in 1964 (Eames 1963, 1972). It is considered likely that the kiln was demolished in 1244 or 1245. The pavement has traditionally been dated to *c.*1240-1244 on the grounds that Henry ordered the building of a *furnus* in 1237, which has been tentatively identified as the same structure as the tile-kiln (Eames 1980, 29). However, it is now considered unlikely that the *furnus* was in fact the tile-kiln (Norton 1996, 91-93, f. 7). It would therefore seem more likely that the pavement dates to the period shortly after the order was issued in March 1244.

The tiled pavement for the King's chapel at Clarendon, made *c.*1244-45, was probably made by the same tilers who had made tiles for Winchester Castle in the early 1240s (Norton 1980, 53; 1983, 79). The Winchester Castle tiles are dated from references to purchases of tiled pavements for the Castle in 1241-42, and fragments from this early group have been found at the Castle and elsewhere in and around Winchester. The existence of wasters from Marwell Manor, south of Winchester, suggests the tiles were produced at a kiln there. This 1240s workshop was probably derived from one working in Normandy in the second quarter of the thirteenth century (Norton 1996, 93; see also Eames 1963).

a. Recovered from finds hut 1952 (acc. no. *1999.34*):

Decorated tiles

762 Design 17 (BM design 625). Fragment of a foliate sprig motif from the top of a segmental tile as used for one of the series in the circular pavement in the King's Chapel. Sc1. Th. 27mm. Cl 1. *c.*1244-45. **Fig 71**
See also Cat 763 and 836.

763 Design 17 (BM design 625). Fragment of the stem of a foliate sprig motif. Scored vertically down the centre of the tile before firing to a depth of *c.*2-4 mm, but never separated. Sc2 (one each on either side of the scored line). Th. 26mm. Cl 1. *c.*1244-45. **Fig 71**
This design is one of the segmental tiles from

the circular pavement in the King's Chapel (see also Cat 762 and 836); it is possible that it may have been scored to produce a half-tile, in case one were needed, to make up the band in the circular pavement, or perhaps to provide a recess in the pavement to accommodate a feature such as a doorway, step, pillar or font, in the chapel. Scored tiles from this pavement have not been noted previously.

764 Probably design 28 (BM design 1296), representing the base of an arcade of pilasters. Sc1. Th. 24mm. Cl 1 or Cl 2.   **Fig 71**

The BM example is edged at the top with a white band and is rebated at the top of the back, for use facing the risers of steps, where tiles of this design would have formed a continuous architectural arcade.

765 Design 19 (BM design 626), a segmental tile representing a large fleur-de-lis with pierced centre. Fragment of a half tile, from the lower part of the tile, with mortar adhering to the outside edge. Sc1. L. 72*mm. W. 68mm. Th. 24mm. Cl 1. *c*.1244-45.
                                                Fig 71

One of the tiles made for the circular pavement in the King's Chapel. The tile was cut in half lengthways down the centre of the tile before firing, as the cut edge is completely glazed. As with Cat 763, this may have been in case a half-tile was needed to make up a space in the pavement or to fit around a feature which cut into it. Cat 371, design 19 (Eames 1991, 111 and fig. 28) is also scored down the centre. Tiles decorated with this design were recorded by Madame Borenius as having been found in the tile kiln at Clarendon (Eames 1980, 186). The same design is also found on rectangular tiles, rebated at the top for use as risers, and with a line of white slip, also associated with Kiln 1.

b. From the excavations of 1961 (acc. no. *1990.24*):

Plain tile

766 Quarter of a square tile, scored on two sides before firing, and separated after firing. Dark green/ brown glaze. Sc1. 75mm x 75mm. Th. 27mm.

Incised or line-impressed tile

767 Triangular tile, scored on all three sides before firing. The surface scored with a double arc, either incised or line-impressed. Pale olive green copper glaze flecked with runs, over white slip. Sco. 57*mm x 67*mm x 80*mm. Th. 26mm.   **Fig 71**

Decorated tiles

768 Design 174. About 3/4 of a tile, 151mm x 151mm. Sc4. Th. 26mm. Cl 1. *c*.1244-45.

The fragment is very damaged and weathered, and may be a waster as the glaze is overfired and bubbled.

769 Similar to designs 91-96. Small fragment with part of head of griffin to the left. Th. 14*mm. W/S.

770 Small fragment of design of a mounted knight, showing a hind leg of the horse above a broad horizontal line. The slip representing the horse's leg has been embellished by hand with impressed decoration. Sc1. Th. 32mm. W/S. *c*.1250-52.   **Fig 72**

This design is the same as BM design 42 and was intended, with BM design 43, to represent a pair of mounted knights in combat. These two designs are the embellished versions of BM designs 1298 and 1299 (the identical inlaid designs, but without the impressed decoration; Eames 1980, 63-64, 192-4). The impressed decoration was presumably intended to represent the knight's armour and the horse's coat. The Salisbury fragment is decorated with the same stamp as the BM tile, a riser (Eames 1980, cat no. 11,750), but is almost certainly from a different tile, rather than being part of the same tile: small dots, as well as the crescent-shaped impressions, decorate the Salisbury fragment, and the tile has a reduced core, while the BM tile is oxidised throughout. It is therefore apparent that the embellished BM tile is not a unique example. Moreover, a recent re-examination of the BM tiles decorated with these designs has revealed a further area of embellishment on the horses' hooves on some of the tiles: an incised curving line beneath the hooves, above which is a series of dots, probably intended to represent horseshoes and nails. Some of these inlaid tiles, otherwise unembellished, nevertheless have this decoration on the horses' hooves, while on other tiles, with identical inlaid designs, this embellished decoration is not present. Evidently varying degrees of hand embellishing occurred on these tiles.

The Salisbury Museum fragment was excavated in 1961 from a section cut into the garden terrace below the Great Hall at the end adjacent to the north kitchen (pers. comm. D. Algar). The fragments in the British Museum were found during the excavations by Borenius and Charlton between 1933 and 1939, and most were found on the site of the King's private chamber block or his adjoining chapel block. One example was found *in situ* facing the end of a 'bench' in the room in the easternmost range excavated in the 1930s (James and Robinson 1988, pl. LXa). This room may have been the chamber of the King's chaplains (Eames 1980, 63-64, and 193; see also James and Gerrard 2007, 191, where the room is identified as the Chamber of the Friars Minor). The fragments of the right-hand tile were found in the ruins of the King's chapel block in 1936. They may have come from the chapel on the first floor, paved *c.*1244-45, or more probably from the ground floor, which was refurbished in 1250 and thereafter known as the Antioch Chamber, because scenes from the siege of Antioch were painted on the walls. The Antioch Chamber was probably paved with the same tiles as the Queen's Chamber, but scenes of combat between knights would have been appropriate subjects for decorating steps or a frieze (Eames 1980, 63-64; see also James and Gerrard 2007, 195). The theme of the Antioch Chamber suggests that the knights may have been intended to represent Richard I and Saladin: one has a cross on his shield and holds a sword and the other has a lance but these are insufficient definitively to prove this. The similar designs found at Cleeve Abbey, dated to 1244-1272 and thought to be derived from the Clarendon designs, appear to represent Richard I, armed with a lance, and Saladin, with a round shield and a scimitar (Harcourt 2000, 47, fig. 14.35-36). It would appear that these riser tiles decorated staircases, steps or friezes, or a series of benches, in several rooms in the royal apartments at Clarendon. They were probably made *c.*1250-52, and possibly in the same kiln as the tiles for the pavement in the Queen's chambers.

c. From the material recovered by Winchester University during survey and management of the site between 1998 and 2004 (acc. no. *2007.9*):

Decorated tiles

Two fragments from the right-hand tile of the pair representing knights in combat (see Cat 770) were recovered from the spoil heaps of the Antioch Chamber:

771 Fragment showing parts of a lance, horse's head and a decorative circle. No evidence of scoops. Th. 21mm. W/S. *c.*1250-52.   **Fig 72**

772 Fragment showing a helmeted head, part of a shield and a decorative circle. No evidence of scoops. Th. 20mm. W/S. *c.*1250-52.   **Fig 72**

This design appears to be the same as BM design 1299, and is unembellished. The single surviving BM fragment showing the helmet is embellished by hand with impressed dots and a lattice of incised lines on the shoulder (BM cat 11,749). The backs of the Salisbury fragments are not cut away to form a riser. Tile fragment (BM cat 11,746) bears the trace of a rebated edge on the back surface: the other surviving fragments are too worn or fragmentary to be certain of this.

d. Casual finds:

Decorated tiles

773 Design 125. Fragment of a half-tile, scored diagonally before firing and snapped to form a triangular tile. Sco. Th. 28mm. Cl 1. *c.*1244-45. From Clarendon Palace (paper label Clarendon House). *1992.7*

774 Fragment showing hindquarters and wing of griffin. Sc2. Th. 25mm. Cl 1. *c.*1244-45. From Clarendon Palace. *2005.73* **Fig 71**

    As designs 73 and 74, and probably the same stamp as 74. The same design is also present on a riser tile, rebated at the top, and with a line of white slip along the top (Eames 1991, 96, design 24), associated with kiln 1.

Salisbury Cathedral

Two groups of tile fragments associated with Salisbury Cathedral (Chapter House and Bishop Beauchamp's Chantry) are recorded here, adding twelve new designs to the Museum's collection of tiles from Salisbury Cathedral (Cat 775-8, 784, 787-8, 796, 803, 809, 814 and 826).

Probably Chapter House

Designs 126, 127, 131, 133, 136, 142 and 148 have been previously recorded for the Chapter House (Eames 1991, 118).

    Here are recorded thirty two fragments (acc. no. *1999.32*) recovered in 1951 by members of the Bishop Wordsworth School Archaeological Society from a dump (containing tile, window glass and leading) exposed south-east of the Chapter House, Salisbury Cathedral. Among these are twenty nine fragments of decorated tiles. Many of the designs among the fragments are represented by complete tiles from the Chapter House pavement now re-sited by the Gorges monument in the Chapel of St Peter and Apostles, (see RCHM(E) 1999, 168, fig. 128). This suggests that this group *may* have come from the original Chapter House pavement (ibid. pl. 6), which was replaced by a Minton copy some time between 1852 and 1858, and that they were thrown out during that period of restoration.

Decorated tiles

Designs intended to be used in borders, tiles often oblong:

775-7 Three fragments. Same stamp; originally tiles of 9 fleur-de-lis, scored before firing and separated, each tile making 3 border tiles. Similar to design 37-38, but not the same stamp. Possibly the same stamp as BM design 1283 (Eames 1980). 775: W. 45mm. Th. 22mm. 776: W. 44mm. Th. 23mm. 777: W. 45mm. Th. 24mm (max). W/S. **Figs 72**

778 Similar to designs 37-39. Fragment of a border tile, scored down the left side; originally a tile of 9 fleur-de-lis, scored before firing and separated. Probably the same stamp as BM design 1281 (Eames 1980), on tiles from Salisbury Cathedral. W. 40mm. Th. 22mm. W/S. (Norton 1996, fig. 3, no. 20, from the Chapter House). 1260s. **Fig 72**

779 Probably the same as design 40; BM design 1239 (Norton 1996, fig. 3, no. 18, from the Chapter House); fragment of one end of the tile. W. 44mm. Th. 23mm. W/S 1260s.

780-783 Four fragments, probably the same as design 41; BM design 1240 (Norton 1996, fig. 3, no. 19, from the Chapter House). 780: W. 45mm. Th. 22mm. 781: W. 45mm. Th. 22mm. 782: W. 44mm. Th. 22mm. 783: W. 45mm. Th. 23mm. W/S. 1260s.

784 Border tile, of quatrilobe flowers. A line scored diagonally at 45 degrees across one flower is probably unintentional, and not deep enough to divide the tile. Probably the same stamp as BM design 1243, on tiles from Salisbury Cathedral (Eames 1980). W. 45mm. Th. 25mm. **Fig 72**

785 Border tile, decorated with quatrilobe flower, probably the same as Cat 784. Scored down both long sides. W. 45mm. Th. 21mm. W/S. **Fig 72**

Lions or griffins in circles with fleur-de-lis in the corners:

786 Probably the same as design 91: fragment - 2 middle feet of left-facing animal (griffin?) in circle. Sc2. Th. 23mm. W/S? or Cl 2. This may be a worn version of the design represented in the pavement in the Queen's Chamber, Clarendon Palace, or possibly a later version of the design (BM design 1868). *c.*1250? (Eames 1980, 187-8; 1991, cat 631-2 and 731: Cl 2). This design is also found in the Muniment Room at Salisbury Cathedral, where the tiles are dated to the 1260s (Norton 1996, 93-95).

787 Fragment showing the forefeet of animal facing right in circle, with fleur-de-lis in corner. Sc2. Th. 21mm. W/S.   **Fig 72**

788 Fragment showing leg of animal in circle. Sc1. Th. 20mm. W/S.   **Fig 72**

Birds addorsed:

789 Design 110. Fragment. Sc2. Th. 21mm. Cl 2 or W/S. Probably BM design 1969; Norton 1996, fig. 3, no. 12, Salisbury Cathedral Chapter House, 1260s.

790 Design 110. Fragment. Sc1. Th. 18mm. Cl 2 or W/S.

791 Design 110. Scored diagonally across before firing, and separated, forming a triangular tile (left side of tile). Th. 21mm. Cl 2 or W/S.

792 Design 110. Fragment. Sc2. Th. 19mm. Cl 2 or W/S.

793 Design 110. Fragment. Sc3. Th. 25mm. Probably Cl 2.

794 Design 108 or 110. Fragment. Sc?0. Th. 20mm. Probably W/S.

795 Design 108. Fragment. Sc2. Th. 18-21mm. W/S.

796 Probably the same stamp as design 108. Fragment. Sc2.Th. 25mm. W/S.   **Fig 72**

797 Similar to design 108-109. Fragment. Sc4.Th. 22mm. W/S.

798 Similar to design 108. Fragment. Sc2. Th. 22mm. W/S.

799 Design 108. Scored down the middle before firing and separated (right side of tile). Sc2.Th. 21mm. W/S.

800 Design 111, fragment. Sc2. Th. 22mm. W/S.

Designs based on fleur-de-lis: single tile and repeating designs:

801 Same as design 126-7. Fragment. Sc0. Th. 22mm. W/S. 1260s (Norton 1996, fig. 3. no. 14; BM design 2194).

Single tile designs based on stiff-leaf foliate crosses and sprays:

802 Same as design 131, cross in circle; fragment of scored half-tile. Sc2. Th. 22mm. This design is represented in the pavement in the Queen's Chamber, Clarendon Palace. W/S. *c.*1250 (Norton 1996, 93-95, fig. 2, no. 7, in Salisbury Cathedral).

Four-tile design based on stiff-leaf foliate sprays:

803 Similar to design 146. Fragment of scored half-tile (scored down the centre and separated after firing; top right-hand side of tile). Sc0. Th. 23mm. W or W/S.   **Fig 72**
      This adds a further element to design 146 as illustrated in Eames 1991,146, demonstrating the presence of a fleur-de-lis or similar element in the top corner of the tile, as on design 145.

Plain border tiles
804 Small square border tile, two edges, two scored edges. White slip beneath clear glaze, fragment. 45mm x 45mm. Th. 24mm.

805 Small triangular tile, dark green glaze. Fragment. 41mm x 41mm x 58mm. Th. 21mm.

806 Small triangular tile. Fragment. 39mm x 33*mm x 50*mm. Th. 20mm. Very worn.

Site of Bishop Beauchamp's Chantry

Twenty five tile fragments (acc. no. *2005.14*) were recovered during superficial excavations on the site of Bishop Beauchamp's Chantry, which was destroyed in 1789. These included twenty two decorated fragments. The tiles cannot have formed part of the chantry structure, unless used as rubble; several show evidence of use in this way. Cat 820-2 appear to have been split on edge and Cat 820 is heavily mortared. Probably, most come from flooring elsewhere within the Cathedral.

Decorated tiles

807 Design 43, fragment. Sc1. Th. 18mm. W/S.

808 Probably the same as design 90. Fragment. Sc1. Th. 25mm. W/S.

809 Probably design 86. Fragment (left rear foot and trefoil in corner). Sc2. Th. 20mm. W/S.

810 Same as design 110. Sc2. W. 137mm. Th. 24mm. ?Cl 2.

811 Same as design 110. Sc2. Th. 20mm. ?Cl 2.

812 Same as design 108 or 110. Sco. Th. 24mm. Cl 2 or W/S.

813 Same as design 108 or 110. Half-tile (left side of tile), scored before firing and separated. Sco. L. 126mm. Th. 26mm. ?Cl 2/W/S.

814 Similar to design 108 or 110, but a different stamp. Half-tile (right side of tile), scored before firing and separated. Th. 26mm. Cl 2 or W/S.   **Fig 72**

815 Same as design 126-127. Sc1 (covered in mortar). Cl 2 or W/S.

816 Same as design 128. Sc2. Th. 25mm. Cl 2 or W/S.

817 Similar to design 131. Sc1. Th. 25mm. W/S.
 This design is represented in the pavement in the Queen's Chamber, Clarendon Palace. *c.*1250? (Norton 1996, 93-95, fig. 2, no. 7, in Salisbury Cathedral).

818 Similar to design 131. Sco. Th. 23mm. W/S. Comment as for Cat 817.

819 Similar to design 133. Sco. Th. 30mm. W/S.

820 Same as design 135. Th. 13*mm. W/S.

821 Similar to design 135-137. Th. 13*mm. W/S.

822 Similar to design 135-137. Th. 14*mm. W/S.

823 Same as design 136-137. One tile, comprising three joining fragments. Sc4. W. 134mm. Th. 26mm. W/S. 1260s (See Norton 1996, fig. 3, no. 13, from Salisbury Cathedral Chapter House).

824 Same as design 136-137. Sc2 (heavily mortared). Th. 24mm. W/S?

825 Same as design 153. Half-tile fragment (left side), scored before firing and separated. Sc2. Th. 25mm. ?Cl 2.

826 Possibly a Lombardic letter E, although there is no band of white slip on either of the surviving edges (compare Eames 1991, designs 3 and 15). Sc 1. Th. 22mm. ?Cl 2.   **Fig 72**

Plain tiles
827 Complete plain border tile. Dark green/brown glaze. Mortar on glazed surface. Sco. L. 129mm. W. 42mm. Th. 20-26mm.
828 Square quarter-tile, white slip, clear glaze. Sco. 70mm x 70mm. Th. 25mm.

829 Small square tile, surface very worn. Two edges, two scored edges. Sco. 42mm x 42mm. Th. 20mm.

Other Provenances

The King's House, The Close, Salisbury
830 Fragment bearing a crude rendering of a design based on 4 fleur-de-lis. Sc2. Th. 25mm. ?Cl 2. From the front garden of King's House, The Close, Salisbury. *1991.50*   **Fig 72**

Similar to design 128 but a variant; compare with other examples of design 128 (Cat 210 and 211) from the Old Deanery, which is next door to the King's House. This Wessex design has also been found on a tile at Orange Grove, Bath (Oliver and Eames, fig. 27, nos. 28-29). See also Norton 1980, fig. 4, no. 23 for another similar example from Christchurch Priory, Hampshire, *c.*1280.

Crane Bridge, Salisbury

Three fragments of floor tile (acc. no. *2008. 1*), two decorated and one plain, were among un-stratified material recovered from the bank of the River Avon during revetment improvements, west of Church House, Crane Street.

Decorated tiles

831   Same as design 108 or 110. Addorsed birds. Fragment. Sc4. 107*mm x 85*mm. Th. 24mm..*c.*1260s. W/S or Cl 2.

832   Same as design 165. A very worn fragment. Sc2. 80*mm x 60*mm. Th. 24mm. W/S.

Design 165 is recorded from other sites within Salisbury. However, the location of the pavement which included this design is un-known.

Plain tile

833   Border tile, scored on one edge. Glossy dark green/brown glaze. Sco. L. 78*mm. W. 62mm. Th. 22mm.

Britford Church

834   Complete plain border tile, dark green/brown glaze, worn. Sco. L. 135mm. W. 45mm. Th. 26mm. From Britford Church. *1999.33*

Gomeldon Deserted Medieval Village

835   Similar to fleur-de-lis design 37/38. Fragment of border tile, scored, with two edges. W. 43mm. Th. 28mm. W/S. From the Gomeldon deserted medieval village excavations. *2001.73*

This fragment, possibly from Clarendon Palace, was found in flint rubble above building 7 and was most probably included with broken roofing tiles brought to Gomeldon for use in hearth construction (Musty and Algar 1986, 142 and 151).

Brown Street, Salisbury

Excavations on the site of 49-51 Brown Street yielded some floor tile fragments (acc. no. *1991.56*), which most probably were derived from Clarendon Palace.

Decorated tiles

836   Design 17 (BM design 625). Fragment. Sc2. 110*mm x 117*mm. Th. 26mm. Cl 1. *c.*1244-45.
Fig 71

The foliate sprig motif on this fragment was used in one of the series of segmental tiles in the circular pavement in the King's Chapel at Clarendon Palace (see also Cat 762-3).

837   Design 164 (BM design 2472). A half tile frag-ment, scored and separated diagonally; edge cham-fered; inlay contracted; Sc1. Th. 22mm. ?Cl 2.

Plain tile

838   Small square border tile with two scored edges. Dark copper green glaze. Sco. 41mm x 41mm x 22mm.

I would like to express my thanks to Peter Saunders and David Algar for their generous help, advice and above all forbearance while this report was written, and to Nick Griffiths for illustrating the tiles to his usual impeccable standards, for his hospitality, and for general advice on Wessex tiles.

BIBLIOGRAPHY

Eames, E. S. 1957-8: 'A tile pavement from the Queen's Chamber, Clarendon Palace, dated 1250-52', *J. Brit. Archaeol. Assoc.* **20** and **21** (for 1957-58), 95-106 and pls. XXXII-XXXV

Eames, E. S. 1963: 'A thirteenth-century tiled pavement from the King's Chapel, Clarendon Palace', *J. Brit. Archaeol. Assoc.* **26**, 40-50 and pls. XXVII-XXX

Eames, E. S. 1965: 'The royal apartments at Clarendon Palace in the reign of Henry III', *J. Brit. Archaeol. Assoc.* **28**, 57-85

Eames, E. S. 1972: 'Further notes on a thirteenth-century tiled pavement from the King's Chapel, Clarendon Palace', *J. Brit. Archaeol. Assoc.* **35**, 71-5

Eames, E. 1980: *Catalogue of Medieval Lead-Glazed Earthenware Tiles in the Department of Medieval and Later Antiquities, British Museum*, vols. 1 and 2

Eames, E. 1988: 'The Tile Kiln and Floor Tiles', in T.B. James and A.M. Robinson, with E. Eames 1988, 127-167

Eames, E. 1991: 'Tiles' in Peter and Eleanor Saunders (eds.), *Salisbury Museum Medieval Catalogue Part I* (Salisbury), 93-137

Harcourt, J. 2000: 'The Medieval Floor Tiles of Cleeve Abbey, Somerset', *J. Brit. Archaeol. Assoc.* **153**, 30-70

James, T. B. and Gerrard, C. 2007: *Clarendon: Landscape of Kings* (Macclesfield)

James, T. B. and Robinson, A. M. with

Eames, E. 1988: *Clarendon Palace: the History and Archaeology of a Medieval Palace and Hunting Lodge near Salisbury, Wiltshire*, Soc. Antiq. Res. Rep. **45**

Moore, C. N. 1969: in 'Excavations and Fieldwork in Wiltshire', *Wilts. Arch. Mag.* **64**, 129

Musty, J. W. G. and Algar, D. J. 1986: 'Excavations at the Deserted Medieval Village of Gomeldon near Salisbury, Wilts', *Wilts. Arch. Mag.* **80**, 127-169

Norton, E. C. 1980: 'The Medieval Floor-tiles of Christchurch Priory', *Proc. Dorset Natur. Hist. Archaeol. Soc.* **102**, 49-64

Norton, E. C. 1983: 'The Medieval Tile Pavements of Winchester Cathedral' in *Medieval Art and Architecture at Winchester Cathedral*, Brit. Archaeol. Assoc. Trans. **6**, 78-93

Norton, C. 1996: 'The Decorated Pavements of Salisbury Cathedral and Old Sarum' in L. Keen and T. Cocke, *Medieval Art and Architecture at Salisbury Cathedral*, Brit. Archaeol. Assoc. Conf. Trans. **17**, 90-105

O'Leary, J. 1991: 'Excavations at Orange Grove and other studies' in P. Davenport (ed.), *Archaeology in Bath 1976-1985*, Oxford Univ. Comm. for Archaeol. Monograph **28**, 1-39

Oliver, R. V. and Eames, E. 1991: 'Floor Tiles' in J. O'Leary 1991, 14-26

RCHM(E) 1987: *Churches of South-East Wiltshire* (HMSO)

RCHM(E) 1999: *Sumptuous and Richly Adorn'd - The Decoration of Salisbury Cathedral* (TSO)

Plate 30. Floor tiles: edge of Cat **737**, showing white slip in shallow depression in the surface of the tile

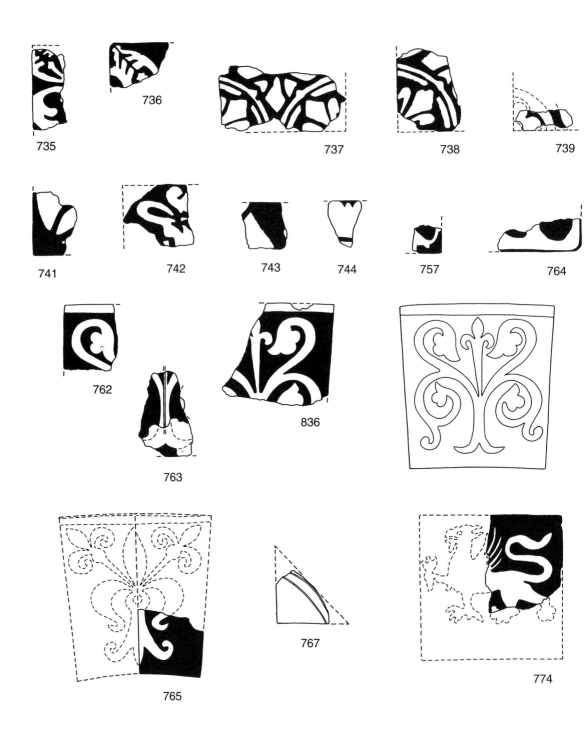

Fig 71. Floor tiles: Cat 735-9, 741-4, 757, 762-4, 767, 774, 836 (1:4)

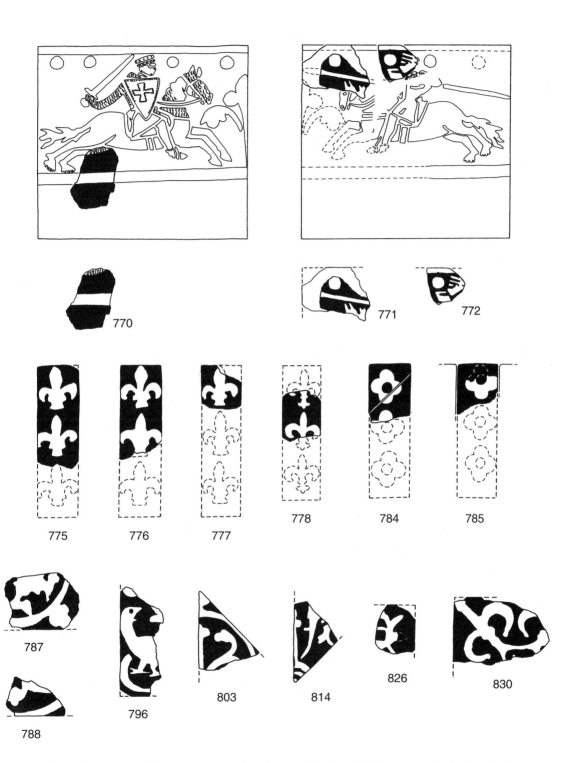

Fig 72. Floor tiles: Cat 770-2, 775-8, 784-5, 787-8, 796, 803, 814, 826, 830 (1:4)

Jettons

by David Algar

INTRODUCTION

Since the publication of the jettons in Part 3 of this Catalogue (Mernick and Algar 2001) two additions to the collection have been made, both previously unpublished English types of early fourteenth-century date and both found within a mile of Old Sarum.

A lead plug with jetton impress is included (Cat 276) and allows reinterpretation of jetton Cat 273 (op. cit., 249) as a permanent seal, possibly from a witch-bottle.

CATALOGUE

Editor's note:

In order to avoid possible confusion in future citation the catalogue here commences at Cat 274, which is sequentially the next catalogue number in the series for this class of object in Part 3 of the Catalogue (Mernick and Algar 2001). Obverse and reverse descriptions are separated by //.

274 English Sterling head type

Sterling head probably Fox Class 15 // long cross patonce, crowned leopard head in quarters; border pellets and trefoils/in each quarter, stroke between triple sprigged trefoils.

Probably second quarter 14th century. D. 20mm. Th. 0.9mm. Wt. 1.94g. Punch mark in the centre of obverse. Found in soil removed from the garden of Roselea, Stratford-sub-Castle. *2002.21* **Pl 31**

This type does not appear to have been published previously. The crowned leopard heads are to be compared with an early silver mark of the London assay office.

275 Exchequer board (Berry Type 2)

Chequered circle of five horizontal and five vertical lines (Berry Type 2) // cross patée with a 6-point star in each quarter; border beaded. Probably first quarter 14th century. D. 19mm. Th. 0.8 mm. Wt. 1.06g, small fragment missing from edge and slightly bent. Pierced in centre from obverse. Found between Cowslip Farm and the River Avon, Salisbury. *2008.12*

Pl 31

Although the obverse is well known and highly appropriate for a jetton it has not apparently been published previously in combination with this reverse, which is itself not apparently hitherto recorded.

276 Lead plug with jetton impress

Irregular lead object *c.*40mm x 28mm. Th. 13mm (max). Wt. 59.3g. This appears to be essentially a lead plug *c.*23mm diameter and 13mm thick. Further molten lead was probably added around this plug to improve the seal. The upper surface impressed with the reverse of a late 15th-century Tournai jetton. Cross potent with angular sprigged quatrefoils springing into the quarters from an inner circle. The legend is lost except for an initial rosette and I, the last letter of the inscription. This almost certainly reads: rosette SIT IIOIIIEII DOIIIIIII (SIT NOMEN DOMINI); for a parallel see Mitchiner 1988, 239 no. 729. Found in the bank of the River Ebble at Homington, Coombe Bissett, and donated by Mr Nick Booth. *2008.15*

Pl 31

In Part 3 of this catalogue series a somewhat similar lead/tin alloy circular flange bearing the impression of a jetton was published (Mernick & Algar 2001, 249). The object was tentatively identified as a dagger pommel. Since then this similar example of a plug bearing a jetton impress has been found. Now, taking these two objects together, it is suggested that they may be seals for containers of some sort. Witch-bottles, used as antidotes to witchcraft, are known from about 1500. German stoneware bottles were favoured containers, and have been found plugged with lead (see Merrifield 1987, 163ff.). The diameters of the plug from Homington and the one already recorded from the River Avon, Salisbury (Mernick and Algar 2001, op. cit.) are appropriate to that for sealing a stoneware bottle.

The deliberate choice of the reverse of particular jettons may be significant as they may bear not only a cross but were also chosen for some possibly perceived protection to be invoked by their inscriptions: on Cat 273 AVE MARIA GRACIA (contracted from 'Ave Maria Gracia Plena': Hail Mary full of grace); and on this example a cross and also SIT NOMEN DOMINI (contracted from 'Sit Nomen Domini Benedictum': Blessed be the name of the Lord), both impressed as mirror images.

Other examples are known, including a find from Bishops Cannings (Wiltshire Heritage Museum, acc. no. 2002.3) that has an impression of a cross (cf. Mitchener 1988, 201, no. 566) encircled by an inscription, of which part reads AVE MARI. There is another without the apparent religious connection from Kingston Lisle, Oxfordshire (Portable Antiquities Scheme database WILT-71DA46) that bears the Austro-Burgundian arms used between 1482 and 1555.

BIBLIOGRAPHY

Berry, G. 1974: *Medieval English Jetons* (Spink, London)

Mernick, P. and Algar, D. 2001: 'Jettons or Casting Counters' in Peter Saunders (ed.), *Salisbury Museum Medieval Catalogue* (Salisbury), 213-260

Merrifield, R. 1987: *The Archaeology of Ritual and Magic*

Mitchiner, M. 1988: *Jetons, Medalets and Tokens, vol. 1: the Medieval Period and Nuremberg*

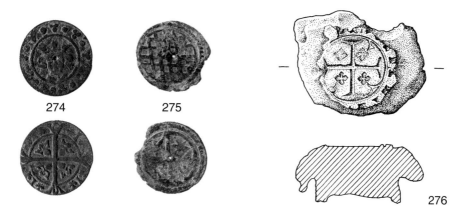

Plate 31. Jettons: English Cat 274-5; Cat 276 jetton impression on lead plug (1:1)

Lead/Tin Alloy Metalwork

by Geoff Egan
with David Algar

INTRODUCTION

Lead/tin alloy metalwork in the Museum was recorded in Part 3 of this Catalogue (Egan 2001). This section includes additional objects, which for ease of future reference are catalogued from number 196 to avoid confusion with the numbering for this class of object in Part 3. The majority were recovered from the River Avon, within the city of Salisbury.

CATALOGUE

DRESS ACCESSORIES

Buckles

These comprise numerous examples of small buckles which seem to have been for shoes (Grew and Neergaard 1988, 75-6). They are of circular, double oval and square or rectangular form and most conform to the types illustrated by Egan and Pritchard 1991, fig. 40, nos. 214 and 227, fig. 53, nos. 350 and 376 and fig. 63, nos. 452-3 and found in London in contexts of the first half of the fifteenth century.

196 Circular with iron pin. D. 15mm. Found in the River Avon, Bridge Street, Salisbury. *1993.1*
Fig 73

There are fifteen other examples from the same source, two from elsewhere in the River Avon (acc. no. *1987.107.15-16*) and one, lacking its pin, from the Drainage coll. (*SD625; 1999R.112.3*).

197 Circular with central bar, shallow V-shaped profile and iron pin. D. 30mm. Found in the River Avon, Salisbury. *1987.107.14*

198 Circular with central bar, beaded border. Iron pin. D. 23mm. Found in the River Avon, Bridge Street, Salisbury. *1993.1*
Fig 73

There are ten other examples from the same source.

199 Oval, double frame, beaded border. L. 24mm. The pin would probably have been of iron. Found in the River Avon, Bridge Street, Salisbury. *1993.1*
Fig 73

For a similar buckle on a low boot, from London see Egan and Pritchard 1991, 87, fig. 53.376.

200 Oval, double frame, similar to above, one loop missing. Surviving L. 16.5mm. Found by the Town Path. *1976.93*

201 Rectangular with central bar, frame bevelled towards the centre. L. 18mm. Found in the River Avon, Bridge Street, Salisbury. *1993.1*
Fig 73

The buckle is sharp from the mould, without a pin and apparently unused. There are three used examples from the same source. A similar buckle with an iron pin is illustrated by Egan and Pritchard 1991, 96, fig. 63.452.

Mounts etc

202 Disc. D. 15mm, with field of dots and four projecting knops around perimeter; flattened central rivet. Found in the River Avon, Salisbury. *1987.107.12*

Brian Spencer (pers. comm.) described this and Cat 205 as belt studs, with a suggested fifteenth-century date. This complete example, and another (acc. no. *1987.107.13*) lacking two of the knops, are further examples of a type of mount already published, Egan 2001, 94 and fig. 31, no. 38.

203 Disc. D. 25mm; with deep concentric mouldings and remains of rectangular loop or two rivets. From the River Avon, Salisbury. *1987.210.3* **Fig 73**

Compare Egan and Pritchard 1991, 179 and fig 114, nos. 927-8 for similar mounts in copper alloy.

204 Disc. D. 28mm; blackletter *ihc*, retrograde, within two concentric circles and an outer ring of pellets; central rivet L. 7mm. From the River Avon, Salisbury. *1987.100* **Fig 73**

A heavy mount, perhaps from an object other than dress. There is a stone mould from Clarendon Palace for casting similar but larger items (Spencer 1990, 39, no.78).

205 Cinquefoil with projecting sepals. D. 17mm. Reverse has raised lattice and stub of central rivet on a seam. Found in the River Avon, Salisbury. *1987.107.11* **Fig 73**

Brian Spencer (pers. comm.) described this as a belt stud, with a suggested fifteenth-century date.

206 Sexfoil, shaped like a Tudor rose, with two whorls of petals. D. 12mm; two rivets. From the River Avon, Salisbury. *1987.210.4* **Fig 73**

Brian Spencer (pers. comm.) suggested a sixteenth-century date.

207 Sexfoil stud. D. 12mm with cylindrical shank, which is hammered and splayed at the back. From the River Avon, Salisbury. *1987.209.13* **Fig 73**

208 Blackletter 'Y'; 27mm x 20mm; two integral rivets. From the River Avon, Bridge Street, Salisbury. *1993.1* **Fig 73**

For examples of letters in iron see Egan and Pritchard 1991, no. 1085.

209 Two interlocking rings; L. 26mm; ring diameter 12mm; rivet at each end. From the River Avon, Salisbury. *1987.210.2* **Fig 73**

210 Three linked rings, openwork fragment. L. 32mm. Each ring originally with four trefoil-shaped cusps forming a cruciform opening in the centre. No obvious means of attachment. Found in the River Avon, Salisbury. *1987.107.17*

Possibly part of a pilgrim or secular badge.

211 Eyelet; abraded; D. 13mm; ring comprising series of radiating struts/petals with six small holes; the central hole has been distorted perhaps by a buckle pin. From the River Avon, Bridge Street, Salisbury. *1993.1*

See Egan and Pritchard 1991, 227.

212 (?)Mount or button; circular, incomplete; D. 12mm; beaded border; irregular voids/gouged holes occupy a considerable part of the projected roundel; no obvious means of attachment. From the River Avon, Bridge Street, Salisbury. *1993.1*

Strap-ends

213 Fragment of strap-end buckle, decorated on one side. L. 30mm. 15th century. Found in the River Avon, Salisbury. *1987.107.10* **Fig 73**

214 Hollow-sleeve form, rectangular, complete with single rivet at top. L. 27mm. W. 18mm. Front is cast with decorative ridges ending in a recessed shield-shaped panel decorated with pellets forming a saltire with quatrefoil of pellets in each quarter. From the River Avon, Salisbury. *1987.98.1* **Fig 73**

215 Hollow-sleeve form, with single rivet-hole at top. Front has kidney-shaped openwork panel; vine-leaf finial with beaded collar. Possibly gilded. L. 32mm. From the River Avon, Salisbury. *1987.98.2* **Fig 73**

This is a more complete example than Cat 56 (see Egan 2001, 95 and fig. 32).

216 (?)Mount or strap-end; 24mm x 13mm; motif in two halves; rebated rectangle with square void, and raised longitudinal bar with five struts attached at right angles and having six engrailed webs between (with two small voids, probably from bubbles during casting); two integral rivets. From the River Avon, Bridge Street, Salisbury. *1993.1*   **Fig 73**
See Egan and Pritchard 1991, nos. 1199-1201.

Brooches

217 Circular, openwork; just under half surviving; original D. 22mm; triple knopped-roundel motifs (trefoils) survive at two cardinal points; beaded border along both edges of raised frame with series of knops; central roundel with raised border, and cross on knop (intended to be retained by a diametrical strut with raised edges); fringe, along part of perimeter, of excess metal from casting; stub of integral pin survives. From the River Avon, Bridge Street, Salisbury. *1993.1*
Fig 73

218 Circular, incomplete with integral pin; D. 29mm; octofoil with central knop, in eight-pointed star against cross-hatched field; border with series of knops on a raised band, surrounded by a beaded perimeter. Found in the River Avon, Salisbury. *1987.202.6*   **Fig 74**

219 Sexfoil, openwork; D. 22mm; central related cross-hatched roundel and knops (the majority with a field of pellets) at the junction of each pair of foils. Integral pin is missing, though the casting seam is visible. Found in box with pilgrim badge Cat 22 (acc. no. *1987.225.15*), from Mr. Brian North Lee. The provenance unknown, but probably from Salisbury. *2008.16*   **Fig 74**

220 Square, openwork; incomplete; 20mm x 19mm; open quatrefoil in centre; beaded, rebated border; series of pelleted roundels along frame, with pelleted roundels surviving at three corners; integral pin. From the River Avon, Bridge Street, Salisbury. *1993.1*   **Fig 74**
See Egan and Pritchard 1991, no. 1358.

Bells

221 Three small rumbler bells. D. 13-15mm. Possibly from dress or from a toy. From the River Avon, Bridge Street, Salisbury. *1993.1*
See Egan and Pritchard 1991, 336

Miscellaneous

222 (?)Mount or pendant roundel; D-shaped fragment, broken off at straight edge; D. 14mm; openwork quatrefoil in ring with circle of pellets between raised edges; corresponding ridges on back and front, adjacent to point of damage to perimeter, and possible broken off stub etc. at middle of these features suggests this was originally part of a larger item. From the River Avon, Bridge Street, Salisbury. *1993.1*   **Fig 74**
Perhaps a pendent variation on Spencer 1990, 112-3 figs. 284 and 286-94, assigned to the early fifteenth century.

223 (?)Mount. Incomplete; 16mm x 15mm, voided shield-shaped frame with bevelled inner and outer edges; the roughness of the former suggests there was originally a central motif; dating uncertain. From the River Avon, Bridge Street, Salisbury. *1993.1*

224 Broad leaf, now lacking means of attachment, 20mm x 15mm, with veining on both faces; the stem curves naturally, crossing a straight moulding seam on one face. From the River Avon, Bridge Street, Salisbury. *1993.1*   **Fig 74**
Compare Bruna 1996, 299 no. 568 for a three-dimensional lead/tin rose with two leaves in the Musée de Cluny (Paris) and see Egan 1998, 195 no. 545 for a three-dimensional ?carnation in lead/tin, assigned to the early fifteenth century. See Mitchiner 1986, no. 488 for an identical leaf.

Mould

225 One part of a multiple stone mould for casting circular (?)buckles, probably of lead/tin. Block of fine-grained mudstone *c.*87mm x 72mm x 23mm with recesses on the two flat faces for casting buckles of D. *c.*44mm (undamaged face) and D. 48mm (damaged face). Sudden contact with cold water when still hot from use could have resulted in the fairly-neat removal of over half of the worked surface, as now evident. The former face retains two small holes for location pins, and a third, larger one (probably added later), to hold the adjacent part of the mould. The latter face has similar provision (though three of four smaller holes are now at broken edges), and there is also a series of tiny, scratched grooves to allow gases to escape. On both faces a groove from the sprue and through the diameter of the products continues below, suggesting there was originally provision for casting further accessories on a part of the stone now broken away. This is the central stone of three, which would have fitted together when in use enabling two buckles of different sizes to be cast at the same time. All edges are smoothed from handling, suggesting the mould saw sustained use in its present, final form. From the River Avon, probably south of Fisherton Bridge, Salisbury. *1987.208*

Fig 74

Although it is suggested above (by GE) that the mould was for casting buckles in lead/tin, there is none in the Museum. However, buckles of copper alloy of appropriate size do occur (see Cat 7, page 92).

The fine-grained stone used for this mould was at a premium, and (like many stone moulds) this one had seen several phases of use, damage and re-cutting, perhaps originally being up to four times its present size. The mudstone is of uncertain age but apparently pre-Jurassic and thus from outside Wiltshire. It could have been obtained originally as a 'foreign' unit within assembled river gravel in Wiltshire. The help of Justin Delair in the identification of this stone is gratefully acknowledged.

For another part of a stone mould for casting buckles, found in Salisbury, see Spencer 1990, 9 and 136 fig. 324.

TOYS

226 Rider on horseback, bent off remainder of object. H. (surviving) 20mm. This much damaged figure is perhaps a mounted knight. The head and arms of the rider and the head of the horse are missing, as are most of the latter's legs, with the exception of the upper forelegs. The body of the horse, which advances to the right, appears to have a grid of straps over the rump. The harness is hung with a series of little bells or pendants. The rider, who faces to the front, wears a vertically-ribbed ?tunic with a studded band across the chest. The rider's right leg is obscured by what appears to be a circular, heavily studded buckler (an hour-glass perforation here is a casting defect). Most likely to be late 13th or 14th century. From the River Avon, Bridge Street, Salisbury. *1993.1*

Fig 74

A limited number of similar equestrian figures are known from London. See Forsyth with Egan 2005, 144-151.

BIBLIOGRAPHY

Bruna, D. 1996: *Enseignes de Pèlerinage et Enseignes Profanes* (Musée National du Moyen Âge - Thermes de Cluny, Paris)

Egan, G. and Pritchard, F. 1991: *Dress Accessories c. 1150-c. 1450*, Medieval Finds from Excavations in London **3**

Egan, G. 2001: 'Lead/tin alloy metalwork' in Peter Saunders (ed.), *Salisbury Museum Medieval Catalogue Part 3* (Salisbury)

Egan, G. 2005: *Material Culture in London in an Age of Transition: Selected Tudor and Stuart Period Finds c. 1450-c. 1700 from Excavations at Riverside Sites in Southwark, South London*, Museum of London Archaeology Monograph **19**

Forsyth, H. with Egan, G. 2005: *Toys, Trifles and Trinkets: Base-metal Miniatures from London 1200-1800*

Mitchiner, M. 1986: *Medieval Pilgrim and Secular Badges*

Spencer, B. 1990: 'Pilgrim Souvenirs and Secular Badges' in *Salisbury Museum Medieval Catalogue Part 2* (Salisbury)

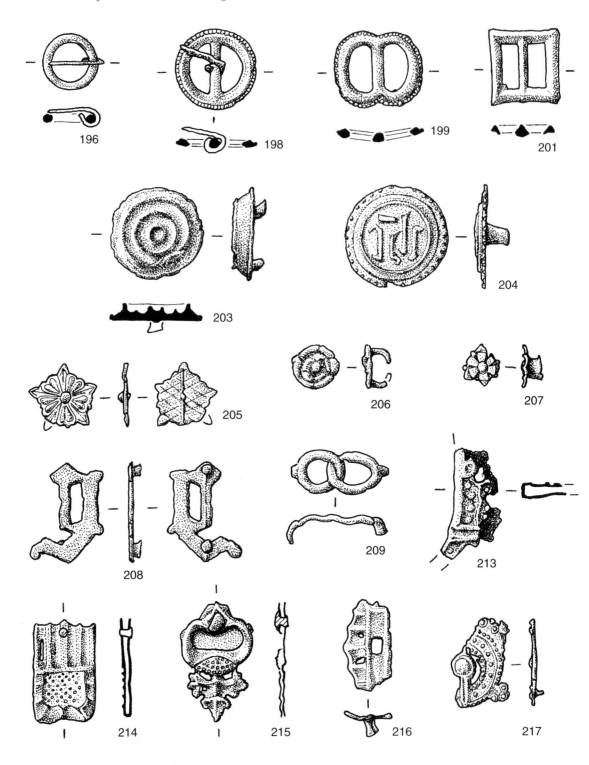

Fig 73. Lead/Tin Alloy: Cat 196, 198-199, 201, 203-209, 213-217 (1:1)

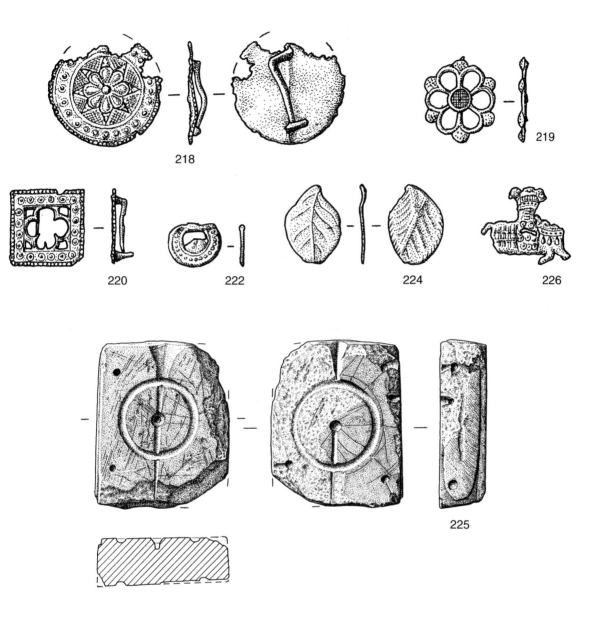

Fig 74. Lead/Tin Alloy: Cat 218-20, 222, 224, 226 (1:1); Cat 225, stone mould (1:2)

Pilgrim Souvenirs, Livery and other Secular Badges

by Brian Spencer
with David Algar

INTRODUCTION

Since the publication of Part 2 of this Catalogue (Spencer 1990), more badges and badge fragments have been added to the collection, including at least twenty two pilgrim and eight secular types not recorded earlier.

Unless otherwise stated all the badges listed here were recovered by metal detectorists from the River Avon, just downstream from Fisherton Bridge, Bridge Street, Salisbury in 1992 and possess the group acc. no. *1993.1*.

In addition, several items published in 1990 and previously in private possession have since been acquired for the Museum collection and have accession numbers *1991.1-9*. These items are mentioned where appropriate in the present catalogue in order that they may now be given a *Medieval Catalogue* number. Further gifts and purchases of items previously on loan were made in 1997. These are listed in the corrigenda on page 331 to bring the record up to date.

With the exception of Cat 229, all the items catalogued here are cast in tin or lead/tin alloy. Cat 300, 306 and 333, and possibly also 258 and 327, show evidence of having been cut with shears, perhaps prior to the recycling of the metal. For other indications of the working of lead and tin in the area adjacent to where these finds were recovered see Egan 2001, 92.

CATALOGUE

Editor's note:

In order to avoid possible confusion in future citation the catalogue here commences at Cat 229, which is sequentially the next catalogue number in the series for this class of object in Part 2 of the Catalogue (Spencer 1990).

Pilgrim Souvenirs

St Osmund of Salisbury

229 Pilgrim badge. A bracteate badge depicting the nimbed and mitred bust of St Osmond flanked by the letters O and S (for Sanctus Osmundus or Signum Osmundi), surrounded by a barbed quatrefoil border, stamped onto a diamond-shaped flan of brass. H. 32mm. Spencer 1990, 14, fig. 7. Found in 1987 in late 15th-century spoil removed from Butler's Wharf, Bermondsey, London. Given by Mr Brian North Lee. *1987.225.29*

St Thomas of Canterbury

Martyrdom of St Thomas

230 Pilgrim badge. The figure of St Thomas is kneeling to the right, with hands clasped in prayer, before an altar. There is the clasp for a vertical pin. Late 14th century. H. (surviving) 24mm. See Spencer 1998, nos. 55 et seq.

Fragment most probably from large elaborate badge depicting the martyrdom of St Thomas.

The scene, known from more complete late fourteenth-century badges, would have shown Becket, attended by Edward Grim, kneeling at an altar with four knights attacking him from behind.

231 Pilgrim badge. Badge in the form of a buckler or hand shield, with a characteristically prominent boss. The boss is ringed by a series of pellets which are repeated at the edge of the shield. No trace of a sword remains. D. 32mm. Second half of the 14th century.   **Fig 75**

This is perhaps part of a souvenir of the sword with which St Thomas Becket was slain. The sword was exhibited to pilgrims at the spot where Becket's martyrdom took place. These badges have been discovered over a wide area, an indication of their popularity. For other examples, found at Canterbury, see Spencer 1990, 19.

St Thomas head reliquary

Throughout the fourteenth and fifteenth centuries the most popular of all Canterbury badges were those commemorating a reliquary known as the Head of Thomas. This took the form of a richly jewelled, mitred bust and contained the portion of Becket's skull that had been hacked off by his assailants. Many forms of the badge exist. Some depict the bust under an elaborate architectural canopy or within a simple frame. There is also a large group where the bust is shown unenclosed, in silhouette, sometimes with the inscription CAPVT THOME or THOMAS. There are two headless examples of souvenirs of this type.

232 Pilgrim badge. Lower part of a reliquary bust. The depiction of the amice is quite plain with a band inscribed :T:O:M:A:S: in Lombardic capitals at the base. The clasp for the pin survives. There is a secondary piercing at the surviving side of the neck. W. *c*.38mm. Early 15th century.   **Fig 75**

233 Pilgrim badge. Lower part of a reliquary bust. The shoulders are covered by a richly adorned amice. The jewelled apparels appear rounded and collar-like. There is an ornate band at the base of the bust above which the front of the amice is embellished with trefoils of realistic leaves. The clasp for the pin survives. W. *c*.26mm. 15th century.   **Fig 75**

For a very close parallel see Mitchiner 1986, no. 447.

234 Pilgrim badge. Mitred bust of Becket flanked by two vertical swords, only one of which remains, set within two joining fragments of a circular frame consisting essentially of a series of close set collets. The vertical pin and clasp survive intact. D. *c*.47mm. Found in the River Avon, Salisbury. *1991.10*
                                        Fig 75

See Spencer 1998, no. 106a for a slightly smaller badge of the same design found by the River Thames near Queenhithe with coins of the early fifteenth century.

235 Pilgrim badge. Mitred head. Prominent side curls protrude from beneath a jewelled mitre. This is from a bust of Becket, perhaps part of a badge similar to Cat 234. H. 20mm. Complete vertical pin, L. 25mm.   **Fig 75**

236 Pilgrim badge. Fragment from the right-hand pier of an architectural canopy, most probably incorporating a pair of lancets beneath a pierced quatrefoil, originally topped with a trefoil pinnacle, of which only one leaf remains. H. 63mm.   **Fig 75**

This is probably from an elaborate badge commemorating the Becket head reliquary. For near complete examples of fourteenth-century date, see Spencer 1998, nos. 87 and 88a-b.

237 Pilgrim badge. Barbed quatrefoil frame with a beaded edge, now lacking the central device. H. 34mm. Late 14th or early 15th century.

Such frames often held an image of St Thomas Becket or a crucifixion scene. See Spencer 1998, no. 109, 110a and 189a, 190.

238 Pilgrim badge. Part of a circular beaded frame enclosing a ?polylobe. Central device lost. D. 27mm.

Compare Spencer 1998, no. 103.

Other badges relating to St Thomas

239 Pilgrim badge. Part of a quatrefoil suspension loop most probably from a Canterbury bell. W. 13mm. Perhaps late 14th century.

The Virgin Mary

240 Figurine. Central part of a draped figure with a conspicuous hexagonal brooch on the breast. H. (surviving) 28mm. Late 13th or early 14th century.
Fig 75

This appears to be a fragment from an example of the figure of the Virgin Mary enthroned as Queen of Heaven. For a complete version of this figure from Salisbury, but in a private collection, see Spencer 1990, Cat 35, fig. 40. The subsequent discovery of a few other examples of these devotional figures has led to the conclusion that they are examples of *sedes sapientiae* and that they are probably of northern French origin. See Wustenhoff 2000.

Our Lady of Salisbury

In these badges, Our Lady is crowned and sceptred and stands supporting a puppet-like figure of Jesus, also crowned, against her left hip. The main distinguishing characteristic of these badges is the linear treatment of the Virgin's garments, the folds of which have become crowded stripes of dot and circle ornament. The badges were all probably made in Salisbury in the fifteenth century.

241 Pilgrim badge. A rather more complete example than that recorded by Spencer 1990, Cat 61, fig. 81. With vertical pin and clasp. H. (surviving) 48mm.
Fig 75

242 Pilgrim badge. Another example as Cat 241, but only the clasp survives. H. (surviving) 39mm.

243 Pilgrim badge. The example illustrated by Spencer 1990, fig. 84 is now in the collection. This has a complete pin and clasp. Found in the River Avon, Salisbury. *1991.1*

Our Lady of Eton

244 Pilgrim badge. Standing, crowned figure of the Virgin, sceptre in right hand and crowned infant Christ in left, within beaded frame, encompassed by a mandorla, the rays of which are tipped with pellets. This badge is almost complete but is unfortunately weakly cast and/or abraded. The complete vertical pin and clasp survive. H. 34mm. W. 20mm.
Fig 76

The cult of the Blessed Virgin of the Assumption was assiduously fostered by Henry VI at Eton College, which he founded in 1440. The souvenirs of the resulting pilgrimage depict the figure of the Virgin (in some instances holding the infant Christ) being borne up to heaven in an almond-shaped mandorla, the rays of which are typically tipped with pellets. This Salisbury find probably dates from the early sixteenth century and derives from earlier, larger Eton badges (Spencer 1990, Cat 45, fig. 58; 1998, nos. 154a-c and 2000, fig. 16).

Unattributed Virgin and Child

245 Devotional badge or pilgrim sign. H. (surviving) 30mm. There is a raised lattice pattern on the back and a complete pin and clasp.   **Fig 76**

Another, but headless, example of this badge, from a private collection, is illustrated in Spencer 1990, fig. 54. The lattice pattern illustrates how the reverse mould was sometimes scored with a knife to ease the flow of metal to the edge of the mould during casting (compare Cat 278 and 294). For other examples of this see the reverse of the badge depicting a garb of arrows, also from Salisbury, published by Spencer 1990, Cat 102, fig. 135 and Spencer 1998, nos. 140-1.

246 Devotional badge or pilgrim sign. The example (then in private possession) illustrated by Spencer 1990, fig. 53 is now in the collection. Clasp only present. 15th century. Found in the River Avon, Salisbury. *1991.2*

The letter V

Letters often formed the substance or the framework of fourteenth and fifteenth century badges and brooches. For an example in this catalogue see Cat 278, where the initial R surrounds the figure of Richard Caister. The letters associated with Our Lady were most frequently the crowned M for Maria, Queen of Heaven and the V for *Virgo*, the Virgin.

247 Devotional badge or pilgrim sign. Crowned V decorated on the sides with a pellet on a cusp and at the base by a cluster of three pellets. 14th-15th century. H. 26mm. See Spencer 1998, nos. 169 and 169a.   **Fig 76**

The Annunciation
As a symbol of innocence the lily stood for the immaculate conception of Christ, the three flowers being taken as signs of virginity before, at and after birth. The Annunciation lily-pot presented a shape suitable for a range of attractive devotional badges.

248 Pilgrim badge. Fragment of a badge celebrating the Annunciation, which is symbolised by the lily, which when complete would have had three flowers in a shapely vase. H. (surviving) 24mm. Traces of what appears to be red pigment survive between the flower petals.   **Fig 76**
  Compare Spencer 1998, no. 149 and Spencer 1990, Cat 51-2, fig. 70-1 for two vases from which the lilies are missing. Several other examples of this badge have been found in fifteenth-century contexts at London and Canterbury. This type of badge is, however, more likely to have been a souvenir of Walsingham Priory, Norfolk, where the Annunciation had a special significance for pilgrims.

The Fleur-de-Lis
The lily was the flower of purity and its heraldic form, the fleur-de-lis, was another ubiquitous symbol of the Virgin Mary.

249 Pilgrim badge. Fleur-de-lis with trace of a beaded frame at the base. H. 22mm. 15th century. Found in the River Avon, Salisbury. *1987.202.2*
  See Spencer 1990, Cat 54-6, figs. 74-6.

The Winged Heart
A winged and wounded heart was another emblem of the Blessed Virgin. On devotional badges the heart was usually pierced by a pair of crossed arrows or flanked by a pair of wings. Sometimes the badge consisted of an angelic demi-figure holding a crowned heart. Examples of both types have now been added to the collection.

250 Pilgrim badge. Crowned heart pierced by an arrow, only the feathered end of which is present. The heart has a beaded border. A vertical pin and clasp survive. H. 39mm.   **Fig 76**
  See Spencer 1998, no. 176c.

251 Pilgrim badge. Another, though slightly less complete, example of this badge. H. 36mm.

252 Pilgrim badge. Fragment of a winged demi-angel holding a crown that would have surmounted a Sacred Heart. No trace of method of attachment remains. H. 27mm.   **Fig 76**
  Part of another similar badge is illustrated by Mitchiner 1986, no. 559. See also Spencer 1998, no. 176d for a complete and more elaborate piece.

The Crowned Sun and Moon

253 Devotional or livery badge. Crowned six-pointed star within a crescent. H. 29mm. If interpreted as a crowned sun and moon, this may also be a badge celebrating the Blessed Virgin. Both the sun and moon were attributes of the Virgin; the crown perhaps signifying her status as Queen of Heaven.
            Fig 76
  An almost identical example was found at York in 2001. For similar but uncrowned badges see below Cat 310, Spencer 1990, Cat 178, fig. 237 and Mitchiner 1986, nos. 672-3.

Crosses, Holy Roods and Holy Blood

The Rood of Grace, Boxley
There are three substantial fragments from rood

badges, Cat 254-256. It is likely that all three badges relate to the Rood of Grace at Boxley Abbey, Kent, a favourite stopping-off place for Canterbury pilgrims in the fourteenth and fifteenth centuries. When complete, these badges would have had an altar at the foot of the Cross inscribed with the word '*gras*' in reference to Boxley's miracle working Rood of Grace. The rood had a life-sized figure of Christ which was denounced as an automaton in 1538 when the image was taken down and destroyed. The changes of facial expression with which the figure had been credited were revealed as having been accomplished by 'certain engines and old wires' (Finucane 1977, 208-10).

254 Pilgrim badge. Central part of a badge depicting the crucified Christ, who is crowned and given the sort of forked beard that was fashionable *c.*1440. The cross is textured with diagonal cross-hatching. Only the stub of a substantial vertical pin remains. H. 53mm.

This badge stands apart through the superb quality both of the composition and of the detail represented through the excellence of the mould-cutting and of the casting.   **Fig 76**

255 Pilgrim badge. Part of a similar badge except that the wood of the Cross is textured with a pattern of wavy lines. The Cross is also represented as breaking into leaf through the use of trefoil shoots. The badge retains part of a vertical pin. W. 38mm. Probably 15th century.

The casting of this badge is above the usual standard.   **Fig 76**

256 Pilgrim badge. Part of a badge of similar proportions and sharing some of the characteristics of Cat 254 and 255, such as the trefoil shoots, but not so finely modelled. H. 48mm.   **Fig 76**

257 Pilgrim badge. Ornamental terminal from the horizontal limb of a rood. W. 19mm.   **Fig 76**

A complete rood badge with identical lateral terminals is illustrated in Mitchiner 1986, no. 156.

Unidentified roods

258 Pilgrim badge. Fragment depicting an arcaded altar, which, when complete, would have stood at the foot of a rood. Two devotees, with garments trailing behind them, kneel on either side of the altar. Only one figure survives on this example and only a trace of the rood remains. The texturing of its wood is to be compared with that of Cat 255. H. (surviving) 12mm.   **Fig 76**

Several related examples are known from sites in London. They may be fifteenth-century variants of Boxley badges, see Cat 254-256 above, but are of entirely different style.

259 Pilgrim badge. Fragment of horizontal limb of rood with ornamental terminal. L. 23mm.

260 Pilgrim sign or devotional badge of circular medallic form on which is depicted a cross with two devotees beneath. D. 21mm.

The badge well illustrates the banality of many products at the bottom end of the medieval souvenir trade. Compare Spencer 1990, Cat 64-5, figs. 86-7.   **Fig 76**

The Five Wounds of Christ.

Badges incorporating five roundels appear to have been very popular in Salisbury, there being no fewer than twelve examples in the collection. They come from numerous slightly different moulds. All the badges of this common type were fitted with vertical pins, the fittings on Cat 263-6 being the best preserved. All probably fifteenth century.

261-264 Devotional badges or amulets. Further examples of the badge recorded by Spencer 1990, Cat 75, fig. 100. H. *c.*20mm.

265 Devotional badge or amulet. Another example, as Spencer 1990, Cat 75, fig. 100.

Found in the River Avon, Salisbury. *1987.190.13*

266 Devotional badge or amulet. Another example of a slightly different version of the badge recorded by Spencer 1990, Cat 74, fig. 99. H. 21mm.

267-269 Devotional badges or amulets. Three examples of another slightly different version of the badge. H. 21mm. Cat 268 is illustrated. **Fig 76**

Other badges relating to Christ

270 Pilgrim badge. Christ's crib viewed from above. The head of the Christ Child is missing but has survived on other comparable badges (van Beuningen and Koldeweij 1993, 132, nos. 69-70; van Beuningen, Koldeweij and Kicken 2001, 356, no. 1493; see also MOL nos. 8657-8). W. 42mm. **Fig 77**

In some instances the subject is depicted in profile (Spencer 1998, 175, no. 195b). In every case the crib is criss-crossed by swaddling bands. The badge possibly commemorated a relic of the Nativity such as the crib at Canterbury Cathedral or the swaddling clothes possessed by Peterborough Abbey.

271 Pilgrim badge or amulet. Two fragments of a flaming star apparently with a central aperture. 14th-15th century.

As Spencer 1990, Cat 79-80, figs. 104-5.

Other saints and cults

St Edward the Confessor, Westminster

272 Pilgrim badge. Crowned bust within a circular frame. D. 24mm. There is evidence for a vertical pin.

See Spencer 1990, Cat 103-5, figs. 136-40.

273 Pilgrim badge. Another example, as Cat 272. D. 22mm. Late 14th century.

274 Pilgrim sign. Studded and buckled garter, lacking the central device. There are traces of a vertical pin with the clasp surviving at the bottom. D. 31mm. Late 14th century. **Fig 77**

Another slightly more complete example of the badge from a private collection is illustrated in Spencer 1990, fig. 143.

St Hubert

275 Devotional badge or amulet. Hunting horn fitted with mounts and strap; the main suspension loop is incomplete. The mouth-piece is to the right. This badge appears to have had a horizontal pin. L. 31mm. 15th century. **Fig 77**

For an almost identical example see Mitchiner 1986, no. 626. See Spencer 1990, 54.

St Leonard

Whether or not he ever existed, St Leonard became one of the most popular saints of the Middle Ages. He was regarded as the patron saint of pregnant women and by the twelfth century had established a reputation as a liberator of prisoners. The French shrine to St Leonard at Noblat, near Limoges, achieved considerable international fame being on one of the routes to Compostela. The centre of the cult in England is uncertain. The priory at Great Bricett, Suffolk, a daughter cell of the house at Noblat is a possibility. The priories of St Leonard at York and at Norwich are also contenders.

276 Pilgrim badge. Figure of St Leonard, lacking head, wearing episcopal vestments and standing on a scroll which reads S LENARD in blackletter. There is a crosier in the left hand; the right is raised in blessing with the saint's emblem, a set of manacles, hanging from the arm. This badge had a vertical pin of which only the clasp remains. H. (surviving) 37mm. **Fig 77**

Two closely related badges, found in the River Thames, were published in Mitchiner 1986, nos. 568-9. See Spencer 1986, 233.

St Michael

277 Pilgrim badge. The armoured legs of the saint stand on a dragon to the left. This badge is fitted with a horizontal pin and clasp. H. (surviving) 34mm. **Fig 77**

Some parallels are to be found among badges originating from Mont-Saint-Michel, such as Lamy-Lassalle 1971, pl. 26-7.

Richard Caister, Norwich

278 Pilgrim badge. Fragment of a badge, which would have depicted Caister set inside his initial letter R. Here, only his head survives within the frame. The frame is a more elaborate version, edged with beaded crockets, of Spencer 1990, Cat 97, fig. 130. See also Spencer 1998, no. 209d. There is a rectangular lattice pattern on the back (see Cat 245 for comment on this), where most of the vertical pin remains. H. 44mm. Late 15th century.   **Fig 77**

Unidentified badges/fragments

279 Pilgrim badge or amulet in the form of a hexagram, a six-pointed star formed by a pair of intersecting equilateral triangles. The inner hexagon forms the frame for a bust of which only part remains. Traces of a vertical pin and clasp survive. H. 39mm.   **Fig 77**
   Throughout the Middle Ages this so-called Solomon's seal was thought to possess supernatural powers. In this instance the 'seal' frames a bust of either a royal saint or an archbishop and thereby provides an example of the way that a secular good luck talisman might be used to reinforce the magic of an ecclesiastical symbol. A similar badge from Dordrecht has been published by van Beuningen, Koldeweij and Kicken 2001, 277 and fig. 755. For details of a secular hexagram brooch from Christchurch, Hampshire see Spencer 1983.

280 Devotional badge or amulet. Part of a circular brooch from the outer edge of which spring various ornaments, which, when complete, might have included miniature busts. H. 32mm.   **Fig 77**
   Such brooches were popular in the fourteenth century. See Spencer 1998, 125-8; van Beuningen and Koldeweij 1993, 289 and van Beuningen, Koldeweij and Kicken 2001, 459.

281 Pilgrim badge. Fragment depicting the lower part of a robed figure. On the right hangs a string of rosary beads. Rosaries displayed in this manner are sometimes a feature of John Schorn's badges.
   Fig 77

282 Pilgrim badge. Lower, rectangular part of a narrow-sided, bead-edged frame. This encloses part of a robed figure apparently with a staff to the left. The canopy within which the presumed saint stands is supported on a bracket, suggesting that a specific carved panel is being commemorated here. The clasp for a vertical pin survives. H. (surviving) 26mm.
   Fig 77

283 Pilgrim badge. Fragment of right-angled frame with external beading. H. 32mm. *1987.209.6.2*
   See Spencer 1998, fig. 108a, 149a where sturdy rectangular frames of the same design enclose a head of St Thomas and an Annunciation scene.

284 Pilgrim badge. Fragment from the left side of an architectural canopy. A crocketed arch is supported by a column topped by a floriated pinnacle. H. 40mm. Found in the River Avon, Salisbury. *1987.107.5*

285 Pilgrim badge. Fragment of ?frame, rosette at one end. L. 25mm. *1987.209.6.1*

286 ?Pendant. Trinket in the form of a tiny left shoe. This rather flat casting, L. 19mm, W. (max.) 7.5mm, has no obvious means of attachment. The broad, flattish-ended toe is characteristic of late 15th/early 16th-century style of footwear. Found in box with pilgrim badge Cat 22 (Spencer 1990, 20-21 and fig. 26), given by Mr Brian North Lee. Provenance unknown, but probably from Salisbury. *2008R.1489*   **Fig 77**
   Probably broken off a pendent pair of shoes, several of which are known in a variety of late-medieval styles from the late fourteenth/early fifteenth centuries in the Netherlands (van Beuningen and Koldeweij 1993, 316 figs. 993-7; van Beuningen, Koldeweij and Kicken 2001, 449 figs. 2004-5). The accompanying roundel

from which the shoes hang on a chain in fig. 993 is paralleled in a wide range of pendants found in England as well as on the Continent (e.g. Cat 287-292 and Spencer 1990, 112-3 and 131 figs. 284-294, nos. 208-9 for ones found in Salisbury). The present item appears to be stylistically the latest known. For the closest pilgrim-related items see Guildhall Museum 1908, 333 nos. 157-9 and pl. 80 nos. 6-8, where similar feet (presumably medieval) are described as attributes of the cult of St. Victor of Marseilles (none of these has been found recently). Geoff Egan kindly contributed the note on this item.

Brooches with suspensory loops

There is a series of very common brooches, which are composed essentially of a small, circular, beaded frame with a loop at its base. Sometimes this loop retains an S-link and very occasionally a further pendant survives below this. Although these brooch frames most frequently enclose a fleur-de-lis which could perhaps symbolise the Blessed Virgin, other devices such as a four-petalled flower, four circles and a trefoil are noted here. These badges all appear to have had a horizontal pin.

287 Brooch or pilgrim sign. Fleur-de-lis within circular beaded frame with trace of a bracket at the bottom. The frame has a small circular perforation. D. 16mm.

See Spencer 1990, figs. 286-88.

288-292 Brooches or pilgrim signs. Fleur-de-lis within circular beaded frame with trace of a bracket at the bottom. Late 14th or early 15th century. Found in the River Avon, Salisbury. *1991.3-7*

These examples, which were in private possession when illustrated by Spencer 1990, figs. 286-290, are now in the collection.

Other brooches with similar beaded frames, but with different central devices:

293 Brooch or pilgrim sign. Flower with four petals and corresponding stamens, surrounded by a circular beaded frame. The horizontal pin is visible

through the open-work. At the foot of the frame is a loop. It is clear from more complete examples that brooches of this type were intended to provide a suitable support for devotional medallions, good luck tokens and trinkets of many kinds, such as a purse or a pair of patens. Late 15th century. D. 14mm.

Fig 77

See Spencer 1980, 31, nos. 149-50; 1998, 158; van Beuningen and Koldeweij 1993, nos. 706, 909 and 993; Bruna 1996, 246-56.

294 Brooch or pilgrim sign. Beaded frame similar to Cat 293 with a complete circular loop at the bottom, but lacking the central device which may have been a lily or a simple cross. Remains of horizontal pin. The reverse bears traces of the raised lozenge pattern comparable with that seen on Cat 278. D. 16mm.

295 Brooch or pilgrim sign. Sprigged trefoil within circular, beaded frame with remains of bracket at the bottom. Vertical pin survives. D. 17mm.

Fig 77

See Spencer 1990, Cat 208-9, figs. 284-94 for similar brooches.

296 Brooch or pilgrim sign. Four circles within circular beaded frame and with a complete horizontal pin and clasp. Found in the River Avon, Salisbury. *1991.8*

This example, which was in private possession when illustrated in Spencer 1990, fig. 293, is now in the collection.

Ampullae

There are two complete ampullae, one of which was mentioned in Spencer 1990 but not illustrated. There are also fragments of five others, three of which appear to be of tin. For the classification of ampullae see Spencer 1971.

297 Ampulla: obv. scallop-shell, type I; rev. saltire in a circle. H. 52mm. Found by the River Wylye, North Street, Wilton. *1991.40*   **Fig 78**

298 Ampulla: obv. scallop-shell, type II; rev. crowned W. H. 57mm. See Spencer 1990, 60.

Found at Milston, Wiltshire. *1989.2*   **Fig 78**

299 Ampulla, mutilated, upper part crushed and contorted: obv. scallop-shell, type II; rev. crowned W. H. 47mm.   **Fig 78**

300 Ampulla cut in half vertically: the looped handle also cut away. obv. six leaf or petal motif; rev. probably a crowned W. H. 46mm. This is probably an example of metal being prepared for recycling for use in other castings.   **Fig 78**

The three fragments which follow are all examples of tin ampullae which have been crudely broken in half about the mid point. Tin-rich metal gave better results for hollow-cast products: see Spencer 1998, 10-11.

301 Lower part of a tin ampulla, broken away above the handles: obv. four leaf or petal motif; rev. shield paly. H. (surviving) 25mm. W. (at handles) 34mm.   **Fig 79**

302 Upper part of a tin ampulla, broken away below the handles and crushed. The top still crimped as originally sealed. H. (surviving) 25mm. W. at handles) 39mm.

303 Upper part of a substantial tin ampulla, broken away below the handles. The top still crimped as originally sealed. The handles are of unusual D-shape, having the straight side at the base, and can be paralleled on only one other of the 27 ampullae in the Salisbury collection. This perhaps indicates that the fragment is from another scallop-shell, type I ampulla as Spencer 1990, Cat 173. H. (surviving) 31mm. W. (at handles) 43mm. Found in the Millstream, near St Thomas's Square, Salisbury. *1987.101*   **Fig 79**

Livery and other Secular Badges

Badges with royal associations

304 Livery or funerary badge. Ostrich feather, the badge of Edward the Black Prince. H. (surviving) 63mm. *c.*1376.

For a slightly more complete specimen see Spencer 1990, Cat 151, fig. 200.

305 Livery badge. Broompod. This badge was described and illustrated in Spencer 1990, 98 and fig. 203 but not given a catalogue number as it was not then in the collection.
1990.61

306 Livery badge. Lion standing left. Foreleg and part of the body of a lion with the mane defined by a series of fine wavy lines. Horizontal pin now pressed flat. Badge apparently cut through from front to back so that only the lower part survives. H. 23mm. Found in the east bank of the Millstream during the construction of Salisbury Library. *1978.142*   **Fig 79**

Mitchiner 1986, no. 695 illustrates another fragment, perhaps from the same mould.

307 Livery badge. Part of lion rampant sinister with mane and tail held vertically, perhaps against side of a frame. The lion is in the attitude of a heraldic supporter. H. 29mm.   **Fig 79**

308 Livery badge. Grotesque lion's head facing, with protruding tongue, enclosed within a circular, beaded frame. There is a trace of a vertical pin. D. 27mm. Perhaps early 15th century.   **Fig 79**

Another version of the livery badge illustrated in Spencer 1990, Cat 168, fig. 224. See also Egan 2001, no. 46 for a possible mount bearing a closely related image.

309 Livery badge. A hart lodged beneath a tree, the hart's head is missing and the tree trunk is folded back. There survives a clasp and trace of a horizontal pin. W. 24mm. Late 14th or 15th century.

Another example of the base metal version of the badge associated with Richard II. Much grander, jewelled forms are depicted in the Wilton Diptych (*c.*1395; National Gallery, London), where they are worn by King Richard himself and by his attendant angels. See Spencer 1990, Cat 157, fig. 207.

310 Livery badge. Fragment of a star of six wavy points clasped by a crescent moon. W. (restored) 36mm. Late 14th or 15th century.

See Spencer 1990, Cat 179-80, fig. 238-9. See also Cat 253 above for another, perhaps related badge. This is possibly a Plantagenet badge of the early fifteenth century.

311 Livery badge or brooch. Star of twelve pearled rays, alternately reticulated. D. 28mm.

Fig 79

Possibly a Yorkist sunburst badge or perhaps purely decorative. See Spencer 1998, no. 291.

312 Livery badge. Hollow tin pendant, the obverse, in the form of a Tudor double rose of five petals upon five petals, the reverse depicting simple, irregular ten-armed cross. Damage at the top has destroyed the attachment ring. D. 27mm. Second half of 15th century. **Fig 79**

Similar to Spencer 1990, Cat 159, fig. 211. See also Mitchiner 1986, no. 963b, which is a closer parallel and the third published piece with a Salisbury provenance. Spencer 1998, no. 290b.

313 Livery badge. Fragment of a swan swimming to the right. Clasp for a horizontal pin. W. 33mm. *1987.209.4* **Fig 79**

For a comparable badge, with swan swimming to the left, see Spencer 1998, no. 281a. See also van Beuningen and Koldeweij 1993, 271.

Other livery and secular badges

314 Livery badge. A right hand to the left proffering a bunch of daisies (incomplete). There are traces of an inscription on the cuff. The badge had a horizontal pin. A neat round perforation in the palm may be a secondary attachment point. H. 29mm. A transverse cut across the lower edge has removed part of the hand and cuff. **Fig 79**

See Spencer 1998, no. 288d for a very similar badge with the inscription *Gratia dei*, which was there tentatively attributed to Humphrey, Duke of Gloucester.

315 Livery badge. Two joined flowers, from a badge similar to Cat 314. H. 20mm.

Talbot badges.

Many of the devices chosen as badges derived from punning allusions to surnames. On this basis, and because it was a symbol of loyalty, a breed of hunting dog, the talbot-hound, now extinct, was adopted as a badge by the Talbot earls of Shrewsbury. Most pewter badges show the talbot seated but occasionally the dog is portrayed *passant*.

316 Livery badge. Talbot squatting on its haunches to the left. The dog's head is missing but its studded collar remains. H. 26mm. Found in the River Avon, Salisbury in 1986. *1989.11*

See Spencer 1990, Cat 173-4, figs. 230-1.

317 Livery badge. Squatting talbot as Cat 316, but this example retains the horizontal pin and clasp. H. 22mm. 15th century. Found in the River Avon, Salisbury. *1989.12*

318 Livery badge. A large part of a smooth-haired animal, with a short tail, running to the right. This is perhaps a talbot. There is a damaged horizontal pin. L. 44mm. **Fig 79**

Strawberry plant

Post-medieval sources ascribe this badge to the Stafford family. However, no documentary record has yet been found of the use of strawberries as a badge by the Stafford dukes of Buckingham in the fifteenth century.

319 Livery badge. The central part of a strawberry plant. The clasp for a vertical pin survives. H. (surviving) 27mm. 15th century.

See Spencer 1990, Cat 175, fig. 232-3.

?Bakers' Company of London

320 ?Livery badge. Fragment of a badge depicting a double layer of heraldic cloud, from which descend the rays of a glory. Of the right hand of God, which issued from the cloud, only the wrist survives. 15th

-16th century. H. (surviving) 18mm. Uncertain provenance, possibly from London. *1999R.1029*
Fig 79

See Mitchiner 1986, no. 930 for a fragment which appears to be from an identical, though also incomplete example of this badge. Here, Mitchiner has suggested that this kind of badge may have been connected with the Bakers' Company of London and that the hand would have held a set of scales symbolising the Bakers' control over the weight and price of bread. This example was found by the River Thames at Billingsgate with coins of Henry VII.

321 Secular badge. Dolphin swimming to right, the eye clearly shown. Vertical pin now bent to the left. L. 21mm.   **Fig 80**

See Spencer 1998, nos. 282, 283 and 283a for badges depicting a dolphin embowed.

Badges associated with hunting

322 Badge. Hawk in perching stance, much as it might be portrayed on a hawking gauntlet. Badge retains its complete vertical pin. H. 40mm. See Spencer 1998, no. 297c.   **Fig 80**

323 Badge. This is a fragment from a bird much as Cat 322. H. 29mm.

324 Badge. Hawk's lure with trace of looped leash at the top. H. 29mm. Perhaps late 15th century. Found in the River Avon, Salisbury. *1991.12*

This badge was referred to in Spencer 1990, 109 and is a slightly more complete example than Cat 197, illustrated as fig. 263.

325 Badge. Man-faced owl. This badge appears to have had a horizontal pin. H. 33mm. 15th century.

For a similar though different casting see Spencer 1990, Cat 201, fig. 269.

Love-tokens and lucky charms

326 Badge. The body and leg stubs of a popinjay facing to the left. There are the remains of a horizontal pin and clasp. H. 36mm.   **Fig 80**

Although the bird lacks its head and long tail, it is clearly another example of the badge illustrated in Spencer 1998, no. 318b. A prototype of this badge, in the Salisbury collection, was mistakenly described as a falcon when recorded in Spencer 1990, Cat 198, fig. 264.

327 Badge. Part of two parallel feathers which are most probably from a popinjay tail. L. 23mm. The fragment is apparently cut across both ends.

328 Badge. Fragment of bird's body to the right with traces of studded collar, such as Spencer 1990, Cat 200, fig. 268. There are the remains of a horizontal pin and clasp. W. 34mm. Found in the River Avon, Salisbury. *1991.11*

329 Badge or amulet. Three fragments forming an open-work purse, side decorated with beaded lattice-work around a central, circular aperture. D. 42mm. This appears to be part of a purse similar to that illustrated in Spencer 1990, fig. 312. **Fig 80**

330 Badge or amulet. Almost complete, flat disc composed of eight open-work panels around a central aperture. This appears to be one half of an open-work container, perhaps a purse, similar to Cat 329 though in design, quite different. D. 43mm.
Fig 80

331 Badge or lover's token in the form of a uniface purse, the upper parts of which are missing. Similar to the purse badge illustrated in Spencer 1990, Cat 222, fig. 313. Retains clasp for a vertical pin. H. (surviving) 18mm. 15th century. **Fig 80**

Many examples of this type of badge have survived. For their significance as good-luck tokens see Spencer 1998, 313-7.

332 Badge or lover's token. Plant with globular buds or fruit on long stalks. This 15th-century badge still has the complete vertical pin and clasp engaged as in use. Found in the River Avon, Salisbury. *1991.9*

In private possession when illustrated in Spencer 1990, fig. 322 but now in the collection.

Triptych panel

333 Pewter panel, probably the left hand leaf of a triptych, decorated with six heraldic shields, three on each face. The arms are simple and probably of no significance. The principal elements are indicated by cross-hatching. The shields on the outer face are from the top (1) on a bend sinister, a wave, (2) saltire, (3) barry of seven. Those on the inner face are (4) fess between six crosses, three and three, (5) paly of seven, (6) fess; on this side the area behind the shields is cross-hatched. The top of the panel is cut at an angle and the sloping edge has a series of indentations to represent crockets. The panel has been trimmed along both long sides, which has removed all trace of the hinges. Probably 14th century. H. 93mm. W. (maximum) 17mm.   **Fig 80**

The base metal triptych was a popular form of medieval artefact which commonly depicted religious scenes. A specimen in Norwich Castle Museum bears devotional scenes: see Spencer 1980, no. 120. Further good examples of triptych panels are in the Canterbury Museum and the Museum of London (MOL 81.148/1).

Mitchiner 1986, illustrates two examples nos. 316-7, which are like the panel above in bearing only heraldic devices. The second fragment, no. 317, from Angel Passage, London, is cut from the top of a panel and bears the same two shields as the Salisbury example, it may well be from the same mould. Triptych panels of this sort reveal a similar decorative technique to that used on some pewter tokens of fourteenth-century date (Mitchiner and Skinner 1983, 49-54 and pls. 2-5) and on certain badge-like artefacts in the form of axe heads (Spencer 1998, nos. 299-302). At the present time much remains to be revealed about the manufacture and purpose of these objects.

At enterprising resorts, pilgrims could buy not only hat badges but other desirable knick-knacks as well. Cheaply-manufactured devotional panels were perhaps offered as a substitute for the ivory tablets and alabaster images obtained only by the well-to-do. Miniature leaded 'shrines' with hinged doors continued to be made in the fifteenth century.

BIBLIOGRAPHY

Bruna, D. 1996: *Enseignes de Pèlerinage et Enseignes Profanes* (Musée National du Moyen Âge - Thermes de Cluny, Paris)

Egan, G. 2001: 'Lead/Tin Alloy Metalwork' in Peter Saunders (ed.), *Salisbury Museum Medieval Catalogue Part 3* (Salisbury), 92-118

Finucane, R. C. 1977: *Miracles and Pilgrims*

Guildhall Museum 1908: *Catalogue of the Collection of London Antiquities in the Guildhall Museum*

Lamy-Lassalle, C. 1971: 'Les enseignes de pèlerinage du Mont St-Michel' in *Millénaire Monastique de Mont Saint-Michel*, vol. 3 (Paris), 271-86

Mitchiner, M. 1986: *Medieval Pilgrim and Secular Badges*

Mitchiner, M. and Skinner, A. 1983: 'English Tokens *c.*1200-1425', *Brit. Numis. J.* 53, 29-77

Spencer, B. 1971: 'A scallop-shell ampulla from Caistor and comparable pilgrim souvenirs', *Lincs. Hist. and Archaeol.* 1, no. 6 (Lincoln), 59-66

Spencer, B. 1978: 'King Henry of Windsor and the London pilgrim' in J. Bird, H. Chapman, and J. Clark (eds.) *Collectanea Londiniensia: Studies presented to Ralph Merrifield.* (London and Middlesex Archaeological Society Special Paper 2), 235-264

Spencer, B. 1980: *Medieval Pilgrim Badges from Norfolk* (Norwich)

Spencer, B. 1983: 'The Pewter Brooch' in K. S. Jarvis (ed.), 'Excavations in Christchurch 1969-80', *Dorset Natur. Hist. Archaeol. Soc. Monogr. Ser.* 5 (Dorchester), 81-3

Spencer, B. 1990: 'Pilgrim Souvenirs and Secular Badges' in *Salisbury Museum Medieval Catalogue Part 2* (Salisbury)

Spencer, B. 1998: *Pilgrim Souvenirs and Secular Badges,* Medieval Finds from Excavations in London: **7**

Spencer, B. 2000: 'Medieval pilgrim badges found at Canterbury' in D. Kicken, A. M. Koldeweij and J. R. de Molen (eds.) *Gevonden Voorwerpen: Lost and Found: Essays for H.J.E. van Beuningen (*Rotterdam), 316-327

van Beuningen, H. J. E. and Koldeweij, A. M. (eds.) 1993: *Helig und Profaan: 1000 Laatmiddeleeuwse Insignes uit de collectie H. J. E. van Beuningen* (Rotterdam Papers **8**, Cothen)

van Beuningen, H. J. E., Koldeweij, A. M. and Kicken, D. (eds.) 2001: *Helig und Profaan 2: 1200 Laatmiddeleeuwse Insignes uit openbare en particuliere collecties,* (Rotterdam Papers **12**, Cothen)

Wustenhoff, J. E. 2000: 'Middeleeuwse tinnen Sedes Sapientiae' in D. Kicken, A. M. Koldeweij and J. R. de Molen (eds.), *Gevonden Voorwerpen: Lost and Found: Essays for H. J. E. van Beuningen* (Rotterdam), 356-9

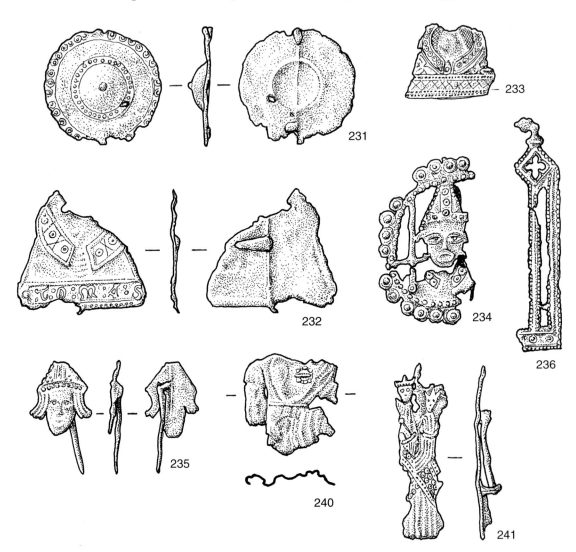

Fig 75. Pilgrim souvenirs: Cat 231-6, 240-1 (1:1)

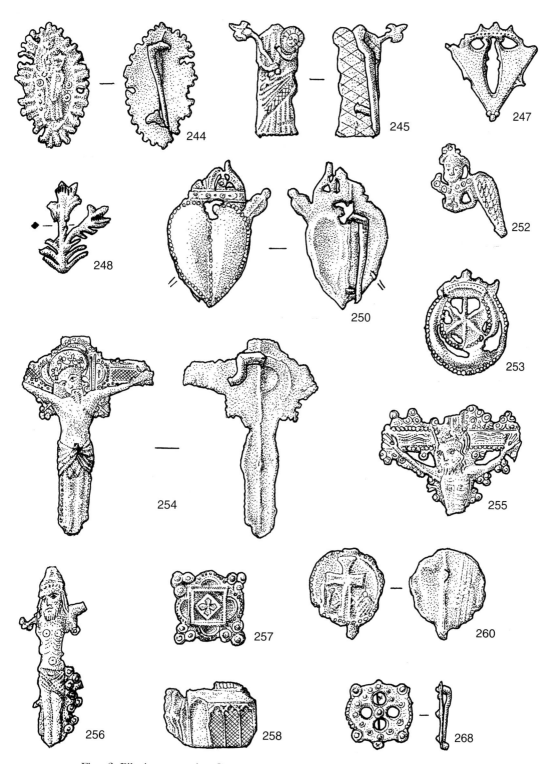

Fig 76. Pilgrim souvenirs: Cat 244-5, 247-8, 250, 252-8, 260, 268 (1:1)

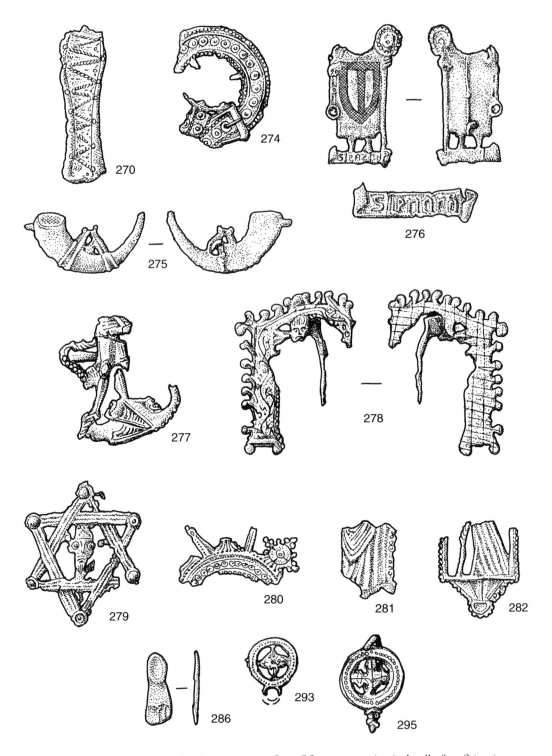

Fig 77. Pilgrim souvenirs: Cat 270, 274-82, 286, 293, 295 (1:1); detail of 276 (2:1)

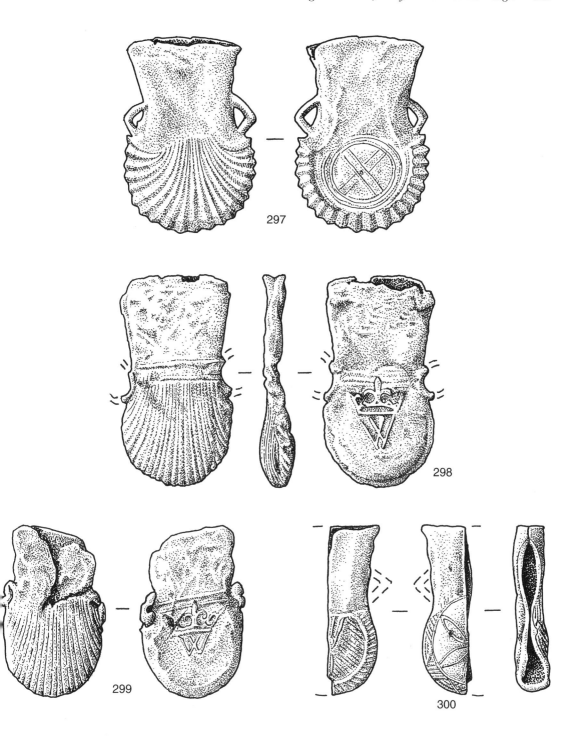

Fig 78. Pilgrim souvenirs: Cat 297-300 (1:1)

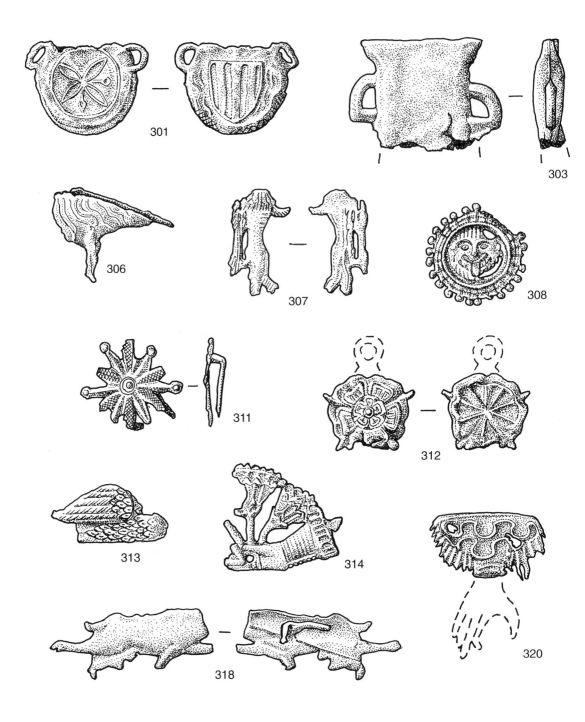

Fig 79. Pilgrim souvenirs: Cat 301, 303 (1:1). Secular badges: 306-8, 311-4, 318, 320 (1:1)

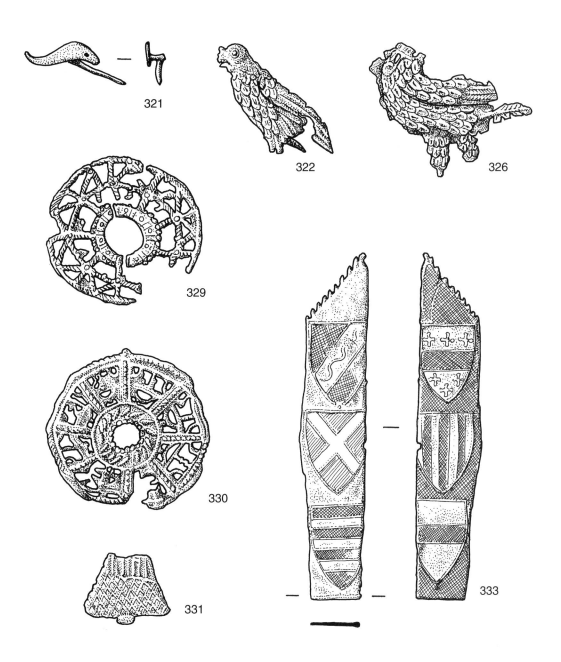

Fig 80. Secular badges: Cat 321-2, 326, 329-31, 333 (1:1)

Pottery and Tile

by Lorraine Mepham
with David Algar
and a note on Raeren stoneware by Duncan Brown

INTRODUCTION

Since publication of the Museum's extensive collection of this category of object in Part 3 of this Catalogue (Musty 2001) there have been three accessions worthy of note and they are catalogued here. The most important is a collection of about eighty fragments of pottery recovered in 1910 from garderobe pits within the castle at Old Sarum, noted in *Wilts. Arch. Mag.* 38, 540, and recently transferred from the Wiltshire Archaeological and Natural History Society to the Museum (acc. no. 2008.17).

Much of this pottery is complementary to the material from Old Sarum already in the Museum; there is a good cross-section here of twelfth- to thirteenth-century wares, almost all representing local ceramic traditions. In the latter part of the period these local wares are comparable to the products of the thirteenth-century kilns at Laverstock (Musty *et al.* 1969), although their date range probably extends into the early part of the fourteenth century. The revised and extended chronology for the Laverstock kiln wares, from the early thirteenth to early fourteenth century, is given in the earlier catalogue (Musty 2001, 138-9). The twelfth-century wares provide evidence of a pre-existing ceramic tradition of very similar sandy wares, almost certainly made in the Salisbury area; examples were found in pits at Laverstock which pre-dated the kilns. There is nothing here, however, either to fill the lacuna of the late Saxon period at Old Sarum, or to augment the as yet sparsely represented later medieval period (later fourteenth to fifteenth century).

As well as this group from Old Sarum (Cat 325-400), there are two single accessions: an unusual lid from Clarendon Palace (Cat 401), and a stamped applied medallion from a fineware jug, from the Millstream in the centre of Salisbury (Cat 402).

CATALOGUE

Editor's note:

In order to avoid possible confusion in future citation the catalogue here commences at Cat 325, which is sequentially the next catalogue number in the series for this class of object in Part 3 of the Catalogue (Musty 2001).

The definition and description of vessel forms throughout this catalogue follows nationally recommended nomenclature for post-Roman ceramic vessels (MPRG 1998), and as such is in accordance with the earlier published catalogue (Musty 2001). References to fabric types, however, have been updated in line with recently published type series for Salisbury and the surrounding area (e.g. Mepham 2000a). This defines, within the overall range of 'South East Wiltshire ware' (or 'Laverstock-type ware'), one coarseware and two fineware fabrics based on the range, size and frequency of macroscopic inclusions (*ibid.*, fabrics E422, E420 and E421 respectively). Given the provenance of the material discussed here, and its likely origin, the terms 'Laverstock-type coarseware' and 'Laverstock-type fineware' are used here.

Many of the Laverstock-type coarsewares in the Salisbury area from at least the eleventh through to the thirteenth century carry a surface treatment known as scratch-marking, formed by the use of a serrated or toothed implement, or possibly a stiff brush, wiped in random strokes across the surface of the vessel. The terms 'scratch-marked ware' and 'developed scratch-mark ware' are not used here as sherds from a single vessel may include both plain and scratch-marked examples. It is clear, however, from subdivision of the coarseware fabric into variants based on the size of the quartz inclusions that there is an overall (but not entirely straightforward) chronological development from coarse to fine inclusions, and from deep to more rudimentary scratch-marking, although, as an arbitrary division, this is difficult to sustain for the purposes of analysis.

Medieval wares other than of Laverstock type are rare in Salisbury; the competition from the local kilns was presumably too strong. Other regional wares do occur occasionally, however, and there are a few examples here, from north Wiltshire ('Crockerton-type' from the Warminster area: see Smith 1997, 21-4) and from west Berkshire/north-east Wiltshire ('Kennet Valley-type': Mepham 2000b).

Pottery from Old Sarum

Globular or Rounded Jars

Jars are the predominant vessel form found from the late Saxon through the medieval period. Those that are found in the Salisbury area have a globular (round-based) profile, later developing into rounded vessels with sagging bases. Many are scratch-marked on the exterior, and sometimes interior surfaces. Four rim profiles were illustrated for the jars from the Laverstock kilns (Musty *et al.* 1969, fig. 7), of which one (type I)

is a late eleventh/twelfth-century form surviving into the thirteenth century. The examples from the Old Sarum collection are a mixture of this early form with two slightly modified variants (types 2 and 3), although the overall profile is unknown.

One base sherd from a sagging base jar is in a non-local fabric, sandy with sparse, coarse, subangular flint inclusions; this can be identified as an example of a type found widely across east Wiltshire and west Berkshire and defined as 'Kennet Valley-type flint-tempered ware', with a wide potential date range spanning the medieval period from at least the eleventh century (Mepham 2000b, fabric E441). Uncommon in the Salisbury area, its occurrence here is of interest.

325-33 Large rim fragments from nine jars, all but one scratch-marked on the exterior. Two examples have finger impressed rims. All are in the typical Laverstock-type coarseware fabric. Late 11th - early 13th century. D. (rim) ranges from 270mm to 390mm. One example is labelled 'Old Sarum 1910'.

334 Sagging jar base, in Kennet Valley-type flint-tempered ware. Late 11th/12th century. D. 205mm.

Pipkins

Pipkins are essentially jar forms, with added handles and, sometimes, tripod feet. The pipkin forms seen here, with squat, rounded profiles, everted rims and sagging bases, are clearly related to the examples from the Laverstock kilns (Musty 2001, no. 33), but differ in the application of a tubular rather than a solid handle, springing from just below the rim. One example shows the mode of manufacture very clearly. The handle was applied to the outside of the vessel just below the rim; the vessel wall was then pushed out and perforated, the excess clay being pushed into the handle to strengthen the join internally. The external join was reinforced by clay drawn out from the rim. All the Old Sarum examples are in the Laverstock-type fineware fabric, and all are partially glazed.

335 Everted rim pipkin with attached tubular handle springing from just below the rim. Partial green mottled lead glaze on exterior surface. 13th/early 14th century. D. (rim) 180mm; handle L. 100mm, handle D. 42mm.   **Fig 81**

336 Everted rim pipkin, as Cat 335, but with slightly narrower and shorter handle. Speckled green exterior glaze, and inside rim. 13th/early 14th century. Handle L. 80mm; handle D. 28mm.

337 Lower part of a very squat, rounded pipkin, with trace of a handle stub. Traces of sparse, clear lead glaze on inner surface. 13th/early 14th century.

Dripping pan

A large dish, generally oval or sub-rectangular, designed to catch the juices from roasting meat. This example is similar to one from the Laverstock kilns (Musty 2001, no. 43), and is in the typical Laverstock-type fineware fabric, but adds a pinched lip and the full handle profile.

338 Three joining sherds from an oval dripping pan. Pinched lip at one end. A short strap handle rises from the middle of one long side. Rich green internal glaze. Traces of exterior sooting. 13th/early 14th century. L. *c.* 220mm; H. 40mm.

Jugs and Pitchers

Jugs are another very common medieval form; in the Salisbury area they occur in both coarseware and fineware fabrics and are usually at least partially glazed. The earliest examples fall within the tripod pitcher tradition, and occur only in coarseware fabrics (Musty 2001, nos. 74-80). A regional type of 'South East Wiltshire pitchers' was first defined by Vince (1981, 311),

who postulated a source in the Salisbury area, as a precursor to the later Laverstock industry, and certainly the fabrics of these vessels can be visually indistinguishable from the thirteenth-century coarsewares. Tripod pitchers were found in a pit at Old Sarum associated with a coin of William I (Stone & Charlton 1935, fig. 5, nos. 17-19, 25, 29), and they are considered to have been in use in the region from the late eleventh to late twelfth century. They are generally glazed, and often carry elaborate decoration using a combination of techniques, e.g. combed and applied motifs. While they do not appear to have been a particularly common vessel form, and could be considered as higher quality 'tablewares', there is no clear evidence that they were restricted to 'high status' sites – as well as examples from Old Sarum and Trowbridge Castle (Mepham 1993), there are also sherds from the village site of Gomeldon (Musty and Algar 1986, 156, fig. 19, nos. 85-7).

Later jugs occur in both coarse- and finewares. The coarseware examples (e.g. Musty 2001, nos. 86-9), which normally have relatively squat, rounded or pear-shaped bodies and strap handles, sometimes with a pinched lip, may be glazed or unglazed, and the glaze when present is often thin and patchy. Decoration is not universal, and is generally fairly simple, comprising red slip-painted linear motifs. The dating for these vessels is uncertain; they are certainly found in thirteenth-century contexts within Salisbury, but their genesis may be earlier.

The fineware jugs of the thirteenth century can be regarded as the epitome of the Laverstock industry (Musty *et al.* 1969, figs. 13-21). These are almost always glazed and are often decorated, sometimes elaborately, with a vibrant polychromatic range of applied and slipped motifs typical of the 'highly decorated' tradition of the thirteenth century. These highly decorated examples are particularly characteristic of the Laverstock kiln products, and are often taken to be typical of that production centre, although excavations in Salisbury have shown that they are in fact fairly rare, plainer variants occurring far more commonly (e.g. Mepham and Underwood n.d.). Perhaps highly decorated jugs were intended for wider circulation rather than local consumption, but the pattern may, alternatively, reflect the relative status of the dwellings excavated within the city. Certainly this small group from Old Sarum includes some elaborately decorated examples.

Tripod pitchers

339 Sherd with vertical bands of horizontal combing with superimposed finger-pressed bands, perhaps forming an angled lattice. Clear lead glaze overall, appearing olive green. Late 11th/12th century.
Fig 81

340 Three sherds, not joining but almost certainly from the same vessel. The combed surface has applied bands forming an irregular wavy lattice, the bands marked with a four-pronged implement. Traces of clear lead glaze. Late 11th/12th century.   **Fig 81**

341 Body sherd with horizontal bands of square-toothed rouletting. Clear lead glaze overall, appearing olive green. Late 11th/12th century.

Coarseware jugs

342 Jug neck, everted, with simple pinched lip and plain strap handle. Scratch-marked. Late 12th/13th century. D. (rim) 125mm.

343 Shoulder and base of neck from jug. Three horizontal bands of thin red slip paint. Unglazed. Interior wiping marks. Late 12th/13th century.

344 Body sherd with applied strips of clay in straight and wavy vertical lines. Traces of painted vertical red slip bands. External clear lead glaze. A second sherd with similar applied decoration could be from the same vessel. Late 12th/13th century.

345 Sagging base sherd with three large discrete thumb impressions forming 'feet', probably from a similar jug form.

346 A strap handle with two rows of elongated finger/thumb impressions that could be from a coarseware jug; alternatively, this could be from a handled jar (see Musty 2001, no. 8). Late 12th century.

Fineware Jugs (globular)

347 Four fragments from the mid section of a globular jug. Neck decorated with a series of vertical applied strips decorated with horizontal incisions and terminating at the lower end with large oval pads bearing vertical incisions. Rich dark olive green glaze overall with brown and green flecking. Late 13th century.   **Fig 81**
   The applied decoration may be deliberately imitative of the strut jugs (see below, Cat 369).

348 Rim/neck fragment possibly from a globular or substantial baluster jug. The heavy rod handle (*c*.30mm x 22mm) has a series of deep slashes down the spine. Pale green glaze with darker streaks. Late 13th century.

349 Body sherd from globular jug with pale olive green glaze and series of vertical red slip stripes. For very similar decoration see Musty *et al.* 1969, no. 109. Late 13th century.

350 Body sherd from globular jug with applied horizontal, finger-impressed strip. Clear lead glaze with dark flecks. Probably comparable to Musty 2001, no. 114. Mid to late 13th century.

351 Body sherd from globular jug with combed panels (chevrons or lozenges?) interspersed with lines of impressed dots. Horizontal bands of dots on the neck. Green glaze overall.   **Fig 81**
   The decorative scheme is reminiscent of the Rouen-style decoration found, for example, on London-type ware jugs of the early thirteenth century (e.g. Pearce et al. 1985, fig. 28, nos. 63-5).

352 Collared rim and bridge spout from a globular jug with a cylindrical neck. The collar is decorated with a series of applied red slip pads, impressed with ring-and-dot motifs. Further applied red slip decoration can be glimpsed on the body. The potter's fingerprints in red clay can be seen inside the rim which he has supported while impressing the pads. Clear exterior lead glaze with green flecks. For the form see Musty 2001, no. 102. D. (rim) 128mm. Mid to late 13th century.

353 Rim and shoulder section from jug, probably globular, with strap handle. One band of horizontal combing visible on neck. See Musty 2001, no. 94. Early to mid 13th century.

354-57 Four bases from globular jugs. All carry pulled down 'feet' formed from discrete groups of multiple thumbing, and bear very sparse speckled green glaze. One base has a horizontal band of fine horizontal combing on the body. D. (bases) *c.* 125mm, 160mm, 165mm, 170mm. Mid to late 13th century.

(Baluster) jugs

358 Two non-joining sherds from the upper part of a baluster jug with plain rod handle. There is a piped vertical rib on one of the sherds. Very speckly green glaze. 13th century.

359 Two joining sherds from the mid section of a baluster jug with poorly attached rod handle stub without the usual thumb pressed thickening at the base. The handle has two horizontal notches, perhaps from a fingernail. The body has at least five horizontal bands of combing. Thinly applied yellowish glaze flecked with green. As Musty 2001, no. 134. Early 13th century.

360 Baluster jug rim with rod handle. Bands of horizontal combing just under the rim, and lower down the neck; probably as Cat 359. Clear lead glaze with green flecks. Early 13th century.

361 Rim and shoulder section of baluster jug with rod handle. The handle is stabbed with six large, deep piercings down the spine. No decoration visible on body. Rich green glaze overall.

362 Baluster jug with rod handle, plain, green glaze.

363-68 Six baluster jug bases, ranging in diameter from *c.* 95mm to 150mm. All are glazed, most sparsely, with a speckled green glaze. One base shows external vertical knife-trimming. One base has deep, continuous thumbing drawing down the vessel wall; two others have lighter continuous thumbing just above the basal angle.

Strut jug

An unusual form of decorated jug, these vessels have four or five thin struts arranged at regular intervals and bridging the rim and shoulder. They were found at Laverstock in kilns 2, 3 and 5 (Musty *et al.* 1969, fig. 21, nos. 166-8). Elsewhere, a possible parallel can be found within the Surrey whiteware industry (Pearce and Vince 1988, fig. 51, no. 8), although the 'struts' in this example are more like subsidiary strap handles. Cat. 347 (see above) may be an imitation strut jug; another example was noted at Laverstock (Musty *et al.* 1969, fig. 21, no. 169).

369 Fragment of jug rim with upper part of arching strut pulled out to two points where it joins the rim. Rich pale green glaze inside and out.

Jugs of various forms

370-73 Four jug rims, two examples collared with vertical combing around collar, and one example with horizontal combing. Fourth example has series of impressed pads below rim, and a strap handle stump; handle is thumb-pressed at edges with two deep stabbed piercings in spine at anchor point.

All these decorative techniques are paralleled at Laverstock, the rim combing seemingly confined to the early/mid thirteenth century kiln products.

374 Fragment of rod handle from a highly decorated jug, circular red slip pads down sides, stamped with ring-and-dot motifs; oval red slip pads down spine, scored to represent leaves. Clear lead glaze overall. Late 13th century.

375-8 Six other rod handles, one with impressed ring-and-dot motifs down the spine, another with diagonal slashes down both sides. Most handles have a heavy single thumb impression at the basal junction.

381 Strap handle with thumb-pressed strip running down the spine. Small glaze spots. Fine sandy fabric, possibly Crockerton-type (north Wiltshire).

382-83 Two strap handles, one with thumb-pressed edges and deep slash marks (some go right through handle).

384-91 Eight body sherds (or groups of sherds), both plain and decorated (combed, slipped and applied motifs).

All these decorative techniques find parallels at Laverstock, and no entirely new decorative schemes are present amongst this material.

Uncertain vessel (?jug)

392 Fragment from the shoulder of a vessel of uncertain form, perhaps a jug, with the stub of a small handle, of which the orientation is uncertain. Series of vertical applied clay strips on body, clear lead glaze overall. D. *c*.100mm.   **Fig 81**

Costrels

The costrel is a container for storing and transporting liquid, generally furnished with means of suspension in the form of small lugs at the rim. They can be of various forms; examples found in the Laverstock kilns are all of cylindrical or barrel-shaped form, although one possible standing costrel was included in the earlier catalogue (Musty 2001, no. 224).

Fragments of five cylindrical costrels are included here, all in the typical Laverstock-type fineware fabric. Final shaping of the costrel bodies was by trimming and wiping lengthways, but these vessels are on the whole not well finished, and their manufacture shows a lack of attention to detail. One of the costrel necks is formed from a cylinder simply luted on to the body (an obvious point of weakness), with no attempt to disguise the join on the exterior. Interestingly, neither of the costrel necks have attached suspension lugs.

393-94 Ends of two costrels of rather crude, unglazed manufacture, D. *c*.73mm and 75mm.

395 Costrel end with traces of green glaze, D. *c*.79mm.

396-97 Necks from two other costrels.

Bottles

These vessels are variously described in the literature as 'bottles' or 'drinking jugs'. They have also sometimes been termed 'measures', as there is a suggestion that they were made in standard sizes to hold specific measures (Pearce *et al.* 1985, 41; Pearce and Vince 1988, 75). Their form and relatively rare occurrence suggests manufacture for a specific function, whatever that may have been, but the fact that they are often fairly crudely formed has been remarked upon.

Several examples have already been catalogued (Musty 2001, nos. 225-33), including some from Laverstock. A date range into the fourteenth century is supported by a stratified group from Clarendon Palace (Borenius and Charlton 1936, 77).

398 Base, probably from a biconical bottle. Unglazed. D. (base) 65mm.

Cistern

This form, designed for the storage of liquids which could then be drawn off by means of a basal spout, is generally considered to be a late medieval form (e.g. Pearce and Vince 1988, 84). Cisterns are not found amongst the Laverstock kiln assemblage and, although this example is in the standard Laverstock-type fineware fabric, it is likely to be of fourteenth-century date or possibly even later. The method of forming the bunghole spout is clearly shown: the body wall was pushed out at this point, and the resulting internal hollow filled in with added clay, then a hole was pierced right through from the exterior, and the spout finally shaped around this.

399 Bunghole spout from a cistern. Traces of yellow flecked green external glaze. Possibly subjected to burning. D. (spout) 46 mm with central perforated hole D. 15mm.

?Roof furniture

Alongside pottery vessels, the Laverstock kilns did produce ceramic roof furniture (although not flat tiles), and this small fragment, in the standard fineware fabric, may be part of one such item, perhaps a finial or louver, although not directly paralleled at Laverstock.

400 Fragment from the edge of a possible finial or louver, with series of thumb-pressed pads below. D. (rim) c.128mm. Areas of green speckled glaze inside and out, with trails of glaze running down towards the pads. **Fig 81**

Pottery from other sources

401 A small sherd with an attached knob handle, probably from a lid. The oval handle has been drawn into two points or 'horns'. Laverstock-type fineware; overall green glaze. From Clarendon Palace, recovered in 1952 from the site of the 1939 finds hut. *2004.44* **Fig 81**

Although there are no parallels from the Laverstock kilns, a similar example is known from the Surrey whiteware industry (Pearce and Vince 1988, fig. 101, no. 393).

Floor tile fragments found at the same time

are included elsewhere in this catalogue (see pages 272-3).

402 Sherd from jug body; applied pad with rather crude stamped bearded face, the pad at the junction of applied strips now detached from the body. The glaze was originally green but is now a slightly metallic green/grey from the conditions in the river bed. Found in the Millstream, behind Tesco, Salisbury. *2005.2.* **Fig 81**

This is an intriguing piece which finds no direct parallel in the Salisbury area. The fabric is fine, but does not exactly match the Laverstock-type fineware fabric; it may instead be a north Wiltshire product, perhaps from the Warminster area (Crockerton-type), although there are no known parallels there either. Stamped bearded faces on applied pads are known from the latest Laverstock kilns, now dated to the early fourteenth century, and are thought to be ultimately inspired by imported French jugs (Musty 2001, 162-3, nos. 201-5), but these are quite distinct stylistically from this example.

403 Three sherds: a rim, a handle and a body fragment. Found near the bottom of a pit containing brazier's waste to the east of 29 Guilder Lane, Salisbury (see page 69). *2009.5*

Duncan Brown has kindly examined these sherds and provides this comment: 'The three fragments of pottery are all Raeren stoneware, a type commonly imported into England in the late fifteenth and early sixteenth centuries. The typical Raeren stoneware form is a globular beer mug with a cylindrical neck, 'D'-shaped handle and a frilled base (e.g. Brown 2002, 68, fig. 30, nos. 303-12). These sherds comprise a rim, a handle and a body fragment and although none of them fit together, the colour and character of the brown salt-glaze and the nature of the grey stoneware fabric suggest they are likely to have come from the same vessel.

'Raeren stoneware was imported into England in large quantities from around 1450 to 1550. The industry itself grew to prominence in the middle of the fifteenth century (Gaimster 1997, 224), and finds of Raeren beer mugs on the wreck of the Mary Rose show that they were still in use in 1545 (Brown and Thomson 2005, 471-2). Large consignments of *cruses* or beer mugs are recorded in the port and brokage books for Southampton, indicating the likely source of the Guilder Lane finds. The Southampton brokage book for 1478 records one basket of

cris' leaving the town for Salisbury, while in the books for 1527 and 1528 four separate consignments of *cruses*, the largest numbering 200 pots, are mentioned (Brown 2002, 133, table 24). This confirms Raeren stoneware as a tradeable commodity at that time, and perhaps shows that it was by no means an exotic ceramic type.'

BIBLIOGRAPHY

Borenius, T. and Charlton, J. 1936: 'Clarendon Palace: an interim report', *Antiq. J.* **16**, 55-84

Brown, D. H. 2002: *Pottery in Medieval Southampton c. 1066-1510*, Southampton Archaeology Monographs **8**, CBA Research Report **133**

Brown, D. H. and Thomson, R. G. 2005: 'Pottery vessels' in J. Gardiner with M. Allen (eds.), *Before the Mast: Life and Death Aboard the Mary Rose* (Mary Rose Trust), 462-477

Gaimster, D. 1997: *German Stoneware 1200-1900* (British Museum Press)

Mepham, L. N. 1993: 'Pottery' in A.H. Graham and S.M. Davies, *Excavations in Trowbridge, Wiltshire 1977 and 1986-1988* (Wessex Archaeol. Rep. **2**), 101-14

Mepham, L. 2000a: 'Pottery' in M. Rawlings, 'Excavations at Ivy Street and Brown Street, Salisbury, 1994', *Wilts. Arch. Mag.* **93**, 29-37

Mepham, L. 2000b: 'Enborne Street and Wheatlands Lane: medieval pottery' in M.J. Allen *et al.* (Technical Reports supporting Birbeck, V., *Archaeological Investigations on the A34 Newbury Bypass, Berkshire/Hampshire, 1991-7*), Wessex Archaeology, 52-66

Mepham, L. N. and Underwood, C. n.d.: 'The pottery' in J.W. Hawkes, 'Excavations in Salisbury 1984-1990' (unpub. rep. for Wessex Archaeology)

MPRG 1998: *A Guide to the Classification of Medieval Ceramic Forms*, Medieval Pottery Research Group Occasional Paper **1**

Musty, J., with Algar, D., Gerrard, C. and Hadley, J. 2001: 'Pottery, tile and brick' in Peter Saunders (ed.), *Salisbury and South Wiltshire Museum Medieval Catalogue Part 3* (Salisbury), 132-212

Musty, J. and Algar, D. 1986: 'Pottery' in J. Musty and D. Algar, 'Excavations at the deserted medieval village of Gomeldon, near Salisbury', *Wilts. Arch. Mag.* **80**, 154-66

Musty, J., Algar, D. J. and Ewence, P. F. 1969: 'The medieval pottery kilns at Laverstock, near Salisbury, Wiltshire', *Archaeologia* **102**, 83-150

Pearce, J. E. and Vince, A. G. 1988: *A dated type series of London medieval pottery. Part 4: Surrey Whitewares* (London Middlesex Archaeol. Soc. Spec. Pap. **10**)

Pearce, J. E., Vince, A. G. and Jenner, M. A. 1985: *A dated type series of London medieval pottery, Part 2: London-type ware* (London Middlesex Archaeol. Soc. Spec. Pap. **6**)

Smith, R. W. 1997: *Excavations at Emwell Street, Warminster: the Early Economy and Environment of a Wiltshire Market Town* (Wessex Archaeology)

Stone, J. F. S. and Charlton, J. 1935: 'Trial excavations in the east suburb of Old Sarum', *Antiq. J.* **15**, 174-92

Vince, A. G. 1981: 'The medieval pottery industry in southern England: 10th to 13th centuries' in H. Howard and E. Morris (eds.), *Production and Distribution: a Ceramic Viewpoint* (Brit. Archaeol. Rep. **S120**), 309-22

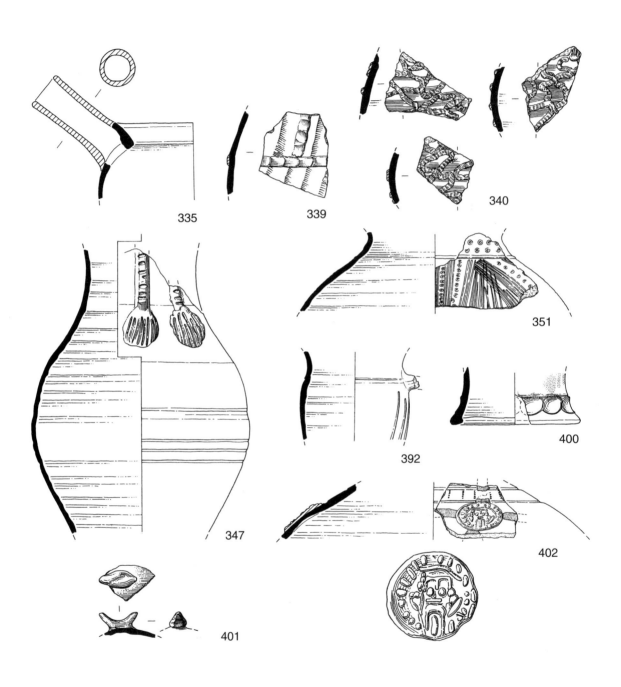

Fig 81. Pottery: Cat 335, 339-40, 347, 351, 392, 400-02 (1:4, stamp 1:2)

Rings

by John Cherry

INTRODUCTION

Since the publication of Part 1 of this Catalogue (Cherry 1991) five rings have been acquired through the Treasure Act. These and one hitherto unpublished ring are recorded here, together with an impression from a signet ring found locally but the whereabouts of which is unknown.

CATALOGUE

Editor's note:
In order to avoid possible confusion in future citation the catalogue here commences at Cat 28, which is sequentially the next catalogue number in the series for this class of object in Part 1 of the Catalogue (Cherry 1991).

28 Copper alloy signet ring with an octagonal bezel with a Lombardic letter T with crown above. 15th century. D. 22mm. From Winterbourne Stoke. *1986.88*   **Fig 82**

Such signet rings with a letter with a crown above were common in the fifteenth century. A similar example with the letter R is catalogued in Cherry 1991, 42, no.19.

29 Silver finger ring, a plain band 2.5mm. in width inscribed with the letters AGLA separated by crosses. Now somewhat distorted to an irregular oval 21x15mm. Wt. 1.15g. 13th or early 14th century. Found at Fifield Bavant. Treasure M&ME T146. *Treasure Annual Report 1998-99* (DCMS), 58 no.118 and fig. 118. *2001.60*   **Fig 82**

Agla is a word formed of the Latin equivalents of the initial letters of the Hebrew phrase Ata Gibor le'olam Adonai, which means 'Thou art mighty for ever, O Lord'. Although it is widely used in the later Middle Ages and the first written reference to it is in the late fourteenth or early fifteenth century, the occurrence of the word on thirteenth or early fourteenth century rings such as this shows that it has a much earlier history. Crosses often separate the letters, and helped to give the inscription an additional protective power against fever. See Evans 1922, 125.

30 Silver finger ring, a plain flat band terminating in two clasped hands at the bezel. Engraved with transverse ridges probably representing the cuffs of sleeves from which the hands emerge. D. 22mm. Wt. 2.65g. Early 16th century. Found at Winterslow. Treasure 2006 T64. *Treasure Annual Report 2005/6 (DCMS)*, 120, no. 436. *2007.41*   **Fig 82**

31 Silver stirrup-shaped finger ring, inscribed outer surface +AIIORVINCX (probably for Amor Vincit). Small knop of metal at the top instead of a stone. L. 31mm. W. 16mm. Wt. 2.83g. 14th century. Found at Codford. Treasure 2006 T236. *Treasure Annual Report 2005/6 (DCMS)*, 117 and 353, no. 420. *2007.42*   **Fig 82**

32 Silver iconographic ring with crudely engraved figures on the two facets of the bezel, the shoulders engraved with stylised leaves. Most of the hoop is missing. L. 21mm (surviving), W. 7.5mm (maximum), Th. 4mm (maximum), estimated diameter *c*. 21mm (17mm internal). Wt. 3.73g. Found at Durnford. Treasure 2005 T175. *Treasure Annual Report 2005/6 (DCMS)*, 119 and 354, no. 426. *2006.46*   **Fig 82**

The two figures are probably saints. For a similar ring see Cherry 1991, no.13.

33 Base silver signet ring, incomplete, broken
at the back of the hoop. Circular bezel, D. 12.3mm
x 13.2mm, inscribed with a grooved R, surrounded
on four sides by a branch, within a circumferential
groove. The shoulders are raised with three facets, all
of which are C-shaped in section. D. 27.6 mm. Wt.
10.15g. 15th century. Found at Laverstock. Treasure
2007 T282. *2008.49*   **Fig 82**

34(i) Impression from signet ring
Impression in red wax of a crowned W within
circular frame D. 13mm. From a late 15th or 16th
century ring, which was found before 1907 in the
bed of the River Nadder at Fisherton Mill (Bowle's
Mill), Salisbury. Present location of ring unknown.
Seal impression no. 347. From the A. R. Malden
collection.   **Fig 82**

For impressions from seals see pages 320-5.

BIBLIOGRAPHY

Cherry, J. 1991: 'Rings' in Peter and Eleanor
Saunders (eds.), *Salisbury Museum Medieval
Catalogue Part 1* (Salisbury), 40-46

Evans, J. 1922: *Magical Jewels of the Middle Ages
and the Renaissance* (Oxford)

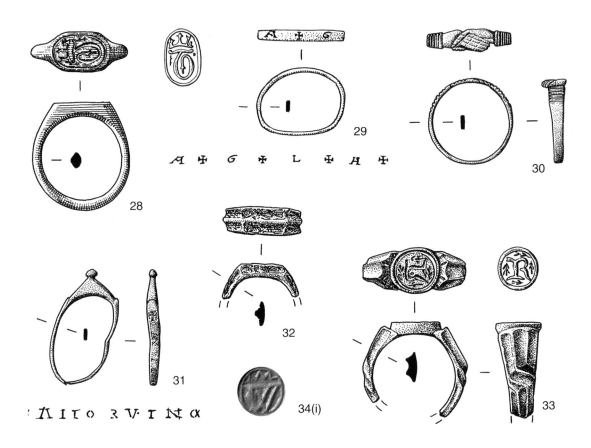

Fig 82. Rings: Cat 28-34 rings (1:1); Cat 34(i) impression from signet ring (1:1)

Seal Matrices and Impressions

by John Cherry

INTRODUCTION

The collection of medieval seal matrices in the Museum was recorded in Part 1 of this Catalogue (Cherry 1991a). This section includes three new matrices acquired by the Museum since then, and a matrix or die from the Old Sarum excavations that was not included in the earlier list.

Here the opportunity is also taken to publish a small number of items from the Museum's considerable collection of impressions and casts of seals: those which represent the discovery of medieval matrices in Wiltshire and those which record impressions of matrices now held elsewhere but which have a close Wiltshire connection. Excluded are impressions of the seals of the Mayors and City, the Cathedral seals and royal seals. For the civic seals of Salisbury see VCH 1962, 178-9, and for the cathedral seals see RCHM(E) 1999, 71 and pl. 53. For an impression taken from a locally-found finger ring see page 318 (Cat 34(i)).

CATALOGUE

Editor's note:

In order to avoid possible confusion in future citation the catalogue here commences at Cat 29, which is sequentially the next catalogue number in the series for this class of object in Part 1 of the Catalogue (Cherry 1991a) and the impressions are distinguished from original medieval objects by the suffix '(i)' in their respective catalogue numbers.

Seal matrices

29 Thomas de Harnham. Lead alloy, pointed oval, ridge and broken loop at the back. Stylised flower of eight petals. Legend (Lombardic) + S᾽ TOMAS DE HARNAM, with reversed N. 13th century. 31mm x 21mm. *1993.31* **Pl 32**

Thomas de Harnam is a surname probably derived from Harnham near Wilton. It has been suggested that this seal belonged to Thomas Harnham, who was the parson at Odstock, a village south of Salisbury, in the second half of the fourteenth century, but the seal is probably too early for that Thomas.

30 Crede Michi. Copper alloy, circular, pentagonal conical handle with pierced loop. A boar's head to the left. Legend (Lombardic) ★CREDE MICHI. 14th century. D. 15mm. H. 16mm. Found at Newton Toney, Wiltshire. *2001.47.1* **Pl 32**

This legend appears with a number of different images. The most frequent is a bird but others are a man, a lion's head, a squirrel, a dragon, or, as here, a boar's head. The seal was probably originally designed for the sealing of letters and the legend was intended to give a similar impression as a formal letter-ending today. For a list of seals with the inscription CREDE MICHI see Harvey and McGuinness 1996, 114.

31 Spes Mea in Deo Est. Copper alloy seal matrix, pointed oval, loop at back. A fish, vertical with head at the top, stylised water to the right. Legend (Lombardic) + SPES : MEA. IN DEO : EST. 13th century. 27mm x 15mm. Found at Amesbury, Wiltshire. *1989.51* **Pl 32**

This is a 'banal' or impersonal religious seal. The fish was a Christian symbol, and the inscription indicates that my hope is in God.

32 Unidentified. Lead seal matrix or die, rounded oval. Classical draped male bust to the right, offset within a broad border 5mm in width, which may have once carried a legend. 13th century. 47mm x 35mm, 4mm thick. Found in a garderobe pit in the Bishop's Palace at Old Sarum in close proximity to a fine gold ring set with an emerald. Cherry 1991b, 41, no. 2. See *O.S. Diary 1912*, p.60; *Proc. Soc. Antiq.* 25, 1912-13, 101 and 103. *OS.C3*   **Pl 32**

This matrix was thought to be a piece of exceptional interest by Sir Arthur Evans when it was shown at the meeting of the Society of Antiquaries of London at which Lt. Col. Hawley reported on the excavations at Old Sarum in 1912. He thought that the head looked at first sight like a classical intaglio, but must be contemporary with the thirteenth-century episcopal ring. Hans Wentzel (Wentzel 1953) discussed the use of classical profiles on French seals and showed that they were used from 1201. The interest of this example is that it is of lead and presumably dates from the early thirteenth century. It is not strictly speaking a seal since it does not have an inscription. Its presence together with a ring with a broken stone may indicate the presence of a craftsman's workshop, possibly a goldsmith's, in Old Sarum.

32(i) An impression of Cat 32 in red wax (seal impression no. 476), probably from the collection of W. P. Spalding of Cambridge.   **Pl 32**

For another unidentified personal seal matrix, circular, octagonal conical handle with pierced trefoil knop in lead//tin alloy from Salisbury see Egan 2001, 98 and fig. 33, no. 76. This seal bears a roughly scratched device rather like a spider's web.

It is also worth noting here the publication of a fourteenth-century copper alloy seal matrix showing a hare, found in Salisbury, in the catalogue of the Schøyen collection (Linenthal and Noel 2004, no. 185).

Official Seal

33 Great Seal of Edward IV affixed to the Tailors' Guild Charter. The Tailors' Guild Charter of 1461 bears an example of the first Great Seal of Edward IV (1461-83).This, of green wax, is broken in two, and is not complete. D. 115mm. It is attached by silk laces in the form of a diamond above the seal, and twisted laces beneath. The charter was presented to the Museum by the daughter of the last Clerk to the Tailors' Guild. *1917-8.28; 1996R.2167*   **Pl 33**

The charter and seal are illustrated in Haskins 1912, pl. facing p. 1. The chapter on the Tailors' Guild is ibid. 98-219, with a translation of the charter on pp.105-8.

Impressions

The collecting of impressions taken both from seal matrices and by copying existing seals was popular in the early and mid nineteenth century. David Williams has traced the development of such a collection in the National Museum of Wales (Williams 1993, 2-3). The collection at Salisbury Museum is a good example of such a collection in a non-national Museum. The Museum was founded in 1860 and possessed such a collection from the beginning. By the time of its 1864 catalogue, it was described in the Medieval Department by James E. Nightingale and E. T. Stevens. It comprised a series of casts of the Great Seals of England (the main seals of the Kings of England from Edward the Confessor to the present Queen [Victoria]), a series of impressions from matrices found locally and the fine collection of seals presented to the Museum by William Osmond, junior (1790-1875). The section on seals was most probably written by James Nightingale (c.1817-1892), although the list of the seals donated by William Osmond appears to be by Osmond himself (*Sal. Mus. Cat.* 1864, 84-89).

The collection now consists of 678 examples, which includes a small number from post-medieval matrices. The impressions consist of casts in plaster, wax, sulphur, or gutta-percha. Gutta-percha was discovered in the 1840s. It was produced by evaporating the milky fluid of the gutta-percha tree and coagulating the latex. An inelastic firm insulator resulted, which was used for the insulation of cables. Items of gutta-percha were brought to Europe from the Malay Peninsula and exhibited at the Royal Society of Arts in London in 1843. It was subsequently discovered to be useful for jewellery and seal impressions. Copies of seal impressions, both plaster and gutta-percha, were often coloured or sometimes gilded.

William Osmond was the stonemason to the Cathedral from 1818. His workshop was at 13 St John's Street, where the stone-carved heading still announces 'Osmond Statuary and Mason'. He was responsible for much repair work at the cathedral, to the Chapter House (1855-63), Choir (1870-7), Nave (1877-8) and also to the Spire. Some monuments in the cathedral are by him. The most important is the tomb of Bishop Burgess (1835), a copy of a fifteenth-century altar tomb. His career shows the importance of the creation of funeral monuments in the revival of the Gothic style. Augustus Welby Pugin, the great pioneer of the Gothic revival, was his friend and described his many wall monuments as 'Osmond's blisters'. Beyond Salisbury, he was responsible for the capitals at the church of St Mary and St Nicholas, Wilton, built by Thomas Henry Wyatt and D. Brandon in 1841-5 (Osmond 2000).

James E. Nightingale, who described the seals in the 1864 catalogue, was a notable local historian, author and collector with a very wide knowledge of medieval art. He catalogued the church plate of the counties of Dorset and Wiltshire, and served as the Honorary Curator of Medieval Antiquities in the Salisbury Museum until 1892 (*Wilts. Arch. Mag.* 26 (1891-2), 290-1).

Arthur Russell Malden (1850-1913), who succeeded James Nightingale as Hon. Curator in 1892, also formed a collection of seals. His interest probably derived from his work as a solicitor in Salisbury where he was a partner of J. K. MacDonald from 1879. He served as Chapter Clerk from 1888, Diocesan Registrar from 1902, and Cathedral Librarian from 1909. Canon Wordsworth said that he possessed 'much diplomatic skill', and knowledge of ancient deeds (*Wilts. Arch. Mag.* 38 (1913-4), 500-501).

Philip Nelson was a Liverpool collector in the first half of the twentieth century (Rushton 2001, 41-8). He corresponded with Frank Stevens, then the Curator of the Salisbury Museum, in the 1930s, and gave the impressions of the Giffard seals and that of Reginald le May (Cat 38(i)-40(i)), which were then in his collection.

Official seals

34(i) Wiltshire Seal for the Cloth Subsidy. Impression in red wax, D. 30mm. Crown over ornate shield with arms of England, sun and rose to sides. Legend (Lombardic) S'SUBC'PANNOR'IN COM'WILTEC'. Probably from the collection of A. R. Malden of Salisbury. Seal impression no. 381.

Pl 34

From a late fifteenth-century copper alloy matrix, now in the British Museum, found either at Westbury, or near Warminster, before 1787 (*Archaeologia* 8 (1787), 450 and 427, pl. 30, fig. 7), Tonnochy 1952, no. 33, and Egan 1995, 53, no. 104 and fig. 24. The matrix of this seal was first published in the *Gentleman's Magazine* for 1787 pl. 2 fig. 6 and then given to the British Museum by Sir Augustus Wollaston Franks in 1851. It is also published in *Proc. Soc. Ants.* 1 (1860), 228.

Aulnagers were officials who marked the measure and quality of cloth. The system began in the late twelfth century. Seals exist both for the office of the aulnager and for the subsidy. This example belongs to the group of seals for the subsidy on cloth. The earliest cloth subsidy seal has been attributed to the reign of Edward I (Linenthal and Noel 2004, no. 25), which is a seal with the King's head (possibly Edward I). The inscription indicates that it is the seal for the subsidy, but does not indicate that it was used for a particular area. Later seals for the subsidy, indicating the area, exist for Kent,

Lincoln and Southampton. This Salisbury seal probably belongs to a reorganisation of the subsidy as a result of an Act passed in the reign of Richard III touching the order of dyeing wool and cloths. The presence of the rose and sun indicates a date in the reign of either Edward IV or Richard III.

35(i) College of St Edmund, Salisbury. Impressions in red wax, pointed oval, 60mm x 38mm. Below an ornate canopy, on a stone corbel, a mitred ecclesiastic, wearing pontificals, is seated, full-faced, blessing with his right hand and holding an archiepiscopal cross in his left. Outside the canopy, on his right side, is a round-based shield bearing: three annulets irradiated. To his left, a similar shaped shield bearing: a chevron between three towers. Below, an ecclesiastic kneels in prayer. Legend (blackletter) S'COE COLLEGU SA EDMUNDI NOVE SAU. Seal impressions nos. 388, 397 and 410.   **Pl 34**

From an early fifteenth-century matrix in the Ashmolean Museum, Oxford. This matrix, in the Rawlinson collection (R97), has a long history. First published by Rawlinson 1720, 247, it was soon after in his collection. There is a sulphur cast in the British Library (Birch no. 3961).

The College of St Edmund in Salisbury was founded in 1268 by Walter de la Wyle, bishop of Salisbury, in honour of Edmund Rich, Archbishop of Canterbury and Treasurer of Salisbury, who died 1240 and was canonised in 1248. The figure is Saint Edmund (Archbishop of Canterbury from 1233 to 1240). His arms are on the shield on the left. The arms on the shield to the right are those of Walter de la Wyle, bishop of Salisbury (1263-1271). St Edmund's church was the church of St Edmund's College founded by Bishop Walter de la Wyle in 1269 for a provost and thirteen priests (RCHM(E) 1980, 35-9). In the fifteenth century a large aisled chancel was built, the north aisle containing a Chapel of St John and the south aisle a Lady Chapel. The fifteenth-century aisled chancel still exists as the present nave; the will of William Mercer (d. 1407) probably refers to it when he mentions the newly built church of St Edmund.

The building of these new chapels suggests that the College was reformed at the beginning of the fifteenth century, from which period the seal might date. It is likely that this is the date of the engraving of the seal matrix.

36(i) Hospital of St Giles, Wilton
Impressions in sulphur, gutta-percha (nos. 302 and 622) and red wax (nos. 287-90), pointed oval, 84mm x 50mm. St Giles, full length, with nimbus, holding a staff and book, under a Gothic architectural canopy. Legend (crude blackletter) S'DOMUS ELIMOSINARE SCI EGEDI IUXTA WILTON. Seal impression no. 591.   **Pl 32**

The fifteenth-century bronze matrix is now in the Schøyen collection (Linenthal and Noel 2004, no. 79). There is a sulphur cast in the British Museum (Birch no. 4339, DC G33). There are casts at Wilton House and Wiltshire Heritage Museum. See also Hoare 1825, 130.

The hospital of St Giles was founded about 1135. A mutilated seal attached to an agreement of about 1275 shows the first seal, which has a cloaked figure with a staff in the right hand (*Wilts. Arch. Mag.* 19 (1881), 342 no. 10). This matrix continued to be used into modern times according to VCH 1956, 364. In the early part of the twentieth century, the hospital was amalgamated with other Salisbury charities.

Personal Seals

37(i) Milo of Gloucester. Impression in gutta-percha, gold coloured, circular, D. 55mm. Mounted knight riding to right, wearing pointed helmet, and mail tunic with shield in left hand and lance with three streamers in right hand. Legend (Lombardic) +SIGILLUM : MILONIS : DE GLOECESTRIA. The lance cuts the legend between the I and A. From the G. B. Mellor collection, no. 13. Seal impression no. 163.

Pl 34

From a silver matrix dating from *c.*1130 found in a field near Andover in 1795. See *Archaeologia*, 14 (1803), 276 and pl. 47 no. 4; *Gentleman's Magazine*, 65 (1795), 737f.; Ellis 2000, 125.

On January 29, 1795 John Selwyn wrote to

the *Gentleman's Magazine* from Ludgershall and sent an engraving, which he had taken from an impression of this seal that had been turned up by the plough about six months before in a field near Andover in Hampshire. The silver seal weighed 3 ounces 3 dwts; it was quite plain on the reverse, and had a neck or loop at the top. The subsequent history of Milo's matrix is complex. It was in a number of collections in the nineteenth century. The copy of the Birch catalogue, now kept in the Department of Prehistory and Europe in the British Museum, records against no. 6064, in a marginal written note, that the matrix was sold abroad in 1903. Its present whereabouts is unknown.

The British Library has two impressions, one in sulphur (xlviii.923) and a much better one in red wax (xxxv.56). There is an impression of Milo's seal at the Society of Antiquaries in London. There were also electrotypes of the seal since Mr Charles Spence exhibited one to the Antiquaries in 1853 (*Proc. Soc. Ants.* 3 (1853-6), 286).

The matrix of Milo is comparable in importance with that of Robert Fitzwalter, found at Stamford, Lincolnshire, and now in the British Museum (Tonnochy 1952, no.332).

Milo of Gloucester was Constable of England and Governor of Gloucester Castle. He succeeded his father in 1126, and died in 1143. He was a faithful supporter and protector of the Empress Maud. He was made a governor of Gloucester by Earl Robert, natural son of Henry I, during his father's reign; and created Earl of Hereford by the Empress Maud in 1141. Sir Robert Atkyns in his *History of Gloucestershire* comments: 'I am confirmed in my opinion of the person to whom this seal belonged from the spot where it was found being in a direct line between the city of Winchester and Ludgershall to which latter place the Empress Maud escaped, on her way to Devizes after having been for some time besieged by the army under the command of Stephen's queen and son in the castle of Winchester; and as Milo, who was doubtless one of the party selected to oppose the pursuit of the enemy, in order to favour his sister's escape, af-

terwards joined her at Gloucester, having passed through the enemy's parties in the disguise of a beggar, it is most probable that he threw away this badge of distinction in the field in which it was lately found, the most easily to effect his purpose.' The matrix does not refer to him as Earl of Hereford and is therefore likely to have been produced before 1141, and most probably soon after 1126. If the seal was superseded by another matrix in 1141, this, rather than some dramatic incident, may have occasioned its disposal. A recent account of the life of Milo of Gloucester is in the *Oxford Dictionary of National Biography*, 22 (2004), 481-3.

38(i) Margaret Giffard. Impression in red wax, circular, D. 21mm. Lozenge shield of arms, three lions walking, within elaborate quatrefoil. Legend (Lombardic) + Sʼ MARGARETI·GYFFARD. Seal impression no. 475. **Pl 34**

From a silver matrix of *c.*1298 found at Codford before 1856. It was exhibited, by H. J. F. Swayne of Netherhampton House, at Warminster on 5th August, 1856. It was later in the collection of Philip Nelson from whom the impression was received. See Nelson 1936, no.59, pl.4, no.4. Nelson exhibited the matrix in the Victoria and Albert Museum *English Medieval Art* exhibition of 1930, no. 299, and it was in the Birmingham exhibition of 1936, 56, no. 394 (in the name of Mrs Lily Court, Philip Nelson's third wife). The present location of the matrix is uncertain. There is an impression in the British Library (XLVII.1439) in green wax.

The seal matrix of Lady Margaret Giffard, who died in 1338. The arms of Gyffard are gules three walking lions silver. She was the wife of John Giffard of Brymesfeld. See *Wilts. Record Soc.* 29 (1974), 26 (foot of fine no. 65, recorded in 1330). There were family involvements in Codford, so the finding of the seal there is appropriate. See *Wilts. Arch. Mag.* 3 (1857), 267.

Philip Nelson, 1936, commented: 'Probably the seal of Margaret Gyffard, second wife of John, Lord Gyffard of Brim[p]sfield, who died 1299. She was previously married to Sir John Neville of Essex by whom she had a son Hugh.

By 1302 she received from her uncle Godfrey, Bishop of Worcester, a legacy of a cup 'the value of 100s. and a clasp or ring the value of 70s.' In 1316 (Duchy of Lancaster Charters L5, no. 68), there is a grant by Dame Margaret de Neville to her son Hugh de Neville of houses in London. To this is attached an oval seal in red wax on which Margaret is standing, a hound at her feet, upon whose robe are three walking lions and to the left and right of whom are shields bearing respectively there walking lions for Giffard and a lion rampant for Neville Around S' Margarete de Nevyle. It appears that on the death of her second husband, she reverted to the name of the first.'

39(i) Thomas Giffard. Impression in red wax, circular, D. 30mm. Shield of arms. Three walking lions and a label of three points hanging by a strap from a two-branched tree. Legend (blackletter) SIGIL-LUM THOME GYFFARD. Seal impression no. 197.
Pl 34

From a late fourteenth-century silver matrix found near Devizes 1854. *Wilts. Arch. Mag* 2 (1855), 291; *Archaeol. J.* 13 (1856), 183; V. & A. Exhibition 1930, 167; Birmingham Exhibition 1936, 58, no. 413. Nelson 1936, no. 83.

This is a fine armorial matrix of Thomas Gyffard. It may be dated to *c.*1380. It was in the collections of John Ellen of Devizes, John Evans, and Philip Nelson, who sent Frank Stevens the impression on 17th April, 1931. The matrix was shown at the Birmingham exhibition of 1936 (in the name of Mrs Lily Court, Philip Nelson's third wife). Its present location is unknown.

40(i) Reginald le May. Impression in red wax, D. 18mm. Shield of arms incorporating the letter R. Legend (Lombardic) S REGINALDI LE MAY. Seal impression no. 473.
Pl 34

From a copper alloy matrix dating from about 1280, apparently found in Salisbury, and at one time in the collection of Philip Nelson from whom the impression was received. See Nelson 1936, no. 57. The present location of this matrix is unknown.

The legend suggests that this is the seal of Reginald le May. Presumably Reginald le May is based on Reginald le Maior.

41(i) Jehan Paumont. Impression in gutta-percha, D. 31mm. Canted shield of three open left hands, surmounted by a helm with unicorn head crest to right, griffon supporters. Legend (Lombardic) JEHAN PAUMONT. Seal impression no. 258. Probably from the collection of J. E. Nightingale of Wilton. There are two other impressions in red wax (nos. 262 and 301).
Pl 34

From a fifteenth-century matrix found at Barford, probably Barford St Martin, by a Mr Clark. The present location of this matrix is unknown.

The device of the shield represents a pun on the French word 'paume' (palm). This and the name indicate that the seal is French.

Impersonal Seals

Religious

42(i) Surrexit Dominus de Sepulchro. Impression in red wax, pointed oval 37mm x 23mm. In the centre the tomb of Christ, with lid at an angle behind. Christ, three quarter length, rises from behind holding a cross shaped staff in his left hand and blessing with his right. To his right two stars and to his left the moon with points upwards. Beneath the scene of the Resurrection, under a trefoil arch, there is a kneeling female figure placing a vessel on a table. Legend (Lombardic) + SURREXIT DNS DE SEPULCRO. Seal impression no. 247. From the collection of J. E. Nightingale of Wilton.
Pl 34

From a matrix of *c.*1260 found between Kingsway and the New Cut, near Wilton, in June 1861. The matrix was at one time in the collection of Philip Nelson. See Nelson 1936, no. 48. The present location of this matrix is unknown.

The figure at the bottom may represent St Mary Magdalene.

43(i) Sit Mihi Propicia Mitis Pia Virgo Maria. Impression in black wax (seal impression no. 224),

pointed oval 45mm x 30mm. Virgin and child beneath triple arched canopy above another figure below architectural canopy, angel supporters. Legend (Lombardic) SIT M' P'PICIA MITIS PIA VIRGO MARIA.
Pl 34

From a ?fourteenth-century matrix found in St Ann Street, Salisbury in 1871. The present location of this matrix is unknown.

The legend may be translated as: O Pious Virgin Mary, may you be beneficent to me.

44(i) Saint Margaret. Impression in red wax, oval 21mm x 16mm. St Margaret standing, facing with cross in right hand. Legend (Lombardic) +SCA MARGARETA ORA P N. Seal impression no. 204. *1931.5*
Pl 34

From a fourteenth-century brass matrix found at Horningsham, Wiltshire in 1863. See *Wilts. Arch. Mag.* 9 (1866), 24. From the clarity of the impressions, the matrix was very worn, particularly in the centre. Its present location is unknown.

45(i) Saint Margaret. Impression in red wax, oval 24mm x 18mm. St Margaret standing with long cross in left hand and dragon under feet. Legend (Lombardic) ★SAUNTA MERGO. Seal impression no. 246.
Pl 34

From a ?fourteenth-century matrix found at Woodford. The present location of this matrix is unknown.

St Margaret was the patron saint of pregnant women. Often shown spearing a dragon underfoot with her cross, since she was thrown into a dungeon where she was swallowed by the devil in the form of a dragon. The cross that she carried irritated the dragon's stomach and it spewed her forth. On a similar seal in the Schøyen collection (Linenthal and Noel, 2004, no. 74), the inscription reads + saunca mergoreta.

46(i) Caput Marie Magdalene. Red painted sulphur cast, D. 22mm. Draped head of Mary half right. Legend (Lombardic) + CAPUT MARIE MAGDALENE. From the William Osmond Jr. collection; in the Museum before 1864. Seal impression no. 111.
Pl 34

From a fourteenth-century silver matrix found on the site of the Priory of St Mary Magdalene at Monkton Farleigh in 1841 during an excavation made by the late Wade Browne Esq. of that place (Jackson 1855, 389 and plate opposite 387, no. 2). There is another impression of this seal in the British Museum (PE OA 8475). The present location of the matrix is not known.

The seal is unlikely to have been that of the Priory but may have been the private seal of a Prior. While the abbey of Vezelay in France claimed to have the body of St Mary Magdalene, in December 1279 another body of the saint was discovered in the crypt of the church of St Maximin in Provence. The head of this latter body was, in December 1283, encased in a golden head reliquary (Haskins 1994, 129-132). It is presumably to this that the seal refers.

See Williams 1993 no. W151 for another seal of the Magdalene.

BIBLIOGRAPHY

Atkyns, Sir R. 1712 (reprinted 1974): *Ancient and Present State of Gloucestershire*

Birch, W. de Gray 1887, 1892: *Catalogue of Seals in the Department of Manuscripts in the British Museum*, vols. 1 and 2

Birmingham Exhibition 1936: 'Heraldic Exhibition' held at the City of Birmingham Museum and Art Gallery

Cherry, J. 1991a: 'Seal matrices' in P. and E. Saunders (eds.), *Salisbury Museum Medieval Catalogue Part 1* (Salisbury), 29-39

Cherry, J. 1991b: 'Rings' in P. and E. Saunders (eds.), *Salisbury Museum Medieval Catalogue Part 1* (Salisbury), 40-46

Egan, G. 1995: *Cloth Seals and Related Items in the British Museum*, Brit. Mus. Occas. Pap. **93** (first ed. 1994, London)

Egan, G. 2001: 'Lead/Tin Alloy Metalwork' in Peter Saunders (ed.), *Salisbury Museum Medieval Catalogue Part 3*, 92-118

Ellis, P. (ed.) 2000: *Ludgershall Castle: Excavations by Peter Addyman 1964-1972*, Wiltshire

Archaeol. Natur. Hist. Soc. Monogr. **2**

Harvey, P. D. A. and McGuinness, A. 1996: *A Guide to British Medieval Seals*

Haskins, C. 1912: *The Ancient Trade Guilds of Salisbury* (Salisbury)

Haskins, S. 1994: *Mary Magdalen: Myth and Metaphor* (New York)

Hoare, Sir R. C. 1825: *The History of Modern Wiltshire: The Hundred of Branch and Dole*

Jackson, J. E. 1855: 'Wiltshire seals', *Wilts. Arch. Mag.* **2**, 387-392

Jewitt, L. F. W. and St John Hope, W. H. 1895: *The Corporation Plate and Insignia of Office of the Cities and Towns of England and Wales*

Linenthal, R. and Noel, W. 2004: *Medieval seal matrices in the Schøyen collection* (Oslo)

Nelson, P. 1936: 'Some British Medieval Seal-matrices', *Archaeol. J.* **93**, 13-44

Osmond, S. 2000: 'A Tall Story?', *Wiltshire Family History* (July 2000), 42-44

Rawlinson, R. 1720: *The English Topographer, or, an historical account of all the pieces, that have been written relating to the antiquities, natural history, or topographical description of any part of England. By an impartial hand*

RCHM(E) 1980: *Ancient and historical monuments in the city of Salisbury*. Vol. 1 (HMSO)

RCHM(E) 1999: *Sumptuous and Richly Adorn'd : The Decoration of Salisbury Cathedral* (TSO)

Rushton, P. 2001: 'A Liverpool collector: Philip Nelson (1872-1953)', *Apollo* (January 2001), 41-8

Salisbury Museum Catalogue 1864 (Salisbury)

Tonnochy, A. B. 1952: *Catalogue of British Seal-dies in the British Museum*

V. & A. Exhibition 1930: 'English Medieval Art' exhibition held at the Victoria and Albert Museum

VCH 1956: R. B. Pugh and E. Crittall (eds.), *A History of Wiltshire* **3** (Victoria County History of the Counties of England)

VCH 1962: 'Seals, Insignia, Plate, Arms and Officers of the City [of Salisbury]' in R. Pugh (ed.), *A History of Wiltshire* **6** (Victoria County History of the Counties of England)

Wentzel, H. 1953: 'Portraits '*á l'antique*' on French medieval gems and seals', *Journal of the Warburg and Courtauld Institutes*, **16**, 342-350

Williams, D. H. 1993: *Catalogue of Seals in the National Museum of Wales, Vol. 1. Seal Dies, Welsh Seals, Papal Bullae*

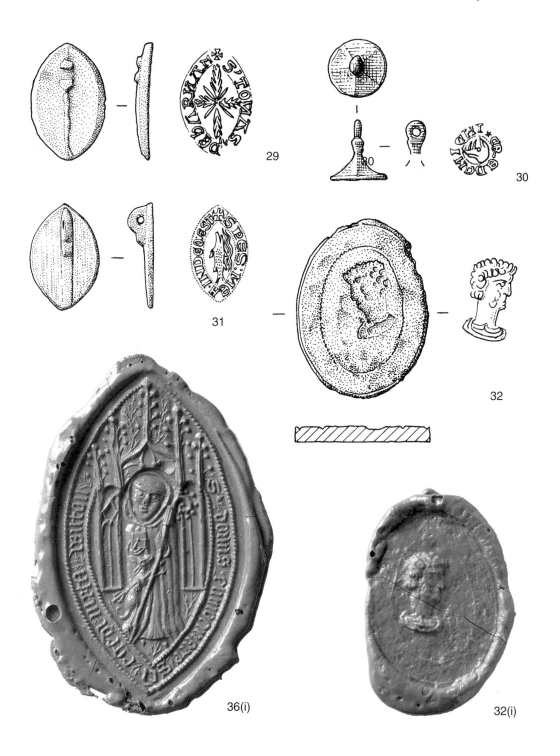

29

30

31

32

36(i)

32(i)

Pl 32. Seal matrices and impressions: Cat 29-32 matrices; Cat 32(i), 36(i) impressions (1:1)

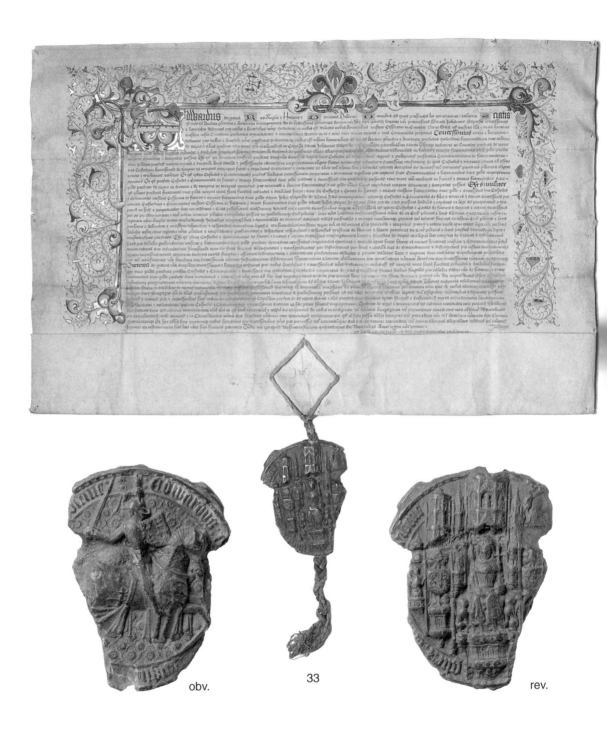

obv.   33   rev.

Pl 33. Seal matrices and impressions: from Tailors' Guild Charter (1:4); Cat 33 seal of Edward IV (1:2)

34(i)

35(i)

37(i)

38(i)

39(i)

40(i)

41(i)

42(i)

43(i)

44(i)

45(i)

46(i)

Pl 34. Seal matrices and impressions: Cat 34(i)-35(i), 37(i)-46(i) impressions (1:1)

Textiles

by Peter Saunders

INTRODUCTION

Since the publication of the textiles in Part 1 of this Catalogue (Crowfoot 1991, 50-3) there is one addition to be made to the two recorded there.

CATALOGUE

3 Twisted rope. Several small fragments. Longest 95mm. D. 10-12mm. Z-twist, made of 3 S-twist threads. Fibre (flax, identified by Wiltshire County Conservation Centre). Pre-Dissolution. From a burial on the site of the former Dominican Friary, Fisherton Street, Salisbury, found during redevelopment of the site (then Moody's furniture repository) in 1977. *1983.111* **Fig 83**

Found in situ beneath the lumbar vertebrae of a skeleton, they are possibly the remains of a belt used as a fastening, perhaps for a friar's habit or, less likely, rope used to hold a burial shroud in place. Three leather shoes (see page 87) and a wooden bowl (see page 207) were found at the same site.

BIBLIOGRAPHY

Crowfoot, E. 1991: 'Textiles' in Peter and Eleanor Saunders (eds.), *Salisbury Museum Medieval Catalogue Part 1* (Salisbury)

Fig 83. Textiles: Cat 3 rope (1:1)

Corrigenda

The opportunity is taken here to make corrections to *Parts 1-3* of the Catalogue. The Museum welcomes its attention being drawn to any errors which may be discovered within this volume.

Part 1

Seal matrices
Page 31 Cat 9: 'a bird above' should read 'a bird below'.

Balances and weights
Page 121 Cat 13: 'écu a la coronne' should read 'écu à la couronne'.

Coins
Page 144 Cat 40: the weight is 1.39 g (24.1 gr.), not 1.30 g (20.1 gr.).

Page 148 Cat 141: 'Given by F. Coster' should read 'Given by F. Carter'.

Page 152 Cat 231: 'Shortt 1959' should read 'Shortt 1969'.

Page 155 Cat 242: 'Tealby', not short-cross, coinage.

Page 157 Cat 288: 'pl 23' should read 'pl 1'.

Page 163: Cat 46 on plate 4 is illustrated upside down.

Textiles
Page 50 Cat 1: the width of woven band is 15.5 mm not 155 mm.

Part 2

Pilgrim souvenirs and secular badges
Since their publication in 1990 twenty three pilgrim and six secular badges, then recorded as loans, have been accessioned into the Museum's permanent collection. They are Cat 7, 11, 12, 41, 51, 52, 54, 59, 68, 84, 94, 97, 98, 100, 106, 107, 110, 121, 125, 126, 128, 131, 143, 167, 177, 186, 189, 202 and 205.

Part 3

Lead / Tin Alloy Metalwork
Page 106 Cat 183 and 184: both are probably those recorded in *O.S. Diary* 1910, 27 and have the old catalogue number *OS. C174*.

Balances and Weights
Page 125 Cat 27: 'apothecaries' should read 'apothecary's'.

Page 126 Cat 31: accession number should read '107.9/1987', not '107.9/1989'.

Pottery, Brick and Tile
Page 166 Cat 226: 'iB5' should read 'iB5A'.
Page 171 Cat 268: add '*OS. C94*'; Cat 269 add '*OS. C95*'; Cat 270 add '*O.S. Diary* 1910, 56' and '*OS. C7*'.

Jettons
Page 214 Fig 77: sum should read '1671 from 6799', not '1617 from 6799'.

Page 223 Cat 47: accession number should read '*11/1992*', not '*111/1992*'.

Page 249: Cat 273 was tentatively interpreted as a dagger pommel but is now, together with Cat 276 (see pages 282-3), considered more likely to be a plug used to seal a witch-bottle.

Index
Page 269 'Salisbury (specific locations), St John Street': add '176'.

Fig. 84 Find spots in the vicinity of Salisbury

Index

by Philip Aslett

The index entries are filed in letter-by-letter sequence and consist of personal names (except donors and depositors), place names and selected subjects. Most English places are identified by historic (pre-1974) county names and parish names. References are to page numbers, except those in **bold** type, which refer to catalogue numbers. Page numbers usually accompany catalogue numbers for the reader's convenience. Moneyers are indexed together under 'moneyers' and do not appear elsewhere in the index.